twentieth-century thinkers

henri bergson
maurice blondel
etienne gilson
jacques maritain
gabriel marcel
nicholas berdyaev
arnold toynbee
edmund husserl
martin heidegger
ludwig wittgenstein
john dewey
sigmund freud
carl jung
miguel unamuno
jean paul sartre
maurice merleau-ponty
paul tillich

twentieth-century thinkers

studies in the work of seventeen modern philosophers, edited and with an introduction by john k. ryan

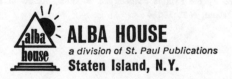

ALBA HOUSE
a division of St. Paul Publications
Staten Island, N.Y.

Nihil Obstat:

    Rev. Peter J. Rahill
    Censor Deputatus

Imprimatur:

    ✠ Patrick A. O'Boyle
    Archbishop of Washington

First printing November 1965

Second printing January 1967

Library of Congress Catalog Card No. 65-17976

Designed, printed and bound in the U.S.A. by the Pauline Fathers and Brothers as part of their Communications Apostolate.

Copyright 1965 by the Pauline Fathers and Brothers, Society of St. Paul, 2187 Victory Blvd., Staten Island, N.Y. 10314

contents

introduction

There are those who hold that the era bearing by its own choice the name modern is drawing to a close, or that even now we are in the first stages of a new period in thought and action. However future historians may appraise our confused and tormented time—whether as the death throes of one cycle or the birth pains of another—it will be necessary for them to base their deepest judgments upon the thought and deeds of the century's thinkers and artists much more than on the acts of those who hold power in government, commerce, and technology. It will not be essential to know the names of all the military leaders who built up the most powerful forces in history and led them to victory or defeat, or to an inextricable confusion of both, but future students will have little understanding of twentieth-century Europe and America if the character and impact of our chief thinkers and their forebears are left unrecognized and unassessed.

With more than a third of its course still to run, our century shows itself to be a greatly productive period in the history of philosophy. It opened with a legacy of established thinkers—Mercier, Eucken, Wundt, Bradley, James, and Royce may be named from among many—and of younger men about to begin distinguished careers as teachers and writers, and its succeeding decades, although filled with turmoil and disaster, have seen sincere and able men and women at work in all branches of philosophy and in its history. Europe maintains its leadership, but America and the Orient take an increasing part in the great discussion that constitutes a search for wisdom. Further evidence of interest is seen in the multiplication of journals, the wide distribution of both the great philosophical classics and lesser works, the great variety of philosophy courses offered in colleges and universities, and the enlarged enrollment in them.

The place that philosophy has taken in the modern world is shown most strikingly by the triumphs of the Marxian doctrine. In conjunction with religion and other forces philosophy had its earlier successes, but there is no past parallel to the translation found in communist countries of a priori doctrine into political institutions, moral practices, and social movements. Yet if no other thinker has had the deep immediate and pervasive impact on the lives of men that Marx has had, every philosopher whose opinions and values are known and discussed by others leaves a mark upon them. The winds of doctrine that blow from lecture halls, or from printed pages as readers turn them over, can have diverse effects. Their sharp blasts can arouse men to thought and action, bring in a clearer air, and sweep away outworn and useless things; at times too they can deface and demolish, or more correctly, cover over things so great and good that beyond them "men can have nothing more profitable in life." Error in men's minds as to such realities, according to Plato, constitutes "the true lie," that most complete and disastrous falsity of which falsity in words is only a simulacrum. Or it can take the form of the misology against which Socrates warns, that distrust of reason and its works seen so often in the anti-intellectualism of our time.

But if we read the best contemporary thinkers with open and independent minds, we find in them new truths that they have labored to uncover, new aspects of familiar things, new questions to answer, new approaches to old problems, and new ways of expressing established truths. For one of us to be a Bergson in style is as impossible as to be an Epictetus, an Anselm, or a Leibniz, but Bergson's way of writing should evoke in us a desire for some personal grace and distinction in speech. None of us can be a Husserl or a Wittgenstein, but they tell us how every generation must grapple with the persistent problems and look for new modes of thinking about them.

As we listen to such men and learn from them, we keep in mind our own standards and our advantages as heirs to the best in Greece and Rome and in the patristic and medieval worlds, along with what has been thought and done in these latter centuries. The critical mind must operate when we read critical philosophers and challenge must be met with challenge. Therefore we reserve our right and we fulfill our duty to reject as well as to accept, remembering with Lactantius that recognition of error is essential to the attainment of truth, and with Seneca that it is unwise and wrong both to trust all men and to trust none. Nor is it illicit for us as students of philosophy to recall the words of St. Paul—he did not hesitate to quote Aratus, Epimenides, and Menander—to the end that "if there is any virtue, any praise of learning" in us, it is because we give ourselvs to the best in Christian culture, and think upon and seek after things that are true, honorable, just, holy, beautiful, and of good report.

The several articles in this volume discuss seventeen of the most renowned and influential of contemporary thinkers. Some of them stand for that great tradition in western thought which flows from the Greeks and Romans through the chief patristic, medieval, and renaissance teachers, and continues unbroken, sometimes in unsuspected places, into our own time. Others speak for very different types of thought, such as nominalism, naturalism, and atheism, and others still for a renewed interest in the philosophy of history, a new method, or new fields of investigation, or in connection with the revival of logical studies that our age has witnessed. Perhaps it is too early to call any one of them great in the sense in which that title is given to Plato and Aristotle and Plotinus, to St. Augustine and St. Thomas Aquinas, or to Kant and Hegel, yet all of them have undoubtedly produced works that in diverse and sometimes discordant modes speak to our world and evoke a response from it. There is more to learn from some than from others, but all of them have much to say to us. Again, because certain voices seem more typical of their time and have commanded a wider hearing than others, we perhaps think of them as more authentic oracles than they may prove to be. Hence in passing judgment it is well for us to remember how quickly a lofty reputation can decline—Spencer and Eucken are modern instances—how names great in one generation can become mere names in another, and contrariwise how thinkers known during life to but a small circle—Kierkegaard and Nietzsche may be named in this regard—can have great influence on succeeding generations. But whatever inevitable critical reactions, changed interests, and altered judgments the future may bring, the twentieth century can well be proud that it has given to history such men as Jacques Maritain, Etienne Gilson, and Luigi Sturzo, and such a woman as Edith Stein, along with so many sincere and able spokesmen for other ways of thought.

John K. Ryan
The School of Philosophy
The Catholic University of America

IN THE GREAT TRADITION
HENRI BERGSON: HERACLITUS REDIVIVUS
MAURICE BLONDEL: THE METHOD OF IMMANENCE AS
AN APPROACH TO GOD
ETIENNE GILSON AND CHRISTIAN PHILOSOPHY
JACQUES MARITAIN: A CHRISTIAN IN PHILOSOPHY
GABRIEL MARCEL: PHILOSOPHER OF
INTERSUBJECTIVITY

henri bergson

HERACLITUS REDIVIVUS
by John K. Ryan

Certain periods in history have a distinctive character of their own, whether good or bad, both while we live them and as we look back to them, and not unnaturally men like best to recall and perhaps idealize times when their country was prosperous and productive and esteemed and envied by others. Such a time in the history of France is the quarter or third of a century before 1914, which with no little propriety has come to be called the *belle époque*. By the 1880's France had recovered both economically and militarily from the disastrous effects of 1870, so much so that Bismarck thought of waging a new war that would crush his victim a second time and perhaps permanently. In the ensuing decades this recovery became more complete and France was not only strong again but led Europe and the world in many ways. In art it had taken on undisputed leadership. It had its wonderful painters—Puvis de Chavannes, Manet, Degas, Toulouse-Lautrec, Renoir, Monet, Seurat, and others, some of them not yet famous but destined to become so—and Rodin as its great sculptor, and it provided a setting for the *art nouveau*. There was a brilliant if not great opera: Gounod lived into this time, while Saint-Saens, Massenet, and Charpentier had their resounding successes, and in the higher reaches of music, César Franck, Ernest Chausson, and Claude Debussy were at work. The theatre had Sardou, Rostand, and Brieux, the novel Zola, Anatole France, Paul Bourget, René Bazin, Romain Rolland, and Marcel Proust, poetry Mallarmé, Valéry, and Péguy, and in all three forms there were lesser figures, many or even most of whom are now almost forgotten. For religion it was not the best of times—it witnessed declining belief and practice, modernist subversion within the Church, and unrelenting anti-Christian assaults from the outside—but neither was it the worst of times. A learned clergy wrote individual books of great value and projected monumental works of scholarship, such as the *Dictionnaire de théologie catholique*, that still stand, a new generation of lay leaders emerged, and faithful Catholics silently built up the strength that sustained France between 1914 and 1918. The physical and biological sciences flourished, with Pasteur as the chief glory of the elder generation and the Curies showing what was to come. There was high ability in government and diplomacy, and in the army there were great soldiers—Foch, Pétain, Gallieni, Joffre, Franchet d'Esperey, and the others who would prove themselves in the coming war. As part of all this latter-day expression of French genius there was an opulent and glittering social life that far surpassed that of cruder and newer nations. Slowly deepening economic and ideological divisions and the constant threat of war could not darken these triumphs of French culture. Nor could so splendid a time be without its philosophers, or perhaps we should say its philosopher. A brilliant era deserved a brilliant thinker, and it found one in the exponent of pan-metabolism and the *élan vital*.[1]

Henri Louis Bergson was born in Paris on October 18, 1859, the son of parents who were Jewish in race and British in citizenship, and he remained a British subject until becoming a French citizen at the age of 21. His father was a musician, as was also his mother, Katherine Lewinson Bergson, and he had the great advantage of a home interested in the arts and things of the mind. He made a brilliant career as a student at two famous and difficult schools, first at the Lycée Condorcet and later at the École Normale Supèrieure. After hesitating for a time between literature and science, he settled on philosophy as his life's work. However, it may be said that as a philosopher Bergson did not forsake literature, and scientific interests are seen everywhere in his writings. Because of his English background, he had certain advantages at school, including a knowledge of the English language and of contemporary British philosophy, such as that of Spencer and

Mill, and he was known among his teachers as being *trés anglais*.
Later in life his thought had affinity with that of William James,
whose friend he became. The names of British and American
philosophers appear frequently in his works, and he shows
considerable knowledge of English literature. After teaching
philosophy at Angers and Clermont-Ferrand, Bergson continued
his career in Paris at the Lycée Henri IV (1889-1897), at his
alma mater, the École Normale Supèrieure (1897-1900), and
thereafter at the Collége de France, remaining there until 1918
when he retired to devote himself to public life. Honors came to
him: he was made a member of the French Academy in 1914,
received the Nobel Prize for literature in 1928, and was president
of the League of Nations Committee for Intellectual Cooperation.

Bergson died on January 4, 1941, in the first year of the Nazi
occupation of France. During his latter years he had become
much interested in mysticism, especially that of its great Christian representatives, and in the Gospels. He had various Catholic
friends, among them Père A. D. Sertillanges, O.P., and Père
Pouget, C.M. However, Bergson did not die a professed Catholic,
as is sometimes thought. In his will, dated February 8, 1937, he
wrote:

> My reflections have led me closer and closer to Catholicism, in which I see the complete fulfillment of Judaism.
> I would have become a convert had I not seen in preparation for years (in great part, alas, through the fault of a
> certain number of Jews entirely deprived of moral sense)
> the formidable wave of anti-Semitism which is to sweep
> over the world. I wanted to remain among those who
> tomorrow will be persecuted. But I hope that a Catholic
> priest will be good enough to come—if the Cardinal
> Archbishop of Paris will authorize it—to pray at my
> funeral. Should this authorization not be granted, it will
> be necessary to approach a rabbi, but without concealing
> from him, nor from anyone, my moral adherence to
> Catholicism, as well as my express and first desire to have
> the prayers of a Catholic priest.[2]

In 1881 when Bergson began his career as a teacher of
philosophy, the French intellectual world worshipped in the two

shrines of natural science and German idealism, and the chief dogmas of the prevailing religions included materialism, determinism, positivism, and atheism, whether formal or arrayed as pantheism. Against all this Bergson reacted in a decisive way. As he later testified, "It was from the idolatry of science that I started out on my intellectual odyssey," [3] and he asserted that his whole endeavor had been to "rebuild the bridge, broken since Kant's day, between metaphysics and science." [4] Thus from the beginning Bergson shows himself to be a philosopher in the truest sense, one affronted by gross error, ready to face basic issues, and working to effect a synthesis between two great kinds of knowledge. As such, he grappled with the fundamental metaphysical problem of being and becoming, and as a student of the history of philosophy he went back to the fifth century before Christ when the problem was first debated by the pre-Socratic philosophers of Greece.

Two men may be taken as representing two opposing views of reality. Heraclitus, the greatest of the early cosmologists, teaches that there is no inert, static being, that whatever is real is constantly changing, that all is active and dynamic, that all things flow, that all is becoming. In contrast to this Parmenides, "the great Parmenides" [5] of Plato's phrase, holds that all reality is static and unchanging, that all is being, that there is no becoming, that there is the appearance but not the reality of movement and change. Since Parmenides' seemingly extravagant doctrine naturally met with attacks from various quarters, his disciple, Zeno the Eleatic, rose to the master's defense. In a series of brilliant and durable arguments Zeno showed some of the difficulties involved in a current theory of motion. Parmenides' denial of real movement contradicts the senses, but his critics' defence of motion challenges reason and logic. Every space, no matter how small, can be dichotomized an infinite number of times; how then can it be traversed in a limited time? No matter how slowly the tortoise apparently crawls along, and no matter with what speed Achilles apparently runs, he can in reality never catch it, since Achilles must always get to where the moving tortoise was before he can get to where it is. There were, of course, philosophical refutations of Zeno's paradoxes, such as Aristotle's, [6] and discussions of them still continue year after year. There is also the

more obvious answer of common sense as put by Democritus the
atomist, Zeno's younger contemporary, who refuted him and Parmenides by getting up and walking about. *Solvitur ambulando.*[7]
Experience has both the first and the last word as to the reality
of movement.

Bergson's answer to Parmenides and Zeno is that of Democritus. A direct appeal to fact is necessary and irrefutable, but at
the same time it requires a commentary. Zeno's paradoxes must
be answered in full since all previous refutations have been abor-
tive, he claims, because of a confusion of space and time. Bergson's philosophy will supply not only a thorough answer to Parmenides and Zeno but as well an energetic and comprehensive
assertion of the Heraclitean doctrine of the universality of change.
The result is the series of books and articles that lead us to call
Bergson *Heraclitus redivivus,* Heraclitus returned to life, and, we
may say, in a greater way. There are four chief works: *Essai sur les
données immédiates de la conscience* (1889), *Matière et memoire*
(1896), *L'Évolution créatrice* (1900), and *Les Deux sources de
le religion* (1932). In addition he published *Le Rire*: *Essai sur la
signification du comique* (1900), *L'Energie spirituelle*: *Essais et
conférences* (1919), *Durée et simultanéité* (1922), and *La
Pensée et le mouvant*: *Essais et conférences* (1934), containing
among other important articles "L'Ame et le corps," "Le Rêve,"
"L'Intuition philosophique," "Introduction à la métaphysique,"
and "La Perception du changement."[8] Three volumes of *Écrits et
paroles* have appeared, and a vast literature has grown up around
his philosophy and life. Because of his great popularity Bergson's
works were soon turned into many languages, and he himself
took particular care with English translations of them. So well
done are the English versions of the four chief works— *Time and
Free Will, Matter and Memory, Creative Evolution,* and *The
Two Sources of Religion and Morality*—and those of *Introduction
to Metaphysics* and *Laughter,* that they may be considered to be
contributions to English philosophical literature just as are the
original works to French.[9]

In his doctoral dissertation,[10] *Time and Free Will,* Bergson
shows his independence of thought both by his subject and by
his approach to it. The problem of free will, he says, is common
to metaphysics and psychology, and he continues with the charge

that both defenders and opponents of free will are in error. They are confused as to space and time, quality and quantity, succession and simultaneity, duration and extension, that is, by the same confusion that has vitiated both ancient and later attempts to refute Zeno's paradoxes. If it can be dispelled, as Bergson thinks it can, then objections to freedom disappear, as will definitions of it and even the very problem itself. Such is his position as stated in the preface to his doctoral dissertation, and his concluding words are that free will has needlessly been for modern thinkers what the Eleatic arguments were for the ancients.

For a solution of the problem, or a way to dispose of it, Bergson turns to our internal experience, to consciousness. In contrast to external things with their fixed dimensions, he finds that our psychic life is devoid of space, and holds that we must not impose the same forms or categories equally on inner and on outward reality. What obtains is the reverse of the Kantian doctrine: it is not that the mind imposes space on things, but rather that spatially determined things impose themselves on the mind. But for Bergson psychic life is neither a unity nor a multiplicity; it transcends both the intellectual order and the mechanical order. For him both finalism, a philosophy of purpose, and mechanism, a philosophy of necessity, have meaning only in the outward realm where space, multiplicity, and an assemblage of pre-existing parts are found. Psychic life, real duration, is entirely different: it means undivided continuity and creative activity. In *Time and Free Will,* with its energetic affirmation of freedom, we find his basic attitudes and concepts already stated: an insistence on the active, the dynamic, the mobile, an appeal to experience, and an attempt to find the truth of things by means of something higher than intellect and reason.

In the January, 1903 issue of the *Revue de Métaphysique et Morale,* fourteen years after *Time and Free Will* and seven years after *Matter and Memory,* Bergson published the short work entitled *Introduction to Metaphysics,* in which he continues to assert certain things found in the earlier books and prepares for *Creative Evolution.* Metaphysics is the science that claims to dispense with symbols, that is, it cannot remain satisfied with describing objects and translating them into different words or symbols.

It wants more than mere relative knowledge; it tries for the absolute. It is not content to know things from the outside but wishes to enter into them. When we want to know a man, even a fictional character, descriptions, histories, and analyses, no matter how detailed and penetrating, always leave us on the outside and in the realm of the relative. Absolute knowledge can be had only by a coincidence with the man himself, and can be attained only by an intuition, an intellectual sympathy, whereby the knower places himself inside the object so as to coincide with what is unique and incxpressible in it.

The essay on metaphysics concludes with nine theses; for most of them, the author says, he has already given partial proof and hopes to demonstrate them more fully when dealing with other problems. The nine theses are as follows: (1) There is an external reality that is given immediately to our mind. Common sense is right in affirming this, contrary to both idealists and realists in philosophy. (2) This reality is mobility. There are no things made but only things in the making, no permanent states but only states that change. Rest is always apparent, or better, relative. Consciousness of our own personal being in its continual unfolding introduces us into the interior of a reality, and thus it is the model on which we must represent other realities. "All reality is therefore a tendency, an incipient direction." (3) Although reality is an unceasing flow, our mind represents states and things. It takes, we may say, instantaneous snapshots of what is indivisibly mobile. Following our natural bent, our intellect proceeds on the one hand by solid perceptions and on the other by stable conceptions. It begins with the unchanging, and makes movement a function of the unmoving. (4) The errors and antinomies of past metaphysicians and the long history of antagonistic schools come from putting ourselves in the unmoving, the static, and waiting there for the moving things to pass, instead of placing ourselves within the moving thing. We can mentally abstract fixed concepts from moving reality, but we cannot rebuild reality, which is always moving, out of fixed concepts. (5) Skeptics, and all those who deny that we can reach absolute knowledge, are as much in error as the dogmatists they attack. Because we cannot rebuild reality out of rigid, ready-made concepts, it does not follow that we are unable to grasp it in some other way. (6) This other way is that of intuition, or intellectual sympathy. The mind must act against itself; it must recast all its categories, and by so doing it will attain to those fluid concepts which alone can follow reality in all its turns and adopt the actual movement of the inner life of things. Only thus can a progressive philosophy be built up, free from the quarrels of past schools. Hence for Bergson to philosophize means that we must invert the habitual direction of our thought. (7) This difficult feat has been accomplished in infinitesimal calculus, and metaphysics should extend the example to all qualities. To do this is not to turn to "that chimera of modern philosophy," a universal mathematics. Metaphysics deals with the realm of quality, and its differentiations and integrations must be qualitative. (8) We are rightly impressed by the long, slow, careful, and successful methods of physical science, but often we mistake "the logical equipment of science" for science itself; we forget that momentary metaphysical intuition from which science itself has sprung. Failure to note this intuition results in the error of looking upon scientific knoweldge as merely relative, whereas the relative is the familiar passage from fixed concepts to moving reality. Intellectual intuition reaches the absolute, and science and metaphysics come together in intuition. (9) It is not true that there is more in the immutable than in the changing, as Plato and Plotinus hold, and that we pass from the stable to the unstable by a process of diminution. The contrary is true. Nor is Kant correct in holding that the intellect can only Platonize, that is, pour all possible experience into preexisting molds. Metaphysics is integral experience.

Bergson's fierism [11] is developed most fully in *Creative Evolution* where he begins by summarizing certain earlier conclusions. Following the principles laid down in the *Introduction to Metaphysics,* to determine the meaning of existence each of us must turn to what he knows best, his own existence. I find that I am subject to constant change: sensations, feelings, acts of will, and ideas succeed one another, and each of them is itself constantly changing. For a conscious being, that is, a being that does not merely view changing and enduring things from the outside but perceives change and endurance in its own innermost reality, to exist is to change, to change is to mature, to mature is to create oneself unceasingly. This consciousness of duration, this concrete duration or real time, is the very stuff of our existence and nothing is more substantial or resistant than it. When he applies this intuition to all existence, reality, whether matter or mind, shows itself to Bergson as a perpetual becoming. Reality is forever making or unmaking itself, but it is never something made and finished once and for all. It is true that in the cosmic reality there is a twofold process, a descent as well as an ascent. Yet matter, the reality that descends, endures only by virtue of that which rises, and life and consciousness are this upward movement. Once we have got at this essential process, we see how all reality derives from it. To place ourselves within the evolutionary process is the true function of philosophy and to be a philosopher is simply for the mind to turn back to itself. To philosophize is the coincidence of our consciousness with that living source from which it flows. It is to make contact with the original creative effort, and to plumb the depths of becoming in general. Such philosophy is a true evolutionism, and a true extension of science, although not of such science as the mechanistic materialism that had developed in the second half of the nineteenth century.

Bergson's method is closely connected with the substance of his philosophy and is an important and instructive part of it. Its principles may be summarized as follows. He is opposed to mere rationalism in method as well as elsewhere. Deduction and induction have their necessary place in the sciences, but they cannot reach ultimate realities. The true method of philosophy is empirical; it is that integral experience which shuns a priori abstractions and turns to our own consciousness. Once a problem has been seen, it must be carefully isolated, as Bergson does with the problems of life, free will, the soul, religion, and morality. Caution must always be exercised, and he is constantly urging such phrases as "if this be so," "as if," and the like. When all available data have been gathered and assessed, further problems may remain. If so, they must remain problems until new evidence is acquired. Thus in *Creative Evolution* he considers the problem of life, but he refrains from considering the problem of the origin of life. A further characteristic of Bergson's method is his effective use of opposing aspects of reality. He contrasts spirit and matter, time and space, the dynamic and the static, the living and the mechanical, quality and quantity, freedom and necessity, intuition and intelligence, interpenetration and juxta-position, the homogeneous and the heterogeneous, the superficial ego and the deep ego, pure memory and habitual memory, intellectualism and mysticism, static religion and dynamic religion, and closed morality and open morality. Matter, the reality that tends downward, is quantified, spatial, rigid, static, necessitated, mechanical, and all of a kind; spirit is qualitative, conscious, dynamic, spontaneous, free, infinitely varied, intuitive, and creative.

Akin to this use of contrast is what may be called Bergson's analogical method. Great as Plato, Aristotle, and Augustine are in their use of figures of speech, they do not approach Bergson in his facility at fashioning vivid and memorable metaphors and similes. Thus he was much impressed by the invention of the moving picture camera and described the intellect as giving a cinematographic view of reality: quick as the camera is, it never gives us anything but still pictures, and so also with the intellect. Again, we can never get a complete view of Paris, no matter how many snapshots we take of it, even though each one, or the total of them, is labeled Paris. A poem may be translated time and time again into all known languages, but we can never know the poem by means of such intellectual efforts; it can be known only by an intuition and by an integral experience of it. A completely free act is like a piece of fruit that has slowly ripened on the tree and has at length dropped easily to the ground. Creation is like a display of fireworks, spraying out from a central point, but the center is itself a spray. On page after page we meet such striking analogies drawn from literature, physical science, and common experience. For Bergson's purposes these innumerable figures of speech are undoubtedly effective and contribute no little to his great success as a writer.

A document that reveals something of Bergson's method and character as a thinker is a letter written in 1912 to Père Joseph de Tonquédec, S.J. In it he writes of the three works that had established his position in contemporary thought:

> The argument of *Time and Free Will* brings into light the fact of free will; that of *Matter and Memory* makes sensible, I hope, the spirituality of the soul; that of *Creative Evolution* brings out the fact of creation. From all of

them emerges the idea of God, creator and free, source
both of matter and of life, whose creative effort goes on
in the order of life through the evolution of species and
the formation of human persons, and consequently the
refutation of all monism and pantheism. However, to go
further and to make these conclusions more precise, I
should take up the study of quite different problems. I
am not sure I shall ever publish anything on that subject. I
will do it only if I get results that appear to me as demonstrable as those of my other works.[12]

In the ensuing years Bergson concentrated on those "quite
different problems," and in 1932 published his conclusions upon
them. *The Two Sources of Morality and Religion* is not a long
book—there are only 165 pages in the closely printed text of
the *Oeuvres* and 306 in the more generously produced English
translation—and it is simple in structure, with four chapters,
headed in order "Moral Obligation," "Static Religion," "Dynamic
Religion," and "Final Remarks: Mechanics and Mysticism." It is
a compact book in every sense and it is difficult to think of a
similar work in modern philosophy that contains so much profound
thought expressed in so arresting and memorable a way.

The first form of morality is biological and social in origin
and issues from the pressure that is exerted on free individuals by
the collective will. A society made up of free wills takes on the
appearance of a living organism. The community has needs, and
social life is a system of habits, whether of command or, more
usually, of obedience fashioned to fulfill these needs. An impersonal order emanates from society bringing us to obey the rules
and customs of society as such. Our social habits involve a sense
of obligation, and that collection of free human beings which is
a society can exist only by imposing obligations on its members.
A force, "the totality of obligation," exerts itself, and if it could
speak Bergson says that it would say, "This must be done because
it must." Obligation is like a habit weighing upon the will, and
each obligation drags behind it the accumulated mass of other
obligations, thus using all of them to put pressure on the will.
Here we find a sort of categorical imperative, since habits have
been formed that imitate instinct. This moral obligation resulting

from group pressure on individual free men is the closed morality of a closed society. Such a situation is not necessarily crude and primitive; it may be highly civilized, as in the contemporary world which contains so many instances of what Bergson describes. Consider what happens under the organized pressures of war: respect for property, human life, and truth is thrown aside, and the opposite becomes a virtue. Quoting the witches in *Macbeth,* Bergson points out that men at war can say, "Fair is foul, and foul is fair." Nor, we may add, need we look further for closed societies and closed moralities than in the Marxist nations, in communities where racism is in control, and in the more diffuse realms of business, publicity, and propaganda.

In his search for pure obligation Bergson has reduced morality to its barest essentials, and in so doing, as he notes, he has reduced the range of morality. Typically, he writes that we can conceive of this bare duty as radiating out, expanding, and being absorbed into something that transfigures it. To reach this new moral obligation and this complete morality, he will reverse his method and move upward. At all times there have been superior men in whom a higher morality has been embodied. He names the sages of Greece, the holy men of Buddhism, the prophets of Israel, and the saints of Christianity. They draw disciples to themselves, and crowds follow them. They ask for nothing, and yet they receive. They do not need to exhort, but simply to be. Their very existence is an appeal to others, and such is the true essence of the higher morality. Whereas natural morality is a restraining or a propulsive force, complete and perfect morality is an appeal and a call to action. The character of the moral hero can be known fully only by personal contact, but each of us has some experience with such a one: we take models, and we ask ourselves what would someone we respect do in a certain case. The source of strength in this higher morality is that it is universal: it considers not merely the advantages of a group or nation, but of mankind. The prophets of Israel transformed the idea of justice, but still kept it to the chosen people. Theirs was an advance, and a second advance, from the closed to the open, was made by Christianity. This was something that mere philosophers could not do. Mankind had to wait for Christianity for the idea of universal brotherhood, which implies equality of rights and inviolability of the person, before it becomes effective.

It is clear that Bergson draws a powerful contrast between
closed, static morality and dynamic, open morality. The one is
infra-intellectual, the other supra-intellectual; the one is a system
of orders imposed by impersonal social needs; the other is a series
of appeals made to our individual consciences by persons who
represent the best that is in humanity. But all morality, whether
downward pressure or upward aspiration, is essentially a manifestation of life itself.

Corresponding to static morality is static or closed religion,
and of static religion the source is what Bergson calls the myth-
making faculty. This power and activity must have arisen from
the need to protect man against certain dangers inherent in our
use of intellect, namely, selfishness, fear of death, and fear of
the unforeseen. Hence looked at in this way, religion is a defense
reaction on the part of nature against the dissolvent power of
the intellect. Fear had a place in the beginnings of religion in
primitive man, but Statius' *Primus in orbe deos fecit timor*,[13] is
not the correct statement. For Bergson, religion is not so much
something dictated by fear as a reaction against fear, and further,
in its beginnings it is not a belief in gods. Nature has worked
towards intelligence at the end of one of the two great evolutionary
lines as a counterpart to the most developed instinct at the end
of the other. Therefore nature will see to it that intellect will
exercise its myth-making power so as to maintain an order that
intellect would otherwise disturb and to protect man against what
is depressing for the individual and disruptive for society. All
religion supplies strength, and static religion attaches man to life.

Just as in the study of morality a passage must be made from
the static to the dynamic, so also in the consideration of religion.
Bergson holds that to arrive at the essence of religion and understand man's history, we must proceed from static, outward religion
to inner, dynamic religion, where again the creative impulse has
carried man on from the infra-intellectual to the supra-intellectual.
Mysticism, which is productive of this higher religion and is in
turn produced by it, lifts the soul up to another level and has as
its ultimate purpose to bring us into contact and as a result into
partial coincidence with that creative effort which life itself dis-

plays. "This effort is of God, if it is not God himself." Bergson gives his own personally verbal definition of the great mystic. He is a man who is capable of transcending the limitations placed on the human species by its materiality, and by so doing he continues and extends God's activity. Complete mysticism is that of the great Christian mystics, such as St. Paul, St. Teresa of Avila, St. Catherine of Siena, St. Francis of Assisi, St. Joan of Arc, and, as Bergson adds, "how many others besides." He proceeds to study mysticism as found in its best representatives, and puts his findings into memorable words that are themselves a contribution to the literature of mysticism.

The mystic has felt truth pouring like an active force out of its first source and into his soul. He is transformed by it, and cannot help spreading this truth, not by words alone but as well by deeds. He is consumed by a love that is no longer simply man's love for God but rather God's love for man, so that in God and through God he too loves mankind with a divine love. The mystic wishes to transform mankind, and he knows that this can only be done by slowly passing on this active force from one man to another. Christianity is mysticism *par execellence,* for its very essence is mysticism, and Christ is the supreme and archetypal mystic. Mysticism and religion continue to interact and to contribute to one another unceasingly. Yet this mutual interaction must have had its start, and at the beginning of Christianity stands Christ. There have been those who have even denied the existence of Christ, but they cannot annul the existence of the Sermon on the Mount along with other words stamped with divinity. For Bergson, the great mystics that he has interpreted and described are "imitators and continuers, original but incomplete, of that which the Christ of the Gospels was completely."[14]

Bergson is not satisfied with the God of Aristotle's philosophy and with the Aristotelian approach to his existence. To establish the existence of God, who is love and the object of love, he appeals to the testimony of the mystics. They testify not only to God's existence, but likewise, he says, to the fact that God needs us just as we need him, and that he needs us solely to love us. In creation, we see God creating creators so as to have others besides himself who are worthy of his love. God has made men free and responsible, and if we lie half crushed beneath the things that we have accomplished, we should still realize that the future lies in our hands. Men must decide whether they wish to live or to die, and whether merely to live, or to make that added effort necessary to accomplish the essential purpose of the universe, "which is a machine for making gods." [15]

Such is the barest summary of the basic theses that Bergson sets forth and defends in his major works, but no summary can give an idea of how eloquently he presents his doctrines and of the richness of detail and illustration with which they are elaborated. He is for the soul, freedom, life, and God, and in view of the time in which he lived and worked he could not escape criticism from those who deny God, repudiate spiritual realities, reject man's personal liberty and responsibility, and reduce life to a material mechanism. But Bergson's philosophy has met severe criticism from other sources as well. His psychology, his natural theology, and particularly his basic metaphysical premise of pandynamism have been subjected to both early and continued scrutiny by competent opponents who are entirely in sympathy with his great aims in philosophy.

Against Bergson's doctrine of free will the criticism is advanced that despite his strong attack on determinism he does not offer an acceptable theory of freedom itself. He is dissatisfied with earlier libertarian doctrines as well as being opposed to determinism, and in reply to his objections traditional defenders of freedom of the will can point out that when we act freely we choose between motives, and that to do so is neither to act without a motive nor is it to be necessitated by the stronger motive. It can be claimed too that his doctrine seems to reduce freedom to mere spontaneity, that he needlessly stresses the rarity of free acts, and that while he objects to any explicit definition of freedom, he implicitly defines it by equating freedom with creative activity. Bergson, it may be said, is more concerned with the fact of freedom than with the reasoned fact, whereas a more acceptable account must probe deeper and show both what freedom is and why.

So also the core theses of *The Two Sources* have been weighed and found wanting. [16] His rejection of rational arguments for the existence of God must be answered like all other such rejections by showing their essential character and value and their place in a complete metaphysics. His own use of the testimony of mystics is faulted as an argument from authority and found to suffer from even more insufficiences than is the usual argument from human testimony. We must distinguish true mystics from the false, but even of the true mystic it may be asked if his personal experience of God can serve as a proof for other men. At best the argument may be described as probable only. Bergson has also been reproved for failing to distinguish clearly between the natural and the supernatural orders, with the result that on the basis of his doctrine mystical experiences could be accounted for in a pantheistic sense rather than as evidence of a transcendent personal God. His account of God as creator in relation to the mystic as well as to the whole of reality lacks the fullness and precision that this essential subject demands.

But the great charge that must be made against Bergson's philosophy is based on his panmetabolism and his failure to provide a sufficient place for substances in his system. For Bergson reality is not merely changing, but rather change itself. Yet all our own integral experience, to use his memorable phrase, is not solely of change but of something that changes. What is real is the child who becomes a man, and not merely "becoming a man," as Bergson holds. In such a doctrine as Bergson's man, a substantial being, the focus it is true of unceasing changes throughout his life but always identical with himself and the abiding subject of change, is presented as a mere process within the cosmic process. God too is not a substantial, or better a supersubstantial being, but again a process, a becoming, an activity, even if that activity is called creation. Bergson rightly thinks of God as unceasing life, action, and freedom, but he errs in thinking that God has needs and potentialities of further development. Along with his preference for becoming to being, he looks upon all acts as involving a transition from the potential to the actual, and sees the mutable as the first as well as the last reality. To his loss, the Aristotelian-scholastic doctrine of God as pure act evaded him. If he had grasped it, he would have seen both in what sense God is immutable because perfect and how his immutable perfection does not make him static and inert but infinitely active. Hence by nature God knows, loves, and does what is best in so complete a way that he is truth itself, goodness itself, and love itself. God is love, and the object of love, as Bergson recognizes. However, as he states his doctrine, it is difficult to satisfy those[17] who hold that Bergsonian theism is essentially a form of pantheism in which God as divine becoming is identified with the cosmic process.

Other strictures have been put on Bergson's philosophy. It is asserted that he has brilliantly used the intellect to depreciate the intellect. He rejects the charge of anti-intellectualism, it is true, but the limits that he places on the powers of reason and intellect and his appeal to intuition provide basis for the charge. Different as he is from Kant, it has been pointed out that he never completely divested himself of early Kantian influences. His use, or overuse, of metaphor, has been instanced as a substitution of sense images for the abstract concepts that must be the tools of the metaphysician. Figures of speech have their value, but they cannot take the place of the rigorous analysis and strict reasoning that philosophy demands. Just as it may be argued that Kant was never able to move from epistemology into metaphysics, so also it may be said that Bergson did not succeed in moving from psychology into metaphysics.

While there undoubtedly are serious errors and deficiencies in Bergson's philosophy, there are as well great good qualities that counterbalance its weaknesses. Some of these virtues have already been named or at least implied, but they deserve repetition and fuller stress. Bergson derives not only from Heraclitus but also from other great Greek thinkers—in varying ways from Socrates, Plato, Aristotle, the Stoics, and Plotinus—and this background adds to the solidity and vitality of his thought. He knows the history of philosophy both ancient and modern and he may be taken as a continuer of its best traditions. While he does not have an adequate knowledge of the chief medieval thinkers, it is significant that he has expressed liking for the passages of St. Thomas Aquinas that he had read.[18] As Jacques Maritain has written, if anyone were to isolate and release what Bergson wished and tried to do in philosophy, "it would yield and order its powers in the great wisdom of Thomas of Aquin." [19] Moreover, like St. Thomas and many other spokesmen both early and late for the *philosophia perennis,* Bergson had profited from study of the Old Testament and the Gospel. Hence in *The Two*

Sources, he does not hesitate to put what he learned to use and to quote from the prophets, the apostles, and Jesus of Nazareth. Neither hostility to religion nor timidity in the face of modern prejudices deprives his work of the wisdom that comes from searching the Scriptures. Here as in so many other ways Bergson provides an example that can be followed. The things that are written in the two Testaments should not lose their efficacy for those who say that they are purely human words, and surely not for others who say that they are God's.

To perceive the nature of the shallow and inconclusive doctrines that dominated in Europe during Bergson's formative years required strength and independence of mind as well as knowledge of better things, and to speak out against them called for courage and integrity of character. The easiest way for young Bergson would have been to go along with the prevailing ideas, but he chose to go against them and was able to rise above them, and for the partial defeat of those nineteenth-century dogmas Bergson deserves credit above all other thinkers of his time. He not only criticized the defects and limitations of others, but he saw facts that had to be accounted for and persistent problems that had to be restated. This is in itself the act of a genuine philosopher, and to strive as long and hard as Bergson did to provide answers is fuller proof of his worth as a thinker. Whatever reservations are made as to his answers, it is still Bergson's endeavor to establish the reality of free will, of a spiritual soul, and of a freely creating God, and to refute pantheism and all other forms of monism; more than this, it is his conviction that he has done so. Maritain rightly makes a distinction between the Bergsonism of fact and the Bergsonism of intention, and while there is regret that Bergson's philosophy is not completely successful, with Maritain we pay tribute to the nobility of his aims.

Bergson is a true synthesist in philosophy. As he has written, every man's doctrine can be reduced to a single proposition, and for him it is, "All is becoming." The theme runs throughout all his works and is developed and applied over and over. Thus in the lesser classic that he produced in *Le Rire: Essai sur la signification du comique* it is shown that we laugh because we are living, social, intelligent beings, and he tells us that for him the things that lead us to laugh are breaks in the flow of life, intrusions

of the material upon the spiritual, and impositions of the artificial
and the mechanical upon the natural and the living. When we
laugh there is "a momentary anesthesia of our feelings;" we become detached from the victim of the slapstick and we are without
sympathy for his plight. Even in these few chapters on the
meaning of the comic element in our lives, brief as they are in
relation to his whole work, Bergson's dominant idea is put to
work. His philosophy here as well as elsewhere shows an inner
consistency, and in him such consistency is a source of strength,
just as it is in Hobbes the materialistic, Hegel the idealist, and
Aquinas the philosopher of being.

The clarity and order with which Bergson presents his doctrines, his wide and solid learning, and his wealth of ideas, together with the felicity of expression that he gives to them, all
assure him of a special place in modern thought. It is worth
noting that Bergson's philosophy derives in part from Schopenhauer. Like Schopenhauer in the first half of nineteenth-century
Germany, Bergson shows himself to be the artist as thinker, and
his way of writing combines with what he has written to make
him a greatly influential figure. His doctrine of all-pervading
mobility has had a deep and abiding impact on literature, music,
and the other arts, on psychology, and on social, moral, and
religious theory as well as on the course of philosophy itself.
His contribution to the flourishing pragmatic movement of the
century's earlier decades is apparent. Many ancestors have been
assigned to contemporary existentialism, and Bergson must certainly be included among them. His influence may be seen in
Maritain's work,[20] particularly his esthetic theory, in the theological
speculations of Maurice Blondel and Le Roy, and in varying
ways in the work of Louis Lavelle, Pierre Teilhard de Chardin,
and Gabriel Marcel. In literature he found a fervent supporter
and channel of influence in Charles Péguy, and the names of
Proust, Joyce, and Shaw are among the many that can be associated with his.

As is often the case with thinkers and makers who have had
great popular acclaim during their own lifetime, an early reaction
set in against Bergson, and as yet there has not been a counter-
reaction, although there are many who are devoted to him and
his work.[21] His books continue to be read and to be made the

subject of specialized studies. Undoubtedly, critical opinion as to the value of his doctrine and the extent of his influence will slowly settle so as to give him a definite and honored place in the history of philosophy. There are certain close parallels between Bergson and Plotinus, of whom he has written, "Il lui fut donné de voir la terre promise, mais non pas d'en fouler le sol." [22] Shall we apply the words to Bergson himself—that he never fully entered into the promised land of metaphysics, the first philosophy and science of God, as Aristotle terms it? If he did not join there the company of Plato and Aristotle and Plotinus and of Augustine and Aquinas, yet he knew of it from his youth, labored all his life to draw near it, and at the end had a vision and promise not only of such a land but of something vastly more.

NOTES

1. This rather stale method of setting the historical scene for Bergson's work has been used with hesitation but I hope some justification, since Bergson belongs so completely to his time and place and yet in his thought rises so far above it.

2. John M. Oesterreicher, *Walls Are Crumbling* (New York: Devin Adair Co., 1952), p. 43. Cardinal Suhard is quoted as saying that in his judgment according to the constant doctrine of the Church Bergson had received the baptism of desire. Cf. Jacques Chevalier, *Entretiens avec Bergson* (Paris: Plon, 1959), pp. 299-301.

3. "Entretien avec Bergson," *La Vie catholique*, X (Jan. 7, 1933) 432, p. 1.

4. *Bulletin de la Société française de Philosophie*, Mai, 1901, pp. 63-64. Both this and the preceding statement are quoted by Stuart E. Dollard. "A Summary of Bergsonism," *The Modern Schoolman*, XX (Nov., 1942) 27.

5. Cf. *The Sophist*, 327 a.

6. Cf. *Physics*, IV, iii; VI, ii, ix; VII, v, viii.

7. "It is solved by walking." Democritus illustrates the scholastic maxim, "Contra factum non valet argumentum: Against fact there is no valid argument." However, his act of walking is not itself a refutation of Zeno, since Zeno does not deny the factual appearance of movement and attacks an opposing theory rather than defends his own. Democritus' appeal to fact is like Dr. Johnson's answer to Berkeley's immaterialism as reported by Boswell. "We stood talking for some time together of Bishop Berkeley's ingenious sophistry to prove the non-existence of matter, and that every thing in the universe is merely ideal. I observed, that though we are satisfied

his doctrine is not true, it is impossible to refute it. I shall never forget the alacrity with which Johnson answered, striking his foot with mighty force against a large stone, till he rebounded from it, 'I refute it thus.' " James Boswell, *The Life of Samuel Johnson*, ed. Roger Ingpen (2 vols; Bath: George Baytun, 1924), I, 286. Berkeley does not deny the reality of the stone and its hardness; what he denies is its materiality.

8. All these works are contained in the one-volume "Édition du Centenaire," published in 1959, and references are to this edition.

9. For these translations see the bibliography.

10. Bergson presented the *Essai sur les données immédiates de la conscience*, together with a Latin thesis, *Quid Aristoteles de loco senserit* (Paris: F. Alcan, 1889), as part of the requirements for his doctorate at the Sorbonne.

11. I use this term from the Latin "fieri," to become, as a name for Bergson's philosophy.

12. Cf. "M. Bergson est-il moniste?" *Études*, 130 (février, 1912) 515.

13. "Fear first made gods in the world." Statius, *Thebais*, Ph. Kohlmann, ed. (Leipzig: Teubner, 1884), iii, 661.

14. *Oeuvres*, p. 1179.

15. *Ibid.*, p. 1245. These are the concluding words of *The Two Sources*.

16. Cf. Jules A. Baisnée, "Bergson's Approach to God." *The New Scholastiscism*, X (April, 1936) 116-44. Archimedes Fornasari, "A Critical Study of Henri Bergson's *Two Sources of Religion and Morality*," pp. 32, an unpublished work done in 1964 in the School of Philosophy, The Catholic University of America, is also valuable. Father Fornasari defends Bergson against charges of anti-intellectualism and pantheistic monism but finds valid criticism for the absence of a final cause. He writes: "The burden of the creative effort is based exclusively on the efficient cause. The reason for his steadfast refusal to admit a final causality operating in the vital impulse may be explained by fear that such causality would destroy the freedom he wants for his vital impetus." p. 27.

17. Cf., e.g., Cardinal Désiré Mercier, "Vers l'unité" in *Revue Néoscolastique*, XX (1913) 253-78.

18. Cf. Raissa Maritain, "Henri Bergson," *The Commonweal*, XXXIII (Jan. 17, 1941) 319: "A few years ago Bergson wrote that although he was little familiar with Thomas Aquinas, yet each time that he had come across one of Aquinas's texts, he had agreed with him, and he readily acceded to his philosophy being placed in the stream of continuity flowing from Saint Thomas."

19. Jacques Maritain, *La Philosophie bergsonienne: études critiques* (3rd. ed. Paris: P. Téqui, 1948), p. 321.

20. For Bergson's deep effect upon the life of Jacques Maritain and his wife, cf. Raissa Maritain, *We Have Been Friends Together*, translated by Julie Kernan (New York: Longmans, Green, 1945).

21. In France there is an "Association des Amis de Bergson" and a journal, *Les Études bergsoniennes*, is dedicated to his work. His books are

kept in print and their popularity is evidenced by the fact that *Le Rire,* first published in 1900, went into its 59th printing in 1959.

22. *Oeuvres,* p. 1162.

BIBLIOGRAPHY

Bergson, Henri. *Oeuvres.* Textes annotés par André Robinet; Introduction par Henri Gouhier. Paris: Presses Universitaires de France, 1959. (Édition du Centenaire)

————. *Écrits et paroles.* Edited by R. M. Mossé - Bastide. 3 vols. Paris: Presses Universitaires de France, 1957-1859.

————. *Time and Free Will: an Essay on the Immediate Data of Consciousness.* Authorized translation by F. L. Pogson. London: George Allen, 1910.

————. *Matter and Memory.* Authorized translation by Nancy Margaret Paul and W. Scott Palmer. London: George Allen and Unwin, 1911.

————. *Creative Evolution.* Authorized translation by Arthur Mitchell. New York: Henry Holt, 1911.

————. *The Two Sources of Morality and Religion.* Translated by R. Ashley Audra and Cloudesley Brereton with the assistance of W. Horsfall Carter. New York: Henry Holt, 1935.

————. *Laughter: an Essay on the Meaning of the Comic.* Authorized translation by Cloudesley Brereton and F. Rothwell. New York: Macmillan, 1911.

————. *An Introduction to Metaphysics.* Translated by T. E. Hulme. Authorized edition, revised by the author, with additional material. New York and London: G. P. Putnam's Sons, 1912.

In addition to works cited in the notes, the following works will be helpful to a student of Bergson's thought.

Benda, Julien. *Trois idoles romantiques.* Genève: Éditions du Mont - Blanc, 1948.

Chevalier, Jacques. *Henri Bergson.* Translated by L. A. Clare. New York: Macmillan, 1931.

————. *Bergson et le Père Pouget.* Paris: Plon, 1954.

Husson, Léon. *L'Intellectualisme de Bergson.* Paris: Presses Universitaires de France, 1947.

Jankélévitch, Vladimir. *Henri Bergson.* Paris: Presses Universitaires de France, 1959.

Maritain, Jacques. *Bergsonian Philosophy and Thomism.* Translated by Mabelle L. Andison. New York: Philosophical Library, 1954. (A translation of *La Philosophie bergsonienne.*)

Maritain, Jacques. *De Bergson à Thomas d'Aquin: essais de métaphysique et de morale. New York:* Éditions de la maison française, 1944.

————. *The Degrees of Knowledge.* Translated by Gerald B. Phelan. New York: Scribner, 1959.

Scharfstein, Ben-Ami. *Roots of Bergson's Philosophy.* New York: Columbia University Press, 1943.

Sertillanges, A. *Avec Henri Bergson.* Paris: Gallimard, 1941.

Sheen, Fulton J. *God and Intelligence in Modern Philosophy.* New York: Longmans, Green, 1935; Garden City, N. Y.: Image Books (paperback).

Stepelevich, Lawrence S. *Henri Bergson's Concept of Man: An Exposition and Critique.* Washington, D. C.: The Catholic University of America Press, 1963. Microfilm.

maurice blondel

THE METHOD OF IMMANENCE
AS AN APPROACH TO GOD

by Bernardine M. Bonansea, O.F.M.

Unlike various other thinkers considered in this volume, Maurice Blondel is little known to the English-speaking world, even within the limited circle of philosophers. None of his works has been translated into English, no comprehensive study has been made of his thought by any of our scholars, very few articles have been written on him in our periodicals, and even his name is seldom mentioned in our manuals of the history of philosophy.

Yet Blondel has been the object of many studies, especially in France and Italy, where he became the center of a heated controversy upon the publication in 1893 of his famous thesis, *L'action; essai d'une critique de la vie et d'une science de la pratique*. While some attacked him for his new ideas, which they closely associated with the invading error of modernism, others praised him for his courage to stand up and defend Christian doctrine against the widely spread rationalism and positivism of his day.

There seems to be no question today as to the orthodoxy and high level of Blondel's thought, which has won the admiration of many outstanding scholars who see in the French philosopher a leading figure in the intellectual movement of the twentieth century. Thus Michele F. Sciacca, professor of philosophy at the university of Genoa and an enthusiastic admirer of Blondel, calls him "the greatest contemporary Catholic thinker."[1] Père Auguste Valensin, Blondel's intimate friend and disciple, praises his master for having given a new orientation to philosophical thinking."[2] Henri Bouillard, S.J., professor at the Institut Catholique in Paris and a recognized authority in Blondelian studies, says that no work has exercised such a profound influence upon the French theology of the first part of the twentieth century as that of Blondel. He adds further that perhaps no other work has so helped contemporary Christian philosophers to harmonize their convictions with their faith.[3] Charles Moeller goes so far as to compare Blondel with St. Augustine and St. Thomas Aquinas, and says that with them "he is one of the three great Christian minds called to reaffirm the meaning of humanism and of the supernatural in our world sickened from atheism and lies." Moeller expresses the belief that Blondel "will become more and more the great dominating figure of our unfortunate twentieth century."[4]

To these testimonies of appreciation of Blondel's philosophy it may be added that when the Archbishop of Aix, Monseigneur Bonnefoy, was prompted by attacks on Blondel to inquire of Pope Pius X what he thought of his philosophy, the Pope replied: "I am sure of Blondel's orthodoxy, and I charge you to tell him so."[5] Pope Pius XI received Blondel in a special audience and expressed to him the hope that his students may be inspired by his same spirit.[6] Pope Pius XII, in a letter written by Msgr. G. B. Montini, the present Pope Paul VI, also commended Blondel's work.[7] These authoritative documents should be enough to dispel any doubt as to Blondel's orthodoxy.

LIFE AND WORKS

Blondel was born at Dijon, France, on November 2, 1861. After preliminary studies in his own town, he obtained his licentiate in literature and his baccalaureate in science and law. In 1881 he entered the École Normale Supérieure of Paris where Henri Bergson had just completed his studies. His masters, Léon Ollé Laprune and Émile Boutroux, two well-known figures in the history of nineteenth-century French philosophy, exercised a considerable influence on the formation of his thought. It was during the second year at the École Normale that he decided on action as the topic for his doctoral thesis. Reportedly, when one of his classmates heard of the choice of the topic, he exclaimed: "A thesis on action, my God, what could that be? The word 'action' does not even appear in Franck's dictionary of philosophy."[8] As

a matter of fact, when Blondel went to the Sorbonne and asked
for approval of his topic, he was told by the secretary that there
would not be sufficient material for such a thesis. As things turned
out, Blondel found enough to write several hundred pages!

It took Blondel ten years of hard work to complete his thesis,
which he presented to the Sorbonne in 1893. After reading the
manuscript, Boutroux, under whose guidance the thesis had been
written and who would be on the presiding board of examiners,
suggested to Blondel to go and see the other members of the
board who, in his own words, had been deeply upset by the
novelty of the topic and especially by his notion of Christian
philosophy. In this way, Boutroux told Blondel, "they will have
a chance to blow up before they do so in public." [9] The defense
of the thesis took place before a packed audience on June 7, 1893,
in a memorable session, full of emotion and heated discussion,
that lasted from three o'clock in the afternoon until seven fifteen
in the evening. It was an historical event, for, as one writer puts it,
not without a little sarcasm, "the great pontiffs of the Sorbonne
presiding at the defense of the thesis had the clear but painful
sensation that a revolution was taking shape. This revolution was
going to shake the very foundations of that spiritual rationalism
which they so well represented. They felt that their power was
coming to an end." [10] Blondel defended himself so well in the
course of the debate that the thesis was unanimously approved
with the marked distinction of the right of publication.

As previously stated, the publication of the thesis, which was
completely sold out in the period of fifteen months, caused a great
stir among philosophers and theologians, both in France and
abroad. Blondel had to defend himself against the attacks of
those Catholics who saw in him a supporter of modernism and
against rationalists who thought he had compromised the rights
of human reason. For the rationalists, says Prof. Sciacca, Blondel
was too much of a Christian; for the Catholics, he was not Christian
enough.[11] As a result of these attacks, Blondel was refused a
professorship at the Sorbonne. However, through the good offices
of his former master, Émile Boutroux, he was appointed "Maître
de conférence" at the university of Lille, and later ordinary
professor at the university of Aix-Marseille, where he remained
until his retirement in 1927. A gradual loss of his sight, which

eventually led to complete blindness, forced him to return to private life. From then on he dictated his works and had philosophical publications read to him.

It was only after forty-one years of intense meditation and profound thinking that his second major work was published. This is the first of a five-volume series which appeared between 1934 and 1937 and includes *La pensée*, in 2 volumes, *L' Être et les êtres*, in 1 volume, and *L'action*, in 2 volumes, the first of which is entirely new, while the second is a partial recast of the 1893 thesis. The five volumes constitute what Blondel calls "his trilogy" and represent the synthesis of his entire philosophical speculation. *L'action*, in both editions, remains however Blondel's most original and perhaps most important work. Between 1944 and 1946 Blondel published two volumes of *La philosophie et l'esprit chrétien*, a treatise on Christian philosophy, which may be taken as his spiritual testament.[12] He died on June 4, 1949, at the age of 88, without having been able to complete a third volume.

Blondel is the author of numerous articles and several other works, in addition to those already mentioned. The following writings are of a special interest to a philosopher: *De vinculo substantiali et de substantia composita apud Leibnitium* (Paris: Alcan, 1893); "Lettre sur les exigences de la pensée contemporaine en matière d'apologétique et sur la méthode de la philosophie dans l'étude du problème religieux," *Annales de philosophie chrétienne*, Jan. - July, 1896; *Principe élémentaire d'une logique de la vie morale* (Paris: Colin, 1903); "Le point de départ de la recherche philosophique," *Annales de philosophie chrétienne*, Jan. - June, 1906; *Le procès de l'intelligence* (Paris: Bloud and Gay, 1922); "Le problème de Dieu et la philosophie," *Bulletin de la Société Française de Philosophie*, Jan. 1930; "Ya-t-il une philosophie chrétienne?", *Revue de métaphysique et de morale*, Nov. 1931; *Le problème de la philosophie catholique* (Paris: Bloud and Gay, 1932); "Pour la phlosophie intégrale," *Revue néoscolastique de philosophie*, May 1934; *Exigences philosophiques du christianisme* (Paris: Presses Universitaires de France, 1950). Posthumous works: *Études blondéliennes* (3 vols.; Paris: Presses Universitaires de France, 1951-1954); *Lettres philosophiques* (Paris: Aubier, 1961).

The Blondelian bibliography, compiled by Father André

Hayen in 1951, includes 1090 entries. Many other works on Blondel have been written since, mostly in French and Italian.[13]

It is the purpose of this study to present the general theme of his philosophy, with special emphasis on his method of approach to God as found in *L'action* and his trilogy.

L'ACTION (1893)

The basic idea of Blondel's philosophy was suggested to him by the atmosphere of religious indifference he found at the École Normale Supérieure when he was student there. He noticed with great concern the almost total lack of interest of his masters and schoolmates in all matters pertaining to religion. Is it possible, he asked himself, that a divorce exists between philosophy and religion, and that religion is of so little importance to a philosopher that he can completely ignore it and even boast of such an attitude? This is how there arose in Blondel the problem that characterizes his entire philosophy. The way in which he would solve it would be by studying and analyzing in a concrete fashion the fundamental issue of human destiny.

The Method of Immanence. — Accepting St. Thomas' principle that the best way to refute an error is to use the very arguments advanced by its defenders,[14] Blondel will take the principle of immanence as a starting point for his dialectic, since immanentism was a current trend in his own day. He will use what later became known as the "method of immanence," which may be defined as the psychological process of posing all philosophical and religious problems by starting from the self. It differs from the "theory of immanence" in that the source of philosophical and religious truth is held to be internal observation rather than consciousness or subconsciousness. The theory of immanence confines its study to the subject and denies or ignores all transcendent reality; the method of immanence, while studying the subject, goes beyond the subject and admits the existence of other realities than the self, and especially the supreme reality of God.[15]

In Blondel's view, the infinite disproportion that we observe between our exigencies in life and our ideals makes us realize our deficiencies and the need for a transcendent and necessary being. Thus the order of nature finds its integration in the supernatural order of grace and revelation as manifested in Christian religion. The method of immanence is therefore, in Blondel's words, the denial of, and the antidote against, immanentism in the strict sense of the term.[16] It is also the best possible method, for traditional metaphysics "is impotent when it is a question of bringing modern spirits to Christianity."[17] He writes in this connection:

> Modern thought considers with jealous susceptibility the notion of immanence as the very condition of philosophy ... If there is one conclusion to which modern philosophy attaches itself as to a certainty, it is the idea, basically justifiable, that nothing can enter into a man which does not come from him, and does not correspond in some fashion to a need for expansion ... There is no truth for him which really matters and no acceptable precept that is not in some way autonomous and autochtonous.[18]

And a little further:

> If the meaning of modern philosophy fails to be grasped by many people, who in our very own time have lived of the past, and if so many current doctrines appear to them enigmatic and vague, it is no doubt because of their failure to show the least appreciation for the principle of this method, a principle that has become and is going to be more and more the soul of philosophy.[19]

Blondel believes that his method of immanence contains a positive affirmation leading to faith. Yet he does not pose as an apologist of Christian religion, as he has often been presented against his explicit statement to the contrary. He is and wants to be essentially a philosopher. The purpose of his dialectic is to show to the intellectualists of his own day that a philosopher cannot be indifferent to the problem of religion, and that Christianity, more specifically Catholicism, is the only answer to the fundamental problem of human destiny.[20] It is important to keep this in mind in order to avoid any prejudicial attitude towards Blondel's system.

Dialectic of Action. —

Yes or no [Blondel asks in his introduction to *L'action*], has human life a meaning, has man a destiny? I act,
but I do not know what action is. I have not wished to
live, and I do not know exactly who I am or even if I
am . . . And yet my actions carry within themselves an
eternal responsibility . . . Shall I say, then, that I have
been condemned to live, condemned to die, condemned
to eternity! How is that possible, and by what right, since
I did neither know it nor will it? . . . The problem is inevitable; man inevitably resolves it; and this solution,
right or wrong, each one carries out in his own actions.
That is why one must study action.[21]

For Blondel action is a complex term that stands for the entire
human experience conceived within the framework of man's basic
needs and tendencies; it is the synthesis of thought, will, and being
itself, the activity of the whole man. The greater and the nobler
is man's activity, the greater and the nobler is his action. In this
sense Blondel can say with St. John of the Cross that to think
of God and to contemplate him is the supreme form of action.[22]
Action is the most universal fact in human life and no one can
avoid it. Suicide itself is an act. Action is also a personal obligation that may demand a hard choice, a sacrifice, and even death.

Blondel's dialectic of action is a description of the real logic
that governs each human destiny. In his own words, "it is the role
of the logic of action to determine the chain of necessities that
compose the drama of life and lead it inevitably to the denoue-
ment."[23] Today, as one author puts it, we would call such an
enterprise a philosophy of existence.[24]

Just as Freud would after him devise a method by which
one can bring to the level of consciousness what is hidden in
the deep subconscious, so Blondel has devised a method of revealing to man what he wills without being aware of it. Freud
calls his procedure "phychoanalysis," to distinguish it from the
ordinary observation of the psychologists; Blondel's procedure
could perhaps be called, with Auguste Valensin, "a metapsychological analysis."[25] It consists not so much in cataloguing the

contents of consciousness as in bringing forth the contents of the will as manifested in action or activity in which it is incarnated.

The dialectic of action is a novelty. It has a characteristic of its own which it derives from the very nature of the problem it aims to solve, namely, the problem of human destiny. Action is essentially an act of the will. To make sure that the need of the supernatural towards which the dialectic tends is found in the will as will and not merely in the will of some individual persons, there is only one way: to start from the most basic and limited act of the will, to show that this act contains inevitably another act, this other a third one, and so on and so forth until one arrives at an act of the will that includes the object desired and fully satisfies man's aspirations. This transition from one act of willing to another is Blondel's dialectic of action. It would be impossible to follow him step by step in such a dialectic, since to do so would amount to condensing into a few pages the substance of a 495-page volume. However, an attempt will be made to give a general idea of its process and its terminus.

As previously stated, for Blondel action is a necessity and an obligation, and even to refuse to act and to do away with one's own life is an action. This same principle must be applied to human willing, which is a characteristic of human activity. The most simple act of willing, no matter how limited its object may be, is still too rich and too involved to serve as a starting point for the metapsychological analysis of the will and its contents. One can always think of willing something less than he actually does. For example, one can think of not willing at all, of making no choice and no decision. Yet to do this is to will something, for any refusal to will is possible only in terms of an act of willing. To refuse to choose is to make a choice.

To show that man cannot live without willing is not enough. One must also show that he actually wills something, for otherwise his act of willing would be a purely negative one. We would have no starting point for our analysis which must lead inevitably to something positive, a definite end. Now the minimum object we can assign to the will, after it has been proved that it is impossible for the will not to will, is to will nothing or nothingness (le néant). This is what Blondel calls the attitude of the pessimist, while in the former case, namely, in the case of a man who refuses

to will altogether and makes no decision as to the purpose of his
life, we have the attitude of the dilettante or amateur.

But is it possible to will nothing or to make nothingness, i.e.,
nonbeing, the term of our act of willing? Evidently not, answers
Blondel, because a negation is only conceivable in terms of an
affirmation. As Schopenhauer had already remarked, even the
man who takes his own life does so only because he would like
to enjoy a better life. It is the love of an ideal being that makes
one hate his present being. Blondel concludes the first phase of
his dialectic of action by saying that the human will always tends
towards *being,* and any statement to the contrary is a contradiction.[26]

Blondel then goes on to study human activity in all its aspects.
He notices everywhere a contrast between action and its realization, between the object willed and the primitive *élan,* the impetus
of the will, or, in his own terminology, between the *volonté
voulue* (the willed will) and the *volonté voulante* (the willing
will). This contrast constitutes the permanent dissatisfaction of
human life, and provides the incentive for further action. When
the extreme limit of what can be willed and desired in the natural
order has been reached, man soon realizes that his willing power
is far from being exhausted. On the contrary, it craves for something more, something that cannot be found in the natural order
where all goods are finite. It is at this stage that the idea of the
infinite comes to man's mind, and with this, the idea of God as
the "unique necessary" which can completely satisfy his aspirations. This idea impresses on action a character of transcendence.
Man wishes to possess God who is somehow present to him; he
wants to become similar to him. But this he cannot do by himself. Hence he must face an inevitable alternative which requires
an option, a decision that concerns the meaning and value of his
whole life.

> Yes or no [Blondel asks at this point], is man going
> to will to live, even to die of it, as it were, by consenting
> to be supplanted by God? Or will he pretend to get along
> without Him, profiting by His necessary presence without
> making it voluntary, borrowing from Him the power to

get along without Him, and infinitely willing without willing the infinite?[27]

Blondel is aware, and states explicitly, that not all men are confronted with this tragic dilemma in the same exacting terms. However, he remarks that once the thought is suggested to a person, in one form or another, that something must be done with his own life, even the rudest and least educated of men realize that they are called upon to resolve this most important problem, the only necessary concern in man's life.

It is at this point that Blondel proposes his theory of the supernatural as the necessary implementation of the natural order, and thus introduces the most crucial and controversial issue of his entire philosophy. He realizes the challenging and provocative character of his doctrine, but he does not retreat. He writes:

> Action is not completely achieved in the natural order. But is not the very term "supernatural" a scandal to the human reason? When a philosopher is confronted with such an unknown [term or reality], is it not true that his attitude is simply to ignore it, or, more resolutely and more frankly, to deny it? No. To deny or to ignore it is against the spirit of philosophy. Far from invading a reserved domain, one must show that any such invasion is impossible, and that it is precisely because of this impossibility that a necessary relation exists [between the natural and the supernatural order]. It is the task of rational science to study the absolute independence as well as the necessity of the supernatural order.[28]

These statements contain the theme of Blondel's concluding treatment of action, namely, the relationship between the natural and the supernatural order. We shall return upon this theme later.

THE TRILOGY

The dialectic of action, whose main traits have just been described, is to a great extent a phenomenology of action. The trilogy, on the contrary, contains what may be called Blondel's ontology. While still retaining the basic ideas of his previous work, in the trilogy Blondel feels that the title "philosophy of action" no longer provides an adequate description of his system. Action presupposes being, and being is intelligible. To be complete, a philosophical system must include the study of thought and being. This is what Blondel proposes to do in *La pensée* and *L'Être et les êtres,* which, together with the new version of *L'action,* constitute what has rightly been called "Blondel's integral realism."

La pensée. — The two volumes of *La pensée* make it clear that Blondel is not so much interested in thought as representation as he is in the intrinsic act of thinking, the very reality and possibility of thinking.[29] He does not present a critique of knowledge, nor does he discuss the value of knowledge as such. Rather, he studies the dynamism of thought in its origin, its development, and the necessary conditions for its fulfillment. In his analysis, he begins with *cosmic* thought, or thought as represented by the inorganic world. It has often been said that the world is a thought that does not think itself. This statement acquires a special meaning in Blondel for whom the world is just as intelligible as it is real. Does the world derive its intelligibility merely from the divine mind on which it depends or from our mind which apprehends it? Evidently not. The world has an intelligibility of its own; it is a subsistent, although incomplete, thought.[30] The world has the characteristics of the one and the many, which are proper to thought. It is in effect a permanent whole, with mutually dependent parts, in a continuous becoming that gives rise to multiplicity and variety. As a result, cosmic thought presents two different aspects: the *noetic,* which stands for the universal and the rational in the universe; the *pneumatic,* which represents the singular, the unique, and the ineffable. These two different aspects of the universe have their counterpart in man's perception of it.

Blondel extends his analysis to *organic* thought and *psychic* thought, and finds in them the same characteristics of unity and multiplicty which belong to cosmic thought but on a proportionally higher level. The principle of unity in organic beings is life, an active and original power that organizes the manifold material into a new reality, an architectonic perfection that makes up for the inadequacy observable in the physical world. The characteristics of life are unity, spontaneity, and "perennity," or a tendency to continue in existence, as manifested in the preservation of the species. These characteristics are even more noticeable in psychic life, which represents a further step in the ascending process of the many towards the one. Psychic thought, roughly called animal consciousness, paves the way for *human* thought, in which Blondel distinguishes again between noetic and pneumatic thought, a duality corresponding to the relationship between the one and the many in the structure of the universe. Noetic thought is simply abstract thought dealing with the universal and the rational; pneumatic thought is concrete thought representing the singular and the unique. Both noetic and pneumatic thoughts coexist in one and the same *pensée pensante* (thinking thought) of which they are but different forms or aspects. Besides, they are so intimately related to each other that they cannot be separated. They are, to use Blondel's expression, "two thoughts in one thought." [81] Yet pneumatic thought is superior to noetic thought because it reveals to us the real in its concreteness rather than by morcellation, as noetic thought does. In pneumatic thought we have real knowledge; in noetic thought we have purely notional knowledge.

By applying to thought the dialectic of action, Blondel proves the radical inadequation between the *pensée pensante* (thinking thought) and the *pensée pensée* (thought that is thought). He discovers at the very heart of thought a drama similar to the one that takes place in action, namely, that the more man comes to know the more he wants to know, and this vital desire for knowledge and truth cannot be satisfied within the limits of his temporal life and the objects of a finite world. This is not merely an empirical fact; it is something essential and intrinsic to human nature. It is not merely an accidental wound that can be cured with the time, but a constitutional disease. Death itself, Blondel says, is the best proof of the inadequacy of human thought, for death is something against man's nature, it is both antiphysical and antimetaphysical.[82] The very idea of death is not possible and real without the implicit certitude that we possess within us something that is immortal. Blondel calls this a sort of ontological argument for the immortality of the soul.

In fact our thought, Blondel argues, cannot know itself except

by understanding a truth that is independent of all transitory
accidents. Essentially the act of understanding transcends time,
for truth has the characteristics of universality and eternity. Hence
the thinking soul belongs to a world superior to that characterized
by simple duration, becoming, or degradation, and an incompatibility exists between the life of thought and the inevitable disappearance of the thinking subject. It is from this incompatibility that
arises the scandal of human reason, the instinctive revolt of our
consciousness, the strange easiness with which, certain of our
impending mortality, we look at it as something hypothetical, unreal, uncertain, and foreign to our concrete preoccupations.[33]

No matter what one may think of this argument, Blondel
goes on to show that the dialectic of thought imposes on us an
option. Shall human thought be confined to knowing and or-
ganizing the finite world, or shall it open itself to a perfection
that it can find neither in itself nor in any object in this world?
This again leads man to God and the supernatural as the only
solution to his crucial dilemma.

L'Être et les êtres. — The same conclusion is arrived at by
Blondel in his dialectic of being, which he develops in *L'Être et
les êtres,* or *An Essay on Concrete and Integral Ontology,* as the
subtitle indicates. Here, however, as one author points out, the
drama of human destiny is enlarged to become a drama of the
universe.[34] Being is a most common term that has its equivalent
in every language and seems to convey the most simple meaning
to everyone who uses it. But is being really so simple as to
make all explanation and analysis useless? Despite its apparent
clarity, Blondel observes, being is one of the most confusing
and equivocal terms of our everyday usage. Its meaning is so
obscure that it borders on mystery. Yet it is impossible, even
mentally, to deny being, for to think is to thing something. The
idea of nothing is but a nothingness of an idea; it is a pseudo-
idea, a fiction.[35] But while we know that being is, we do not know
what it actually is; we believe in being.[36] Hence an analysis of
being is necessary.

In his analysis, Blondel attempts to prove that none of the
beings of our experience fits into the concept of being in the
strict sense of the term. Being is not a mere abstraction but a
concrete presence; it is not something that is most universal and

common (*ens generalissimum et commune*), but an irreducible singularity. The term being is a proper, incommunicable, and substantial name.[37] The beings of our experience have an objective reality—Blondel was not an idealist—and to this extent they have some sort of being, but they never completely realize in themselves the notion of being as such. There is only one being, he concludes, that fully realizes this notion, so that we can say of it without any qualification, "it is." That being is *l'Être en soi et par soi* (Being in itself and by itself), God.[38]

The dialectic of being leads once more to the crucial alternative of an option for God or against God. As a rational being, man has the power to divert himself from his end. However, his refusal to possess Being becomes for him a positive privation, since the universal order from which he excludes himself subsists against him. By failing to choose God, he fails to achieve his eternal destiny.

L'action (new version). — This same theme is restated in the new version of *L'action,* the third part of the trilogy, where the problem of action is approached from the metaphysical viewpoint of the relationship between the secondary causes and God as pure act. Action, by its very nature, tends towards an end which is also a good, or good itself. The study of action, even in its lowest form of physical operations, shows that the intimate dynamism of nature is but a progressive realization of the metaphysical principle that all beings tend to be similar to God (*omnia intendunt assimilari Deo*). It is only to the extent that this tendency and aspiration is accepted and effectively carried out by spiritual beings, that we can properly speak of them as free agents and true secondary causes participating in the sovereignty of the unique primary cause.[39]

The action of secondary causes is essentially a becoming, a transient reality, a movement from the imperfect to the perfect. However, becoming does not exclude a determinate orientation, an internal finality, a rigorous judgment. That is why a critical study of secondary causes and transient actions can and must lead to the idea, the affirmation, the absolute and necessary truth of a pure act. In it alone are to be found the perfect intelligibility and the substantial specification of a permanent and immutable action, an action with no stagnation, inertia, or sterility. In pure

act alone action receives its formal specification precisely because, in it, determination of action is inseparable from its exercise, which is always actual and fecund. On the contrary, the
specification of the action of secondary causes can only be determined by the end they are supposed to attain, an end that is
not merely their cause, but can become their life and their
reward as well.[40]

It would be wrong, therefore, to look for a true and complete
definition of action in the immanent series of secondary causes,
whether taken separately or in the totality of the universal order.
The essence of action can only be found in an absolute being,
in a being in which transcendence is fully immanent to itself.
This is so true that if, by a pure hypothesis, the only kind of
action were a becoming, there would be no action properly speaking. If our acts are in effect always of a transitional nature,
as we know them to be by experience, it is precisely because we
are constantly tending towards the eternal and pure act, in which
being, knowledge, and will are joined together in a perfect unity.[41]

The tragic dilemma that confronts man in his desire to become
similar to God and the realization of his own inadequacy are
reasserted by Blondel in the second volume of *L'action* in essentially the same terms as in his 1893 dissertation.

The directive idea and unifying principle of the entire trilogy
is best summarized in Blondel's own words that everywhere, in
thought, being, and action, we are confronted with a duality that
becomes known to us only because of a natural tendency towards
unity. Everywhere we meet, at the heart of all contingent reality,
an inadequation which, far from discouraging, opens up a new vista
and stimulates us to a further action in view of a superior end.
Thus in all we are and in all we know, will, and do an infinite is
everywhere present which we must acknowledge in our mind
and accept in our actions.[42]

A philosopher, it has been said, expresses only one idea in
his lifetime. Blondel did not think otherwise. He writes: "All
philosophical endeavor only translates a primitive and permanent
idea and intention which would seem to be contained in one word,
but which many assembled books do not exhaust."[43] The idea
that Blondel tried to convey to the intellectuals of his own day
was in answer to a question raised at the École Normale Supé-

rieure in Paris by one of his schoolmates: "Why should I be obliged," his friend asked him, "to investigate and to pay attention to an event which happened 1900 years ago in an obscure corner of the Roman empire, when I glory in ignoring so many other important historical events?"[44] Blondel's answer to his friend is that Christianity is not merely a thing of the past but an actual reality that concerns every man, and the philosopher perhaps more than any other. He proves this, or at least he attempts to do so, by showing that in our thought there is more than our thought, that in our being there is more than our being, and that in our action there is more than our action. In his analysis of thought, being, and action he arrives at one and the same conclusion, namely, that in the very immanence of our own spontaneous life a transcendent being is revealed, for the relative and the contingent is not intelligible except in terms of the necessary and the absolute.[45]

NATURAL AND SUPERNATURAL ORDER

Before concluding this study, we feel the need of stating very briefly what seems to be Blondel's position on the relationship between the natural and the supernatural order, since a clear notion of his teaching on this delicate subject is necessary for the understanding of his entire philosophy.

According to Blondel, the existence of the supernatural order is a fact that is known to us exclusively by faith and revelation. The supernatural order is in no way due to man; it is absolutely gratuitous on the part of God. This is Blondel's firm belief as a Catholic—all agree in saying that he was a sincere and devout Catholic—and the teaching that can be gathered from his writings, especially those of a later date, when he felt the need of defending his own position against the attacks of some theologians.[46] Yet, in Blondel's view, a philosopher can arrive at the idea of a supernatural order even without the help of revelation, since this order must appear to him as the necessary integration of the order of nature.

Contrary to what has been affirmed by some of his critics, Blondel does not study the relations existing between pure nature or nature in the theological sense of the term, which is a pure abstraction, and the supernatural order. He always considers nature as found in concrete and actual reality, a nature which has de facto been raised to the supernatural order. The supernatural is, therefore, for Blondel something that must be reckoned with even by a philosopher. To refuse to accept the supernatural is not the same thing as to reduce oneself to the order of pure nature, just as any attempt to build up a philosophical system that prescinds from the supernatural is not the same thing as to deny the existence of the supernatural as such.

The exact point of demarcation between the natural and the supernatural order is not clearly stated by Blondel, who on the other hand is very explicit in his teaching that once the supernatural is presented to our mind we have no choice but to accept it. To refuse it, or even to refuse to act, is to renounce the divine call and expose ourselves to the most serious consequences for having failed to achieve our eternal destiny, the very purpose of our earthly existence.[47] It is in the light of these principles that Blondel can advance his theory of a hypothetical necessity of the supernatural and claim for Christian philosophy the exclusive right to be called a true and genuine philosophy.[48]

One may question the correctness of some of Blondel's statements, especially in his early writings, which taken separately may give the impression of a systematically antagonistic attitude towards traditional scholastic philosophy and even of an open rejection of some of its fundamental tenets. However, when such statements are considered in their proper context and within the general framework of his entire system, they lose part of their challenging nature and become more understandable. They can, at any rate, be corrected and made to harmonize with Christian teaching in the light of his later declarations.

It is our conviction that despite its inevitable inaccuracies and shortcomings Blondel's system stands out as a landmark in the history of human thought.[49] It represents a vigorous and original attempt to rethink man's basic philosophical problems from the point of view of his concrete life, his inner desires and aspirations, his many failures and disappointments, and the evident but painful realization of his own inability to solve the problem of human destiny. The value and constructive nature of Blondel's system appears even more evident when compared to certain contemporary philosophies that have captured the imagination of the public and won acceptance among various categories of people but are purely negative in their approach to reality and the basic problems of man. Whereas the anguish and anxieties that beset twentieth-century man have often led thinkers to a philosophy of despair and of the absurd, these very anxieties and basic inadequacies become for Blondel the starting point and springboard for his ascent to God by calling man's attention to the perennial and vital truth of the Augustinian saying, "You have made us for yourself, and our heart is restless until it rests in you." [50] This is Blondel's message to his twentieth-century fellow men, who in the midst of the most confusing ideologies often lose sight of the fact that man has a fundamental tendency towards the infinite. It is hoped that his message will not go unheeded and that history will assign him that place among the great minds which a thinker of his stature so rightly deserves.

NOTES

1. Cf. *Il problema di Dio e della religione nella filosofia attuale* (3d ed. rev.; Brescia: Morcelliana, 1953), p. 322.

2. "Maurice Blondel et la dialectique de l'action," *Études,* 263 (Oct.-Dec., 1949), 145.

3. Cf. *Blondel et le christianisme* (Paris: Éditions du Seuil, 1961), p. 16.

4. Cf. *Au seuil du christianisme,* Cahiers de "Lumen Vitae," IV (Bruxelles: Éditions universelles, XVI, 1952), p. 97.

5. Katherine Gilbert, *Maurice Blondel's Philosophy of Action* (Chapel Hill, N. C.: University of North Carolina, 1924), p. 4.

6. Fiammetta Vanni Bourbon di Petrella, *Il pensiero di Maurice Blondel* (Florence: L'Arte della Stampa, 1950), p. 21.

7. As reported by M. de Solages in the *Bulletin de littérature ecclésiastique* and quoted by Paul E. McKeever, "Maurice Blondel: Figure of Controversy," *American Ecclesiastical Review,* 126 (Jan.-June, 1952), 444.

8. Fiammetta Vanni, *op. cit.,* p. 10. Adolphe Franck's Dictionary of philosophical sciences was the one commonly used in France at that time.

9. *Ibid.,* p. 11.

10. Eugène Masure, "Le témoignage d'un théologien," *Les études philosophiques,* New series, 1 (1950), 54-55. Blondel reports that after the defense of his thesis one of the judges asked him whether his "manifesto" was the work of a solitary man, a "savage," or the beginning of a campaign against an independent and secularized philosophy. "It is the work of a 'savage'," he answered, "but against a new type of barbarians and for

the defense of civilization." Cf. Maurice Blondel, *Le problème de la philosophie catholique* (Paris: Bloud and Gay, 1932), p. 18, n. 1.

11. Sciacca, *op. cit.*, p. 323.

12. The two volumes of *La philosophie et l'esprit chrétien* have been published in Paris by the Presses Universitaires de France in the following order: Vol. I, *Autonomie essentielle et connexion indéclinable*, 1944; Vol. II, *Conditions de la symbiose seule normale et salutaire*, 1946.

13. Here are the principal works on Blondel's philosophy arranged according to a chronological order: Joseph de Tonquédec, *Immanence; essai critique sur la doctrine de M. Blondel* (Paris: Beauchesne, 1913); Katherine Gilbert, *Maurice Blondel's Philosophy of Action* (Chapel Hill, N. C.: University of North Carolina, 1924); Paul Archambault, *Vers un réalisme intégral; l'oeuvre philosophique de M. Blondel* (Paris: Bloud and Gay, 1928); Frédéric Lefèvre, *L'itinéraire philosophique de Maurice Blondel* (Paris: Spes, 1928); Fr. Taymans d'Eypernon, S. J., *Le blondélisme* (Louvain: Museum Lessianum, 1933); R. Garrigou - Lagrange, *God, His Existence and His Nature*, tr. Dom Bede Rose (St. Louis: Herder, 1934), I 40-60; Auguste Valensin and Yves de Montcheuil, *Maurice Blondel* (Paris: Gabalda, 1934); Paul Archambault, *Initiation à la philosophie blondélienne en forme de court traité de métaphysique* (Paris: Bloud and Gay, 1941); Blaise Romeyer, *La philosophie religieuse de M. Blondel* (Paris: Aubier, 1943); J. Roig Gironella, *Filosofia blondeliana* (Barcelona: Ed. Balmesiana, 1944); Henry Duméry, *La philosophie de l'action* (Paris: Aubier, 1948); Various Authors, "Il pensiero filosofico di Maurizio Blondel," *Attualità filosofiche*, Atti del III Convegno di studi filosofici cristiani, Gallarate 1947 (Padua: Editoria Liviana, 1948), 251-368; Fiammetta Vanni Bourbon di Petrella, *Il pensiero di Maurice Blondel* (Florence: L'Arte della Stampa, 1950); Paolo Valori, S. J., *M. Blondel e il problema d'una filosofia cristiana* (Rome: "La Civiltà Cattolica," 1950); Various Authors, "'En hommage à Maurice Blondel," *Les études philosophiques*, Nouvelle série, 1 (1950), 5-104; Various Authors, *Teoresi*, 5 (1950), commemorative volume dedicated to M. Blondel; Aloisius Sartori, *Filosofia e cristianesimo in "La philosophie et l'esprit chrétien" di Maurizio Blondel* (Padua: Typis Seminarii Patavini, 1953); Henry Duméry, *Blondel et la religion* (Paris: Presses Universitaires de France, 1954); Romeo Crippa, *Il realismo integrale di M. Blondel* (Milan - Rome: Bocca, 1954); Albert Cartier, S.J., *Existence et vérité; philosophie blondélienne de l'action et problématique existentielle* (Paris: Presses Universitaires de France, 1955); Maria Ritz, *Le problème de l'être dans l'ontologie de Maurice Blondel* (Fribourg, Switz: Éditions Universitaires, 1958); Leo J. Zonneveld, C.I.C.M., *Maurice Blondel's Approach to God* (Washington, D. C.: The Catholic University of America, 1960), M. A. Thesis; Henri Bouillard, *Blondel et le christianisme* (Paris: Éditions du Seuil, 1961).

14. *Contra gentiles*, Book I, chap. 2, n. 3.

15. "L'immanentisme est un système qui nie ou néglige toute réalité transcendante, qui aboutit à enfermer le sujet en lui-même. Or M. Blondel a

affirmé très fortement la necessité pour le sujet de sortir de son immanence, de reconnaître des réalités differentes de la sienne et en particulier celle de Dieu." Tonquédec, *op. cit.*, p. 8.

16. Cf. André Lalande, *Vocabulaire technique et critique de la philosophie* (Paris: Presses Universitaires de France, 1960), p. 469. It is worth mentioning that Blondel has contributed several articles to this classical dictionary of philosophy, which is thus a valuable source for the understanding of some of Blondelian terms.

17. Maurice Blondel, "Lettre sur les exigences de la pensée contemporaine," as reported in *Les premiers écrits de Maurice Blondel* (Paris: Presses Universitaires de France, 1956), pp. 5-6.

18. *Ibid.*, p. 34.

19. *Ibid.*, p. 39.

20. Blondel affirms explicitly the agreement of philosophy with Catholicism: ". . . . la philosophie essentielle 'convient' pleinement et librement avec le catholicisme, dont elle peut même, dans le sens que nous avons dit, épouser le nom, sans perdre le sien; à ce prix seulement, la philosophie réelle et réaliste peut coopérer, sans présomption ni hybridation, à cette oeuvre indivise et distincte foncièrement dont nous parlèrent saint Bernard et saint Bonaventure avant Deschamps, et qui, parce qu'elle forme une vivante trame de deux tissus allogènes mais anastomosés, semble en effet comporter une double appellation quelque peu hybride." *Le problème de la philosophie catholique*, pp. 175-76. Hence Duméry's pertinent observation: "Pour Blondel il ne peut y avoir une métaphysique du bouddhisme au même titre que du christianisme. La philosophie de la religion est necéssairement et intrinsèquement philosophie de la religion chrétienne. If faut même dire, d'après Blondel, que *la* philosophie est essentiellement *catholique*, car en toute rigueur elle n'a place dans son registre rationnel que pour une notion du surnaturel expressément et littéralement définie au sens catholique." *Les études philosophiques*, Nouvelle série, 1 (1950), 37, n. 2.

21. *L'action* (1893), reprint (Paris: Presses Universitaires de France, 1950), pp. vii-viii.

22. Lalande, *Vocabulaire, op. cit.*, pp. 20-21.

23. *L'action*, p. 473.

24. Henri Bouillard, S. J. "The Thought of Maurice Blondel: A Synoptic Vision," *International Philosophical Quarterly*, 3 (1963), 396.

25. "'Maurice Blondel et la dialectique de l'action," *art. cit.*, p. 149.

26. *L'action*, p. 38.

27. *Ibid.*, pp. 354-55.

28. *Ibid.*, p. 389.

29. *La pensée*, I, *La genèse de la pensée et les paliers de son ascension spontanée* (Paris: Presses Universitaires de France, 1948), p. 3.

30. *Ibid.*, p. 34.

31. *La pensée*, II, *Les responsabilités de la pensée et la possibilité de son achèvement* (Paris: Presses Universitaires de France, 1954), p. 13.

32. *Ibid.*, p. 179.

33. *Ibid.*, pp. 178-79.

34. Bouillard, *art. cit.*, p. 401.

35. *L'Être et les êtres* (new ed.; Paris: Presses Universitaires de France, 1963), pp. 43-44.

36. *Ibid.*, pp. 35, 325, 359 and 455.

37. *Ibid.*, pp. 46, 48, 54 and 387.

38. *Ibid.*, pp. 45, 46, 60 and 67.

39. *L'action*, I, *Le problème des causes secondes et le pur agir* (Paris: Presses Universitaires de France, 1949), p. 200.

40. *Ibid.*, pp. 202-203.

41. *Ibid.*, pp. 192-94.

42. *L'action*, II, *L'action humaine et les conditions de son aboutissement* (new ed.; Paris: Presses Universitaires de France, 1963), p. 14.

43. *Une énigme historique: le "Vinculum substantiale" d'après Leibniz et l'ébauche d'un réalisme supérieur* (Paris: Beauchesne, 1930), p. 116.

44. *Le problème de la philosophie catholique, op. cit.*, p. 11, n. 1.

45. Archambault, *Initiation à la philosophie blondélienne, op. cit.*, pp. 77-79.

46. See, for example, *L'action*, I, p. 190, n. 1, where Blondel explains his thought concerning man's exigency for the supernatural order: "Qu'on ne prenne pas à rebours ce terme d'*exigence*. L'absolue et inaliénable transcendance de Dieu exige que cette incommensurabilité métaphysique demeure ontologiquement intacte et moralement inviolable. Bref, elle exige que, dans ses plus extrêmes condescendances, rien ne soit exigible d'elle. Loin donc d'interpréter nos assertions comme si l'hypothèse que nous examinons ici pouvait être réalisée par nous, ou même requise de notre part, nous voulons signifier expressément ce qu'il y a d'innaturalisable en elle. Dès lors que l'on comprend cette hypothèse telle qu'elle est, on est prémunit contre tout danger de semi-rationalisme, de modernisme et de naturalisme immanentiste." To make his mind even more clear as to the absolute gratuitousness of the supernatural order, he states further: "Il est donc nécessaire de maintenir que, pour une si merveilleuse élévation, l'initiative vient absolument et totalement de Dieu qui, par une grâce prévenante, donne à l'être contingent de quoi donner le nécessaire et naître à nouveau, *dat nobis Deus gratis id quod illi dare debemus necessario ad salutem.*" *Ibid.*, p. 191.

47. Cf. Yves de Montcheuil, *Maurice Blondel: Pages religieuses* (Paris: Aubier, 1942), Introduction, pp. 40-43 and 55. See also McKeever, *art. cit.*, p. 444.

48. Cf. *Le problème de la philosophie catholique, op. cit.*, pp. 31-39, where Blondel speaks of the hypothetical necessity of the supernatural order, and pp. 136-57, where his notion of Christian philosophy is discussed and defended. Blondel's teaching on the relationship between the natural and the supernatural order is the object of a special study by Bouillard, *Blondel et le christianisme, op. cit.*, pp. 67-131. For a critical evaluation of Blondel's doctrine cf. Valori, *M. Blondel e il problema d'una filosofia cristiana, op. cit.*, pp. 225-34.

49. Sciacca calls Blondel's "integral realism" the most original, organic, and complete system of Catholic philosophy that has been devised since Antonio Rosmini. Cf. *Il problema di Dio e della religione nella filosofia attuale, op. cit.*, p. 337. Valori speaks of Blondel's system as of "a kind of modern *Summa Theologiae*," *op. cit.*, pp. 232-33, while Carlo Giacon praises it as one of the most forceful invitations to contemporary philosophy to retrace the way to the rational acceptance of Christian ideals. *Attualità filosofiche, op. cit.*, p. 324.

50. St. Augustine, *The Confessions*, translated with an Introduction and Notes by John K. Ryan (Garden City, N. Y.: Doubleday, 1960), Book I, chap. 1, n. 1, p. 43.

etienne gilson

AND CHRISTIAN PHILOSOPHY
by John F. Wippel

At first sight the very term "Christian Philosophy" appears to be self-destroying. If philosophy is to remain philosophy, if it is to be an investigation carried out under the light of natural reason, how is it to be described as Christian? Insofar as it is philosophy it would seem to admit of no direct reference to faith or to theology. Be that as it may, this is not the viewpoint of Étienne Gilson. Perhaps no other name has been linked more closely to a defense of the Christian character of patristic and medieval and Thomistic philosophy. In order to understand more clearly how he gradually arrived at his notion of Christian philosophy and at his present views as regards the interrelationship between philosophy and theology, one may turn to his own works and in particular to his recent intellectual "autobiography" entitled *The Philosopher and Theology*.[1] In the opening pages Gilson notes how deeply familiar with certain fundamental theological notions any well instructed Catholic should be. Perhaps without realizing it, in learning his catechism and his creed, in his high school religion courses and thereafter, he has assimilated a set of beliefs which will serve him to his dying day. In the Apostles' creed he finds answers to some of the most profound questions that have plagued philosophers and theologians from time immemorial. If he does not know many things at this point in life, yet he believes a great deal as regards the origin and nature and destiny of man, and the existence and nature of God. More than that, and this is significant in Gilson's eyes, he has become familiar with some profound metaphysical notions without having attempted in any way to separate them from his religious beliefs. Witness his surprise, then, when he comes into contact with a set of purely philosophical propositions for the first time, many of them treating of notions which until now he had accepted on faith. Now some of these same truths are presented to him as rationally demonstrable.

GILSON'S DISCOVERY OF MEDIEVAL PHILOSOPHY

Apparently Gilson himself underwent a similar experience when he first came into contact with philosophy as such. For some reason, as he now confesses, his good marks not withstanding, he seemed to understand very little of it. Failing to resolve the matter by his own reading, he then began to study philosophy formally at the University of Paris. In spite of diversity in outlook among his professors there, they were agreed on one point at least, and this a rather negative one. Each was convinced that he was a pure philosopher, free from any kind of religious influence in his philosophizing. One might be Protestant, Jewish, or Catholic, but this would never be reflected in one's teaching. And yet, Gilson notes that as a young Catholic student there he felt no particular embarrassment. If he had now entered into a different world, he was prepared. He expected no "revelation" as to what he should hold as true. His religious faith had already decided that issue. Now he would test his own thought and investigate the foundations of that faith.

At the same time, Gilson notes his amazement on coming into contact with certain Catholic theologians who seemed to be defending a kind of primacy of reason. They made great efforts never to believe in any truth which reason could also establish. Apparently their motives were apologetic. In an age of scientism and rationalism, they undoubtedly hoped to appeal to non-Catholic scholars by this emphasis on unaided reason. But if they were right in asserting reason's rights when it comes to knowing truths such as God's existence, Gilson found it far more difficult to understand why they judged belief or continued belief in these same truths to be impossible. Granted that the Vatican Council teaches that human reason can arrive at certain knowledge of God's existence, Gilson would not and will not concede that the Council condemns belief in his existence or rejects such as impossible.[2] He loves to hearken back to a catechism of his youth with its statement: "I believe that there is a God because He Himself has revealed His existence to us." Only then does the 1885 edition add: "Yes, reason tells us there is a God because, if there were no God, heaven and earth would not exist." Gilson contrasts this catechism with a 1923 version which begins its discussion of the existence of God with a number of philosophical arguments, and only thereafter notes the fact that God has revealed his existence. Finally, in seeming despair, he quotes a 1949 version: "I believe in God because nothing can make itself." After noting the questionable philosophy involved in this reply— the omission of an important step, the proof that something has been made or created—Gilson calls for a restoration of faith to its proper place.

> If I believe in the existence of God nothing untoward will happen on the day when some unbeliever will question the validity of my proofs. My religious life is not founded on the conclusions of any philosopher ... But if I have first been taught to hold that God exists on the strength of demonstrative reasoning, and only later to believe it, it is to be feared that the reverse will happen ... The man who thinks he knows that God exists and then realizes that he no longer knows it also realizes that he no longer believes it.[3]

But to return to Gilson, the youthful student of philosophy, one now finds his philosophical research gradually carrying him to similar convictions as regards the mutual interrelations of philosophy and theology. At this point in his career he had as yet enjoyed no direct contact with scholastic philosophy. At the same time, certain historical canons were accepted by practically everyone in university circles at Paris. One of these maintained that there are really only two philosophical periods in history, the ancient and the modern. The latter begins with Descartes and comes after the period of antiquity as though nothing had intervened. Between the decline of the Greeks and Descartes there was nothing but darkness, the darkness of the Middle Ages. At best, one might admit there had been a scholastic theology, grounded on revelation and thus the very antithesis of philosophy. Yet Professor Lévy-Bruhl suggested to Gilson as a research project the theme Descartes and Scholasticism. His 1913 thesis, *La liberté chez Descartes et la théologie,* was the result. Some of his conclusions were rather surprising. A number of philosophical positions were common to scholasticism and Descartes and apparently had passed from the former to the latter. At the same time, however, metaphysics as found in Descartes seemed to have undergone a decline. As Gilson sums it up: "On all these points the thought of Descartes, in comparison with the sources from which it derives, marks much less a gain than a loss."[4] Yet this conclusion seemed to violate the generally accepted law. If Descartes had borrowed metaphysical notions from the scholastics, one could hardly continue to maintain that he came after the Greeks as though nothing had existed in between.

The problem was to become more complicated. What had preceded Descartes seemed to have been theology. It appeared, then, that the theology of the scholastics had, at least in part, been transformed into philosophy in Descartes. However, unless there had also been some philosophy in scholasticism, how could Descartes have borrowed metaphysical notions therefrom? This raised another problem. How was one to account for the presence of philosophy in medieval scholasticism? By appealing to Aristotle, no doubt. And yet, the very notions which Descartes had retained from scholasticism seemed to be absent in Aristotle: the existence of one supreme being, creative cause of the universe, infinite and free, and a theory of man endowed with personal immortality. Not finding these notions in Aristotle, Gilson concluded that philosophy had changed considerably due to its contact with Christian theology. Consequently, he found himself forced to account for a twofold transition: from Greek philosophy to Christian theology, and from Christian theology to modern philosophy.

With this background in mind Gilson then turned to a deeper study of Thomas Aquinas. Restricting himself in the main to Thomas' theological writings, his research resulted in the first edition of his *Le thomisme* in 1919.[5] He notes that it received sharp criticism, especially along three lines. Maurice De Wulf of Louvain pointed out certain weaknesses from the metaphysical standpoint. Gilson grants the justice of this criticism. Secondly, Gilson had followed a theological order of exposition rather than a philosophical. He continues to do so today. Finally, at least one Catholic theologian objected to his speaking of a "philosophy of Saint Thomas," apparently holding to the view promoted by De Wulf according to which all the scholastics maintained a common "scholastic synthesis" consisting fundamentally of the philosophy of Aristotle. Apparently stirred on by these rebukes, Gilson determined to test this final point. Was the philosophy of St. Thomas to be identified with that of the other scholastics? He concentrated on Bonaventure and published *La philosophie de saint Bonaventure* in 1924.[6] His conclusion was that Bonaventure differed from Thomas on such fundamental notions as being, cause, intellect, and natural knowledge. Now he had discovered two medieval philosophies, or so he thought. For then the Dominican, Pierre Mandonnet, entered the discussion. Admitted that Gilson's presentation of Bonaventure's doctrine was sound enough, Mandonnet objected to the title. No doctrine wherein the distinction between faith and reason was so vague could rightfully be styled philosophy. The book should rather be called the "Theology of Saint Bonaventure." Gilson now found himself in the middle. One critic contended that Thomas Aquinas was the only medieval philosopher. Another denied that he had a distinctive philosophy of his own, suggesting rather that he shared in the "common scholastic synthesis." And then another Dominican, Gabriel Théry, struck the final blow. Granted that the doctrine of Bonaventure is a theology, so too is that of Aquinas. Both are theologians. Gilson had simply selected certain propositions from their writings and constructed philosophies. Gilson himself admitted the justice of this final criticism, and seemed to find himself where he had begun. There were no medieval philosophies, only theologies. Thomas Aquinas was not a philosopher, but a theologian! Reviewing matters, then, Gilson noted the following: 1) a series of propositions concerning God, man, and the universe, which could have been taught by the medieval theologians as well as by certain modern philosophers; 2) the fact that most of these were to be found in the *theological* writings of the great medieval thinkers; 3) the fact that in every comprehensive presentation of these same theses, the medievals had not followed the philosophical but the theological order (descending from God to creatures rather than ascending from creatures to God).[7] The problem now arose as to finding a name flexible enough to cover so complex a doctrinal situation.

Gilson's subsequent research in medieval philosophy reinforced his conviction that a number of metaphysical conclusions are to be found there which cannot be simply identified with the philosophy of Aristotle, or with that of any other Greek thinker. As he sees it, only ignorance of the history of philosophy can lead one to proclaim the middle ages a long period of philosophical stagnation. In *The Spirit of Mediaeval Philosophy* he set forth a series of issues whose full philosophical development was due, in his eyes, to inspirations stemming from Christianity. Without denying the heavy debt of medieval philosophy to the Greeks, his purpose in this work was to emphasize the distinctively Christian elements, or more accurately phrased, those philosophical notions which appear there because of Judeo-Christian influences.[8] Gilson's thesis is that philosophy did receive new impulses and insights and, consequently, did attain to new heights precisely because it was exercised under Christian conditions. In this, of course, he is diametrically opposed to the position taken by Émile Bréhier in 1928 and again in 1931 and thereafter in the great debate concerning the possibility of a Christian philosophy.[9] Without spelling out in detail the particulars, a survey of the titles of some of the lectures in *The Spirit of Mediaeval Philosophy* will suffice to indicate areas where Gilson finds this positive Christian influence: "Being and its Necessity", "Beings and their Contingence", "Analogy, Causality and Finalty", "The Glory of God", and "Christian Providence". It was only after he had completed the lectures which make up this monumental work, save for the first two, that the term "Christian Philosophy" occurred to him as best suited to describe the type of philosophizing characteristic of the Middle Ages. With this in mind he devoted the first two chapters to this notion.[10] Gilson's research had now convinced him that there was a philosophy in the Middle Ages, to be sure, but a Christian philosophy.

CHRISTIAN PHILOSOPHY

In attempting to understand precisely what Gilson means by Christian philosophy, one should never forget that for him it was originally a name which designated certain historically observable realities, namely the philosophical doctrines which are to be found in the writings of the Fathers and the scholastic theologians. The historical premise on which the title rests is the existence in these thinkers of certain philosophical doctrines which are met in their works for the first time in this precise sense and form.[11] One may ask why so many philosophers did in fact turn to Christianity to find a more satisfying solution for their philosophical difficulties. Gilson would refer one back to the very beginnings of Christianity. For a St. Paul, to be sure, Christianity is not simply another philosophy, but a religion which surpasses all that is normally known as philosophy. Christianity offers salvation by faith in Christ and is contrasted with the wisdom of the Greeks. If certain Pauline texts seem to reject Greek philosophy, their real intent, according to Gilson, is to "set aside the apparent wisdom of the Greeks which is really folly, so as to make way for the apparent folly of Christianity which is really wisdom." For the salvation preached by Christ is the true wisdom.[12] But this seems to leave us with the problem of Christian philosophy. Faith may free one from the need for philosophy, but why, then, did some of the earliest writers of the patristic age gain philosophically by accepting Christianity? Gilson loves to cite Justin as a prime example. After his long search among the various Greek philosophies, Justin eventually came to the conclusion that Christianity itself is the only "sure and profitable philosophy." Referring to his conversion to Christianity, he notes that it was by becoming a Christian that he really became a philosopher. After seeking truth by reason alone and failing, Justin accepted the truth proposed by faith. Thereupon, his reason found satisfaction as well. For Justin, then, the happiest philosophical situation was no longer that of the pagan but that of the Christian.[13] In the second chapter of *The Spirit of Mediaeval Philosophy,* Gilson detects a similar pattern in Augustine, Lactantius, Anselm, and Aquinas. For each of these thinkers Christianity was a way of salvation. In addition, faith offered a certitude not provided by reason alone. Yet, in each of these men, reason had its role to play in Christian life, at least to the degree that they aspired to understand the content of revelation. And in every case, because reason existed under Christian conditions, Gilson finds its lot greatly improved.

For Gilson, then, "the content of Christian philosophy is that body of rational truths discovered, explored or simply safeguarded, thanks to the help that reason receives from revelation." [14] Unless the formula, Christian philosophy, is to lose all force, "it must be frankly admitted that nothing less than an intrinsic relation between revelation and reason will suffice to give it meaning." [15] This is not to say that the Christian philosopher will confuse philosophy with theology. Rather, he seeks to determine whether, among those truths he holds on faith, there are not some which reason can also establish.

> In so far as the believer bases his affirmations on the intimate conviction gained from faith, he remains purely and simply a believer, he has not yet entered the gates of philosophy; but when amongst his beliefs he finds some that are capable of becoming objects of science then he becomes a philosopher, and if it is to the Christian faith that he owes this new philosophical insight, he becomes a Christian philosopher. [16]

Gilson goes on to tell us what he means by Christian philosophy.

> Thus I call Christian, *every philosophy which, although keeping the two orders formally distinct, nevertheless considers the Christian revelation as an indispensable auxiliary to reason.* [17]

Or again, he describes it as follows in his *Elements of Christian Philosophy.*

> Such as it is described in this epoch-making document [*Aeterni Patris*], Christian philosophy is that way of philosophizing in which the Christian faith and the human

intellect join forces in a common investigation of philosophical truth.[18]

Certain comments are in order if one will be fair to Gilson.
First of all, he insists that the orders of philosophy and theology be
kept formally distinct. In the formal order, one is concerned with
the essence of the thing. If it is of the essence of philosophy to
operate in the light of natural reason, it is of the essence of
theology to proceed under the light of revelation.[19] The two
orders are formally distinct. Consequently, one will never find
a simple abstract essence or quiddity to conform to the notion
of Christian philosophy. What is envisioned is rather a concrete
historical reality, something to be described rather than defined,
and something which includes "all those philosophical systems
which were in fact what they were only because a Christian
religion existed and because they were ready to submit to its
influence."[20] Gilson suggests, in fact, that failure to make this
distinction lies behind much of the controversy between philosophers and theologians as regards the notion of Christian Philosophy.[21] The distinction proposed here seems to correspond with
a distinction developed by Jacques Maritain in his doctrinal
solution to the problem. Maritain distinguishes between the
nature (or essence) of philosophy, considered in itself and abstractly, and the state in which it exists in a given subject. In
terms of its nature and as abstracted from its concrete conditions
of existence, philosophy is a purely natural and rational discipline.[22] Considered in this way, then, philosophy is simply that,
pure philosophy. It is not Christian. But Maritain contrasts this
with philosophy considered according to its state, as found in
the man who philosophizes. Here, because Christians also philosophize, one may speak of a Christian philosophy. Here there
will be a difference between the Christian and non-Christian
philosopher. For the Christian believes that fallen nature is
elevated and strengthened by grace. Furthermore, he finds that
his faith reveals certain truths to him which unaided reason
would, in fact, fail to attain.

He also believes that if reason is to attain without admixture
of error the highest truths that are naturally within its ken

it requires assistance, either from within in the form of inner strengthening, or from without in the form of an offering of objective data.[23]

For Maritain, then, Christian philosophy is not a simple essence but something complex, an essence plus the given state in which the Christian thinker finds himself. Because of its Christian state philosophy receives a certain guidance from the faith without thereby ceasing to be philosophy. For it will always judge things in accord with its own principles and norms. This will apply even to the philosophical consideration of those naturally knowable truths which were not, in fact, clearly and accurately attained apart from some influence of Christian revelation.[24] Maritain's distinction, then, between philosophy considered according to its nature and philosophy considered in its concrete state of existence seems to correspond to Gilson's distinction between philosophy considered formally, or in the abstract, and philosophy taken as a concrete historical reality, found in philosophers. Gilson also grants that one will never find a simple abstract essence to correspond to Christian philosophy. What he intends to describe is rather a concrete way of philosophizing. It should not be forgotten, of course, that Gilson originally arrived at this notion by way of historical research, to resolve an historical problem. Nonetheless, he has referred to Maritain's study as the natural doctrinal complement to his historical investigations and has expressed his agreement with it.[25] If one objects that, since philosophy is distinct from faith, the latter can have nothing to do with the former save in some purely extrinsic way, Gilson will no doubt agree that such is true in the formal order. But taken as a concretely observable reality, such will not be true of Christian philosophy. Here its Christian condition and mode of existence must be taken into account.

A second point should also be kept in mind in Gilson's description of Christian philosophy. An *intrinsic* relation between revelation and reason must be admitted. It does not suffice to say that Christian philosophy will refer to faith and revelation as a negative norm, warning reason when it is in danger of contradicting revealed truth. It will do this, of course, but more. For Gilson, Christian philosophy also involves the positive contri-

butions which philosophy has received from its Christian state
of existence. At the very least this implies that philosophy has
discovered certain naturally knowable truths only at the positive
suggestion of revelation. Once these truths have been pointed out
by faith, of course, the Christian philosopher is invited to investigate their rational foundations. In line with this, Gilson
sets down certain typical characteristics of the Christian philosopher. Granted that he has the right to investigate each and every
philosophical problem, in fact he is selective. Questions concerning the existence and nature of God, and the origin and nature
and destiny of man will be of paramount importance. A second
characteristic of Christian philosophy has been its tendency to
systematize. This is understandable, for in the Christian view of
things, there is a fixed frame of reference, man in his relationship
to God. Finally, Christian philosophy has the necessary material
at hand for its completion. To illustrate this point, Gilson appeals
to Thomas, *Summa contra gentiles,* 1, 4, where he notes that it
was fitting for God to reveal certain truths which human reason
can also attain. For, as Gilson interprets Aquinas here, truths of
this type (including certain truths necessary for salvation) would
otherwise be grasped only by a few. The reasons offered by
Thomas confirm Gilson in his view that the Christian will do well
to philosophize from within the faith. Without revelation the
majority of men would never attain to these truths either because of a lack of native ability, or a lack of time for research, or a
lack of interest in such matters. And even those who did finally
succeed would do so only with great effort, after a long period
of time, and at the risk of spending the greater part of life in
ignorance of such truths. Again, the human intellect is so
weakened in its present state that, unless it were reinforced by
faith, that which might seem clearly demonstrated to some would
remain doubtful to others. In the concrete existential situation,
then, man has need of divine assistance in such matters. If this
is not an optimistic view of the results to which unaided reason
can attain in practice, Gilson insists that it is the view of Thomas
Aquinas as regards such metaphysical truths.[26] He urges the
Christian who would philosophize to keep this judgment in mind,
always making the necessary distinctions, of course. A true philosophy, considered formally in itself, will stand or fall in virtue of

its own rationality. Such a philosophy, however, has not been constructed in fact without the help of revelation, "acting as an indispensable moral support to reason." Both history itself and the words of Aquinas point to this conclusion. If, then, one does find in history an influence exercised on the development of metaphysics by revelation, the reality of Christian philosophy is historically demonstrated. This, of course, is what Gilson claims to have done.[27]

PHILOSOPHY AND THEOLOGY

One problem remains to be settled. If one follows Gilson in his historical development of the notion of Christian philosophy and agrees with him that, while distinct in the formal order, philosophy and religious faith are in fact found together in the believing philosopher, what remains of the distinction between philosophy and theology? Once again, in order to understand the notion of philosophy more fully, Gilson directs our attention to it in its relationship to theology. He has insisted that the truly original philosophical contributions of Thomas Aquinas are to be found in his theological writings. This squares, of course, with the Gilsonian view that the Christian who philosophizes does not find himself in the same state as the pagan. One must admit, then, some real connection between natural theology, on the one hand, and revealed theology on the other. Two reasons point to this conclusion. First of all, in the past the greatest masters of natural theology have also been professional theologians. Secondly, every historical attempt to separate philosophy from theology has, in Gilson's opinion, ended in disaster. It is not enough to restrict the role of faith to a negative norm. Placed by God at the disposal of all, philosopher and non-philosopher, faith not only teaches those truths which one may not contradict. To the degree that some of the revealed truths admit of rational demonstration as well, as with the preambles of faith, the believing philosopher is invited to seek to demonstrate and to understand such truths insofar as this is possible.[28]

To return to philosophy and theology as found in Thomas Aquinas, Gilson notes that in his time the theologian who used philosophy in his work was normally not described as a philosopher, but as a philosophizing theologian (*philosophans theologus*), or more simply, as a philosophizer (*philosophans*). The term philosopher was usually restricted to pagan thinkers. The thirteenth century theologians do not seem to have explicitly considered the possibility of a person who would be at one and the same time a *philosophus* and a *sanctus,* that is, one sanctified by baptism.[29] As regards Aquinas in relationship to Aristotle, Gilson judges it an oversimplification to say that Thomas simply "baptized" the Stagirite. In his commentaries on Aristotle, whenever Thomas finds him contradicting Christian teaching, he either admits as much or at the very least does not force conclusions upon him which he did not expressly defend. Thus, Aquinas never uses the term *creatio* to describe the causality of the First Mover in his commentary on the *Metaphysics.* Yet he did attempt to remove from Aristotle alleged contradictions to Christian truth which are not clearly there, but which commentators such as Averroes seemed to find there. In Gilson's view, if one will speak of a Thomistic "baptism" of Aristotle, this took place in his theological writings.[30] After having purified Aristotle, Thomas noted certain shortcomings in his thought. Here he found it necessary to complete him. And yet, Aristotle was the philosopher *par excellence* and seemed to represent the best that unaided reason can achieve without the help of revelation. In his theologizing, however, Aquinas needed an adequate philosophy. To the degree that none was at hand he found it necessary to develop his own, which Gilson describes as a "reinterpretation of the fundamental notions of Aristotle's metaphysics in the light of Christian truth." Gilson cites the Thomistic notions of being, substance, and efficient cause as illustrations.[31]

This Thomistic development of the Aristotelian metaphysics was the work of a teacher of Christian truth and, as Gilson will insist, a teacher of Christian *theology.* In line with his theological mission, then, Aquinas found it necessary to develop a philosophy. But as Gilson interprets him, this philosophy is a *part* of Thomistic theology.

> This philosophy, which, according to Thomas himself, is part of his theology, appeals to no revealed knowledge; it is purely rational in both principles and method, and

still, it is irreducible to the philosophy of Aristotle if only
for the reason that the first principle of human knowledge,
being, is not understood by Thomas and Aristotle in the
same way.[32]

If one asks, then, is there any philosophy in the works of Aquinas,
Gilson will reply affirmatively. But he will insist that it is always
there in order to aid man in his knowledge of God. Thomas has
worked out a philosophy with theological goals in mind. Here
Gilson cites with full approval Thomas' reply to the objection that
the Christian monk should not busy himself studying Letters.
Thomas replies (*Summa theol.*, II-II, 188, 5, ad 3) that monks
should devote themselves to a study of the doctrine which is
"according to godliness." They should interest themselves in
the various branches of secular learning only insofar as such
ministers to sacred doctrine. For Gilson this is a perfect expression
of Thomas' attitude regarding philosophical speculation. Thomas
never forgot that he was a religious. He would interest himself
in philosophy to the degree that it could be of service to sacred
science. Once more, suggests Gilson, Thomas will not be overly
concerned in freeing his philosophy from all theological influences
and goals.[33]

As we have now seen, Gilson's historical research had convinced him there was such a thing as Christian philosophy.
The fact that this philosophy had been worked out by theologians under the guidance of faith and for theological purposes
continued to perplex him, eventually leading him to his present
view that Christian philosophy should in some way be included
in sacred theology. To account for this, he determined that the
notion of theology would have to be broadened. According to a
widely held view, conclusions deduced from naturally known
premises are strictly philosophical. Gilson does not object. But
many go on to conclude from this that philosophical reasoning
has no function in theology. They would restrict theology to
the task of deducing conclusions from premises, one at least
of which is known by faith. Gilson finds such a view acceptable
so far as it goes, but entirely too restrictive. If it is true that
strictly theological conclusions do not enter into philosophical
demonstrations, it does not follow that purely rational conclusions

cannot contribute in some way to theological investigation. In fact, as Gilson sees the situation, it is of the essence of scholastic theology to employ philosophical reasoning. In his own words: "Because it draws on faith it is a scholastic *theology,* but because of its distinctive use of philosophy, it is *scholastic* theology."[34]

For Thomas, of course, theology or divine science is twofold. There is a theology in which divine things are not considered as the subject-matter of the science, but rather as the principle of the subject-matter. This is natural theology or metaphysics. There is another which considers divine things in their own right as its subject-matter. This is the theology which is taught in Scripture and which we know as sacred or supernatural theology (cf. his commentary on the *De Trinitate* of Boethius, V, 4). This theology, sacred theology, differs generically from natural theology.[35] Gilson defends this distinction, but also sounds a note of warning. Some fail to distinguish between the formal order, where such distinctions do apply, and the concrete order. In the formal order, sacred theology and metaphysics are generically distinct. But he suggests that the concrete order is of greater interest to Thomas here.[36] It would also seem to be in the concrete order that Gilson's "broadened" notion of theology finds its full application. In the concrete order sacred science notes certain possibilities for philosophical reasoning of which philosophy, left to its own devices, would remain unaware. The philosophy which the theologian applies in his theology remains philosophical in its nature, formally considered. But it is now employed in a higher task, the theological, and subjected to a higher light, that of the theologian, and thereby becomes a part of theology. One might object that theology itself is degraded insofar as it uses philosophical reasoning. Thomas faced such an objection in the *Summa theologiae.* If sacred science borrows from the lower sciences, it would seem to be inferior to them. He replied that sacred teaching does not receive its principles from any lower science, but immediately from God by revelation. Therefore, it does not receive from the other sciences as from its superiors, but rather uses them as its inferiors and handmaids. On the other hand, according to Gilson, this does not imply that philosophy's condition is worsened by its theological state of service. On the contrary, to serve as the handmaid of theology is its highest honor. If some of the Patristic writers had found that the most favorable situation for philosophy was not that of the pagan but that of the Christian, Gilson insists that in the same fashion philosophy as its exists within theology is in far better position than any kind of separated philosophy. However, it has also been objected that such a view turns philosophy into theology and thereby destroys one or the other or both. In his commentary on the *De Trinitate* of Boethius Thomas had faced a similar charge. He had been accused of mixing the water of philosophy with the wine of Scripture. He had replied that in a mixture both component natures are changed, resulting in some third substance. Here, however, there is no mixture. Philosophy passes under the authority of faith and thereby water is changed into wine. Gilson interprets this to mean that philosophy is *changed into theology* by being so used.[37] The nature of theology is not thereby destroyed and apparently, in line with what we have already seen, philosophy retains its own principles and method.

Far from being harmed by this change, Gilson suggests that it is rather a kind of "transfiguration" for philosophy. He concludes from all this:

> ... the nature of the doctrine in the *Summa Theologiae* should be clear. Since its aim is to introduce its readers, especially beginners, to the teaching of theology, everything in it is theological. This does not mean that the *Summa* contains no philosophy; on the contrary, it is full of philosophy. Since the philosophy that is in the *Summa* is there in view of a theological end, and since it figures in it as integrated with that which is the proper work of the theologian, it finds itself included within the formal object of theology and becomes theological in its own right.[38]

As found in the theological writings of Thomas Aquinas, then, (and this is where one must look to find his own philosophy, according to Gilson), philosophy is there in view of a theological end. Consequently, it will be included within the formal object of theology and will thereby become theological. This seems to be Gilson's final conclusion. If in the concrete order the philosophy of Aquinas is not separated from his faith and his religious convictions and if it is thereby rendered a Christian philosophy, it now seems that insofar as this Christian philosophy was constructed by a theologian in theological writings and for theological goals, it has been changed into theology. It is perhaps this final point which has raised the greatest number of protests, even from among those who would defend some kind of Christian philosophy. In line with the above, Gilson now broadens the notion of Christian philosophy itself. It will now refer to any usage of philosophy made by the Christian in the service of theology and, in its most comprehensive meaning, "transcends the distinction of scholastic philosophy and scholastic theology." For it is now taken to apply to the use the Christian makes of philosophy in either philosophy or theology insofar as he joins religious faith and philosophical reasoning.[39]

PRACTICAL CONSEQUENCES

Gilson is not content to stop with a purely historical investigation of Christian philosophy. If, as he judges to be the case, the Christian philosophy of Thomas Aquinas was at the same time a part of his theology insofar as it served as its instrument, and if it was thereby changed into theology, what of the Christian who would philosophize today? He could, of course, attempt to philosophize without any reference to his religious belief. But such is not the ideal for the Christian philosopher. Granted the formal distinction between philosophy taken abstractly and Christian belief, the two should not be *separated* in fact. However, Gilson goes even farther. If philosophy and theology are also generically distinct when considered formally, or in the abstract, nonetheless, the modern Christian who wishes to philosophize today, above all, the modern Thomist, should proceed in the same way as did Thomas in his day. If philosophy not only ministered to but was changed into theology by being used as its instrument in the writings of Aquinas, it would seem to follow that the Christian who wants to philosophize today should first study theology. Then he will follow the order proposed by Thomas in his theological works, and will be in position to profit from the positive contributions which theology has to make to philosophy. Consistent as he is, Gilson does not stop short before such a conclusion. In a lecture originally given at the Aquinas Foundation at Princeton University, March 7, 1953, he discusses this very issue. Basing himself on certain texts of Aquinas he concludes that, according to Thomas himself: 1) young people are not yet ready to study metaphysics; 2) "youth" ends at fifty; 3) the ancient philosophers used to wait until the latter part of their lives to study metaphysics.[40] Gilson notes that this is verified by his personal experience. For he recalls his own difficulties as a youth of twenty in attempting to understand metaphysical questions in spite of his great interest therein.

But the question arises, how did Thomas himself study and teach metaphysics before he was fifty? He died at the age of forty-nine and composed his *De ente et essentia* when only thirty-one. In Gilson' view there was no contradiction or inconsistency in Thomas' position. For he did not regard himself as a philosopher but as a theologian. If Thomas advised young people against studying metaphysics and natural theology and ethics, he did not say they are not ready to study revealed theology, including the philosophy it may contain. As he saw it, the pure philosopher, the man who would philosophize without the guidance of revelation, had best wait until late in life to take up the study of metaphysics. But as a Christian and a religious he had studied philosophy while still a "youth" in order to become a theologian. His advice, as interpreted by Gilson, would be: if one wishes to become a metaphysician, he can hardly begin too late; if he wishes to become a theologian, he can hardly begin too soon.[41] Gilson suggests that Thomas objects to the early study of metaphysics because of its exceedingly abstract nature. Religion, on the other hand, can provide a concrete approach to certain notions presented abstractly by metaphysics. If the notion of "pure act" elicits little response from a class of undergraduates, a term such as "God" will fare much better. For he is already known to them by reason of their previous religious training. Gilson grants that one cannot substitute the teaching of theology for metaphysics in Catholic colleges today. Nevertheless, insofar as possible, one should "recreate around our teaching of philosophy a like religious atmosphere." The best way to teach something of metaphysics to young people is to introduce them to the relevant parts of Thomistic theology. And as regards institutions preparing future theo-

logians, the answer is clear. If one will teach such students some
metaphysics and ethics, let him teach them "straight theology."
For as Gilson conceives it, such a theology, if is really Thomistic,
will include that Christian philosophy which serves as its instrument and handmaid.[42]

CONCLUDING REMARKS

Our purpose here has been to expound Gilson's views on
Christian philosophy and its relationship to theology as objectively
and accurately as possible. Since these views have been roundly
criticized and highly praised many times before, it is not our
intent to repeat old charges or to prolong the controversy. However, a certain amount of positive work has been done in this
area rather recently, and we judge it appropriate to briefly indicate
some points which might be of interest to the reader. As regards
the medieval situation, Anton Pegis has made a highly suggestive
distinction in a recent work, *The Middle Ages and Philosophy*.
There he speaks of a certain ambivalence of medieval philosophy.
Considered as a philosophy, one finds that it was developed
in a religious atmosphere under the influence of a Christian
Weltanschauung. For this reason, one is not surprised to note that
it bears the marks of its Christian origins and is, in fact, a
Christian philosophy. At the same time, however, one finds that
this same philosophy was used as an instrument of theology
and thereby involved in a task which carried it beyond the realm
of philosophy. Pegis and Gilson would agree, then, that it was
developed by theologians in order for them to create and perfect
their theologies. Consequently, continues Pegis, one must distinguish between its "Christian character as a philosophy and its
theological state of service." Precisely here is the ambivalence of
medieval philosophy. On the one hand it was a Christian philosophy: *philosophy,* because it was a work of human reason operating according to its proper light; *Christian,* because it was elaborated under the influence of revelation. On the other hand, it was
not only a Christian philosophy, but was developed within a
theology and served as its instrument. As Christian this philosophy
remained philosophical in substance, and for that reason deserves
to be called Christian philosophy, not Christian theology. But as
a theological instrument it was involved in a labor which was

imposed upon it neither as philosophy nor as Christian. Pegis stresses this distinction, then, between the Christian character of medieval philosophy and its theological state of service. Granted that it is one and the same Christian philosophy which was also used by theology, that which makes it Christian philosophy cannot be identified with that which makes it theological. One must not confuse "what is Christian in the philosophy to be found in the *Summa* with what is *in addition* theological in the use that St. Thomas made of it." If, then, the Christian philosophy of Thomas Aquinas is not to be reduced to the philosophy of Aristotle, as Gilson has so effectively argued, at the same time it should not be *"equated* with the service to which he put philosophy in the interpretation of *sacra doctrina."* [43]

As regards the contemporary situation, it would seem that a similar distinction might be applied. Once again it will be one thing to say that the Christian should not abstract completely from his faith while philosophizing and that his philosophy may well profit from this contact with the faith and thereby become a Christian philosophy. It is something else again to conclude that this philosophy, because it is Christian, is *for that reason* a part of theology and changed into theology as water is changed into wine. It may indeed be used by the theologian for theological purposes and will then be placed in the ambivalent position ascribed by Pegis to medieval philosophy as it appears in the writings of theologians. Even then, it will be Christian philosophy for one set of reasons, and theological for another. But as regards the modern Christian who would philosophize, would it not be possible for him to philosophize as a Christian, ever open to positive suggestions arising from his faith, *without thereby becoming a theologian?* If such is the case, this would seem to indicate the possibility of a Christian philosophy which is not at one and the same time a part or instrument of theology. (Here perhaps we part company with Pegis.) [44]

One way in which philosophy may be Christian without thereby being changed into theology is suggested by certain writers who distinguish between two different moments according to which a given science may be considered: the "moment of discovery" and the "moment of proof." Often enough those who reject the notion of Christian philosophy do so because they view it only

under the second moment, that is, as a completed set of propositions including principles, proofs, and conclusions. Here they
rightly maintain that nothing pertaining to faith or theology can
enter in. To admit the contributions of faith into the process
of proof itself would be to destroy the philosophical nature of
the science in question. However, one can also consider philosophy in its course of development, that is, in its process of
inquiry or its moment of discovery. In the positive sciences one
may move from a given working hypothesis and work backwards,
as it were, in an effort to establish this hypothesis scientifically.
And if such a method may be employed in other sciences, there
seems to be no reason to deny its usefulness in philosophy.[45] For
the Christian at any rate, it would seem that certain revealed
data might serve as such working hypotheses for philosophical
investigation. While continuing to assent to them as objects of
faith, he would now investigate them "as antecedently probable
results of rational proof." Because such truths guide his research
and serve as "leading questions," he will then operate as a Christian philosopher. However, neither faith nor theology will enter
in positively when it comes to the formulation of the rational
evidence in the moment of proof. Here purely philosophical
criteria must be applied.[46] This, then, would seem to be one
way in which philosophy would be Christian in its course of
investigation without thereby being changed into theology. In
its moment of proof, however, it will be pure philosophy. For
there "it shows none of its Christian character formally as such."
On neither count, however, will it be described as theology.[47]

NOTES

1. Trans. Cécile Gilson (New York: Random House, 1962). For what
follows cf. cc. 1 and 2.

2. *Ibid.*, pp. 73-84. Cf. also "What is Christian Philosophy?" *A Gilson
Reader*, ed. Anton Pegis (Garden City, N. Y.: Doubleday Image, 1957), pp.
181-2, and 190, n. 4, where Gilson writes: "According to Thomas Aquinas,
everybody is held *explicitly* and *always* to believe that God is and that he
aims at the good of man." Gilson observes that there is no reason to
think that Thomas is rejecting his other thesis that one cannot believe
and know the same thing at the same time. In *Christianity and
Philosophy*, trans. R. MacDonald (New York: Sheed and Ward, 1939)

he challenges the view which denies that the existence of God can ever be an object of faith. As Gilson sees it, God's existence must be accepted on faith by those who have not yet attained to demonstrative knowledge of it. Cf. pp. 61-67. Then he goes on to suggest that it might be compatible with Thomistic teaching to say that in one sense the. existence of God as known by us is not identical with the existence of God as believed by us. For the Christian continues to say "Credo in Deum" even after he has become a philosopher. This will not be impossible in Thomism because one would then have faith and knowledge *de eodem* but not *secundum idem*. Cf. pp. 70-71. In the *Elements of Christian Philosophy* (New York: Doubleday & Co., 1960), pp. 25-27 and in his *Introduction à la philosophie chrétienne* (Paris: J. Vrin, 1960), pp. 13-25, Gilson makes the same point. The philosophers should never forget that God has revealed his existence. Again, it is by an act of faith in the God of Moses that the theologian begins his research. To know that God exists will not dispense the Christian from believing in Him whose existence is revealed by divine revelation. For the affirmation of God by faith is specifically distinct from the affirmation of God by philosophical reason. Belief in God is, for the believer, the first real grasp of that God who is the author of the economy of salvation and the first step on the path leading to man's ultimate supernatural end in the beatific vision. Granted that the existence of God can be demonstrated by natural reason, Gilson is not so sure that every man can be certain that his own reason is infallible in its effort to achieve such demonstrative knowledge. While pursuing the rational effort in its every detail, Gilson urges the believer to preserve his faith in that Word which reveals this truth to the simple as well as to the wise. Cf. *Introduction..*, p. 21. He finds no contradiction between such a view and the proposition that it is impossible to believe and know one and the same thing at the same time. He continues: "Nous ne pouvons pas croire, d'un acte de foi surnaturel, que Dieu soit le Premier Moteur Immobile, ou la Première Cause Efficiente, ou le Premier Nécessaire; tout cela, que le philosophe démontre, relève de la raison naturalle, non da la foi. Aussi bien ces conclusions ont-elles été découvertes par des hommes tels qu'Aristote et Avicenne, elles n'ont pas été révélées par Dieu. Il est vrai que, si le Dieu de la révélation existe, il est le premier moteur, le premier efficient, le premier nécessaire et tout ce que la raison peut établir touchant la cause première de l'univers, mais si Yahvé est le Premier Moteur, le Premier Moteur n'est pas Yahvé. Le Premier Efficient ne m'a jamais parlé par ses prophètes et je n'attends pas de lui mon salut. Le Dieu dont le fidèle croit qu'il existe, transcende infiniment celui dont le philosophe prouve l'existence." *Ibid.*, pp. 21-22. Cf. the *Elements...*, p. 286, n. 15: "... while the God of faith is also the Prime Mover, the Prime Mover is not the God of faith."

3. *The Philosopher and Theology*, p. 72. Cf. pp. 65-72 as well as *Christianity and Philosophy*, pp. 74-77,

4. *The Philosopher and Theology*, pp. 88-89. Cf. also *God and Philosophy* (New Haven: Yale Paperback, 1959), pp. xii-xv.

5. *The Philosopher and Theology*, pp. 88-91. The fifth edition of a considerably revised *Le thomisme* has appeared in English under the title: *The Christian Philosophy of St. Thomas Aquinas*, trans. L. K. Shook (New York: Random House, 1956).

6. *The Philosopher and Theology*, pp. 91-92. *La philosophie de saint Bonaventure* has appeared in English as *The Philosophy of Saint Bonaventure*, trans. I. Trethowan and F. J. Sheed (New York: Sheed and Ward, 1938).

7. *The Philosopher and Theology*, pp. 93-95. For Gilson's view that much of modern classical philosophy owes a far greater debt to Christian influences than is generally recognized, cf. *The Spirit of Mediaeval Philosophy*, Gifford Lectures 1931-1932, trans. A.H.C. Downes (London: Sheed and Ward, 1936, repr. 1950), pp. 13-19. The notes of the French original (*L'Esprit de la philosophie médiévale* [Paris: J. Vrin, 1932] 2 vol.) have been considerably shortened in the English version. For his criticisms of attempts to reconstruct a Thomistic philosophy by following the philosophical order, cf. *The Christian Philosophy of St. Thomas Aquinas*, p. 442, n. 33. To do so is to present a *"philosophia ad mentem sancti Thomae* as though it were a *philosophia ad mentem Cartesii."* (p. 443). Cf. also pp. 21-22. Gilson finds this distinction between the "philosophical order" and the "theological order" in the *Summa contra gentiles*, II, c. 4. *Elements of Christian Philosophy*, p. 290, n. 42.

8. *The Spirit of Mediaeval Philosophy*, p. 207. Cf. also the concluding pages of Gilson's *History of Christian Philosophy in the Middle Ages* (New York: Random House, 1955), pp. 540-545.

9. For brief surveys of this controversy cf. E. A. Sillem, "Notes on Recent Work. Christian Philosophy," *The Clergy Review*, XLVI (1961), pp. 151-158 and M. Nédoncelle, *Is There a Christian Philosophy?* trans. I. Trethowan (New York: Hawthorn Books, 1960), pp. 85-99.

10. *Christianity and Philosophy*, pp. 93-94. On previous usage of the term "Christian philosophy" cf. *L'Esprit de la philosophie médiévale*, pp. 413-440; *The Christian Philosophy of St. Thomas Aquinas*, p. 441, n. 19; "What Is Christian Philosophy?" *A Gilson Reader*, pp. 178 ff., 186, 190, n. 6; *The Philosopher and Theology*, pp. 175 ff. Cf. also E. Sillem, *op. cit.*, pp. 149-152 and M. Nédoncelle, *op. cit.*, p. 85. For a brief historical survey of philosophy in Christian times and of Christian philosophy as understood by Nédoncelle, cf. cc. 1-4 of the same.

11. Gilson (*The Christian Philosophy of St. Thomas Aquinas*, p. 441, n. 20) refers to his *Christianity and Philosophy* as follows. "The basic idea in this book is that the phrase 'Christian philosophy' expresses a theological notion of a reality observable in history." Cf. also "La possibilité philosophique de la philosophie chrétienne," *Revue des sciences religieuses* XXXII (1958), p. 168.

12. *The Spirit of Mediaeval Philosophy*, pp. 20-22.

13. *Ibid.*, pp. 23-28. For Justin cf. his *Dialogue with Trypho*, cc. 2-8.

14. *The Spirit of Mediaeval Philosophy*, p. 35. Cf. "What Is Christian Philosophy?" *A Gilson Reader*, pp. 177-79.

15. *The Spirit of Mediaeval Philosophy*, p. 35.

16. *Ibid.*, p. 36.

17. *Ibid.*, p. 37. Cf. *Christianity and Philosophy*, pp. 100-101.

18. p. 5. Gilson insists that his view of Christian Philosophy squares with that advocated by Leo XIII in the Encyclical *Aeterni Patris*. He is convinced that the Encyclical points to far more than a merely negative role for faith as regards human reason. As he interprets it, a positive influence is called for by words such as the following: "Those, therefore, who to the study of philosophy unite obedience to the Christian faith, are philosophizing in the best possible way; for the splendor of the divine truths, received into the mind, helps the understanding, and not only detracts in no wise from its dignity, but adds greatly to its nobility, keenness, and stability." (Cited in his "What Is Christian Philosophy?" *A Gilson Reader*, p. 186). Cf. *Christianity and Philosophy*, pp. 91-102 and *The Philosopher and Theology*, pp. 175-190.

19. *The Philosopher and Theology*, p. 192. Cf. *The Christian Philosophy of St. Thomas Aquinas*, pp. 20-23.

20. *The Spirit of Mediaeval Philosophy*, p. 37. Cf. p. 36. "In this sense [considered according to its formal essence] it is clear that a philosophy cannot be Christian . . . and that the idea of Christian philosophy, has no more meaning than 'Christian physics' or 'Christian mathematics'." Cf. *Christianity and Philosophy*, pp. 95-96.

21. *The Spirit* . . . , p. 36; *The Philosopher and Theology*, pp. 192 ff.

22. "Viewed as a formally constucted philosophy, Thomistic philosophy —I do not say Thomistic theology—is wholly rational: no reasoning issuing from faith finds its way into its inner fabric; it derives intrinsically from reason and rational criticism alone; and its soundness as a philosophy is based entirely on experimental or intellectual evidence and on logical proof." *An Essay on Christian Philosophy*, trans. E. H. Flannery (New York: Philosophical Library, 1955), p. 15.

23. *An Essay on Christian Philosophy*, p. 18. Cf. pp. 15-18. Cf. also Maritain, *Science and Wisdom*, trans. B. Wall (London: Geoffrey Bles, 1940, repr. 1954), pp. 79-80, 90-93, 97. We are here limiting ourselves to Maritain's treatment of speculative philosophy. For him, speculative philosophy is Christian only by reason of its state, not by reason of its specifying object. Practical philosophy, on the other hand, will be Christian by reason of its state and by reason of its object. Cf. *Science and Wisdom*, pp. 100, 127. For his general treatment of the Christian character of moral philosophy cf. the same, pp. 107-27 and Part II, as well as *An Essay on Christian Philosophy*, pp. 38 ff. and 61-100. To return to his consideration of the Christian character of speculative philosophy, he distinguishes between *objective* data which philosophy may receive from faith and from theology, and *subjective* aids and reinforcements. The objective data refer primarily to revealed truths of the natural order, i.e., those data which philosophical

reasoning should be able to attain but which, in fact, the great pagan thinkers did not clearly grasp in their fullness. "Moreover, these *objective data* are also concerned with the repercussions of truths of the supernatural order on philosophical reflexion: and here the connexions and echoes really extend indefinitely." *Science and Wisdom*, p. 80. For more on these objective aids, cf. *An Essay on Christian Philosophy*, pp. 18-24. By subjective reinforcements he refers to philosophical wisdom insofar as it is a *habit* of the intellect. As an intellectual habit, philosophical wisdom may be aided by higher habits such as the habit of faith, theological wisdom, and contemplative wisdom, provided, of course, that the philosopher is a Christian. Here Maritain speaks of a "dynamic continuity of *habitus*" which will reinforce philosophical activity subjectively by vivifying and purifying the philosophical *habitus*. Cf. *An Essay . . .*, pp. 24-29, and *Science and Wisdom*, pp. 80, 86-90. For a detailed exposition and criticism of this aspect of Maritain's theory cf. A. Naud, *Le problème de la philosophie chrétienne. Eléments d'une solution thomiste* (Montreal: Faculté de Théologie, 1960), pp. 13-34. However, Naud emphasizes this notion of the subjective *confortations* so greatly that he may possibly minimize the importance of the *objective* contributions to philosophy by faith and theology in Maritain's theory.

24. *An Essay on Christian Philosophy*, p. 29.

25. Cf. *L'Esprit de la philosophie médiévale* (2d ed. Paris: J. Vrin, 1944), pp. 439-40, n. 80. Though we have not found any detailed treatment in Gilson of Maritain's distinction between objective aids and subjective reinforcements (cf. n. 23) from which philosophy will benefit under Christian conditions, Gilson seems to emphasize the former without rejecting the latter in any way. In fact, in the present reference he tells us why. Granted that that which is most vital is the work of revelation and grace in the soul of the believing philosopher and granted that without this there would be no Christian philosophy, yet for the observer and in particular for the historian of philosophy the only means available to detect this inner action is to examine the outward evidence, i.e., philosophy with revelation and philosophy without revelation. This is what Gilson has attempted to do, and this is why he has said that history alone can give meaning to the notion of Christian philosophy. He continues: "Je dirai donc que la philosophie chrétienne n'est une réalité objectivement observable que pour l'histoire, et que son existence n'est positivement démontrable que par l'histoire, mais que, son existence étant ainsi établie, sa notion peut être analysée en elle-même et qu'elle doit l'être comme vient de le faire M. J. Maritain. Je suis donc entièrement d'accord avec lui."

26. *The Spirit of Mediaeval Philosophy*, pp. 37-40. Cf. "Thomas Aquinas and Our Colleagues," *A Gilson Reader*, p. 296, n. 7; "What Is Christian Philosophy?" *A Gilson Reader*, pp. 179-182; *Christianity and Philosophy*, pp. 60-61; *Elements of Christian Philosophy*, pp. 24-25.

27. Cf. in particular *The Spirit of Mediaeval Philosophy* and his *History of Christian Philosophy in the Middle Ages*. As regards individual thinkers, cf. also: *The Christian Philosophy of Saint Augustine*, trans. L.E.M.

Lynch (New York: Random House, 1960); *The Philosophy of Saint Bona-*
venture; The Christian Philosophy of St. Thomas Aquinas; Elements of
Christian Philosophy; Introduction à la philosophie chrétienne; Jean Duns
Scot. Introduction à ses positions fondamentales (Paris: J. Vrin, 1952).

28. *Christianity and Philosophy*, pp. 77-79.

29. Cf. "Thomas Aquinas and Our Colleagues," pp. 288-289; *Elements*
of Christian Philosophy p. 12; *The Philosopher and Theology*, p. 194.

30. *Elements of Christian Philosophy*, pp. 13-14. For this same point,
that Thomas' most original philosophical contributions are to be found in
his theological writings, cf. also *The Christian Philosophy of St. Thomas*
Aquinas, p. 8.

31. *Elements of Christian Philosophy*, p. 15. Granted that these same
terms are also found in Aristotle, Gilson insists that in Aquinas they have
taken on new meaning. In his eyes the most distinctive feature of Thomistic
metaphysics lies in a "certain metaphysical notion of being tied up with a
certain notion of the Christian God." *Ibid.*, p. 6. To set forth this notion in
some of its most important metaphysical ramifications is the avowed purpose of his *Elements of Christian Philosophy* as well as his *Introduction à*
la philosophie chrétienne. Here again Gilson finds further evidence for a
positive influence of revelation and theology upon philosophy because he
regards it as highly plausible that the original inspiration for the Thomistic
understanding of *esse* as act is to be traced back to the well known biblical
text: *Ego sum qui sum* (Ex., 3:14). Having been prompted by this text to
conclude that God's essence is "to be" (*esse*), Thomas would then have
easily moved to composition of essence and "to be" in all creatures by way
of contrast with God. Once more he would have followed the theological
order rather than the philosophical. Cf. *Elements* . . . , pp. 124-135; *Intro-*
duction . . . , pp. 45-58. For difficulties involved in any purely philosophical
approach to the essence-existence composition, cf. *Introduction* . . . , pp.
98-109.

32. *Elements of Christian Philosophy*, p. 282, n. 6.

33. *Ibid.*, pp. 19-20 and 283, n. 11. Cf. *The Christian Philosophy of*
St. Thomas Aquinas, pp. 6-7.

34. *The Philosopher and Theology*, p. 98. Cf. "St. Thomas and Our
Colleagues," *A Gilson Reader*, pp. 293-294. For Gilson, of course, this broader
view of theology is that of Thomas himself. Cf. *The Christian Philosophy of*
St. Thomas Aquinas, pp. 9-10. To designate those philosophical elements
"which have been integrated with a theological synthesis" Thomas used
the term *revelabilia*. For further discussion of the *revelabilia* cf. *ibid.*,
pp. 9-15.

35. *Summa theol.*, I, 1, 1, ad 2.

36. *Elements of Christian Philosophy*, p. 27. Cf. *Introduction à la*
philosophie chrétienne, pp. 112 ff. and 132.

37. *Elements of Christian Philosophy*, pp. 34-37; 289-90, n. 36; *The*
Philosopher and Theology, pp. 100-101; "Thomas Aquinas and Our Col-

leagues," *A Gilson Reader*, pp. 293-4. For Thomas, cf. *Summa theol.*, I, 1, 5, obj. 2 and reply; *Expositio super librum Boethii de Trinitate*, q. 2, a. 3, ad 5. For fuller treatment of the nature of theology, cf. G. Van Ackeren, *Sacra Doctrina. The Subject of the First Question of the Summa Theologica of St. Thomas Aquinas* (Rome: Catholic Book Agency, 1952). Cf. Gilson's chapter entitled "Sacred doctrine" in the *Elements of Christian Philosophy*, pp. 22-42.

38. *Elements . . .* , p. 42.

39. *The Philosopher and Theology*, p. 198.

40. "Thomas Aquinas and Our Colleagues," *A Gilson Reader*, p. 286.

41. *Ibid.*, p. 289.

42. *Ibid.*, pp. 290-94. Cf. "What is Christian Philosophy?" *A Gilson Reader*, pp. 188-190.

43. A. Pegis, *The Middle Ages and Philosophy* (Chicago: Henry Regnery, 1963), pp. 71, 77, 81. Cf. pp. 69-81.

44. Cf. Pegis, *op. cit.*, pp. 77 ff. and 86. Because of his insistence that Thomistic philosophy cannot be extracted from the theological writings and the theological context in which it is found without thereby doing violence to that philosophy itself, Gilson would undoubtedly also reject such an application of the distinction in question to it.

45. Cf. G. P. Klubertanz, "Metaphysics and Theistic Convictions," in *Teaching Thomism Today*, ed. G. F. McLean (Washington: The Catholic University of America Press, 1963), pp. 278-282; A. Naud, *Le problème de la philosophie chrétienne . . .* , pp. 35-62; G. Grisez, "The 'Four Meanings' of Christian Philosophy," *The Journal of Religion*, XLII (1962), pp. 113 ff.

46. Klubertanz, *op. cit.*, pp. 281-2.

47. *Ibid.*, and p. 293; Naud, *op. cit.*, pp. 72 ff. One might also ask whether such a philosophy will be *intrinsically* Christian in its moment of discovery. As we have seen, both Maritain and Gilson would apparently reply that philosophy may be intrinsically Christian in its concrete state of existence. Naud (*op. cit.*, pp. 91 ff.) rejects the view that philosophy might be intrinsically Christian, though he is there directly refuting Maritain's view of an intrinsic *confortation* of the philosophical habit by a higher habit. Klubertanz (*op. cit.*, p. 279) comments on philosophy in its moment of discovery: "It is in this area that I believe there can be a positive influence of the Faith upon philosophy, to render it intrinsically Christian." There seems to be some similarity, at least, between this distinction of philosophy in its moment of discovery and its moment of truth, on the one hand, and the Gilson - Maritain distinction between philosophy concretely considered (according to its state of existence) and philosophy taken in the abstract (according to its essence). If, according to the present distinction philosophy is Christian only in its moment of discovery, according to Maritain and Gilson it is Christian only in the concrete, in its Christian state of existence. But for Gilson, at any rate, such a philosophy will not only always exist under Christian conditions in the concrete, but also within a theology and will thereby be theological as well.

BIOGRAPHICAL NOTE

Étienne Gilson was born at Paris, June 13, 1884. After receiving the License in philosophy in 1905 and completing his *agrégation* in philosophy, he was awarded the Doctorat ès Lettres by the Sorbonne in 1913. He then began to teach at the University of Lille, but his career was interrupted by the outbreak of the First World War. He served as an officer in the French Army Machine Gun Company at Verdun and was captured in February, 1916, later being awarded the Cross of War for his valor during that campaign. During his period of imprisonment he profited from his contact with fellow-prisoners in order to master English and Russian. In 1919 he resumed his teaching duties, this time serving as professor of the history of philosophy at the University of Strasbourg. In 1921 he became professor of the history of medieval philosophy at the Sorbonne. Maintaining his position there until 1932, he also served as exchange-professor at the university of Brussels in 1923. In 1926, during his first trip to America, he received an honorary doctorate from the University of Montreal, lectured during the summer session at the University of Virginia, and served as exchange-professor at Harvard University during the first semester. It was also in 1926 that, together with Gabriel Théry, O.P., he became cofounder of the *Archives d'Histoire doctrinale et littéraire du Moyen Âge.* In 1929 he contributed to the founding of and became Director of Studies at the Institute of Mediaeval Studies in Toronto. In 1931 and 1932 he was invited to deliver the Gifford lectures at the University of Aberdeen. (This series was eventually published under the title *The Spirit of Mediaeval Philosophy.*) In 1932 he became professor of history of philosophy of the Middle Ages at the Collège de France. During the first semester of the academic year of 1936-1937 he delivered the William James Lectures at Harvard University, and in 1937, the Richards Lectures at the University of Virginia. Continuing his teaching at the Collège de France during the war years (1941-1944), he was selected for membership in the Académie Française in 1946. In 1951, at his own request, he retired as professor at the Collège de France and took up full time teaching duties at the Pontifical Institute of Mediaeval Studies in Toronto. In 1955 he gave the Mellon Lectures at the National Gallery of Art in Washington. At the present writing Professor Gilson is still active and continues to lecture on a wide scale. In recent years his intensive literary activity has continued and, as has been noted, three of his most important works on Christian philosophy and theology appeared in 1960: *Le philosophe et la théologie, Introduction à la philosophie chrétienne,* and the *Elements of Christian Philosophy.* He has won international recognition not only for his contributions to the history of medieval philosophy and his views on Christian philosophy, but also for a challenging and highly influential presentation of Thomism as an authentic "existential" philosophy. Because of Gilson's voluminous literary output, no attempt will be made here to list all of his writings. For a complete catalogue of his works through 1958, one may consult C. J. Edie, "The Writings of Étienne Gilson Chronologically Listed," *Mélanges offerts à Étienne Gilson de l'Academie Française*

(Toronto: Pontifical Institute of Mediaeval Studies, 1959), pp. 15-58. In the present study we have restricted ourselves to those writings which are relevant to the topic at hand, the notion of Christian philosophy and its relationship to theology. For a relatively brief listing of Gilson's books and longer articles of broader philosophical interest, the reader may consult A. Pegis, "The Writings of Etienne Gilson," *A Gilson Reader*, pp. 347-51. Consultation of the various selections in this same volume, *A Gilson Reader*, will also serve to introduce the reader to Gilson's contributions to varied fields of philosophy.

jacques maritain

A CHRISTIAN IN PHILOSOPHY
by Paul K. K. Tong

If one wishes to grasp the *élan vital* of the philosophy of
Maritain, it is necessary to keep in mind that he is first and fore-
most a Christian and only secondarily a philosopher. His philosophical works are the product of a man thinking and laboring in the
state of a lived and experienced Christianity. He never feels that
he has to apologize to any one for his faith, and he does not
consider his faith a weakness in his philosophizing, but looks
upon it as a source of light and strength. Because of his lived
Christian faith he is able to philosophize both profoundly and
enlighteningly. It may be said that Maritain is a great philosopher
because he is a great Christian. In keeping with these things, the
present essay endeavors to portray his philosophical temper and
system as primarily a result of Christian experience. Its first
part is concerned with Maritain's defense of philosophy as a valid
science which is demonstrated by an analysis of the theory of
knowledge; the second part deals with his philosophy of the
real as a further development of the *philosophia perennis*.

I. IN THE DEFENSE OF PHILOSOPHY

When Maritain entered upon the philosophical scene, positivism was the prevailing doctrine, and philosophy was no longer
looked upon as a form of valid knowledge, but was either totally
rejected or absorbed into science. It was taken for granted that
all knowledge is scientific knowledge, outside of which there

is only the dark region of emotional, unverifiable, and meaningless utterance. What is meaningless to a scientist is simply *per se* meaningless. Maritain traces the origin of this philosophical degradation to Descartes, who first attempted to unify all knowledge univocally by means of the sole criterion of mathematical certitude. Thus theology was the first victim to be eliminated from the field of science, because it could not measure up to that criterion. Following the Cartesian revolution Kant regarded metaphysics as *a priori* knowledge and not a knowledge by demonstration. Finally positivists made a complete denial of philosophy as a science. With the great advances of the physical sciences modern positivists have become even more firmly set in their bias. They rarely speak of philosophy except to expose its pretenses to science. Certain positivists, like Moritz Schlick, equate the total realm of science with a system of experimental statements. Since philosophy is not a system of such statements, it is not, therefore, a science. Thus philosophy is not considered a system of cognition but rather a system of acts. Schlick writes:

> It was one of the most serious errors of former times to have believed that the actual meaning and ultimate content was in turn to be formulated in statements and so was representable in cognitions. This was the error of 'metaphysics'. The efforts of metaphysicians were always directed upon the absurd end of expressing the content of pure quality (the essence of things) by means of cognitions, hence of uttering the unutterable. Qualities cannot be said. They can only be shown in experience. But with this showing, cognition has nothing to do.[1]

Positivists of the analytic school also eliminate metaphysics from the realm of science because it has no verifiable meaning. Rudolf Carnap believes that all philosophy of value and normative theory in logical analysis yield at best only the negative result that the alleged statements are entirely meaningless,[2] and A. J. Ayer summarizes the position of present-day positivists in this way:

> ... They divided significant propositions into two classes; formal propositions, like those of logic or pure

mathematics, which they held to be tautological, in a sense
that I shall presently explain, and factual propositions, of
which it was required that they should be empirically verifiable. These classes were supposed to be exhaustive; so
that if a sentence succeeded neither in expressing something
that was formally true or false, nor in expressing something
that could be empirically tested, the view taken was that
it did not express any proposition at all. It might have
emotive meaning but it was literally nonsensical.

Metaphysical utterances were condemned not for being
emotive, which could hardly be considered as objection-
able in itself, but for pretending to be cognitive, for mas-
querading as something that they were not.[3]

The analysts may be right in asserting that metaphysics is
meaningless according to the rules of logical analysis, but they
are wrong in concluding that it has no meaning at all. They fail
to realize that philosophy belongs on a different level of science,
or in Maritain's terms, to a different degree of science. Maritain's
practical orientation in philosophy has been towards reclaiming
its rightful position in the hierarchy of the sciences. He has
labored untiringly over the philosophical system of St. Thomas
Aquinas and demonstrated the validity of philosophy as a science
from the critique of human knowledge. He demonstrated that the
unity of knowledge is not, as Descartes holds, univocal, but analogical and hierarchical, in which distinct degrees of knowledge
constitute definitive realms of science and differ from each other
according to levels of intelligibility. This is true, he holds, because there are objects of knowledge whose intelligibility is immersed in matter, and because without matter these objects can
neither exist nor be conceived. This is the realm of natural
science and the philosophy of nature. Secondly, there are objects
of knowledge whose intelligibility is separate from matter, even
though such objects cannot exist without sensible matter. These
objects make up the realm of mathematics and its related sciences.
Finally, there are objects of knowledge whose intelligibility is
completely separate from matter. Such objects can exist without
matter, and may never have existed in matter at all. This is the
realm of metaphysics, or first philosophy. Thus in the hierarchy

of sciences, philosophy occupies the highest position and is truly the queen of sciences. To verify such a hierarchial division of sciences, Maritain follows the teaching of St. Thomas Aquinas and offers the following proofs.

1. *All sciences are about being.* Being is the total realm of reality, outside of which there is only nothingness. Therefore all sciences must be concerned with being or the properties of being. There is no science of nothingness. Thus the *primum notum,* the immediate evidence of human knowing, is the omnipresence of being as the term of knowledge. As Yves Simon says, "Every representation concerning the observable world shows a dualistic or bipolar character in as much as it refers to an intelligible object expressing itself through a stream of sense appearances (accidents of things) and a stream of sense appearances stabilized by a center of intelligibility. (essence of things)"[4] In empirical investigations the scientist is interested only in the measureable phenomena of his object, but implicitly and obscurely he is also concerned with its being as well. In all knowledge, therefore, we know the modes of the thing and the being of the thing, even though implicitly. The root of unity in knowledge is the value of being, whether known directly as it is, or indirectly through its modes of operation. According to Maritain, being is the matrix of all knowledge even for strictly *deontologized* knowledge such as scientific knowledge whose signs and symbols can be only grasped and manipulated by the intellect in the form of second-hand beings or *entia rationis.*

Maritain further argues that this doctrine is verified by the reflective philosophy of the logicians of science who do not deal with experimental procedures, the ways and means of observation and measurement, but state what the *nature* of science is and what the ways of *knowing* are. Their judgments are not concerned with concrete, measurable phenomena as such, but the nature of being. Thus all sciences are finally resolved in being, not in phenomena. Maritain accepts the traditional definition of science as perfect knowledge which the mind under the compulsion of evidence, points to the reasons in things for being. It is *cognitio certa per causas;* a knowledge through causes.

From his consideration of the ways of human knowing Maritain establishes that being is the ultimate foundation of all knowledge because being is absolutely and simply the first object of the human intellect in all its modes of knowing. Being as unfolded in sense intuition is this or that concrete existing thing; being as exhibited in scientific knowledge is the universal, intelligible natures of things; in metaphysical intuition, being is known as being. Hence being is the primordial and total object of knowledge into which all human knowledge is resolved. Maritain concludes that every attempt by the positivists to eliminate the notion of being refutes itself.

2. *All knowledge is of the necessary.* The intelligible natures or essences with which scientific knowledge is concerned are not contingent but necessary. Knowledge of the singular, contingent thing as contingent is impossible. Each single event is the end-product of an almost infinite number of causes, and to understand the event, it would be necessary to understand the relationship among all these causes as well. Moreover, to almost every rule that one can formulate about the concrete individual there are an enormous number of exceptions. These causes and exceptions are beyond reckoning by any human created mind, and consequently they are neither of utility nor of interest for knowledge.[5] Therefore the contingent singular thing is not the *formal* object of science. Science bears directly on a necessary object which the mind conceives from the concrete singular thing and which guarantees the stability of human knowledge. The intelligible necessities in the object of science are unfolded in ideal constancies and permanent determinations immanent in the object as presented to the mind in the universality of its concepts. These are essences and they are the locale of intelligible necessities. Thus "the universality of the object of knowledge is the condition of its *necessity,* in itself the condition of perfect knowledge or science. Exactly as knowledge can only be of what is by necessity, there can only be knowledge of the universal."[6]

The universal intelligibles are perceived by the mind by the act of abstraction. In it the mind draws out of the singular thing only those determinations which are an integral and necessary part of its being. Such a process negates the possibility of a science of the singular. However, all intelligible universals are not of the same degree but are determined in rank by the degree of immateriality they represent.

3. *Immateriality of knowledge.* Knowledge is immaterial in

a twofold way: from the aspect of the thing known, or the trans-objective subject, as Maritain calls it, immateriality corresponds to its intelligible form, (*ratio formalis sub qua*); from the aspect of the knower, or the cisobjective subject, immateriality is commeasurable with the cognitive faculties, that is, the knowing subject must rise above matter (*lumen intellectuale*). In the Aristotelian and Thomistic tradition, to know is to become *the other*. Thus knowledge implies a union between the knowing subject and the known object and this can only be an immaterial union. In every material union there arises a third term but in knowledge there is no such third term. The knower, while remaining himself, becomes the thing known and identifies himself with it. Maritain writes: "Thus, a material being can become *other*, i.e. it can itself change or be modified, but it cannot become *the other*."[7] In knowledge, therefore, there is an immaterial union, an immaterial superexistence of the subject.

A question presents itself: What is this immaterial union present in human knowing? In other words, in what manner is the knower the known? Or how does the known thing exist in the knower? As is evident, the thing known cannot be present in the knower as it is in its natural state of being, *esse naturae*. When a stone is known, it does not exist in the mind as a physical thing; it exists in the knower in a special manner which the ancients call *intentional being, esse intentionale*. This intentional presence of the object in the knower and the intentional transformation of the knower into the object are the function of both the immateriality of the cognitive faculty and the intelligible forms of things, even though these intelligible forms in material things are only in a state of potency and become actual when they are apprehended. This is the epistemological foundation and justification of the Thomistic thesis of the commeasurability of knowledge with immateriality. Since objects of knowledge have different degrees of immateriality, there are many degrees of knowledge or science. Therefore the same thing may be an object of different sciences, each of which considers a particular intelligible aspect of the thing, and penetrates into different levels of its intelligibility. Hence Maritain writes:

If a figure of speech be permitted here, let us say that

the work of the intellect can be compared to an immaterial magic. From the flux of singular and contingent things, as given to the apprehension of the sense, a first glance of the intellect reveals the world of corporeal substances and their properties. A second glance reveals quite another universe, the ideal world of the extended number. A third glance discloses still another, wholly different universe, the world of being as being and all the transcendental perfections common to spirits and bodies, wherein we can attain purely spiritual realities, and the very principle of all reality, as in a mirror.[8]

Thus through the critique of knowledge Maritain discovers the principle of differentiation of human sciences in the degrees of abstraction that grade each science according to the immateriality of its object. Philosophy, above all first philosophy or metaphysics, is a science, it is a valid form of human knowing concerned with an objectively distinct branch of knowledge, constituting a really autonomous discipline, possessing its own means of exploring this field of knowledge.

Philosophy, therefore, is not a sort of extension of the empiriological sciences, nor is it a sort of mythology, fit only to satisfy our emotional needs. Empiriological sciences do not tell us *what* a thing *is,* because they do not reveal to us the very being of things. Since they provide a knowledge only of the proximate causes of things, they can never satisfy the mind which always raises questions of a higher order, that is, questions as to the ultimate causes of things. Hence Maritain believes that science depends on philosophy and that it inspires the mind with a desire for philosophy. Every scientist consciously or unconsciously asserts —*in actu exercito*—a certain number of metaphysical propositions which may concern the reality of the sensible world, the existence of things outside us.

Moreover, philosophy is not only a science; it is also wisdom, which is the knowledge of ultimate causes. Because it is wisdom, it has the function of ordering human knowledge: *sapientiae est ordinare.* The empiriological sciences cannot be above or transcend themselves. It is philosophy, a higher science by nature, which binds together in harmony the whole universe of knowledge by assigning the natural limits and subordination of the different sciences.

Philosophy, being wisdom, is useless. As Maritain points out, it is of no service because it is beyond all service; it is useless because it is *superuseful*. As a Chinese philosopher, Chaung-Tsu, once said, "Only those who already know the value of the useless can be talked to about the useful". Although it is of no practical use, philosophy is the measure of the values of all practical utilities. Philosophy is not a means; it is an end, a fruit, a good at once self-justifying and delightful; it is knowledge for the free man, the freest and by nature the most regal knowledge. In fine, *philosophy does not reveal truth to serve us, but truth for us to serve.*[9]

II. PHILOSOPHY OF THE REAL

Anyone familiar with the history of philosophy is aware of the conflicting schools of thought. It may be said that there are almost as many systems of philosophy as there are philosophers. This has been a scandal to many and has often led to a belief that of itself the human mind is incapable to attain any truth. Consequently advocates of fideism, skepticism, agnosticism, relativism, and their like crowd the pages of the history of philosophy. This pessimistic mood is more evident today than in former times. It is the fashion to make no commitment whatever to any philosophy. The accepted attitude of many professional philosophers is expressed by this often repeated question: Who is to say that one philosophy is better than another? It is considered a doctrinaire attitude to hold that there is a true, valid system of philosophical discipline, and to do so is held tantamount to contradicting all historical evidence. To Maritain such a relativistic attitude to philosophy is most offensive. He believes every philosophy gives us some knowledge of the real. Indeed, there is no completely erroneous philosophy, nor can there be one. Every error contains a grain of truth; absolute error is unintelligible. In an erroneous judgment at least the terms are true, although their affirmation or negation is not. Even in error human reason in some fashion reaches the real. Every system of philosophy tells us something about the real and a false philosophy only fails in giving us a complete and coherent picture of reality and takes a certain aspect of reality for the whole of reality. Idealism as a philosophical system is false because it reduces all realities to mental realities, yet it does tell us something about the ideal realities; positivism is false as a philosophy since it limits the realm of reality to sole quantified realities, yet it does tell us something about quantified realities. Therefore although different philosophers see realities differently, that is no reason for us to despair and claim that they do not see reality at all.

Maritain is not an exponent of intellectual despair. He believes that a true philosophical system is not only possible, but actually realized in the *philosophia perennis*. As represented by the Aristotelico-Thomistic system, it is the best philosophical system thus far developed. He further indicates that Thomism is not a system fully completed and closed within itself but a system that continually expands and deepens as man's knowledge of reality expands and deepens. Thus Thomism, as Maritain views it, transcends time because truth is not a function of time but based on the real and is valid as long as reality endures. Truth transcends locality, nationality and race, because it is the expression and product of reason which is everywhere the same. Therefore, the *philosophia perennis* is impervious to time and is the common legacy of mankind. For Maritain Thomism has inexhaustible possibilities of invention and progressive synthesis.

Of Maritain's many contributions to Thomism the most outstanding among them is his explicit formulation of St. Thomas's thought on *esse*, which he considers the ground and the stuff of all reality and the core of St. Thomas's philosophical system. Maritain looks upon St. Thomas as the most existential of the philosophers, because in his thought *esse* has sole and absolute primacy. However, it must be added that the existentialism of St. Thomas is a world apart from the phenomenological existentialism of today. In this latter essences or natures are abolished in favor of existence and thus intelligibility itself disappears. Existentialism of this sort is self-destroying. St. Thomas, on the other hand, affirms the primacy of existence while preserving essences or natures. The intelligibility of the real is not abolished but enhanced, since it is essence that *esse* actuates in the real.

What is *esse?* It may be described as the act of existing by which being triumphs over nothingness. The *esse*, Maritain says, by virtue of which I myself and things exist, transcends concepts and ideas; it is a mystery for the intellect. But intellect lives on this mystery, because the act of existing is the very object of every achieved act of the intellect and of every judgment. The act of existing provides ground and center for the intelligible structure of all reality. In its supreme uncreated plenitude *esse* activates and attracts to itself the entire dynamism of nature. *Esse,* therefore, is the act of all acts; the perfection of all perfections; the ground of all that is real.

Esse as an exercised act must be exercised by something, namely, a subject or an existent which the scholastics call the *suppositum. Actiones sunt suppositorum.* An essence can receive *esse* only by exercising it, that is, only if it is placed in an existential state. This state of exercising existence is precisely the state of the existent. The existent, then, is the ultimate subject of reality, the absolute value of ontological contemplation. On the other hand, the total existential value of the existent is found in *esse,* the exercised act. By their essence the existents are diverse and so the exercised act is also diversified. However, this diversification is not equivocal, but analogical, since the exercised act is always in proportion to the essence or nature. The supreme existent is the *esse plenum* at the ontological peak—*Ipsum Esse Subsistens.*

However, the existent, the supremely concrete reality, the singular, incommunicable, irreducible reality, is beyond intellectual concept or idea. Thus it is not a pure intelligible because it is superintelligible. It is not an essence or nature apprehended by abstraction. *Esse,* the exercised act, cannot be grasped by a concept through formal abstraction. According to Maritain, "The trans-objective subjects do not give themselves up to us as objects." St. Thomas uses the term *separatio* instead of *abstractio* in regard to the existential knowledge of *esse. Separatio* is an act of judgment not of apprehension, although it is had in the same instant when apprehension is had. When we know what a thing is, we also instantaneously know that it is. Maritain calls this existential knowledge the ananoetic intellection, a knowledge through analogy. It is only through analogy that the subjects of metaphysics are known. Primarily, we know the analogue as considered in the inferior analogates, namely the created existents. This is the field called by Maritain the trans-sensible. However, metaphysics also opens on to the causes of these analogates, the superior analoguates of being. This second realm is called the trans-intelligible because our knowing power is not proportionate to it. Hence ananoetic intellection is an imperfect knowledge just as perinoetic intellection is imperfect; the second is on account of the subintelligibllity of its objects, while the first is on account of the superintelligibility of its objects.

Ananoetic intellection, whether of the trans-sensible or of the transintelligible, is genuinely had not through pure rational analysis but only through intuition. All rational analysis of *esse* leads only to the logical necessity of an intuitive knowledge, but does not cross its threshold. Only through intuition is the act of existing known.

Many scholastic thinkers have rejected Maritain's term intuition, which is considered foreign to the vocabulary of traditional metaphysics. Maritain, however, claims that it is St. Thomas's doctrine and that it is inherent in his exposition of knowledge.[10] This intuition is eidetic or abstractive, and is clearly distinguished from the intuition effected through sympathy or anguish of the will as found in Bergson and modern existentialism. Nor is such intuition the same as intuition of Platonic essences, since *esse* is definitely and emphatically not a universal. Maritain describes abstractive intuition as eidetic visualization of the act of the transobjective subject, autonomous, essentially diversified, and with all its transcendental and analogical value. It is an intellectual perception, and the intellectual *habitus* of this perception is cause and effect of such intuition. This reciprocal causation means that the metaphysical *habitus* is had at the same time as the intuition. If it is asked how this is possible, Maritain answers that the intellect, by the very fact that it is spiritual, proportions its objects to itself by elevating them within itself to diverse degrees which are increasingly pure in spirituality and immateriality. It is within itself that this intuition attains reality, stripped of its real existence outside the mind and disclosing, uttering in the mind a content, an interior, an intelligible sound or voice, which can possess only in the mind the conditions of its existence one and universal, an existence of intelligibility in act. Once had, such an intuition cannot be lost, but only a few privileged minds ever have attained to such a height.[11]

Once we appreciate the metaphysical role of *esse,* we can have a correct approach to other philosophical problems as presented in epistemology, psychology, natural theology and ethics. *Esse* exercises the cardinal function in all these branches of philosophy.

In epistemology, whether there is a question of sense knowledge or of intellectual knowledge, there is the encounter of the acting knowing power of the cisobjective subject with the act of the existing trans-objective subject. The product of human knowledge is the final activity, the immaterial existence of *esse intentionale.* The whole integrating and vitalizing principle of man in all his diverse properties and activities, powers, acts, and habits, in his *esse,* in which his soul is substantially united to his body, as one agent. In ethics, man, the whole man, is considered in his entire existential state—his personal behavior—in all its dimensions of family, society, and the world at large.

It is most significant that *esse* plays the central role in the proofs of God's existence, since creation is an existential communication. *Esse* as uncreated, the *esse plenum,* is the efficient, exemplary, and final cause of participating and created *esse.* Maritain's new approach to God is based on this intuitive knowledge of *esse.* He writes:

> In the created realm reason confronts Being and labors to conquer it, both to transfer Being into its own immaterial life and immaterially to be or become Being. In perceiving Being Reason knows God—the self-subsisting Act of Being—in an enigmatic but inescapable manner.[12]

Maritain maintains that once a man attains the intelligible perception of the act of being, he immediately and inevitably perceives in some fashion the act of being as such, the *esse plenum.* In the perception of the act of being, one also perceives the contingency of this act as found in oneself or in things. His analysis is as follows:

> I see that my Being, first, is liable to death; and second, that it depends on the totality of nature, on the universal whole whose part I am. I see that Being-with-

nothingness, as my own being is, implies, in order to be, Being-without-nothingness,—that absolute existence which I confusedly perceived as involved in my primordial intuition of existence. And I see that the universal whole, whose part I am, is being-with-nothingness, from the very fact that I am part of it; so that finally, since the universal whole does not exist by itself, there is another Whole, a separate one, another Being, transcendent, self-sufficient and unknown in itself and activating all beings, which is Being-without-nothingness, that is, self-subsisting Being, Being existing through itself.

Thus, the inner dynamism of the intuition of existence or of the intelligible value of Being, causes me to see that absolute existence of Being-without-nothingness transcends the totality of nature—and makes me face the existence of God.[13]

The present study has been restricted to certain fundamental things in Maritain's metaphysics and theory of knowledge, but there are many other subjects in his philosophy which deserve study. Thus he has written on political philosophy and esthetics and his influence in both fields has been extensive. By way of conclusion Maritain's philosophical spirit as a guiding light for those engaged in philosophy must be stressed. First of all, it is his conviction that genuine philosophical activity demands the engagement of the whole person in all his existential dimensions. The philosopher's intellectual *habitus* is nothing else than the actualization of symbolic compenetration of the dynamic energies of his whole being. Any attempt to philosophize apart from one's existential condition is superficial, useless, and even impossible. For a Christian to attempt to construct an achristian philosophy is a futile undertaking because it is not genuine or authentic.

Another facet of Maritain's philosophical spirit is his contempt for passing modes in philosophy. He is definitely not a philosophical man of fashion. Throughout his life he has labored against the tides of his time because he has had a clear vision for the real, the truth, and the good and no power could force him to betray it. He believes that truth has nothing to do with fashion. If one tries to be fashionable in philosophy, he will find it impossible to keep up with the pace. It is now Cartesian, now Kantian, now Hegelian, now Marxian, or now Bergsonian. Now it is linguistic analysis, now phenomenological existentialism, and one knows not what will be the fashion of tomorrow. Search for truth requires courage as well as detachment from worldly interests. A philosopher should not be tempted by either personal ambitions or temporal advantages. Intellectual integrity is more precious and necessary to a philosopher than to a scientist, since true wisdom cannot coexist with falsity or weakness.

The greatness of a philosopher is not determined solely by his intellectual genius, but also by the scope of his philosophical vision. A great philosopher must embrace in his heart the whole universe of reality; anything less will not do. Past philosophers often went astray when they mistook a part for the whole of reality. Such men had only a partial vision and were blind to the rest. Their philosophical teachings are unsatisfactory since they cannot lead man to the totality of being and integral truth.

Finally we may regard Maritain's philosophy as a case study of a Christian in philosophy, whose reason operates actually within Christian revelation freely and gladly through the very movement of his faith. He is an example of the cooperation of human freedom with God's grace. Whoever denies the possibility of such cooperation must necessarily deny the possibility of a Christian philosophy. Let me repeat, Maritain is a great philosopher because he is a great Christian. In a positivistic age Maritain is indeed a rare and precious phenomenon. His spirit gives courage to the weak, his vision enlightens the poor-sighted, and his doctrine, like that of his master, St. Thomas Aquinas, is part of the wisdom of the ages.

NOTES

1. Moritz Schlick, "The Turning Point in Philosophy," *Logical Positivism,* ed. A. J. Ayer, (Glencoe Illinois: The Free Press, 1959), p. 56.

2. Rudolph Carnap, "The Elimination of Metaphysics Through Logical Analysis of Language," *ibid.* p. 61.

3. *Ibid.,* Introduction, p. 10.

4. Yves R. Simon, "Maritain's Philosophy of Science," *Thomist,* Vol. V, (New York: Sheed and Ward, 1942), p. 34.

5. Cf. "Reflections on Necessity and Contingency," *Essays in Thomism,* (New York: Sheed and Ward, 1942), p. 34.

6. Jacques Maritain, *The Degrees of Knowledge,* translation from the fourth French edition under the supervision of Gerald B. Phelan, (New York: Charles Scribner's Sons, 1959), p. 35.

7. *Ibid.,* p. 112.

8. *Ibid.,* p. 37.

9. Cf. *ibid.,* p. 5.

10. Cf. St. Thomas Aquinas' *Commentary on the De Trinitate of Boethius,* Questions V and VI.

11. Readers interested in Maritain's doctrine of intuition are referred to the recent work by Laura Fraga de Almeida Sampaio C. R. *L'intuition dans la philosophie de Jacques Maritain* (Paris: Librairie philosophique J. Vrin, 1963).

12. Jacques Maritain, *The Range of Reason,* (New York: Charles Scribner's Sons, 1952), p. 87.

13. *Ibid.,* p. 89.

BIOGRAPHICAL NOTE

Jacques Maritain was born on November 18, 1882 in Paris, the son of Paul Maritain, a lawyer, and Geneviève Favre, daughter of Jules Favre, who had been a member of Parliament during the reign of Napoleon III. Both parents were of the Protestant faith. Maritain attended the Sorbonne where he met his future wife, Raissa Oumansoff, a Russian Jewish fellow student. During his college years, Maritain befriended Charles Péguy, the publisher of the *Cahiers de la Quinzaine,* who urged Maritain and his fiancée to attend Henri Bergson's lectures at the Collége de France. Subsequently Maritain became an ardent follower of Bergson. He and Raissa Oumansoff were married in November, 1904. The next year they encountered Léon Bloy, a militant Catholic layman, and in 1906 Jacques and Raissa were baptized in a Montmartre church with Bloy as their godfather. Later in the same year Maritain received a fellowship to study biology in Germany under Hans Driesch. After returning to Paris in 1908 he accepted a commission to act as editor of the *Dictionnaire de la vie pratique,* and began to study St. Thomas Aquinas. He published his first article, "Reason and Modern Science," in 1910 in the *Revue de Philosophie.* In 1911 he took a position as instructor of philosophy at the Collége Stanislas and in 1914 accepted the chair of philosophy at the Institut Catholique of Paris. In 1917 a committee of French bishops requested Maritain to undertake the task of composing a series of philosophical textbooks. He accepted but finished only two works in the series: *Introduction to Philosophy* and *Formal Logic.*

When in 1926 Pope Pius XI condemned the Action Française, Maritain defended the Pope's action in his *Primauté du spirituel.* In 1932 he published his *magnum opus, The Degrees of Knowledge,* which was followed by *A Preface to Metaphysics* in 1934, *Science and Wisdom* in 1935 and *True Humanism* in 1936. In 1940 Maritain, together with Raissa and her sister

Vera Oumansoff, came to the United States for a lecture tour. When the Second World War broke out in Europe, his family settled down in New York City and Maritain taught philosophy first at Columbia University, then for a year at Princeton University, and later at the Pontifical Institute of Medieval Studies in Toronto. After the war he was appointed by the French Government to be ambassador to the Vatican and held that post for three years until he resigned in 1948 and became professor of philosophy at Princeton University. Maritain now is living in retirement in France and is reported to be working on the second volume of *Moral Philosophy*.

Maritain is a prolific writer. Donald D. and Idella Gallagher in *The Achievement of Jacques and Raïssa Maritain* list 75 books and several hundred articles written by him up to the year 1962, and 122 books or parts of books and 513 articles written about his philosophy, all of which is a clear indication of his productivity and influence. Maritain's major books are now available in English. The following bibliography lists only the chief works pertaining to the various fields of philosophy.

1. Logic: *An Introduction to Logic*. Translated by Imelda Choquette. New York: Sheed and Ward, 1937. Revised and republished in 1946 as *Formal Logic*.
2. Epistemology: *The Degrees of Knowledge*. Translated from the fourth French edition under the supervision of Gerald B. Phelan. New York: Charles Scribner's Sons, 1959.
3. Philosophy of Nature: *Philosophy of Nature*. Translated by Imelda C. Byrne. New York: Philosophical Library, 1951.
4. Metaphysics: *A Preface to Metaphysics*. New York: Sheed and Ward, 1939.
   Existence and the Existent. Translated by Lewis Galentiere and Gerald B. Phelan. New York: Pantheon Books, Inc. 1948.
   Science and Wisdom. Translated by Bernard Wall. New York: Charles Scribner's Sons, 1940.
   St. Thomas and the Problem of Evil. Translated by Mrs. Gordon Anderson. Milwaukee: Marquette University Press, 1942.
   The Range of Reason. New York: Charles Scribner's Sons, 1952.
5. Natural Theology: *Approaches to God*. Translated by Peter O'Reilly. New York: Harper, 1954.
6. Moral Philosophy: *Moral Philosophy*. New York: Charles Scribner's Sons, 1964.
   The Rights of Man and Natural Law. Translated by Doris C. Anson. New York: Charles Scribner's Sons, 1943.
7. Political Philosophy: *Man and the State*. Chicago: University of Chicago Press, 1951.
   Scholasticism and Politics. Translation edited by Mortimer J. Adler. New York: Macmillan, 1940.
   True Humanism. Translated by Margot R. Adamson. New York: Charles Scribner's Sons, 1938.

Ransoming the Time. Translated by Harry Lorin Binsse. New York: Charles Scribner's Sons, 1941.

Christianity and Democracy. Translated by Doris C. Anson. New York: Charles Scribner's Sons, 1944.

The Person and the Common Good. Translated by John J. Fitzgerald. New York: Charles Scribner's Sons, 1947.

8. Esthetics: *Creative Intuition in Art and Poetry.* (The A. W. Mellon Lectures in the Fine Arts) New York: Pantheon Books, 1953.

Art and Scholasticism. Translated by J. F. Scanlon. New York: Charles Scribner's Sons, 1930.

Art and Poetry. Translated by Elva de P. Matthews. New York: Philosophical Library, 1943.

gabriel marcel

PHILOSOPHER OF INTERSUBJECTIVITY

by Sister M. *Aloysius Schaldenbrand, S.S.J.*

Gabriel Marcel has often drawn attention to the fundamental polarity of his thought, namely, its attraction to the opposing
poles of individuality and universality.[1] To understand his philosophic effort it is essential to situate it within this basic tension.
For out of the conflicting inclinations to individuality and universality there emerges a mediating synthesis: the "concrete universal." Not that the mediating synthesis of concrete universality
arises in the Hegelian manner. Rather, it arises in the privileged
sphere of intersubjectivity and is the work of freedom.

But it is important to observe the existential origins of the
individual-universal polarity. Gabriel Marcel himself underlines
the fact that his youthful philosophizing was held fast in the
powerful grip of abstract speculation in the classic German style.[2]
Whoever reads attentively the first *Metaphysical Journal* or the
recently published *Fragments* finds no difficulty in verifying the
German idealist domination.[3] Reflecting retrospectively, Marcel
observes today that what especially attracted him to these abstruse
forms of philosophizing were (a) their logical rigor and (b) their
ability to transcend the monotonous and trivial round of everyday life. As a possible and partial reason for his susceptibility to
such philosophical formalism, Marcel suggests his German ancestry: on his mother's side, his grandparents were Jewish and
came from the region around Mainz.

If the youthful Marcel was, on his own admission, a prisoner
of abstract metaphysical systems, he was nevertheless an im-

patient prisoner. The will to transcend everyday experience was countered by a will to affirm the concrete in all its irreducible originality. In this connection it is possible that paternal heredity played a relevant part, for Marcel's father was a man who held in highest esteem the concrete of art and history. It was he who introduced young Gabriel to many plays and who thus contributed, perhaps decisively, to his love of the theatre.[4] What is certain in any case is that love of music and the drama, with their implied privileging of individual beings and ultimate mystery, set the problem for Marcel: how reconcile these apparently contradictory aspirations, the one to abstract and rigorous thought, the other to concrete experience?

A first step toward reconciliation appears in what can be called a "quest of presence." This quest began very early. When Marcel was only four years old, his mother died suddenly. Shocked by the abrupt loss and confused by its unsettling effect upon his family, he decided very early that he would one day find out what happens to the dead.[5] Much later, as a young man assisting the Red Cross during the first World War, his search opened out to include those killed or missing in action. Deeply moved by the grief of their afflicted families and friends, he found himself consciously rejecting the abstractionism of his former speculation. More and more, too, he was drawn by the Absolute Presence whose "primacy" he had felt, however obscurely, since the beginning of his search. Finally, in 1929, he embraced the Christian faith by entering into the Roman Catholic communion. Twelve years later his beloved wife, who had been a devout Protestant, joined him there.

Yet universality was not put to rout by the individual. Even before he was able to justify it philosophically, Marcel wagered for a presence of the universal *in* the individual. He made his own the words of E. M. Forster: "It is individual life and it alone which holds up the mirror to infinity."[6] In the difficult task of vindicating reflectively the "concrete universal," the French philosopher found especially helpful the work of the English philosopher, F. H. Bradley, and that of certain American philosophers— in particular, Josiah Royce, William James, and William Ernest Hocking.[7] The contribution of American thinkers to the thought of Gabriel Marcel has, perhaps, not been sufficiently remarked by American philosophers.

But the reconciling of universality and individuality in the concrete universal must finally be understood in terms of the intersubjective dialogue, and it is here that the unique quality of Marcel's work comes to the fore. This brief essay therefore takes as central reference point the intersubjective mystery. Its divisions treat succesively (a) the meaning of intersubjectivity, (b) its dramatic movement, and (c) its ontological bearing.

THE MEANING OF INTERSUBJECTIVITY

To define intersubjectivity may seem an easy matter. What can this awkward term mean if not simply "the relations between subjects"? But Gabriel Marcel contends that "relations between subjects" is precisely what it cannot mean.[8]

It is important to follow the meaning of Marcel here, for it leads to the heart of his existential philosophy. The focal point of his objection is the term "relation." No relation is conceivable, he argues, apart from its terms. Now, nothing can fulfill the function of a term which cannot be "given" in the strong sense. By "given in the strong sense," Marcel means "given as an object." To be given as an object is, as the etymology of the word suggests, to be thrust out before the mind like a boulder on a path. But to be so given is impossible for subjects exactly inasmuch as they are *subjects*. Hence, the phrase "relations between subjects" cannot define intersubjectivity because it is in itself a meaningless phrase: its terms, "relations" and "subjects," cancel each other out.[9]

Not only is relational language meaningless here; it is dangerously misleading. To posit relations between subjects is to denature subjects. It is to confuse them with objects, for it is to suppose that they can function as terms, as "givens."

But if subjects are not given as objects, how are they given? For it seems clear that they must somehow be given or we could not speak of them at all. In replying to this question, Marcel invokes a reality at the center of his reflections: subjects are given, he avers, precisely as *presences*.[10]

To define "presence" rigorously is impossible. There can be no

question of grasping this reality with conceptual tools manu-
factured for gripping objects. If "presence" is to be reached at all,
it can only be by way of certain experiences which evoke it. Marcel
suggests as an example the sort of experiences connected with a
funeral. The automatic delivery of stereotyped formulas of con-
dolence may result in no appreciable awareness of presence, whereas a look or an intonation may witness undeniably to presence.[11]

From the foregoing example, however, it would be wrong
to conclude that the evidence of presence is a strictly private or
incommunicable affair. There is question here of an "open communion of selves": a communion which avoids the extreme of a
flat universality open to "just anybody," as well as the equally
ruinous extreme of a "myself alone" subject.[12] In touching upon
this question, Marcel opens a path to a type of universality that
he calls "concrete" and which it will be necessary to revisit at
length.

But the communion of selves extends not only *horizontally*
to include all those capable of sharing in it. It also extends *ver-
tically,* so to speak, since a quasi-infinite number of variations in
degree or depth likewise characterizes presence: a passerby asked
for information may respond in a way that clearly indicates concern or a "being-with" which, though fleeting, can make a
significant difference to the tired traveler.[13] From a simple instance
like this one which lies very near the base, examples of presence
move in an ascending series toward ineffable heights. It is enough
to think of devoted friendships, genuinely familial relationships,
the intimacies of conjugal love.

What distinguishes these variations, from one another is the
quality of the "with" or, from a slightly different point of view,
the authenticity of the "thou."[14] The intimacy of the "with"
and the authenticity of the "thou" are, in fact, correlative. That is,
the more intimate an experience of being-with, the more genuinely
"thou" is the thou. To be treated as an object is equivalent to
being denied as a thou. But this, in turn, means nothing else than
exclusion from a certain community, from a certain being-with.

When reflection replaces the word "with" in this clarifying
context, it becomes clear that it does not really refer to a relation.
It refers rather to a unity of a supra-relational kind. To reflect
on the supra-relational unity which the word "with" signifies is

to discover how poor and inadequate our logic is: "Apart from
juxtapositions pure and simple, it is in fact incapable of expressing relationships of an increasing intimacy." [15] By a devious route,
it seems, this discussion of intersubjectivity has come back to the
denial which was its starting-point. But the meaning of this denial,
it can at least be hoped, now stands out with greater clarity.

New light can be cast upon intersubjectivity as a supra-relational unity by applying to it the distinction, today become
classic, which Marcel makes between a problem and a mystery.
Perhaps the clearest statement of this distinction occurs in the
entry of the *Metaphysical Journal* that records the original insight: [16]

> A problem is something met with which bars my passage.
> It is before me in its entirety. A mystery, on the other
> hand, is something in which I find myself caught up, and
> whose essence is therefore not to be before me in its
> entirety. It is as though in this province the distinction
> between *in me* and *before me* loses its meaning.

Applied to the subjects of intersubjectivity, this distinction is
clarifying: these subjects are on the side of mystery; they are
together within a supra-relational unity; they are not opposite
one another as things that can be observed, defined, manipulated.

It is, of course, always possible to make a problem of the subject. Not only is it possible, but it is the ever-present and never
fully vanquished temptation. To treat the subject as an "it," to
submit him to calculations and techniques, to exclude him from
the human community—this is the beginning of a host of aliena-
tions whereby the world becomes an immense documentary film
and man the fascinated, impotent spectator of his own destruction. [17]

The whole point of Marcel's prolonged reflection on "existence"
or "incarnation" or the "body-subject"—the terms are finally equivalent—is to recover the mysterious root of communion: human
existence as being-in-the-world. [18] For, if the human existent cuts
the "umbilical cord" which unites it to the world, it destroys itself. When, therefore, Marcel shows the impossibility of identifying self and body-subject in the manner of a crude materialism
and, at the same time, insists on the inverse impossibility of dis-

tinguishing self and body-subject in the manner of an arid intellectualism, he has but one fundamental aim: to reaffirm a primal unity which is betrayed as much by an oversimple identification of self and body-subject as by an exteriorizing of self and body-subject. The nonobjectivity of this primal unity is absolutely prior. Only a tenacious holding to its priority, beyond and despite provisional concessions to "objectivity," can preserve human being from self-destruction.

But tenacity in holding to existence as a primal unity is possible only through a privileged type of reflection which Marcel calls "recollection." Of recollection he writes: "(It) is the act by which I recover my being as a unified whole, with this recovery or *reprise* assuming the aspect of a relaxation or release."[19] Two precisions implied here are worth noting: (a) Since recollection recovers the primal unity, it moves toward mystery and not toward problems; that is, it goes directly counter to the direction of the problematizing regard which looks outward in disregard of existence, dissolves the unity of concrete experience into diverse spatio-temporal objects, divorces these from the conceiving subject, and develops them in the direction of the various sciences. In contradistinction, recollection is self-recuperative; far from losing itself in the object, the self here recovers itself within its experience of the real. (b) Precisely as an act of "abandon" or release, however, this self-recuperative act is neither introversive nor introspective; rather than "withdrawal from," it is "abandon to . . ." or "relaxation in presence of . . ." Marcel deliberately leaves the objects of the prepositions unspecified, but one thing is certain: recovery of self-presence is indissolubly tied to other presences.

With this mutual implication of self-recovery and other presences, the essential reference of recollection to intersubjectivity becomes clear. Self-recuperation is an indispensable condition of being with another, for to whom is the other present if not to the self? Yet, reversely, the other's presence is an indispensable condition of self-recovery, since it is thanks to the other that significant self-differentiation becomes possible. Common experience bears out this mutuality of implication. At no time is a self more deeply present to itself than when intimately with another.

Contrariwise, a self only superficially present to others is but superficially present to itself.[20]

But if mutual presence depends upon an act of recuperative reflection, this act of recuperative reflection depends, in turn, upon an exercise of freedom. Marcel writes of recollection: "(It) is possible only *by* and *for* freedom."[21] That is to say, opening oneself to another is a free act, forasmuch as it is an act of welcoming responsivity. What is more, this exercise of freedom is *for* the liberation of self and other: nothing so effectively overcomes alienation, nothing so furthers and favors the becoming of self and other as this mutuality of presence implied in recuperative reflection.

Why intersubjectivity is "betrayed in its essence" when it is translated into object-language is by now apparent. The subject *as subject* is nonobjective. To reduce him to a sum of data manipulated by psychological and sociological laws is to miss him in his truth. Explained in categories of causality, the subject as subject disappears. For the subject *is* subject in the measure that he is free—which is to say that what he bears within himself comes to light for himself and others only after he has been put to a test. Why dramatic expression is pre-eminently the language of intersubjectivity by this becomes abundantly plain: being above all existential, it deals with the subject as deciding for himself.[22]

THE INTERSUBJECTIVE DRAMA

It is important to recognize that articulation of the drama with existential philosophy in general and, in the case of Marcel, with intersubjectivity in particular is neither something contrived nor something accidental. What is in question is not merely a more or less commodious expression in dramatic terms of a truth acquired elsewhere and by other methods. Marcel insists: Within the drama itself, existential thought achieves its actuality and becomes manifest; existential thought enters into possession of itself *in* and *through* the dramatic situation. In the drama itself the intersubjective mystery comes to be unveiled, not simply to the audience but also to the dramatist-philosopher. That is why the philosopher-dramatist appears to Marcel as a phenomenon "perfectly normal." [23]

Certainly Marcel is advised of the risks attending this articulation. If, for example, the dramatist is not really a dramatist at all but merely a puppeteer, his work will hardly project light on the intersubjective mystery. Puppets are objects, not subjects. If an author turns to the drama for didactic reasons, matters become even worse. Then the play becomes a technique of indoctrination and, in its deeper meaning, represents an assault upon the subject. It is, in fact, by this line that Marcel divides existential thought from *existentialism*: Existentialism, not unlike other "isms," is a "fall" from open existential enquiry to a closed, imprisoning system. [24]

Where the dramatic work of Marcel himself is concerned, there can be no doubt of its crucial importance as prospecting and illumining his philosophic insights. Hardly a significant theme of his philosophy can be found which is not in some way announced in earlier plays. Nor is it at all unusual to find Marcel discovering at a much later date new meanings of certain dramatic events or personages. As for the clarifying power of the plays, Marcel affirms it with increasing vigor as he enters more fully into possession of his thought. Thus, in a very recent statement, he has this to say of his theatre: "Far from being a mere *hors-d'oeuvre,* it clarifies the philosophic work to such an extent that the latter risks being misunderstood if the dramatic work is not known." [25] To take account of the dramatic work of Marcel thus becomes a necessity for those who would enter deeply into his philosophy of intersubjectivity. Given the extent of his theatre and the limits of this essay, however, difficult choices had to be made. The three plays presented here were chosen on the grounds that they illumine, at progressively deepening levels, the intersubjective mystery.

In a work called *La chapelle ardente,* Marcel explores an area of the greatest importance for a philosophy of intersubjectivity: that of egotism.[26] Aline Fortier, the main character of the play, announces an important theme appearing only much later in the philosophical work, namely, the theme of having and being. From this point of view, she exemplifies impressively the coming to actuality within the dramatic situation of what will finally be recognized as a philosophic insight of major importance.

The action takes place at the end of the first World War in the country home of a retired French colonel, Octave Fortier. His wife, Aline, is entirely devoted to mourning their only son, Raymond, who was killed at the front. For her husband, whom she holds responsible for Raymond's death, she feels a mixture of horror and resentment. It was Octave who, after all, encouraged the boy to enlist and who afterward offered no objection to the dangerous mission which was to take his life. Living with the Fortiers is Mireille, Raymond's fiancée. Toward her Aline acts as a "mother," for the very presence of this orphaned girl serves to remind her of her dead son. It is around Mireille's destiny that the play revolves.

When a vigorous and handsome young man, resident of a neighboring estate, becomes visibly attracted to Mireille, Aline is immediately disturbed. Thanks to her influence over Mireille, a powerful influence by virtue of her apparently total dedication to her son's memory, she succeeds in discouraging the courtship. Not content with that, Aline persuades Mireille to marry instead a very sickly nephew of the colonel, André, who is an invalid and whose condition has just been pronounced hopeless by a cardiologist. Mireille, of course, is under the impression that she has arrived freely at this sacrificial decision in honor of Raymond's memory. As for Aline, she has carefully hidden from herself her own decisive part in the unhappy marriage.

The play does not really conclude to anything. Mireille and André achieve a weak intimacy which, to André perhaps, appears as happiness. Aline continues to be everywhere, managing to work evil in all her attempts to do what, in her own judgment, seems only good. Mireille, who sees in retrospect the tyranny of Aline and the fanaticism of her "mourning," speaks out sharply against her. But when Aline tries to leave, both André and Mireille call her back. They know that they will "never get rid of her." Besides, she is not really an evil woman—she is merely "a woman to be pitied."

Marcel, writing of Aline much later, agrees with André and Mireille. She is not a wicked woman, for she has no ill-will. At the root of her destructive influence, he finds this anomaly: Aline is a "haver"; all her acts are governed by a kind of possessiveness. Is it Raymond that she possesses? Marcel thinks not. It is rather *herself* that she asserts possessively. Raymond has been incorporated into herself, her *moi,* and Mireille likewise, through her connection with Raymond, makes part of her idolized *moi.*[27]

The analysis of the *moi,* i.e., the possessively asserted self, is one of the most impressive examples of Marcel's phenomenological reflection. The *moi* rises up on the ground of that initial experience of presence which is called the "sense of existing" or of "being-in-the-world." Very early in the development of the human existent, this vague awareness of existing combines with an urge for recognition. When the urge for recognition expresses itself possessively—when, that is, it claims attention for the self to the exclusion of others—the *moi* is born. It is important to underline: the act of asserting the self before others to the exclusion of others is what constitutes the *moi.*[28]

Two implications deserve drawing out: (1) The *moi* is not an isolated reality. It requires others for its assertive act, even though these others serve merely as amplifiers or resonators. (2) The *moi* does not pre-exist its act. It exists as a certain way of putting itself forward before others, of claiming attention at the expense of others.

The assertive act of the child is especially revealing, for adults too cleverly dissimulate this act. Take the child who has just picked a bouquet of flowers for his mother: "Look," he exclaims, "I picked these!" In effect he is saying, "It was I who am here now who did this excellent thing. It was nobody else. Be sure to give the credit to nobody else." To be noticed especially is the *whole* which the bouquet and the child form: the bouquet is incorporated into the *moi.* Possessive incorporation, grown enormously complex in adults, is the reason for the impossibility of assigning limits to the *moi.* In the case of Aline, Raymond formed part of her ego or *moi;* yet her "mourning" could appear noble and disinterested to herself and the younger Mireille precisely because the extent of her *moi* was not known to either of them.

If the *moi,* through its act of possessive incorporation, eludes any precise delimiting of its frontiers, it is nevertheless paradoxically true that it tends inevitably to think of itself in terms of an enclosure. Why? Marcel finds at the root of this tendency not love but anxiety. The *moi* is best compared to a man with an abscess at the root of his tooth who "experiments cautiously with heat and cold, acid and sugar, to get relief." What anguishes the *moi* is the experience of a rending contradiction: it is torn between the *all* which it desires to possess or monopolize and the *nothing* which it obscurely feels itself to be. For it is vaguely aware of its emptiness, its impotence, its terrifying vulnerability. As a consequence, its assertive act resembles a moving and highly sensitive enclosure. That is, the anxious *moi* expresses itself protectively, as does the man with an abscessed tooth, emphasizing now this and now that zone of its experience according as this or that zone is liable to attack, mobilizing its "space" all the more fiercely as the world becomes more threatening.[29]

The "enclosure" illustrates what Marcel elsewhere calls "the dialectic of having." The possessor is finally possessed by his possessions. For the more he is a "haver," the more his possessions have him in that all his time and energy must be put to their defense. Aline's utter devotion to her Raymond—that is, her *moi*—left her no respite; she was driven to a frenzied maneuvering in order to save from destruction this idol into which she had incorporated, not the dead only, but the living as well.

To be remarked, finally, is the "obturating effect" of the enclosure. The *moi* does not allow others to appear in their otherness or, equivalently, in their truth. For the *moi* others count only in relation to itself, only as amplifying or resonating its self-enjoyment. But, inasmuch as this self-enjoyment is never free of the gnawing anxiety at the root of the enclosure, it is clear that others are always experienced ambivalently by the *moi*—that is, as desirable and necessary but also as secretly threatening. A clear instance of such an ambivalence can be seen in Aline who is at once a "mother" to Mireille and an executioner because Mireille is at once a comfort and a threat.

In the second of the plays chosen as guide into the intersubjective mystery, *Le chemin de crête,* the situation is still more complicated.[30] How does the *moi* discover itself? Is the self condemned to a fundamental ignorance of itself? These are the questions raised by this drama of the self's ambiguity.

Ariane Leprieur, wife of Jerome Leprieur, suffers chronically from bad health. But she appears as an admirable, even a saintly wife: She supports financially her husband, an indigent art critic, with gracious forbearance. When she learns that he is having an affair with a young violinist, Violette Mazargues, she makes it a point to meet the girl and explain to her that she knows everything but bears no grudge. Finding that her husband's mistress also needs money to get medical care for a child born of an earlier and unfortunate liaison, Ariane again shows herself generous. It even happens that, in the course of the piano lessons which Ariane has asked Violette to give her, a strange intimacy develops between the two women and Violette ends by feeling a sincere affection for Ariane.

Jerome, infuriated by his wife's behavior, wants to seek a divorce. Again Ariane proves herself understanding. She suggests to Violette that, after all, Jerome has no money and could never live without it. Accordingly, she offers to support the couple secretly.

But it is precisely at this moment that Violette realizes what has happened. If Ariane had tried by every deliberate and malicious means available, she could not more effectively have destroyed the bond between Jerome and herself. She has, in fact made their marriage impossible. In face of Violette's bitter accusations, Ariane remains silent. Afterwards she assures Violette that she forgives everything. Violette, on her side, is no longer sure of herself. Perhaps she has unjustly accused Ariane. At this point, Ariane begins to doubt herself. Is Violette right? Has she really acted maliciously in all this? Desperately Ariane seizes upon the one recourse that occurs to her: a public confession, a posthumous diary published while she is yet living. Even an act of such "heroic" sincerity gives no indubitable assurance, however. Could it not be a final and ultimate hypocrisy—playing the saint in the grand manner?

The drama ends on this sombre note. Ariane has no illusions; she sees the dubiety of a literary escape. She has no recourse but a kind of inarticulate cry to no one in particular, for she is a woman without faith.

Thus, none of the problems raised by the play is resolved. On the contrary, at its close the very possibility of intersubjective communion appears problematic. Those who see in the "religious existentialism" of Marcel only a failure of philosophic nerve would do well to attend to his theatre.[31] If the ontological mystery fecundates finally a "philosophy of hope," it is from the farther side—not the hither side—of despair.

In *Le dard,* the third and last of the plays considered here, a path out of the labyrinth is opened.[32] But this drama is by no means an optimistic work. Rather, the light shines in darkness.

Eustache Soreau, born a member of the laboring class but an excellent and hard-working student, manages to obtain a teaching position in a Paris lycée. He has married the daughter of a wealthy politician and his father-in-law has generously used his political influence to advance his academic career. But this good fortune is not without its drawbacks. Eustache had been active in the socialist party in the days before his marriage and his new bourgeois status makes him suffer from a guilty conscience. His distress is increased by the gibes of Gertrude Heuzard, a girl who had worked with him as a militant socialist worker. She has lost her teaching position for having disseminated revolutionary propaganda in the classroom; hence, Eustache experiences her very existence as a constant reproach. Goaded by his bad conscience, he vents his anger and resentment upon his wife, Beatrice, whom he really loves. On her side, Beatrice is well aware of her husband's "moral disease" and responds with deep, compassionate affection.

At this point Werner Schnee, a German singer of Lieder and friend of Eustache during happier days, takes refuge at the Soreau home. Werner has left Germany because of the brutal treatment suffered by his friend and accompanist, Rudolph Schontal, at the hands of the Nazis. Rudolph is, in fact, dying in Switzerland as a result of his injuries. But Gisela, Werner's wife, has no sympathy for Rudolph and very little patience with her husband's gesture of solidarity. Her single desire is to return at once to Germany.

Almost immediately the latent hostility between Werner and Eustache becomes manifest. Werner, genuinely artistic and a lover of men, finds the ideologizing habits of Eustache disturbing. He accuses Eustache of a partisan spirit. Eustache reacts furiously. What makes matters worse for him is his growing awareness of his wife's sympathy for Werner.

Driven by some madness, Eustache betrays Werner by informing Gisela that her husband has refused an offer of Nazi protection in Germany. She flies into a rage, leaves Werner, and eventually returns to Germany with a baron whose security is assured.

Werner then decides to return to Germany without Nazi protection. He realizes that he can look forward only to arrest and, perhaps, death. But, aware of his rare ability to touch men's hearts, he is persuaded that his gift of music should be shared with the unfortunate victims of Hitlerism. Aware, too, of his love for Beatrice and of her love for him, he feels certain that remaining in France would mean for both of them an irresistible temptation.

In the concluding scene of the play, he explains his plan to Beatrice who finds it impossible to follow him to these heights. Werner, fearing that she will weaken and abandon Eustache whom she now despises, appeals to her in memorable words: "You cannot leave him. You must remember that you are the wife of a pauper . . . . Poverty is not lack of money or success. Eustache has had money, he has had success. He has remained poor and grown poorer still." When Beatrice protests that she is not strong enough, Werner answers: "You will think of me as I think of Rudolph. Later on I shall be in you as a living presence, as Rudolph still is in me . . . . If there were only the living, Beatrice . ."

These last words of Werner to Beatrice announce the fundamental exigence at work in the philosophic thought of Gabriel Marcel, namely, "to restore to human experience its ontological weight." Eustache is poor not because he lacks money or success but because he lacks the "riches" of being. What makes Eustache poor is, in last analysis, "the spirit of abstraction." It is this spirit which impoverishes men in the truly radical sense, for it robs them of their freedom to enter into the authentic human community whose bond is the concrete universal. To those who would enter into the authentic human community, however, the final word of Werner to Beatrice is a promise: "Later on I shall be in you as a living presence, as Rudolph still is in me." By fidelity—a fidelity which is nothing less than a continual renewal of presence—the way is opened. For, according to a significant entry of the *Metaphysical Journal,* "Fidelity is the place of Being." [33]

INTERSUBJECTIVITY AND BEING

The theatre of Marcel makes it dramatically plain that fidelity, the "place of being," is by no means readily accessible. *Homo viator* is beset at every step of the way by the *moi* or, equivalently, "the spirit of abstraction." But it is time now to ask directly: what does Marcel intend by the "being" whose "locus" is fidelity?

In probing this difficult question, it is useful to take up some indications given by Marcel in a recent publication. He is there searching into the meaning of the programmatic formula of 1932: "to restore to human experience its ontological weight." Since, according to the explicit testimony of Marcel, "ontological weight" is equivalent to "weight of being" or "weight with respect to being," these clarifying remarks are strictly to the point.[34]

Characteristically, the first precision made here excludes from being anything that might be compared to an object. In more positive terms, this means understanding being as a *verb* rather than as a noun. Looking back to his essay of 1933, "On the Ontological Mystery," Marcel regrets that a formulation found there might encourage a substantive interpretation of being. At that time he had written: "Being is what resists or would resist a reductive analysis bearing on the immediate data of experience."[35] Such a formulation he finds unacceptable today, for it invites the view that being is "something residual."

If the irreducibility of being is not to be linked with something residual, to what does it belong? Marcel suggests linking the irreducibility of being to an experience, an experience inaccessible to the methods of science or critical analysis. But he adds that a formula of this sort is still unsatisfactory because, by assimilating being to experience, it risks all the confusions of psychology and psychologism.

Beyond psychologism is the properly philosophic view of human existence as an "in-between," i.e., as a "between" of being and non-being which is called upon to *be*. In this perspective, being emerges as the plenitude or totality to which human being always and everywhere aspires. Here again, however, language is misleading. It could lead to an assimilation of being to the ideal. But this assimilation Marcel vigorously rejects, since "between being and the ideal there is a radical opposition."[36]

In itself the meaning of totality or plenitude seems unobjectionable, and Marcel seeks only to refine its meaning. On the one hand, he points out, it cannot be an ideal or abstract totality. What is required is a *concrete* totality or plenitude. On the other hand, there can be no question of an objective whole subject to fragmentation or division into parts. That is to say, the totality or plenitude in question must be nonobjective.

To bring out his meaning, Marcel suggests as a clarifying image the concrete totality of an orchestra performing a polyphonic work: Each performer plays his part in the work, but it would be foolish to identify this whole with the arithmetical sum of its parts. To do so would be to misunderstand completely the meaning of a musical whole. It is perhaps best to approach the meaning of this peculiar kind of totality from the experiential viewpoint of the instrumentalist. At first the instrumentalist experiences only his own part because he must be very conscious of the part entrusted to him and must concentrate upon it in order to play it well. But little by little he becomes aware of the whole work. And there is every reason to believe that, thanks to his awareness of the whole, the interpretation of his own part will be transformed. From this it is obvious that the concrete whole, i.e., the performance of the polyphonic work, cannot be compared to an ideal. In fact, from the viewpoint of the composer, the whole *precedes* the parts; the parts, in other words, can be conceived by him only as functions of the whole.

Marcel is, of course, well aware that the image of an orchestra performing a polyphonic work is not without its perils.[37] What he wants to suggest is simply this: Any human experience lends itself to a transformation somewhat comparable to the transformation of the instrumentalist's experience during an orchestral performance of a polyphonic work.

It is no accident that, in attempting to understand better the "weight of being," reflection is finally brought to bear upon the concrete universal. Neither is it an accident that the clarifying image invoked here is a musical image. Of music Marcel writes: [38]

> I think I can say without hesitation that it is music, and music almost exclusively, which has been for me an unshakeable testimony of a deeper reality in which it

seemed to me that everything fragmentary and unfulfilled
on the sensory level would find fulfillment.

Through music, then, the "weight of being" can be, not defined certainly, but evoked: "The greatest musical works seemed
to invoke directly a certain communion. I speak of communion,
for each of those involved is not just anyone, and still less are
they representatives of thought-in-general, the *Denken Uber-
haupt* of Kant and the Kantians." [39] Precisely this type of universality—this concrete universality—illumines the vocation of
Werner Shnee: Werner, the singer, is a mediator and what he
mediates is the work of the great creative artists. But, clearly, he
cannot make their work admirable to just *any* listener:

> In this domain there is no room for just *anybody,* since
> there are people to whom an art will always remain some-
> thing alien . . . . And the existence of these 'outsiders'
> does not detract from the universality of the message, for
> this universality, in terms of logic, must be conceived not
> in extension but only in comprehension.

From the mediating power of music, however, it would be
false to conclude that the "weight of being" derives from an
aesthetic experience. What gives the great creative works their
power is rather their attestation to being. But works of art are
not the only witnesses to being. The person-witness, the "thou,"
is a privileged mediator of the riches of being. "He attests by
his being," Marcel writes, "to that mode of being toward which
I am groping." [40] Moreover: "From the moment that I benefit
from this attestation, it may well be that I aspire to become a co-
witness with this other being." Of the life that arises out of this
aspiration, Marcel says that it is finally "inseparable from love."

To the question: what is meant by the "weight of being"?
a response is now possible. Marcel, having carefully qualified it as
tentative and approximative only, nevertheless states it simply:
"What I have called the ontological weight of human experience is
the love which it is able to bestow." [41] This recent attempt to
elucidate being recalls a much earlier entry of the *Metaphysical*

Journal which reads: "Love ... is the essential ontological datum." [42]

But Marcel hastens to add that, in speaking of love here, he intends it in its "deepest, widest, and least psychological sense." To psychologize the love in question would be ruinous. Just as ruinous would be an understanding of it in terms of the old intellectualist-voluntarist controversies. [43] Marcel is by no means here opposing love to intelligence and then opting for the primacy of love with respect to intelligence.

As a corrective to any such restrictive reading of the love which is the "essential ontological datum," it is well to recall Marcel's predilection for the metaphor of light. [44] When, for example, he attempts to say *what* is being attested by the person-witness, he has recourse to this metaphor: "What is disclosed to me is that this other person bears in himself a certain life and that he radiates this life like a light." The "life" of the person-witness gives, radiates, is generous as *light* gives, radiates, is generous. That is to say, this "life" gives or radiates itself *in disclosing*. There can, then, be no question here of an opposition between love and understanding, for here there is question of a luminous giving.

But what is the meaning of this "life" which luminously gives itself? It is perhaps best understood from the side of him who experiences its "appeal," who responds to its "call." From his side the life of the person-witness appears as a sign, as a promise. It is a sign and promise of what he *would be* but is not yet. If, then, the appeal or call of the person-witness takes hold of him, it is because there is at work in him a desire to *be*, an exigence to *be* more and more fully. [45]

To *be* more and more fully is to advance more and more deeply into the mystery of "presence." For Marcel, it seems safe to say, being and presence are somehow one. This becomes especially clear when he speaks of the human vocation in terms of a movement from existence to being: what distinguishes the varying "levels" mounting from existence to being are variations of presence. [46] Pure spatio-temporal existence is nonconscious and nonfree; hence it is closed to presence. Being, on the contrary, is existence raised to free and conscious awareness. Because the human existent is an "in-between"—that is, a spatio-temporal reality which is conscious and free—he is capable of, and called to, an ever-deepening experience of presence.

Once understood that presence and being are somehow one, it becomes possible to see why fidelity is called "the place of being." For fidelity is a free and creative continuation of presence, and presence is—in its fullest significance—the "being of communion" created in and by a reciprocal engagement. In love's communion, existence is raised to ineffable heights of being or, what comes to the same thing, to an ineffable experience of presence.

Fidelity, insofar as it aspires to unconditionality, is even the "place" of Absolute Being. An unconditional fidelity, a fidelity which yields neither to separation nor death nor treason, implies at its base an act of "absolute recourse." For only the Absolute Being can assure against failure and loss the "being of communion."[47] Nor can this Absolute Being be an abstraction. He who is the sustaining Principle of a communion without condition or limit must finally be the Absolute Thou.[48]

To understand the indissoluble bond between fidelity and being in the philosophy of Gabriel Marcel is to understand why his philosophy of being must be a philosophy of intersubjectivity. Once being is understood in terms of presence, the privilege of the "object" wavers and the category of encounter gains the preeminence.[49] Then there is no escaping the dictum: "Love . . . is the essential ontological datum."

NOTES

1. *The Existential Background of Human Dignity* (Cambridge, Mass.: Harvard University Press, 1963), pp. 19-22; *Du refus à l'invocation* Paris: Gallimard, 1940), pp. 192-93; *Homo Viator*, trans. Emma Craufurd (New York: Harper Torchbooks, 1962), pp. 136-37.

2. *Existential Background*, pp. 19-20.

3. *Journal métaphysique* (Paris: Gallimard, 1927); *Fragments Philosophiques*, 1909-1914 (Louvain: Nauwelaerts, 1962).

4. *Existential Background*, pp. 25, 34; for a good account of Marcel's early life, see: Roger Troisfontaines, *De l'existence à l'être* (Paris: J. Vrin, 1953), pp. 18-24; Gabriel Marcel, *Présence et immortalité* Paris: Flammarion, 1959), pp. 132, 182; for Marcel's own account of his entry into the Catholic Church, see: *Etre et avoir* (Paris: Aubier, 1935), p. 30.

5. *Existential Background,* p. 25.

6. *Du refus,* p. 192.

7. *Existential Background,* pp. 1-3, 68.

8. On serait d'abord tenté de definir l'intersubjectivité simplement comme la relation entre les sujets. Mais justement, c'est là une définition qu'il convient d'écarter, ..." Unpublished introduction to an intended American edition of the plays: *Le chemin de crête* and *Croissez et multipliez.*

9. *Ibid.*: ". . . il ne peut y avoir de relation qu'entre des *termes.* Mais seules des données objectives peuvent faire fonction de terme; j'entends par là des données au sens fort du mot, c'est-à-dire placées en quelque sorte devant l'esprit qui les considère. Mais le propre d'un sujet véritable, c'est-à-dire d'un être entendu dans sa qualité d'être ou d'existant, consiste justement à ne pas pouvoir être donné de cette façon."

10. *Ibid.*: "Il n'est un être pour moi que s'il est une présence, et ceci veut dire que d'une certaine manière il m'atteint *par le dedans* et me devient au moins jusqu'à un certain point intérieur."

11. *Existential Background,* p. 67.

12. *Ibid.* pp. 67-8.

13. *Ibid.,* pp. 39-41.

14. *Ibid.,* pp. 39-41, 66-67, 130. To illustrate the meaning intended by the term "thou," Marcel cites the example of a man who has just received two letters. He reads the letter from A without emotion; it is filled with information about an absent acquaintance, a mere "someone." When he reads the letter from B, however, everything is changed; he is truly *with* B. About him it is impossible to reason impersonally; the threshold of intersubjective communion has been crossed: *Journal métaphysique,* pp. 291-93.

15. *Existential Background,* p. 41.

16. *Being and Having,* trans. Katherine Farrer (Westminster: Dacre Press, 1949), p. 100.

17. *Du refus,* p. 32. A frequent theme in the work of Marcel is the depersonalization which accompanies the unrestrained application of "standardizing techniques." He admits that technological advance does not by its nature comport this disastrous effect. Yet he insists that in fact it has proved itself to be a grave threat to subjectivity: *Man Against Mass Society,* trans. G. S. Fraser (Chicago: Regnery, 1952); *L'homme problématique* (Paris: Aubier, 1955), pp. 60-61.

18. *Journal métaphysique,* pp. 113, 122-24, 278, 310; *Du refus,* pp. 22-47; *Existential Background,* pp. 45-47. Marcel's analyses of the body-subject as irreducible to an instrument of the "self" and of sensation as irreducible to telegraphic models illustrate well the subtlety and rigor of his method.

19. *Existential Background,* p. 86.

20. *Du refus,* p. 50.

21. *Ibid.,* p. 35.

22. "Mais l'expression dramatique est existentielle par excellence, parce

que l'être est ici traité comme sujet et eventuellement comme décidant de soi." (Introduction to the intended American edition of the two plays: *Le chemin de crête* and *Croissez et multipliez.*

23. *Ibid.*: "Il est donc en réalité parfaitement normal que le philosophe existentiel se fasse dramaturge."

24. *Ibid.*: "Il convient néanmoins de souligner l'extraordinaire difficulté que comporte une telle entreprise et les risques auxquels elle est exposée, pour peu qu'intervienne de la part de l'auteur quoique ce soit qui ressemble à une intention didactique, à un souci d'endoctrinement. Dans cette mesure en effet, la pensée existentielle dégénère en existentialisme, c'est-à-dire en un système dont l'auteur devient prisonnier."

25. *Ibid.*: "Car ce théâtre, bien loin d'être un simple hors-d'oeuvre, éclaire à tel point l'oeuvre philosophique elle-même que celle-ci, s'il est méconnu, risque de rester incomprise."

26. Published in *Trois Piéces* (Paris: Plon, 1931); American edition: *Three Plays: A Man of God, Ariadne, The Funeral Pyre* (New York: Wang and Hill, 1958.

27. *Existential Background*, p. 104.

28. It should be noted, it seems, that the desire for recognition is not inevitably or incurably narcissistic; thus, Paul Ricoeur discerns, beneath its aberrant forms, an authentic request for recognition: *Finitude et culpabilité: L'homme faillible* (Paris: Aubier, 1960), pp. 136-40.

29. *Existential Background*, p. 102.

30. (Paris: Grasset, 1936); American edition: *Ariadne* in *Three Plays: A Man of God, Ariadne, The Funeral Pyre.*

31. Marcel has, in the past, preferred to describe his thought as "neo-Socratic" and has disclaimed the "existentialist" label. Today he seems willing to acknowledge that his thought is "existential," but he continues to refuse any part of "existentialism." (see footnote 24) He is averse also to the categories: "Catholic philosopher" or "Catholic writer": *Existential Background*, p. 113. He fears "misdirected proselytizing" and is, in any case, anxious to avoid everything that may prove "incompatible with that intellectual honesty which has constantly appeared to me as the first duty, not only of the philosopher ... but also of the writer; and by this I mean in particular the novelist or dramatist."

32. (Paris: Plon, 1938).

33. cited in *Existential Background*, p. 64.

34. *Ibid.*, p. 76.

35. *Philosophy of Existence*, trans. M. Harari (New York: Philosophical Library, 1949), p. 5.

36. *Existential Background*, pp. 77-78.

37. *Ibid.*, p. 78. Inasmuch as the symphony presupposes the composer who has thought it through, this metaphor may invite a "fall" into the pre-critical dogmatism which claims to explain particular experience via an all-inclusive thought. But, Marcel adds, "it would be hardly less arbitrary to deny a priori the existence of such a thought."

38. *Ibid.,* p. 21.

40. *Ibid.,* p. 79.

41. *Ibid.*

42. "L'amour ... est à mes yeux de qu'on pourrait appeler la donnée ontologique essentielle." *Etre et avoir* (Paris: Aubier, 1935), p. 244.

43. Marcel is impatient with such controversies: "L'erreur volontariste apparâit dans toute sa gravité, pour autant du moins que la volonté se distingue de l'intelligence, cette distinction n'ayant d'ailleurs que la valeur la plus superficielle. Une volonté qui ne serait pas intelligente ne serait qu'une impulsion, une intelligence dont la volonté serait absente serait devitalisée." *Le mystère de l'être* (Paris: Aubier, 1951), Vol. II, p. 179.

44. Marcel is very fond of the metaphor of light. He envisions the possibility of a "metaphysic of light" whose stages he suggests: Physical light assists the recognition of generosity; reflection on generosity gives man access to a metaphysical light: *Ibid.,* pp. 119-22.

45. The expression "exigence of being" refers to a basic point of Marcel's philosophy. It is experienced as an urge for "vertical" transcendence. That is, the satisfaction required by this exigence does not lie outside the person in things, objects of what Marcel calls "horizontal transcendence," but in an inner enrichment of the subject. Thus, the exigence of being arises out of the self's depths and seems to be a presentiment of, a striving after, an appeal or call for, the fulness of being: *Ibid.,* Vol. I, pp. 47-66.

46. The word "levels" is not altogether satisfactory inasmuch as it suggests sharp, 'measurable gaps.

47. *Du refus,* pp. 199, 217-18; *Etre et avoir,* p. 16.

48. *Etre et avoir,* p. 63.

49. It should be noted that Marcel uses the term "object" as meaning "that which is before me and does not take account of me." By definition, then, the object refers to the impersonal, to "thought-in-general." *Existential Background,* pp. 26, 40.

BIOGRAPHICAL NOTE

Gabriel Marcel was born at Paris in 1889. He studied philosophy at the Sorbonne and later followed with keen interest the lectures of Bergson at the Collège de France. After teaching philosophy at lycées in Vendôme, Sens, and Paris, he accepted a post as drama critic and editor of works of literary criticism. Soon he was publishing numerous dramatic and philosophic works of his own; of these many works the bibliography below includes only the major titles. Official recognition of his contribution to French literature and philosophy came in 1947, when he was awarded the *Grand Prix de Littérateur de l'Académie française,* and in 1952, when he was elected to *l'Académie des Sciences Morales.* An able lecturer, Marcel has traveled widely throughout western Europe and the Americas. Two lectureships in particular—the Gifford lectures at the University of Aberdeen in

1949-1950, and the William James lectures at Harverd University in 1960—enabled him to achieve syntheses of his thought which, though tentative and approximative only, are nevertheless very clarifying; hence, the published account of both series—the Gifford lectures as *The Mystery of Being*, the William James lectures as *The Existential Background of Human Dignity*—are of exceptional interest and importance.

Major Philosophical Works of Gabriel Marcel (chronological arrangement).

————. *La métaphysique de Royce*. "Philosophie de l'esprit." Paris: Aubier, 1945; English translation: *Royce's Metaphysics*. Translation by Virginia and Gordon Ringer. Preface by William Ernest Hocking. Chicago: Henry Regnery Company, 1956. (First published in *Revue de métaphysique et de morale*, 1917-1918.)

————. "Existence et objectivité." appendice dans *Journal metaphysique*. 13e edition. Paris: Librairie Gallimard, 1935. (First published in *Revue de métaphysique et de morale* in 1925.)

————. *Journal métaphysique*. "Bibliotheque des idées." 13 éditions. Paris: Librairie Gallimard, 1935: English translation: *The Metaphysical Journal* .Translated by Bernard Wall. Chicago: Henry Regnery Company, 1952. (First published by Gallimard in 1927.)

————. *Position et approches concrètes du mystère ontologique*. "Philosophes contemporains." 2e édition. Introduction par Marcel de Corte. Paris: J. Vrin, 1949: English translation in *The Philosophy of Existence*. Translated by Manya Harari. New York: Philosophical Library, 1949. (First published as an appendix to the play *Le monde cassé*. Paris: Desclée de Brouwer, 1933.)

————. *Etre et avoir*. "Philosophie de l'esprit." Paris: Aubier, 1935; English translation: *Being and Having*. Translated by Katherine Farrer. Introduction by D. M. Mackinnon. Boston: Beacon Press, 1951.

————. *Du refus à l'invocation*. 11e édition. Paris: Gallimard, 1940.

————. *Homo viator: Prolégomènes à une métaphysique de l'espérance*. "Philosophie de l'esprit." Paris: Aubier, 1944: English translation: *Homo Viator: Introduction to a Metaphysic of Hope*. Translated by Emma Craufurd. Chicago: Henry Regnery Company, 1952.

————. *Les hommes contre l'humain*. Paris: La colombe, 1951. English translation: *Man against Mass Society*. Translated by G. S. Fraser. Foreword by Donald MacKinnon. Chicago: Henry Regnery Company, 1952.

————. *Le mystère de l'être*. "Philosophie de l'esprit." Tome I: *Réflexion et mystère*. Tome II: *Foi et réalité*. Paris: Aubier, 1951: English translation: Vol. I: *Reflection and Mystery*. Translated by G. S. Fraser. Chicago: Henry Regnery Company, 1950: Vol. II: *Faith and Reality*. Translated by Rene Hague. Chicago: Henry Regnery Company, 1951.

————. *Le déclin de la sagesse*. Paris: Plon, 1954: English translation: *The Decline of Wisdom*. New York: Philosophical Library, 1955.

_____. *L'homme problématique.* "Philosophie de l'esprit." Paris: Aubier, 1955.

_____. *Présence et immortalité.* "Homo Sapiens." Paris: Flammarion, 1959.

_____. *The Existential Background of Human Dignity.* Cambridge: Harvard University Press, 1963.

Major Dramatic Works of Gabriel Marcel (chronological arrangement).

_____. *Les coeurs des autres.* Pièce en trois actes. "Les cahiers verts." Paris: Grasset, 1921.

_____. *Un homme de Dieu.* Pièce en quatre actes. "Les cahiers verts." Paris: Grasset, 1925.

_____. *Le monde cassé.* Paris: Desclée de Brouwer, 1933.

_____. *Le chemin de crête.* Paris: Grasset, 1936.

_____. *Le dard.* Paris: Plon, 1938.

_____. *La soif.* Pièce en trois actes. Paris: Desclée de Brouwer, 1938.

_____. *L'Emissaire.* Published in *Vers un autre royaume,* Paris: Plon, 1949.

_____. *La chapelle ardente.* Pièce en trois actes. Paris: La Table Ronde, 1950.

_____. *Rome n'est plus dans Rome.* Pièce en cinq actes. Paris: La Table Ronde, 1951.

_____. *Three Plays: A Man of God, Ariadne, The Funeral Pyre.* Preface on the drama of the soul in exile. London: Secker & Warburg, 1952.

_____. *Croissez et multipliez.* Pièce en quatre actes. Paris: Plon, 1955.

_____. *Mon temps n'est pas le vôtre.* Pièce en cinq actes, avec une postface de l'auteur. Paris: Plon, 1955.

_____. *La dimension Florestan.* Paris: Plon, 1956.

_____. *Three Plays.* New York: Wang & Hill, 1958.

_____. *Le signe de la croix.* Paris: Plon, 1961.

BEING, MIND, AND SPEECH
EDMUND HUSSERL AND THE PRINCIPLES OF
PHENOMENOLOGY
MARTIN HEIDEGGER: DASEIN AND THE
ONTOLOGICAL STATUS OF THE SPEAKER OF
PHILOSOPHICAL DISCOURSE
LUDWIG WITTGENSTEIN: PHILOSOPHY AS LINGUISTIC
ANALYSIS

edmund husserl

AND THE PRINCIPLES OF PHENOMENOLOGY

by Robert Sokolowski

Edmund Husserl was born in Moravia, a part of the Austrio-Hungarian empire that now belongs to Czechoslovakia, in 1859. He studied mathematics at Vienna and became interested in philosophy through the influence of Franz von Brentano. Husserl always retained his interest in science, and his *Habilitationsschrift* was written to explain the concept of number; it was later expanded into his first book, the *Philosophy of Arithmetic*.[1] After completing his education at Vienna, Husserl worked as Privatdozent at Halle and in 1900 and 1901 published the two parts of his *Logical Investigations,* a work in which he attempts to explain the origins of the basic concepts in logic.[2] He was invited to teach at Göttingen in 1901, and remained there until 1916. During this period of his life, he published what is perhaps his major work, the first volume of *Ideas*.[3] It is an introduction to phenomenology and was to be followed by two more volumes in which the new science would be developed more completely, but these volumes never appeared. In 1916 Husserl was invited to Freiburg and remained there the rest of his life. In 1929 he published his *Formal and Transcendental Logic,* and in 1931 there appeared a French version of some lectures given at Paris, under the title of *Cartesian Meditations*.[4] His lectures concerning time and our consciousness of time were published by Heidegger in 1928.[5] In 1929, Husserl retired as professor at Freiburg and lived a quiet life in that city until his death in 1938 at the age of eighty-seven.

To all external appearances, his life was uneventful. It was a scholar's life, one devoted to teaching and writing; the impression left by Husserl on those who knew him was that of a good, friendly man, one who had a sincere interest in his students and friends, somewhat conservative in outlook, tastes, and even politics.[6] He has left the philosophical world perhaps the most abundant documentation it possesses on any thinker in its history, for all his papers have been preserved at the Husserl Archives at Louvain.[7] They comprise not only his formal compositions, the material he prepared for publication or delivery in classes and lectures, but also reams of informal, personal philosophical reflections, the result of his habit of writing while he thought over philosophical material. The philosophical movement he stimulated, phenomenology, has dominated continental thinking through the first half of the twentieth century, and even those thinkers who have taken his place in the hegemony of European thought owe much to him.

●

In the book that sets out the program his philosophy is to follow, the first volume of *Ideas,* Husserl formulates the rule that is to guide all his investigations. He calls it the principle of all principles; it states that only immediate intuition is to be considered the ultimate norm and criterion for what is said in philosophy.[8] That which is given in direct intuition is to be taken simply as it is given, with the fullness and the limitations it possesses. The principle of all principles is Husserl's attempt to avoid bringing to human experience any preconceived notions and theories that would block an accurate description of what is given. Reality is to be described simply as it presents itself, no more and no less. Any statement based on such direct givenness thus is an absolute beginning, a true *principium* in the original sense of the word. Husserl's philosophy is to be built upon the principles given in direct experience.

We would expect this manifesto to lead to a philosophy like that of Bergson, where the immediate data of consciousness are also given universal philosophical jurisdiction. We would expect elaborate and vivid descriptions of human experience, of emotions of intuitions of values and beauty, of various creative processes of mind and imagination. Such descriptions are indeed found in Husserl's followers, especially in the sensitive analyses of the French school of phenomenologists, but they are not found in Husserl. His own analyses have none of the elegance and subtlety of Sartre, Merleau-Ponty, or Ricoeur; they are repetitive and heavy, his examples are always the same, his style is laborious and confusing. Much of his writing deals with logic, psychology, and the essential structures of things; there is no attempt to re-capture the living moment or recreate the sudden experience in a philosophical impressionism.

How is this to be reconciled with the principle of all principles? Husserl does feel that descriptions such as those done by other phenomenologists must be carried out in order to fulfill the aim he envisions for phenomenology. However, description for its own sake is not enough. It must be founded on a solid basis. Its method must be given a foundation and justification if it is not to dissolve into sporadic, haphazard remarks that never fit into a coherent, structured, and rational pattern. Only when a founda-tion is given can individual descriptions be fruitfully made accord-ing to scientific order, in the sure path of science. Husserl does not attempt to carry out the science himself, but only to start it. This is the part of phenomenology that he reserves for himself: the groundwork, laying of foundations, justification of first assumptions and first principles.[9] He deals with the problem of beginnings, and the attractive descriptions of complex experience lie far from this point. He is not a popular philosopher because both his way of writing and the subjects he writes about are too technical for general appeal. He is a professional, a scholastic, who deals with material that is recondite but of basic importance for more attractive aspects of philosophy.

Husserl is so far removed from the vivid descriptive philosophy of Bergson or Sartre that what he does say seems at times to be bland and pedestrian. He deals with such primitive and funda-mental subjects that he seems to do little more than state the obvious: perception is the basic form of knowledge, sensations function in knowledge, all inner experiences are temporal. Even some of his concepts seem to be so formal and basic as to be utterly devoid of any concrete value and real reference. The concept of evidence, for instance, means the givenness of that which consciousness perceives; but this seems to be so intangible and vague as to apply to anything at all. It is so formal that we hardly know what to say about it. Husserl is so concerned with the skeletal form of experience that he robs it of all immediacy and life; indeed, he offers very few examples to concretize the relentless formalism of what he says.

One reason for this difficulty is that Husserl chooses to deal with such simple, fundamental elements of experience that it is difficult to say much about them at all. Another reason is that Husserl's statements seem much more formal and empty when they are taken out of the context of his overall development. What he says has more content and importance if it is taken in its proper place in the evolution of his thinking. Husserl's philosophical development has to be taken as an organic whole, and every statement he makes has to be interpreted as a stage in the growth of this organism. There is no such thing as the definitive, final philosophy of Husserl. There is no set of clear cut theses that summarize his thinking. He is not a system builder but a searcher for beginnings, and his philosophy is precisely this search. The process it goes through, the paths it follows at this or that time, are important in determining any individual statement made along the way. The process of Husserl's thought is not an unnecessary adjunct that can be thrown away when a certain conclusion is reached; only when the conclusion is seen to be the result of this particular process can it be properly understood. When a statement or concept is placed into its context, then it acquires a meaning that surpasses the literal sense of the words that comprise it, and the apparent empty formalism of what Husserl says is filled with more content and significance than could be seen at first.

For example, Husserl's doctrine on time states that the present instant is not an atomic, dimensionless unit, but that it contains within itself a protention into the future and a retention of its past. This claim does not seem particularly significant, but it does acquire importance when we realize that such a concept of time is central to his way of explaining how consciousness can know its own existence and structure.[10] The doctrine of retention allows Husserl to say that consciousness holds its past states in its present awareness, and thus is able to reflect on itself. If we enlarge our horizon further, this self-awareness of consciousness allows him to claim that consciousness is experienced as an absolute, as something whose existence and structure cannot be doubted. Thus the doctrine of time expands its influence into the problem of the absolute in Husserl's philosophy. The bland statement about the present implying a protention and retention thus loses its formalism and earns much more content and significance when seen in a wider context.

Husserl's principle of all principles also seems to be almost tautological: we can affirm only what is directly given in experience. It becomes significant only when we see how and why the quest to be faithful to this principle leads him to turn from the real world to subjectivity, and then from subjectivity to the present instant of experience. The principle itself is almost a platitude, but the way it works out is not. The process is more concrete and vivid than the principle, though of course it makes no sense without the principle. The same could be said of Husserl's concept of evidence, of constitution, or of intentionality.

It is true that in any philosophy statements cannot be taken out of contexts, that answers can be understood only when cushioned by their questions, but it is especially true in Husserl because his entire philosophy is simply an attempt to get at the ultimate foundations of consciousness and reality. Its entire structure is fashioned by this searching process. It is like an organism whose component structural parts influence and shape one another in their own growth; when his inquiry leads to a readjustment of this or that teaching, the whole philosophy must shift to accommodate it. When he realizes that his search has not penetrated deeply enough, when he must focus on a still deeper aspect of consciousness and reality, then the whole structure that had allowed him to come this far, and to make this new insight, becomes rearranged to suit the new project. The old structure is not thrown away, but it is intrinsically reformed. Thus it is never adequate to state abruptly what Husserl thinks, unless one can locate his doctrine in his general development. His statements and concepts do remain formal and empty unless they are placed in the living context of his thinking, unless both their sources and their consequences are shown. His philosophy has to be approached in this developmental way. At the present state of re-

search on Husserl's thought, many concepts in his thinking have
not yet been so examined, and any attempt to present a definitive
synthesis of his philosophy would be premature at the present
time.

•

Husserl wants to establish philosophy as a rigorous science,
and the science he envisions is called phenomenology. As the
etymology of the word suggests, it will be the science (logos) of
what appears (phenomenon). It will study appearances. The immediate inclination is to think of this in Kantian terms, where
phenomenon is contrasted to noumenon, to the thing in itself.
According to Kant and the British empiricists, what appears to us
is a veil behind which reality hides. We know only our own
sensations and our subjective states, but we do not know the
thing in itself, which somehow causes these sensations. Consciousness, in this perspective, is self-enclosed and insular.

Husserl's concept of consciousness is quite different. For him,
consciousness is by nature intentional; it puts us into contact with
the thing itself. When we know the structure of something, this
structure is not merely a form we impose on our sensations to
organize them, but is the structure of the real thing. Any penetration of this structure is a penetration into the nature of the
thing. Husserl's concept of intentionality, which he obtained from
Brentano, is the decisive factor in a major change in the current
of modern philosophy and reintroduces an element of realism
that had been absent since the Aristotelian and scholastic tradition
was questioned by Descartes.[11]

If intentionality is conceived in this way, then its correlate, the
phenomenon, can no longer be taken in the Kantian sense.[12] Phenomenon is now to be taken literally as that which appears: the
real thing that manifests itself to an intentional consciousness.
The thing is as it appears; it does not hide behind appearances, but
shows itself in them. It becomes possible, in this perspective, to
talk about the thing in itself and its ontological structure. The
science of phenomena therefore is the science of things that
appear, as they appear. The notion of appearance does not imply
an obstacle that somehow limits our knowing, a barrier that

must be overcome if truth and reality are to be obtained. Rather, there is truth in the appearances of things, and things are to be taken as they appear, no more and no less.

Intentionality and phenomena, as Husserl understands them, are correlative to each other. Because consciousness is intentional, we can say that reality is directly revealed to it, and because reality is manifest as phenomenon, consciousness is said to be intentional.[13] Furthermore, the correlation can be carried into the various concrete forms of both consciousness and reality; specific types of reality call forth a particular form and activity of consciousness in order that they can be revealed. Certain types of consciousness are correlated to certain regions of reality. Thus reality and consciousness are correlated not only in their static, formal relationship to one another, but also in the concrete, active processes that each undergoes in relation to the other.

Husserl's concept of constitution appears in connection with this correlation. Constitution is the process by which phenomena appear to consciousness; they are said to constitute themselves in consciousness. And since the process by which reality appears is correlative to the process by which consciousness knows the world, constitution also refers to the activity of consciousness which allows reality to manifest itself. The real world is said to be constituted by consciousness; this does not mean that consciousness makes or causes the world or the distinctions found in it, but simply that consciousness must be present to the world in order to allow the appearance of the world to take place. There is no "truth in itself" in the world apart from consciousness; truth implies, by its very nature, a correlation to consciousness. It must be constituted by consciousness if it is to exist at all. And since "reality" is simply the world when considered as true (*verum*), reality must be constituted by consciousness. Such constitution takes place in the process of appearing the world goes through when it becomes a phenomenon for intentional consciousness.

We have discussed three concepts that are closely interwoven in Husserl's philosophy: intentionality, phenomenon, and constitution. Intentionality and phenomenon are correlative to one another; they cannot be understood, in the technical sense Husserl gives to them, unless they are taken together. Reality is a phenomenon, it "truly" appears (apears as that which it truly is), only to a consciousness that is intentional. The Kantian insular consciousness could not allow the meaning that Husserl gives to phenomenon. And since intentionality and phenomenon are correlative, the doctrine of constitution expresses how their correlation is realized. It describes how the correlation exists and how it is carried out; it tells how reality, or various regions of reality, appear to consciousness, and how consciousness allows them to appear. If phenomenology is to describe the constitution of values, tools, social reality, physics, or any region of our world, it will show how such types of objects become manifest to consciousness. It will be the science of their appearing, phenomenology.

Our discussion of intentionality, phenomenon, and constitution seems to pay no heed to our own prior warning that Husserl's concepts can only be understood in the context of his development. In fact, we have not presented his thought in any concrete form. The triad of terms we have discussed forms only a bare framework, a structure of great generality whose meaning and value depend on how the structure is to be made concrete. We must look to various stages in Husserl's career to see how he conceived of intentional consciousness, what he felt could be a phenomenon for consciousness, and how the process of constitution is to be conceived and described. Important changes took place in each of these points, and the changes themselves are significant for the interpretation of Husserl's thought.

In Husserl's first published work, the *Philosophy of Arithmetic,* the triad intentionality-phenomenon-constitution is not yet explicitly formulated, but its seeds are already present. Husserl wants to explain the basic concept of arithmetic, the concept of number. After lengthly analysis, he concludes that numbers can be explained only by the mental activity of collecting; numbers are ideal entities, they have a certain structure and even an existence of their own, but they owe both their existence and their structure to the numbering mind.[14] Husserl gives no theory of consciousness as a foundation for this process, he does not elaborate a theory of reality as correlate to conscousness, he does not even use the terms "intention," "phenomenon," and "constitution." Still, in the correlation between numbers and the acts of numbering or collecting, we do find an anticipation of the intention-phenomenon correlation, and a foreshadowing of the process of constitution.

Husserl's work on arithmetic provoked some sharp reactions, and he felt that he could not proceed with further mathematical analyses until he had cleared up some more fundamental questions dealing with logic and the nature of science in general. His *Logical Investigations* are the fruit of this new development of his thought. In this work, the triad of intention, phenomenon, and constitution is found, but still not as explicitly and clearly as it will be in his later works. The theme of intentionality is most extensively developed. Husserl claims that there are many types of intentional acts: perception, evaluation, anticipation, desire, etc., and he attempts to explain their structure. In his structural analysis he distinguishes acts from sensations, and shows the role of sensations in intentionality. He goes on to show the relative dependence or interconnection of one type of act upon another, with the act of perception being given the fundamental role: perception is the type of intentionality upon which all other acts must be founded. Finally he analyzes a class of acts that is particularly important in problems of logic and the foundation of science: the acts that form logical entities, such as relations, conjunctions, states of affairs, judgments, universals, and so on. Such logical entities are called "categorical objects" by Husserl, and the acts that constitute them are called "categorical acts." [15]

Although intentionality receives most attention in the *Investigations,* the concept of phenomenon is present also, but in a rather restricted way. The phenomena that Husserl is most concerned to explain are categorical objects. In the first part of the *Logical Investigations,* Husserl argues at great length to show that logical entities, such as judgments or relations, have a certain objectivity and reality of their own. Naturally, they do not exist in the same way that material things exist, but they have an ideal existence that must be recognized. The Pythagorean theorem, for instance, is a reality; an ideal reality, but still one with a structure and existence that cannot be denied. We can experience the theorem, we can find it repeated several times as one and the same logical entity. The theorem thus appears to us; it is a phenomenon whose appearing must be explained. [16]

Categorical objects are explained in much the same way as

numbers are accounted for in *Philosophy of Arithmetic;* a logical entity is the result of the mind's operation of judging, collecting, universalizing, relating, and the like. Categorical objects are thus "constituted" by the mind. Husserl frequently uses the term "constitution" to name the process by which categorical objects become formed, become phenomena for consciousness. However, his use of this term is not limited to the formation of categorical objects. He also uses it to explain the formation of any object of consciousness at all, whether categorical or simple, like a material thing, where no logical formation is involved. The concepts of constitution and phenomenon are not limited to categorical objects in the *Investigations,* but cover the awareness we have of any objectivity at all. Still, categorical objects do receive the bulk of Husserl's attention; simple objects are treated only briefly, and only as a basis for his analysis of categorical objects.

After the *Investigations,* Husserl turns his attention to a wholly new dimension of experience, to the problem of time. His lectures of 1904-1905 on this subject were published later by Heidegger. The intention-phenomenon-constitution triad undergoes an adjustment in them. Theoretically, the major question in the lectures is the problem of objective time; how does objective time, the time we measure with clocks and in which material, physical processes take place, become a phenomenon for consciousness? It would seem that the general path of Husserl's studies on this problem should be similar to what he does in the *Investigations*: objective time is the phenomenon to be explained, it appears to intentional consciousness, and the process by which it appears is the constitution of time. In fact, most of Husserl's analyses in the lectures veer off into another direction. The problem of objective time is only briefly treated, but the question of inner time, of the temporality that belongs to consciousness itself, is given much study. One third of the triad thus becomes the almost exclusive focal point of the lectures. Intentionality itself is explored almost to the exclusion of objective time and its constitution.

Why should inner time become so important to Husserl at this point? It is important because it is necessary in explaining intentionality itself. Although consciousness is correlated to reality as a phenomenon, it is aware of more than reality. It is also aware of itself. Consciousness does not only know reality, it also knows itself. Furthermore, this knowledge of self is not an accessory, unessential adornment to knowledge of reality; unless we are aware of ourselves, we do not know reality, for if we did not know ourselves, we would not recognize reality as something distinct from ourselves. Consciousness of another as other requires some consciousness of self. Thus if it is to be possible for reality to become a phenomenon, then there must be self-consciousness in intentionality. If reality is to be constituted, self-awareness on the part of consciousness is necessary. It turns out, therefore, that the triad of phenomenon, intention, and constitution cannot be realized or explored without an investigation of this new dimension of self-consciousness. Husserl feels that inner temporality is what makes self-consciousness possible.

The explanation Husserl gives for inner time is based on his peculiar concept of the present instant: the present is not a clearly defined unit, but is a flowing structure with a horizon, an extension, into the future and past. The present is accompanied by a protention into the future and a retention of the past. Making use of the concept of retention, Husserl shows that we can be aware of our own intentional acts only because they are extended in inner time; at any present instant, I am aware not only of the immediate present, but also of elapsing instants, the parts of my inner experience that have just occurred. Thus I can keep in consciousness an extended intentional act, and can reflect upon it. Husserl analyzes not only acts but also sensations in this way, and shows how all elements in consciousness need inner time in order to be experienced by consciousness itself. Inner temporality is the necessary condition for consciousness, and since consciousness is necessary for reality to appear as a phenomenon and for constitution to take place, inner time is also required for these other two elements of our basic phenomenological triad.

In his next published work, the first volume of *Ideas,* Husserl goes back to the same general problem and method that mark the *Investigations,* but deepens and expands what is achieved in the earlier work. Whereas the *Logical Investigations* are concerned primarily with logical, categorical objects, the *Ideas* have no such restriction. They are directed to all of reality as a phenomenon. Husserl explicitly says that it is not enough to treat judgments, relations, and logical entities as constituted by consciousness; we must also see that all of reality acquires its sense and its structure as phenomenon through intentional constitution.[17] Thus his concept of phenomenon explicitly reaches full application to all of reality. Every region of reality has its own mode of appearing; other people appear to us in a manner different from the way physical reality appears, the plant and animal world has its proper way of appearing, esthetic objects and values are phenomena in still a different way, and so forth. The structure of each of these regions is peculiar to each and must be described with whatever idiom it possesses. Phenomenology is the science that gives the logos of each region as it appears.

Thus the scope of "phenomenon" is widened in *Ideas* I, and its correlative, intentionality, must also be expanded. Intentionality is no longer described chiefly in function of its categorical activity; it now is taken as the correlate to all of reality. Many more operations of intentionality must consequently be described; its function in constituting each region of reality is to be examined. Husserl sketches how such description is to be carried out. As a correlate to each type of real object, certain intentional acts must be performed, and they must be done in conjunction with certain sensory data. Thus there are two levels of analysis, one which examines acts, and another which studies sensations. The complex pattern of acts (called "noeses" by Husserl) and sensations (called "hyletic data") that is necessary for a certain region of reality is then to be studied and described. In carrying out such description, we explain the constitution of the object in question. For instance, the constitution of material things involves certain coherent patterns of sensory data, and also a combination of noeses appropriate to them. We have to be able to perceive various sides of the thing being constituted, see it from different angles, experience casual action and reaction on the part of the subject, and so on. Constitution of values, on the other hand, requires additional noeses of evaluation, comparison of values, choices of means to attain values, and the like. Constitution of a tool would require still different acts: the process of learning how to use the tool, how to adapt it to new circumstances, etc. Such subjective activity is necessary if the sense of tools or values are to be made phenomena for us. Without such noeses the realities, the "noemas," cannot appear. Thus the phenomenological triad of phenomenon, intentionality, and constitution acquires a much more comprehensive scope than it enjoys in Husserl's earlier works.

After *Ideas* I, Husserl did not publish any significant material for about fifteen years. The next step in his thinking is expressed in two works that date from approximately the same time, *Formal and Transcendental Logic* and the *Cartesian Meditations*. These two works reflect two major stages in Husserl's prior thinking: *Formal and Transcendental Logic* is similar in its general scope to the *Logical Investigations,* and *Cartesian Meditations* resembles *Ideas* I very closely, both in content and in structure. *Formal and Transcendental Logic* attempts to explain logical entities primarily, and the rest of reality is given only brief and incidental treatment. *Cartesian Meditations* deals with the ample scope that marks *Ideas*: all of reality, with the sense and structure it has, is treated as constituted by subjectivity. However, despite this parallelism with earlier works, there is one glaring difference between the earlier and later books. In the interval following *Ideas* I, Husserl's thinking goes through one especially significant change: it becomes much more concerned with the historical dimension of reality and consciousness. Even in *Ideas* I, Husserl's thought deals with static reality. Reality and consciousness are correlated to one another, but this correlation is removed from any reference to concrete historical situations. Noeses and nocmas are taken as pure essences, abstracted from any involvement or change that would result from historical contexts. In both *Cartesian Meditations* and *Formal and Transcendental Logic,* historicity becomes a dominant theme. The appearing of reality to consciousness is no longer taken simply as the correlate of consciousness. It is also seen to be the result of a genetic process, an evolving development. Reality as phenomenon is not only dependent on a present, correlative consciousness, but also on what this consciousness has achieved in the past. The sense of things depends on their history.

Thus the phenomenological triad acquires a still deeper dimension. Phenomena are not simply revealed by a sudden, atemporal insight, but require growth and tradition in order to become manifest. The noema of "person," for instance, is not disclosed immediately when one man experiences another; for the sense of "person" to be constituted, the laborious experience of history is needed. True, even primitives have a concept of person, but it is not as fully elaborated as that found in advanced cultures, and the refined notion is dependent upon the history of the advanced culture that possesses it. The reality known as "person" cannot manifest itself fully in a primitive culture, it cannot become a phenomenon there in the same way it is able to appear in a culture with a deeper tradition. Likewise, the sense of "tool" appears more fully in an IBM culture than in the stone age. The historical dimension must be taken into account in the appearing of phenomena.

The subjective side of the triad is likewise historical. Consciousness in a primitive culture is not able to carry out the acts necessary to reveal certain phenomena. The capacity of subjectivity also depends on its tradition and history. This is true, furthermore, not only on the scale of national or world history, but even in the case of individuals. At different stages in a person's life, some noetic activity is still impossible and must await development of a richer personal history and tradition before it can be realized. Our past is not shed when we advance in age; it enters into our capacity to know and act and either opens or closes horizons of knowledge and activity to us.

The third member of the phenomenological triad is also affected by Husserl's new concern. Constitution is now expanded into the problem of "genetic" constitution. The process by which reality appears as a phenomenon, the process by which consciousness allows reality to become a phenomenon, is a historical process, and we must be concerned with history if we are to explain it.[18] Husserl says that the structure and meaning of any reality bear in themselves a "sedimented" history; present day mathematics carries within itself the history the concept of number has gone through. The contemporary noema of "society" carries the sediment of tribal society, urban formation, aristocracy, monarchy, and democracy that have entered into its constitution. We cannot understand how society appears to us now if we do not examine its genesis. Even on the individual level, we must inquire into the pattern of genesis that our own convictions have grown through if we are to understand how and why they appear to us as they do. We look at the world with history-laden eyes, and the world appears to us only through the light of history. The history Husserl means is, of course, not simply a sequence of events; it is the successive series of insights that takes place in the course of events and gradually constitutes the meanings that appear in the world. Thus the formal structure of phenomenon, intentionality, and constitution takes on a new dimension in Husserl's thought.

In the *Formal and Transcendental Logic* and *Cartesian Meditations,* the genetic aspect of constitution is treated chiefly as regards the individual, personal consciousness. The genesis that occurs in the life of each ego is the focus of Husserl's attention. In another work published after his death, but partially published while he was still alive, Husserl elaborates genetic constitution on the larger, world scale.[19] The whole history of man, and especially Western or European history, is conceived as a teleological process by which reason reveals the structure both of reality and of itself. The correlation between reality and consciousness is conceived on a grand scale, and its social and historical aspects are explicitly treated. Similarly, the process of constitution joining both consciousness and reality is envisioned in the wider context of universal world history.

Thus the phenomenological triad reaches the furthest point of development that it is to attain in the lifetime of Husserl. The manner in which it is worked out, the way it is itself genetically constituted in Husserl's thought, puts flesh and substance on the bare structure of the triad itself. Husserl's own philosophical career shows what it means to study reality as a phenomenon, to study consciousness as that which allows reality to become a phenomenon, and to study constitution as the process by which this takes place. He shows how intricately complex is the simplest human experience; even handling a tool or admiring a landscape carries within itself the sediment of century long culture and the tradition of each person's own lifetime. It entails in us a complicated but ordered tissue of sensory data and intentional acts. All this complexity, however, is unified in the single simple meaning that is disclosed to us. Phenomenology, the science of phenomena, is to show the complex process by which reality is so manifest. Husserl did not carry out the project of actually describing the ways in which various types of reality appear;

his task was to give the guidelines and overall structure in which such a project could be realized. A major part of this task is realized in his description of the general relationship between reality and consciousness, his analysis of the structure of consciousness, and his indication of the various aspects of constitution that must be taken into account. Another part of his task is carried out in another line of thought that we have not discussed until now, his enigmatic doctrine of the epoché or transcendental reduction.

●

The part of Husserl's philosophy we have been describing has been accepted by many philosophers in Europe, who have attempted to carry out the phenomenological program sketched by him. His doctrine on transcendental reduction, however, has been something of a philosophical scandal to most, and it seems that its philosophical career terminated with Husserl's death.[20] And yet it is the subject to which he devotes more effort than any other, and which he considers the cornerstone of his work. It is the problem of foundations *par excellence,* the question which raises, Husserl feels, the most profound and searching analysis not only into the basis of phenomenology and human science, but even into the ground of reality as a phenomenon. The reduction leads us, Husserl claims, to the ultimate foundation that allows reality to appear. Whether we are to agree with it or not, therefore, we must understand it in order to see Husserl's thought in proper perspective.

What does the epoché mean? Let us discuss it as Husserl presents it in *Ideas* I, where it is comprehensively treated for the first time in the works published during his lifetime.[21] In normal human experience, we carry on our activity with the implicit assumption that the world really does exist as we perceive and affirm it. We maintain a tacit but constant belief in the real existence of the world. This normal human state is called by Husserl the "natural attitude." Husserl feels that in order to begin phenomenology we must radically change this attitude; we must suspend our tacit affirmation of the real world. Husserl emphasizes that this is not a Cartesian doubt. We do not seriously or fictitiously doubt that the world is there, we simply suspend our normal, implicit affirmation of its reality. We neutralize our belief in the real world. When we succeed in doing so, we have entered into the "phenomenological attitude." Such neutralization is appropriately called the epoché. In Hellenistic thought, "epoché" is used to name the restraint, the hesitancy one should practice in judgment. Husserl's epoché is such an intellectual restraint. We refrain from asserting the existence of things and the world.

Many questions immediately arise. Why should this peculiar thing be done? Even if the epoché is not a Cartesian doubt of the world, why should we still bother to suspend our judgment of the reality of the world? What purpose does it serve? Husserl's reasons are based on his desire to make phenomenology a rigorous science. A rigorous science must be composed of assertions that are absolutely certain. There must be no doubt or even vagueness attached to them. A rigorous science can admit no unjustified assumptions, and it cannot allow any statements whose certitude needs the futher test of subsequent experience to uphold them. Its assertions must be definitively clear and unquestionable. In two words, the statements in a rigorous science must be apodictic (allowing no doubt) and absolute (allowing no subsequent development or adjustment).

Husserl feels that such rigorous criteria cannot be met by any statements based on the evidence we have of the real, material world. The real world, which in normal experience is the material world, cannot allow us to make absolute and apodictic judgments about itself, because the way in which material things appear to us is never absolute. It is never exhaustive. Whenever we experience a material thing, we always know it only partially. Material things are spatially extended, and hence can present only one face to us at a time. They manifest themselves by showing a series of profiles, a continuum of aspects, which essentially cannot be shown or experienced at one instant. We can see only one side of this desk at a time, can perceive only one sound at a time, and can feel only one part of a thing's surface and texture at one time. We cannot, Husserl claims, have the entire thing before us, totally and absolutely; it can never be fully transparent to consciousness. This is an inherent limitation in the way material things can appear to us. It is not an accidental psychological limitation on our part, but rather an inherent restriction in the way things exist and appear. Spatially extended, material reality is never totally transparent to consciousness; it is known only partially, by profiles.

If this is the case, then consciousness can never make an absolute statement about material things, because it can never have the total continuum of profiles before itself; the continuum would not be a continuum if it were totally present at one instant. The continuum of profiles always extends into the future and thus introduces a necessary component of vagueness, obscurity, and uncertainty. We can never state apodictically how the continuum will develop in the future; it may always be the case that our expectation becomes unfulfilled, that the thing we are experiencing is not really what we thought it was, or even that it does not really exist at all, but was a mistaken perception. Thus no statement about material things can be absolute. The nature of material reality is not capable of allowing absolute statements to be made about itself. The way material reality appears and is a phenomenon is not capable of supporting absolute affirmations.

It is for this reason that Husserl wants to suspend judgment about material reality at the beginning of his rigorous science. He does not want his pure science contaminated by statements that have this element of fallibility and intrinsic limitation.

Let us suppose then that we carry out the epoché and suspend our affirmation of the real, material world. Can we now make any judgment at all? In rejecting the imperfect judgments warranted by material reality, have we not forfeited the power to make any assertion at all? What is there left to make statements about, if reality is "put into parentheses"? Husserl feels that there is still something we can talk about: subjectivity or consciousness itself. Consciousness does not have the limitations inherent in material reality. It does not exist in a material way, it is not extended in space, and consequently it does not appear through a profile continuum. Both in its existence and its appearing it differs radically from material reality. When it appears to itself in self-consciousness and reflection, it is transparent to itself. There is no need to wait for subsequent profiles to reveal what consciousness is. It is totally and immediately present to itself. Therefore, it is possible for consciousness to make apodictic

and absolute statements about itself, because the existence and
appearing of consciousness are able to warrant such statements.
Both the existence and the structure of consciousness can be
asserted absolutely. The rigorous science that Husserl could not
ground in the real world is now found to be possible on the basis
of consciousness. Phenomenology, the science with no presuppositions or assumptions must be the science of consciousness, for
nowhere else is such a science possible.

Thus Husserl's epoché has a double function: it is to turn
us away from reality, to dissuade us from building our final, absolute science on the fragile basis of the material world, and it
is to make us turn towards subjectivity, there to discover the
one true basis for an ultimate science. This turn to subjectivity
is the transcendental reduction, the restriction of our attention
from its natural attitude towards the world to the new, phenomenological attitude focused on subjectivity. Phenomenology is not to
be carried out in the natural attitude, but in the reflective, phenomenological attitude. In order to begin phenomenology, we must
carry out this reversal in the focus of our thinking, for only
then do we enter into the domain that Husserl claims as the field
of phenomenological study.

What happens now to the real world? Are we to discard it
as something entirely outside the scope of phenomenology? No,
the real world, with all its various regions, structures, and types,
is retained in phenomenology, but simply as correlative to
consciousness.[22] The consciousness that the epoché discloses is
an intentional consciousness; it is essentially orientated towards
the world. We would falsify consciousness if we were to deny
this intentionality, and in order to speak about intentionality, we
must speak about its correlate, the world as phenomenon. Thus
the world is slipped back into the domain of phenomenology,
but it is the world taken as a phenomenon, the appearing world.
The world phenomenology speaks about is not the world naively
affirmed in the natural attitude, where it is taken as something
existing in total independence of consciousness. After the epoché,
the world is taken only as a correlate of consciousness, as a
phenomenon, in the technical Husserlian sense of that term.
Phenomenology studies the appearing of the world.

When the world is taken in the natural attitude, as something independent of consciousness, then it cannot support apodictic and absolute judgments; but when it is taken as correlative to consciousness, then this correlation can be studied in a rigorous science, because apodictic and absolute statements can be made about it. Only consciousness can allow absolute statements to be made, but if reality is considered as correlative to consciousness, then it too enters into the apodicticity and absoluteness that a science of subjectivity enjoys. Reality can be included in Husserl's rigorous science.

Thus the argument has made a curious turn. The argument explaining the epoché seemed at first to be concerned only with marking out the nature and structure of subjectivity. It seemed to want only to show how subjectivity exists and how it appears in an absolute manner. The argument does achieve this, Husserl feels, but at the same time it makes us revise our estimate of reality. It makes us look at reality in a new way, as something correlated to consciousness and therefore appearing to consciousness. In turning from the natural attitude to the phenomenological attitude, we see material reality in a new way. This is the reversal of focus, the change in perspective, that must be made in order to enter the point of view of phenomenology.

Thus Husserl's argument concerning the epoché simply gives a reasoned basis for the fundamental structure we have described in the phenomenological triad: the correlation between reality as phenomenon and consciousness as that which allows the phenomenon to appear. We no longer have to accept the correlative structure uncritically, we now have a reasoned introduction to it. The structure is, as we have seen, the guiding pattern for Husserl's phenomenology, and the argument that establishes it is certainly to be considered a critical point in his phenomenology. It is for this reason that he gives so much study and analysis to the problem of reduction and epoché; it is the problem of the beginning of phenomenology.

The consciousness that Husserl's epoché is supposed to disclose should not be misunderstood as an ordinary thing in the world. It is radically different from any "mundane" sort of existent. It is not a member of the world, because the whole world is by definition that which is correlated to consciousness. The whole world and all the things in it are intentionally constituted by consciousness; therefore consciousness, the transcendental ego which is correlated to the world, cannot be classed as another thing in the world. Husserl's concept of the ego is in the Platonic-Augustinian-Cartesian tradition, for he conceives of it as radically and fundamentally distinct from the objects it knows and constitutes.

The problem of transcendental reduction absorbed Husserl throughout his life, and was the stimulus for some of his most provocative inquiry. We have presented it in the form it takes in *Ideas* I. Later Husserl calls this way of reasoning the Cartesian way to reduction, because it resembles in some points the thought in Descartes' *Meditations*. Husserl subsequently develops other "ways to reduction" in his later works, but always retains a predilection for the Cartesian way, even when he subjects it to criticism and almost rejection in his final works.[23] Another argument he uses, perhaps less striking than the Cartesian way, is the "ontological" way to reduction. In this Husserl argues that a rigorous science must not leave any dimension of its subject matter uninvestigated. But a science that studies reality in the natural attitude, such as physics or biology, does leave one major dimension of reality untouched; it entirely neglects to study reality insofar as it is correlated to subjectivity. Husserl compares sciences in the natural attitude to the knowledge that two-dimensional creatures would have of three-dimensional reality: they would be blind to a full knowledge and explanation of what reality is like.[24] This is the case, he claims, for men who examine reality as an independent existence in itself, apart from its correlation to consciousness. All natural sciences, therefore, need to be complemented by phenomenology, which will study specifically the correlation between reality and subjectivity, and thus fill in the gap left empty by other sciences.

Whatever the difficulties attendant upon Husserl's theory of reduction—and they are many—his zealous treatment of this problem raises an important question for contemporary philosophy. It is the problem of how philosophy is to begin. Somehow, the philosopher looks at the world in a way different from the natural scientist and even perhaps the ordinary nontechnical person. There is a point of view, an insight, an intuition, or some activity he carries out that makes him see the world in a "metaphysical" and philosophical way. How is this to be explained? More difficult still, how is this insight or intuition to be communicated to people who profess not to share it? What sort of words, what sort of argument can be used? This is a problem that was treated with uncommon persistence by Husserl. We may dislike the Cartesian overtones in his argument, we may justly question the numerous clear insights he claims to have into the structure of subjectivity, we may indeed disagree with his attempt to make subjectivity the bedrock of all philosophy; still, the type of problem he deals with here is important enough, and his treatment of it is original enough, to merit careful examination.

●

Husserl's influence on contemporary philosophy has been extensive. The phenomenological development in both Germany and France has produced many fine analyses and descriptions of various forms of human experience. The philosophy inaugurated by Husserl leads to a concern with the concrete, real experience, and shies away from the apriorism of earlier thought. His stress on the diversity of human experience and regions of reality has helped overcome philosophical reductionism and the attempt to turn philosophy into psychology or some empirical science. His concern with essences has helped dispel positivism in European thinking.

Husserl's own philosophical development serves to point out some weaknesses in his philosophy, weaknesses and omissions that he tries to overcome in his subsequent thinking. As long as such failings were peripheral or secondary, it is possible for him to correct them and still maintain the general structure of his philosophy. On one point, however, it would be impossible for Husserl to change without a wholesale revision of his entire thought. This point is the nature of subjectivity.

Husserl has almost a Platonic conception of subjectivity. He claims that it is possible to intuit directly our own consciousness and to construct an entire scientific description of the structure of consciousness. We can, he claims, perceive the nature and structure of our consciousness with more clarity and distinctness than we have in perceiving the nature and composition of the material

world. Consciousness is translucent to itself; it possesses itself totally and completely, with no umbrage or vagueness. This is indeed a
Cartesian conviction. Consciousness and its reflection upon itself
is the basis of all philosophy, the foundation upon which the edifice
of knowledge is to be built.

Is such complete self-knowledge possible? Does human consciousness have such direct access to itself? Are Husserl's elaborate
descriptions of the structure of consciousness and its acts really
the result of an inward gaze, or are they not rather inferences
from what consciousness does? For instance, Husserl claims to
analyze the activity of judging; is his analysis and description based
on a look he has taken inside consciousness, or is it a statement
of what consciousness must have done, in order to have produced
a judgment? Husserl's noetic analyses seem to be projections
of noematic structure into noeses. Our criticism is supported
by the course his own philosophy takes. Towards the end of his
development, Husserl tends to turn away from noetic analysis,
and steers towards noematic analysis alone. Furthermore, German
philosophy after Husserl has also called into question his "Pla-
tonism," and a more Aristotelian concept of the soul's knowledge
of itself has come to the fore. Consciousness knows itself not by
a translucent self-consciousness, but by inference from its operations. It knows its own structure not by privileged insight into its
own being, but by seeing how it operates in the world and then
reasoning to its own nature. The fact of self-consciousness is not
to be denied, but this self-consciousness is not angelic or Platonic;
it is human and finite.

If subjectivity is denied an absolute insight into its own nature,
then it cannot be the first principle of philosophy, as Husserl would
have it. Insight into subjectivity is not the sole condition for entry
into the philosophical point of view; instead it becomes necessary
to examine not only subjectivity, but reality as well as a fundamental element in philosophy. It is true that consciousness must
be studied as that which allows reality to become a phenomenon,
but it is also true—and Husserl neglects this point—that reality
must be studied as that which·becomes a phenomenon. The metaphysical structure that allows reality to manifest itself, the structure
that allows it to be intelligible and knowable, must be treated in
philosophy. The two difficulties we mention in Husserl's thought

are basic to his philosophy and have been criticized in the course of philosophy following him. They should not, however, blind us to the weighty contributions he has made to contemporary thought, and to the many new perspectives he has opened to philosophical inquiry.

NOTES

1. *Philosophie der Arithmetik,* Vol. I (Halle: C. E. M. Pfeffer, 1891).
2. *Logische Untersuchungen,* Part I (Halle: Max Niemeyer, 1900); Part II (Halle: Max Niemeyer, 1901).
3. *Ideen zu einer reinen Phänomenologie und phänomenologischen Philosophie,* Vol. I (Halle: Max Niemeyer, 1913). This edition is hard to find now, and a new edition in the series *Husserliana* is generally used (The Hague: Martinus Nijhoff, 1950). Our references will be to the *Husserliana* edition. There is an English translation by W. R. Boyce Gibson, but it needs revision (London: George Allen and Unwin, 1931).
4. *Formale und transzendentale Logik* (Halle: Max Niemeyer, 1929). *Méditations cartésiennes,* trans. G. Peiffer and E. Levinas (Paris: A. Colin, 1931). A critical edition of the German text is to be found in *Husserliana* under the title: *Cartesianische Meditationen und Pariser Vorträge* (The Hague: Martinus Nijhoff, 1950), and there is an excellent translation by Dorion Cairns: *Cartesian Meditations* (The Hague: Martinus Nijhoff, 1960). Our references will be to the *Husserliana* edition, since Cairns gives the pagination to that edition in his text.
5. *Vorlesungen zur Phänomenologie des inneren Zeitbewusstseins* (Halle: Max Niemeyer, 1928). The lectures were originally given in 1904-1905. An English translation has been made recently: *The Phenomenology of Internal Time-consciousness,* trans. J. S. Churchill (Bloomington: Indiana University Press, 1964).
6. An attractive cameo of Husserl's personality can be found in a letter he wrote to Dorion Cairns, published in *Edmund Husserl* 1859-1959, ed. H. L. Van Breda and J. Taminiaux (The Hague: Martinus Nijhoff, 1959), pp. 283-285.
7. We have described the work done at the Archives in a notice: "The Husserl Archives and the Edition of Husserl's Works, *The New Scholasticism,* 38 (1964), pp. 473-482.
8. Cf. *Ideen* I, pp. 52-53.
9. *ibid.,* p. 5.
10. See our study *The Formation of Husserl's Concept of Constitution* (The Hague: Martinus Nijhoff, 1964), pp. 79-80.
11. Husserl modifies Brentano's concept of intentionality. Cf. H. Spiegelberg, *The Phenomenological Movement,* Vol. I (The Hague: Martinus Nijhoff, 1960), pp. 107-108.
12. Husserl explicitly opposes the Kantian concept of phenomenon; cf. *Ideen* I, pp. 98-100.

13. The importance of the correlation between consciousness and reality and the impact it has on Husserl's thought is shown in the following commentary he makes, in the late 1930's, on the beginning of his own philosophy: "The first breakthrough of this universal correlation-apriori between objects of experience and ways of being given (during the time I was working out my *Logical Investigations*, about the year 1898) struck me so profoundly that ever since then, my entire life's work has been dominated by the task of systematically working out this correlation-apriori." *Krisis der europäischen Wissenschaften* (The Hague: Martinus Nijhoff, 1954), p. 169, n. 1.

14. Cf. *Philosophie der Arithmetik*, pp. 82-90.

15. Categorical objects and categorical acts are the main objects of study in Husserl's *Investigations*. The entire sixth investigation, which is the culminating point of the book, deals especially with them.

16. Part One of the *Logical Investigations* is called a "Prolegomenon" to pure phenomenology. It is dedicated exclusively to showing that logical entities and mathematical entities cannot be reduced to psychic events, and that they cannot be studied by psychology. The *Prolegomena* are an attack on psychologism.

17. Cf. *Ideen* I, pp. 146-147.

18. Cf. *Cartesianische Meditationem*, pp. 103-106.

19. *Krisis der europäischen Wissenschaften*. Part of this work had been published in the review *Philosophia*, I (1936), pp. 77-176.

20. Cf. the remark by E. Levinas in the volume, *Husserl* (Cahiers de Royaumont, Philosophie III, Paris: Editions de Minuit, 1959), p. 118.

21. The reduction is already explicitly mentioned in some lectures given by Husserl in 1907 and posthumously published as *Die Idee der Phänomenologie* (The Hague: Martinus Nijoff, 1950). Anticipations of it can also be discerned in the *Logical Investigations* and Husserl's lectures on time.

22. Cf. *Ideen* I, pp. 118-119.

23. In *Krisis*, pp. 157-158, Husserl seems to reject the Cartesian way to reduction, but his criticism of it is merely based on the fact that it is easy to misunderstand. He does not find anything intrinsically wrong with it. The ontological way to reduction is best developed in *Krisis*, pp. 105-193.

24. The metaphor comes from the geometrical image used by Helmholtz. Cf. *Krisis*, p. 121.

martin heidegger

DASEIN AND THE ONTOLOGICAL STATUS OF THE SPEAKER OF PHILOSOPHICAL DISCOURSE

by Thomas Prufer

Heidegger[1] re-originates philosophy in the difference and interplay between being (*Seiendes*), the to-be (*Sein*), and *Dasein*: man as the only being which questions the to-be is its presencing or thereness (*Da*) in differentiation from being. The question concerning being as being is transcended ("destruction of the history of ontology", "surpassing of metaphysics") toward the more radical question concerning the to-be itself, the most questionable theme. The dis-coveredness of beings in their beingness (*Seiendheit, Seiendsein*) presupposes pre-predicative and unthematic openness and standing out into (*ek-stasis,* "exsistence") the to-be as other than beings ("ontological difference"); but the to-be, obscured by beings which it lights and withdrawn into coveredness by being, is forgotten, and this forgottenness is itself forgotten. The history of the to-be is the epochs or difference of ways the to-be sends and withholds itself, goes forth and returns, promises and loses its saying (*Sage*): presencing out of absence (*physis*), being insofar as it is (*das Sein des Seienden, das seiend-Sein*), object for subject, position (*Setzung, Ge-stell*).

Since the to-be is hidden, what manifest being can we question concerning it, what horizon can we open for reading its meaning? —man himself, the only available being concerned with the to-be, man as called hearer, care-taker, forgetter and questioner standing out from beings toward the to-be as veiled and reserved. The method of investigation is phenomenological: letting be seen that which shows itself in the way in which as self-manifesting it uses itself to show itself. Truth as un-concealment and un-forgetting (*a-letheia*) is the inseparability of dis-closedness and re-collection from hiddenness and finitude. We can speak of the veiled to-be only by manifesting ourselves as *Dasein,* but because *Dasein* is ec-centric, Heidegger holds his humanism to be a *lucus a non lucendo.* The difference between that from which we question and the theme concerning which we question is constitutive of philosophy; that difference is *Dasein* itself as finite transcendence.

The phenomenological analytic of *Dasein* begins with ourselves as we are proximally and usually or in our everydayness and evidences through such pre-theoretical structures as instrumentality, thrownness, they (*das Man*), inauthenticity, fallenness and call that we cannot catch up with (*einholen*) our being as disengaged from being always already in the world with others. Heidegger shows our fundamental way of being as dis-posed attunement (*Gestimmtheit*); we are in concern and dread. But the analytic of *Dasein* is neither of man as man (anthropology) nor of being as being (metaphysics), but of man in his ordinary way of being toward the to-be in differentiation from beings; thus concern and dread are neither ontic (moral or psychological) states nor abstract principles but ontological perspectives. Concern is the way in which we find ourselves as always already thrown forward toward . . .; dread is the *pathos* of being toward the not of being as a whole, toward the to-be which makes beings be but which is not a being. The naught (*Nichts*) is the to-be in differentiation from the perspective of worldliness. Temporality is the unity of being always already in and with anticipating the not yet; being-toward-death is being always already thrown forward toward the coming nihilation of to-be-in-the-world-with-others. The ontological constitution of historicity is based on *Dasein's* anticipatory openness to the source: is-as-having-been (*das Gewesen, das Gewesende, das Gewese*) still coming to manifestation through re-appropriation or re-petition (*Wiederholung*). *Dasein*-in-world is before-between-beyond consciousness-of-objects. Being ec-static toward the to-be, *Dasein* illuminates a purview in which beings can be obvious or show themselves standing over against. Projection (*Entwurf*) of the to-be by *Dasein* (the later formulation: the to-be constitutes or "throws down" *Dasein* as its presencing in differentiation among

beings) opens and frees the ontological space in which beings
are encountered: world.

There being no adequate manifestation and speaking of the
to-be in differentiation, the reversal (*Kehre*) which goes beyond
the phenomenological analytic of *Dasein* toward another use of
language (viz., appropriation of obscured origins by bringing to
word the unspoken out of which primordial and originating say-
ings are said) shatters against the impossibility of bringing to
adequate manifestation through speech what is most hidden; but
this reversal is anticipated in the analysis of *Dasein* as the phenomenon which manifests the to-be by questioning it. The *logos*
of the to-be in differentiation is silence, but to be silent is possible
only for a speaker, whose speech is answer to a call (*Geheiss,
Anspruch*). The later Heidegger transcends a dialectic of phenomenology and silence and speaks the unspoken out of which *Sein
und Zeit* was brought to word: a saying of the sending (*Geschick,
Ueberkommnis, Zuwurf, Brauch, Er-eignis*) of the hidden to-be.
The difference (*Zwiefalt*) or split (*Riss, Schied*) between the to-be
(*Sein, Anwesen*) and its epiphany or availability-(*Dasein, Denken*)-in-being-(*Seiendes, Anwesendes*) is unfolded or borne out
(*Austrag*) of the differentiating middle (*to auto*): presencing
withdrawal (*a-letheia*) and the gathering-forth-into-un-hiddenness
(*logos*) of hiddenness *as hidden.*

The beginning as the beginning of . . . leaves itself behind and
is hidden in what has been begun. To begin as different from what
is begun cannot be preserved without the mediation of a more
original moment. Heidegger goes forward by taking a step back
into the possibility of a position; this step backward has various
forms: the destruction of the history of ontology and the overcoming of metaphysics, the re-appropriation of primordial *logoi,*
speaking the unspoken out of which *Sein und Zeit* was spoken;
finally he moves back into the differentiation process in which the
differentiated (the silent and the spoken, the hidden and the
manifest) are differentiated.

●

Philosophy today is in a crisis of self-understanding, but this
state of crisis is not unusual; philosophy is perennially in crisis

because its specificity is perennially being blurred or destroyed and absorbed into something not itself. The perennial resolution of this perennial crisis is reflection on the nature of philosophical discourse, and this in turn is inseparable from reflection on the ontological status of the philosopher as speaker. *Who* is speaking when the philosopher speaks? Where does the philosopher stand in being? What is the philosophical voice or *persona?* From what perspective and to whom does the philosopher speak?

Whoever speaks about the relation between *a* speech and *a* world cannot speak about this relation in *that* speech and in *that* world. So Wittgenstein,[2] the third figure beside Husserl and Heidegger dominating contemporary philosophy by radical reflection on the nature of philosophical discourse, and therefore also on the status and perspective of the philosophical speaker. The philosopher, in seeking the adequate *logos* of all forms of human speech about all that is for man, would seem to have to speak from outside the human world and in a more than human language. Does not the radical and universal intention of philosophy to speak the adequate *logos* of being destroy the philosopher as a human speaker who can be heard by others? Does it not force him into non-sense and silence? Is the radical and universal intention of philosophical discourse in conflict with the humanness of the speaker of that discourse?

There is no philosophy without speech, and speech implies that the speaker has listened and could be heard. There is no speech, and therefore no philosophy, without voice and address,[3] constituents of the rhetorical situation. Although the principle of organization of perfected theoretical discourse is the order of what is spoken about without reference to the perspective of the speaker or to the determination of his speech by the character of the listener and by the available means of communication, there is no discourse which is not also rhetorically organized. Because there is no human truth without discussion and no discussion without the presence of many in differing perspective to each other, contemplation is inseparable from politics; and if rhetoric is the mode of discourse proper to the political, there is no science without rhetoric. The isolated mind, the mind which does not listen and speak, or in Hegelian terms, the consciousness which is unconcerned with recognition by another consciousness does not exist as philosopher—even for itself; it will either have knowledge unmediated by the presence of others, and then it is god-like, or, without testing by other minds, it will be opinionated or in error; private mind is either *apathes* or without form.[4]

To be for us is in speech, and this *logos* is common: "the waking share a common world, but when asleep each turns away to the private" and "those who make sense must be confirmed by what is common, as a city relies on its ways."[5] We know through the sharing of words, and to seek together in speech the illuminating conditions of the actuality of ordinariness, there must be experiences and views common to the seekers, that is, as speakers we are most of the time not distinguished from ourselves as taken up with others. The autarkical contemplative life of the silent stranger is the life of separate intellect, without body and friends, without scene and city, without action and use. But a mind shorn of agency ceases to exist in our world.[6] Although the wise is separated,[7] philosophy is not wisdom but the common search out of the commonplace for wisdom. "We must be silent about that about which we cannot speak," but "he who never says anything cannot be silent . . . being silent authentically is possible only in genuine discourse. To be able to be silent, *Dasein* must have something to say."[8]

Just as there is no speech without common world with others, so speech is inextricable from the *phainomena*. There can be no adequate discourse (transcendental *logos* as the parametric form of all forms of speech: both the exhaustive system of notation or mirroring mind and the *a priori* structure of all possible experience) because its speaker would have to speak from outside world and could not be heard in world. We speak of speech as of a condition of the actuality of the way world is for us proximally and usually, that is, as spoken, but to speak of speech we must also speak of world as of that about which speech ordinarily speaks. "To bring speech as speech to speech"[9] is impossible without bringing world to speech, and although world is always already there for us as spoken, it is never adequately spoken and reflected without redundancy or omission.

Let us formalize the case against the possibility of philosophy as conditioned speech about the unconditioned or as *human* investigation of *first* principles: the following alternatives seem to be exhaustive: (1) the principles of a system can be thematized for investigation only within a metasystem; therefore either there are no first principles because the regress is infinite (meta- n plus 1 system) or first principles cannot be thematized for investigation and we are dogmatists; (2) investigator, investigation, and investigated coincide, so that the philosopher himself is the first principle investigated by philosophy; but if investigator and investigated are identical, why is there need for investigation? (3) we are encompassed and exceeded by what is first, which therefore can never show itself to us "as it is in itself"; but surely the purpose of investigation is to reveal the investigated as itself, irrespective of the perspective of the investigator; must we not know the different itself if we know the difference between it itself and it for us? but if we know it, is it not itself for us?

The difficulties can be put in another form: Plato's *Republic* or Kant's *Critique of Pure Reason,* for example, are works which present themselves to the reader as accounts of the meaning of mind. Where, then, in these accounts do we find an account of the mind which writes them? Plato, the author, is not Socrates, the protagonist. Is Kant's mind somehow beyond the Aesthetic, Analytic, and Dialectic? That is, if philosophy is an account of the whole, then the philosopher who is accounting for the whole must also account for himself and for his accounting. The philosopher cannot be outside the whole, the account of which he gives, for outside the whole there is nothing; nor can he, it would seem, be merely a part of the whole, for then he would be able to present an account which is more than himself and his accounting.[10] Therefore the philosopher must be the same as the account or *logos* which he speaks, and since he is speaking of the whole, he he must be the whole, so that the categories of spectator and participant break down. In short, how do the philosophical speaker, his act of speaking, his speech, and what he speaks about stand to each other?

Or put in still another way: insofar as philosophy speaks about itself, it is involved in the paradox of the word "word"; insofar as philosophy speaks about the presuppositions of speech, it is involved in the paradox of the word "silence." What then does it mean to say that philosophy speaks about itself as inquiry into the foundations of speech? Heidegger speaks of "the dis-appearing (*entscheinende*) word for word." [11]

However this may be, philosophy's power to give answers is never adequate to its power to raise questions, although questions are asked in order that we may find answers. "Human reason has this peculiar fate that in one species of its knowledge it is burdened by questions which, as prescribed by the very nature of reason itself, it is not able to ignore, but which, as transcending all its powers, it is also not able to answer." [12]

Philosophy, perhaps more than any other human endeavor, is shadowed by the temptation to give itself up, and this because the gap between its intention and achievement is so great. The infinite and accurate statement of being is never actual; hence the temptation to unarm the philosophical *eros*. And whence the power to resist this temptation? Once having raised philosophical questions and thereby having lost the innocence of a naive consciousness living straight away into the world, we realize that the non-philosophical dimensions of human experience, that is, ordinary life and the arts and sciences, are encircled by a last horizon, the horizon of philosophical questions or of questions beyond which there is no meaningful human questioning, questions which are implied by all other questions. To raise the ultimate questions is an act prescribed by the very nature of reason and once reason has grasped its own nature, that is, has raised these questions, it can never forget them without destroying itself; but reason also destroys itself if it arrogates the power to answer these questions adequately. The philosophical life is the erotic life par excellence, and *eros* neither achieves plenty nor is it satisfied in poverty. From the point of view of ordinary life and of the arts and sciences, a point of view from which more can be achieved because less is intended, philosophy often seems presumptious nonsense. And philosophy's preoccupations with reflection on its own act usually leads to oscillation between confessing its failures and renewing its pretentions; no comfortable calling, but if, having discovered philosophy, we reject it and attempt to return to ordinary life and to the arts and sciences, we know them to be ungrounded because questions concerning their hidden presuppositions, although repressed, have not been entirely forgotten. Some philosophers have turned philosophy against itself and argued philoso-

phically for the meaninglessness of philosophical questions, but we
know of none who has done this consistently; he has remained
silent.[13] If we throw out architectonic discourse, the house, in
which in our innocence of philosophy we could take our rest,
collapses.

What has this rhetoric on the *pathos* of the philosophical experience to do with Heidegger? Let us present Heidegger's *Dasein*
by contrasting it with Husserl's transcendental subjectivity.[14] For
Husserl the *epoché* disengages transcendental subjectivity from
human consciousness living straight away into the world (*die
Welthabe des Weltkindes*) or from consciousness immersed in
the world without radical reflection on the conditions of the
possibility of this its mundane experience. To paraphrase a
passage from Husserl's *First Philosophy*:[15] "If I criticize my
mundane experience, I see that the factually experienced world
does not have to be. Assuming that this world were not, that my
body were not, that I as human being were not, the pure I would
nevertheless remain untouched by this world-annihilation. The
contingency of the world does not affect the I in its purity; the
pure experience of the I which no longer draws its meaning from
mundane experience does not disappear with the negation of the
world." The subject-aspect of the world is radicalized until it
swallows up the whole world and thereby itself insofar as it is
worldly;[16] this radicalization of subjectivity ends in a solitariness
which is the methodological requirement of a truly first philosophy.[17] For Heidegger, on the other hand, *Dasein* as *ek-stasis*
toward the to-be in differentiation from beings *and* as the way
we are usually and proximally in the world with others (*Alltaeg-
lichkeit, Mitsein*) are inseparable. (Compare the Husserlian
principle of adequate self-givenness with the Heideggerian *a-
letheia*: the truth-process as un-concealment is *essentially* inseparable from a matrix of obscurity.)

There are two crucial difficulties in Husserl's position, difficulties of which he was aware[18] and which flow, first, from the
paradoxical continuity and distinction between the human I and
transcendental subjectivity, and, second, from the conflict of the
principles of evidence and transcendentality. In an essay published
in 1933,[19] Eugen Fink speaks of the *pathos* of phenomenology
which results from the tension between the diverging Egos which

remain nevertheless united. He speaks further[20] of the paradox which results when the transcendental point of view is communicated within the world. "There is a necessary and essential conflict in phenomenological discourse between the mundane meaning of the words and their indicated transcendental meanings."[21] And both Heidegger in his comment (1927) on Husserl's summary of transcendental phenomenology for the *Encyclopaedia Britannica* and Sartre in his essay *The Transcendence of the Ego* (1937) put a finger on these difficulties.

First, how can the differentiation of transcendental subjectivity from worldly consciousness be reconciled with their continuity in the one I of the philosopher? Second, with what kind of evidence can transcendental subjectivity present itself to itself? What is "the pure experience of the I"? Since every meaning lives on credit from an evidential experience and presumes on the evidence of the self-presentation of the meant itself, either an evidential experience of transcendental subjectivity is presumptively possible or at least not contradictory, or transcendental subjectivity cannot be meant at all. Were transcendental subjectivity to be given in evidential and eidetic experience, *to* whom would it be given? To itself. Would then the subject-object polarity collapse into identity or would we require a trans-transcendental principle to constitute the evidence of transcendental subjectivity given as an object? Can the condition of the possibility of experience be itself experienced? Does the pure use of mind or the use of mind to know mind in differentiation from world end in the paralogism that the self as knower and the self as known are both the same and different?

For Husserl there are two last principles: the transcendental Ego or the ultimate subjective principle, and evidence or the ultimate objective principle, and these two principles would seem to be in conflict. Either transcendental subjectivity can presumptively be given in evidence and then it would no longer be transcendental subjectivity as constituting all objects but a constituted object, or it cannot be given in evidence; in that case, since valid meaning implies evidence, transcendental subjectivity is not a valid meaning. If the evidence-principle applies only to the object-pole and not to the subject-pole, where do we draw the right to speak of the subject-pole at all? If the subject becomes object, then it falls under the principle of evidence.

Husserl answers that transcendental subjectivity is self-constituting and that "the pure I can be posited as an object (*ist gegenstaendlich setzbar*) by the self-same pure I." [22] It is perhaps the difficulty in understanding what this means which led Sartre to deny that consciousness flows from an Ego at all (consciousness is rather impersonal spontaneity and negating immersion in the world) [23] and which led Heidegger to circumvent the subject-object problematic by beginning behind it (the existentials of *Dasein* are pre-theoretical) and ending beyond it (the to-be is not an object). [24]

Husserl himself indicates a resolution of the difficulties by an analysis of the essential temporality of transcendental subjectivity. When I shift from thinking about the world to thinking about myself thinking about the world, what was only an act, the act of thinking about the world, becomes also an object—of another act, and the subject of this new act, of the act of thinking about myself thinking about the world, is a new and different subject, although it is continuous with the first subject, the I who thinks the world. This new and different subject is not yet itself also an object, but it can become an object, that is, I can think about myself thinking about myself thinking about the world. This Chinese box structure continues and once again a new and different subject acts, a subject which is not yet itself object, but can become one. There are three points to be noticed: (1) the Ego splits into retentional and protentional Egos: the Ego which *was* only subject *is now* also object, and the Ego for which that Ego becomes object *will be* itself object for another Ego, and so forth; (2) these many Egos all belong to the same stream of phases resulting from the possibility of reflection latent in the unreflective act of living straight away into the world; (3) there is a new and unobjectified act of "I think" which thinks the first act of " I think" as object, a new and unobjectified act which is not yet but which can become in turn also object, but of course for another act which is not yet objectified. This means that the Ego is *essentially* dispersed or distended because it is essentially withdrawn from and can never be exhaustively caught up with by its own power of self-objectification. It is the temporality of reflection which makes self-objectification possible and adequate self-objectification impossible. That lived act is always ahead of thematized act, that

every thematized act was first lived and not yet thematized, and
that lived act is nevertheless to be thematized—this is the primordial time-constituting principle of transcendental subjectivity.[25]

Heidegger's *Dasein* is neither unworldly nor presumptively
transparent to itself, although the mode of being of *Dasein* is not
that of other beings, and the self-possession of *Dasein* is of a
marked kind precisely because man as *Dasein* is that being which
raises the question concerning the meaning of the to-be in differentiation from every kind of being and thus calls himself into question.
According to an early formulation,[26] "transcendental constitution
is a central possibility of the existence of the *factual* self." As
thrown, inauthentic, and fallen, *Dasein* cannot catch up with itself
as disengaged from world, and this because *Dasein* is the worldly
standing out toward the to-be as veiled and withdrawn.

For Heidegger a neutral or an absolute perspective would be
against the very meaning and possibility of philosophy, but the
human perspective,[27] which is neither neutral nor absolute, is
nevertheless ec-centric toward the center, toward the to-be in
differentiation from beings. *Dasein* as finite transcendence, the
world-grounding act by which *Dasein* is open to that which is
ob-vious or over against, is always already, even in the pre-
theoretical mode, a primordial lighting by the meaning of to-be in
differentiation, albeit unarticulated and unthematic. The ontic
markedness of *Dasein* is to be ontologically, that is, to encounter
beings within the horizon of the to-be in differentiation, but ontology is inseparable from finitude because the lighting of the to-be
is in the mode of a questioning of the veiled.

The presencing of *Sein* is time, and *Sein* is "e-venting appropriation" (*Ereignis*) because there *is* no lighting which lights the
lighting (*Sein*) of beings: *"Sein kann nicht sein. Wuerde es sein,
bliebe es nicht mehr Sein, sondern waere ein Seiendes."*[28] ("To-be
cannot *be*. If it were, it would no longer remain to-be, but would
be a being.")

Dasein (later written as *Da-Sein*) is both the philosopher and
the theme of philosophy; it is the way the eternal *aporema*[29]
arises: the mutual constitution of the to-be in differentiation and
everydayness, veiledness and dis-coverdness, forgottenness and recollection, *ek-stasis* and worldliness, silence and speech. In his
essay on Hoelderlin's poem "Homecoming", Heidegger speaks of

the to-be as both self-giving and reserved, near and far, approaching but yet unfound and still sought after.[30] We hear echoes of Socratic ignorance, Platonic *eros,* and Aristotelian *episteme zetoumene,* the paradigms of philosophical experience.[31]

NOTES

1. Born in 1889 in Messkirch, Baden, of Alemann-Swabian background; 1915-1923, teaching at Freiburg i.B. (with the exception of 1917-1919, military service); 1923-1928, professor at Marburg; 1928, Husserl's successor at Freiburg; 1933-1934, Rector; November 1944-1951, forbidden to teach by the Occupation; 1952, emeritus. William J. Richardson, S. J. *Heidegger: Through Phenomenology to Thought,* The Hague: Nijhoff, 1963, is the best study in English of Heidegger; it contains a bibliography of his published work inclusive of *Kants These ueber das Sein* (1961), of English translations which appeared before August 15, 1962, and of selected studies. See also Albert Chapelle, *L'ontologie phénoménologique de Heidegger,* Paris: Editions Universitaires, 1962; Bertrand Rioux, *L'être et la vérité chez Heidegger et saint Thomas d'Aquin,* Montréal - Paris: Presses de l'Université de Montréal, Presses Universitaires de France, 1963; Otto Poeggeler, *Der Denkweg Martin Heideggers,* Pfullingen: Neske, 1963.

2. *Tractatus,* no. 5. 6 to no. 5. 641.

3. See "Voice and Address," Craig LaDrière, *Dictionary of World Literature,* ed. Shipley.

4. "... the case of the *isolated* philosopher who is completely disinterested in the opinion that other men have of him. This attitude is not in itself contradictory ("absurd"), if the philosopher believes that he may attain the Truth by some direct personal revelation of Being or by an individual revelation proceeding from a transcendent God. But if he does believe this, he will have no philosophically valid reason for *communicating* his knowledge (orally or in writing) to others (unless it be for the purpose of obtaining their "recognition" or admiration, which is excluded by definition). Hence if he is truly a philosopher, he will not do so (the philosopher does not act "without a reason"). Hence we will know nothing about him; we will not even know whether or not he exists and, consequently, we will not know whether he is a philosopher or simply a lunatic. In my opinion, moreover, he will not even know it himself, since he will be deprived of any sort of social testing or criticism which alone is capable of weeding out "pathological" cases. In any event, his "solipsist" attitude, which excludes discussion, would be fundamentally anti-Socratic." Alexandre Kojève, "Tyranny and Wisdom," in Leo Strauss, *On Tyranny,* Glencoe, Ill.: The Free Press of Glencoe, 1963, p. 168.

"... contemporary logical empiricism escapes from the range of the Critical philosophy, and belongs to a new emergent phase ... it shifts the locus of logical analysis from thought to language, and in doing so implicitly rejects the formal dualism which characterizes the two earlier periods of modern philosophy alike. For it substitutes for the "I think" the "I say," and thought becomes that aspect of speech which makes it intelligible—its logical structure. Speech is public. It is at once thought and action, or rather a unity of which "mental" and "physical" activity are distinguishable but inseparable aspects; and as a result it establishes communication, and introduces the "you" as the correlative of the "I." For if the "I think" logically excludes the second person, the "I say" makes the second person a logical necessity. The "I say" is logically incomplete. To complete it we must formulate it as follows: "I say to you; and I await your response." John Macmurray, *The Self As Agent*, London: Faber & Faber, 1957, pp. 73-74.

The principles "withdraw from the city" and "live hiddenly" do not exclude friends from the Garden.

5. Heraclitus, fr. 89, 114. Silence is by excess or defect, godlike or animal. See Heidegger's commentary on a line from Stefan George's poem "Das Wort": *Kein ding sei wo das wort gebricht,* in his essay "Das Wort" in *Unterwegs zur Sprache,* Pfullingen: Neske, 1959, pp. 236-237.

6. John Updike, *Pigeon Feathers* (Crest ed.), p. 160.

7. Heraclitus, fr. 108; Aristotle, 1178a22.

8. Wittgenstein, *Tractatus,* 7; Heidegger, *Sein und Zeit,* sec. 34.

9. Cf. Heidegger, *Unterwegs zur Sprache, op cit.,* pp. 241-268.

10. The position that the philosopher is the whole or the theme of philosophy need not be only Hegelian; cf. Aristotle, *de anima* III, 8 (*anima quodammodo omnia*) and Aquinas, *de veritate* I, 9 (*reditio completa intellectus in se ipsum*). *Anamnesis* and *illuminatio* as theories of knowledge can be seen in the context of the question: "How can one who is not the whole give an account of the whole?"

11. Heidegger, *op. cit.,* p. 237.

12. Kant, Preface to the 1st ed. of *Critique of Pure Reason.*

13. Cf. Aristotle, *Protrepticus,* fr. 2 (Ross).

14. See Thomas Prufer, "A Protreptic: What Is Philosophy?" in *Studies in Philosophy and the History of Philosophy,* vol. II, edited by John K. Ryan, The Catholic University of America Press, Washington, D. C., 1963, pp. 1-19, esp. 14-18.

15. *Husserliana* VIII, 72-74.

16. *Ibid.* VI, 183, 25. "Durch transzendentale Reduktion meiner als dieses Ego innewerdend habe ich nun einen Stand ueber allem weltlichen Sein, ueber meinem eigenen Menschsein und menschlichen Leben. Eben diese absolute Stellung ueber allem, was mir gilt und soll je gelten koennen mit all seinem moeglichen Inhalt, muss notwendig die philosophische sein." Husserl, "Phaenomenologie und Anthropologie," *Philosophy and Phenomenological Research* II (1941), p. 10.

17. *Husserliana* VI, 187, 35 to 188, 2.

18. E.g. *Tijdschrift voor Philosophie* **XII** (1950), p. 268; *Husserliana* VIII, 72, 23 ff.

19. *Kantstudien* 1933, p. 356.

20. *Ibid.*, p. 381.

21. *Ibid.*, p. 382.

22. *Husserliana* IV, 101, 20-21.

23. Insofar as there is no word interpolated between understanding and consciousness of understanding, Sartre speaks of "the silence of consciousness." *Literary and Philosophical Essays* (Collier ed.), p. 172.

24. "Alle Wendung zum 'Objektivismus' and 'Realismus' bleibt 'Subjectivismus': die Frage nach dem Sein als solchem steht auserhalb der Subjekt-Objekt-Beziehung." *Nietzsche*, Pfullingen: Neske, 1961, vol. II, p. 195. "...dass dieses Zwischen als Vorgriff ueber das Ding hinausgreift und ebenso hinter uns zurueck." *Die Frage nach dem Ding*, Tuebingen: Niemeyer, 1962, p. 188.

25. *Erste Philosophie*, Lecture 40 and Appendix XVII. For a critique of the view that consciousness is the self knowing itself as an object (the view caricatured by G. Ryle as "taking a peep into a windowless chamber" and by B. Lonergan as "taking an inward look"): Aliud enim est esse conscium; aliud autem est scire (scientia proprie dicta) se esse conscium. Illud omnium est, cum nihil aliud sit quam ipsa mentis praesentia sibi; quae quidem praesentia eo ipso efficitur quod natura nostra sensitiva vel intellectualis sive apprehendo sive appetendo actuatur; necque quidquam refert quodnam obiectum vel apprehendatur vel appetatur, cum conscii et conscie alia apprehendamus et appetamus, neque ideo conscii efficiamur quod in nos ipsos convertamur, cum conscientia ex parte ipsius subiecti convertentis inveniatur, et non ex parte obiecti ad quod convertamur. Bernard Lonergan, *De Deo Trino* II, editio tertia, Romae, 1964, p. 156.

26. *Tijdschrift voor Philosophie* XII (1950), p. 274.

27. *ta prota theorein* is inseparable from *anthropina phronein;* but this does not mean that first philosophy and anthropology are the same; cf. Aristotle, *Nicomachean Ethics* VI, 7.

"Existenz—zeitweilig in 'Sein und Zeit' gebraucht als die ekstatische Instaendigkeit in der Lichtung des Da des Da-seins.

"Instaendigkeit in der Wahrheit des Seins, gegruendet auf die ausdrueckliche Gruendung der ontologischen Differenz, d.h. der Unterscheidung zwischen Seiendem und Sein. Ausserhalb aller Metaphysik und Existenzphilosophie.)" Heidegger, *Nietzsche, op. cit.*, vol. II, pp. 475-476.

Husserl interpreted *Sein und Zeit* as an anthropology: *Husserliana* V, 140; "Phaenomenologie und Anthropologie," *op. cit.*, pp. 1-2.

28. Heidegger, *Kants These ueber das Sein*, Frankfurt a/M: Klostermann, 1963, p. 35.

29. Aristotle, 1028b2-4.

30. "...die Unterkunft der Ankunft des Ausbleibens...das Versprechen im Entzug." Heidegger, *Nietzsche, op. cit.*, vol. II, pp. 353-359, 367-369, 389-390.

31. Note on *Geist* in relation to *Dasein* and transcendental subjectivity: Hegelian *Geist* is both reflected totality or the perspective of all perspectives and each of those perspectives for which the exhaustive *logos* of being is

still veiled but which are nevertheless on the way toward this *logos*. *Geist* is both eschatological and cyclic because the *pleroma* of mind, for which all, including itself, stands revealed, nevertheless remembers and recounts *da capo* the way which it generates and constitutes in order to come to itself, a way, "the toil of science," which passes through all the types of relation between self and other in so far as these have not yet been reconciled to each other and *aufgehoben* in each other. The beginning of the *Phenomenology of Spirit* (*PhG*) presupposes but is silent about what is to come; the end surpasses but remembers what has gone before. ". . . a circle of progressive embodiments, which looked at in one respect still exist beside each other, and only as looked at from another point of view appear as past. The grades which *Geist* seems to have left behind it, it still possesses in the depths of its present." (*Phil. of History*, "Intro.", *ad fin.*) At the end of the drama of consciousness the author himself appears on the stage to recite and comment on his own work.

The *PhG* can be interpreted in two senses in accord with the ambiguity of the word *phainomenon*, which means both *id quod videtur* and *id quod lucet* (cf. *Sein und Zeit*, sec. 7): ". . . this pathway to science is itself *eo ipso* science. . . ." (*PhG*, "Intro."): (1) the journey from experience to science from the perspective of experience, or science itself seen from a less than total and adequate, that is, from a non-scientific perspective: "Now because this exposition (*Darstellung*) has for its object only phenomenal knowledge, the exposition itself seems not to be science, free, self-moving in the shape proper to itself, but may, from this point of view, be taken as the pathway of the natural consciousness which is pressing forward to true knowledge" (*ibid.*); (2) that which is seen as beyond all possibility of negation and discussion, or that which is non-dialectical because, already containing all difference of perspective and all negation within itself, there is nothing outside it which could complement or refute it: "The terminus is at that point where knowledge is no longer compelled to go beyond itself, where it finds its own self, and the notion corresponds to the object and the object to the notion" (*ibid.*).

ludwig wittgenstein

PHILOSOPHY AS LINGUISTIC ANALYSIS

by Robert Sokolowski

Words are a very interesting and puzzling part of our world. Considered in one way, they are simply acoustic vibrations or marks on paper, but the effect they have on human beings makes them quite different from ordinary physical marks and sounds. Words have the peculiarity of transmitting meaning. When the physical vibration that is a spoken word strikes a person's ear, a meaning, to put it grossly, enters that person's mind. As a result, the listener is not only thereby enabled to think differently, but his view of reality changes also. He sees the world in a new way because of the effect words have upon him. As Plato puts it in the *Cratylus,* "Regarding the name as an instrument, what do we do when we name? . . . Do we not give information to one another, and distinguish things according to their natures?"[1] Words communicate, and they help us to see, in a new, deeper, and richer way, the natures of things.

This peculiar and crucially important function of words is the type of enigma that philosophical problems are made of, and the history of philosophy has many instances of thinkers who have attempted to explain the nature of language. Parmenides and Heraclitus mention the problem, and Plato's own theory of language has much to tell us after almost twenty-five centuries. Aristotle, the Stoics and the Epicureans, the medieval logicians and nominalists, all treated the origin and nature of words. In modern times, German philosophy, in the work of Herder, von Humboldt, the neo-Kantians, and Heidegger, has carried on extensive research into language. Twentieth-century British philosophy has been most conspicuous of all in working this rich vein, and its way of doing philosophy has come to be called linguistic analysis. G. E. Moore, Bertrand Russell, A. J. Ayer, Gilbert Ryle, J. L. Austin and many others represent this philosophical trend, but above them all stands the figure of Ludwig Wittgenstein, whose name is practically synonymous with linguistic philosophy.

Wittgenstein was born in Vienna in 1889, of Saxon parents. The atmosphere of his home was very artistic, and he took from it an especially fine sense of music which shows in the composition of his writing.[2] He was interested in engineering as a young man, and studied that subject in Berlin. In 1908, at the age of nineteen, he went to study engineering at Manchester, England. His study of mathematics led him to certain philosophical problems and finally prompted him to enter Cambridge University as a student of philosophy. He studied there from 1911 to 1914, and was influenced by Bertrand Russell and by the writings of Frege, whom he had come to know in Germany. He was also a friend of G. E. Moore.

When the 1914-1918 war broke out, Wittgenstein joined the Austrian army, was captured by Italian forces in 1918, and spent several months as a prisoner, chiefly in a camp near Monte Cassino. Even during the war he continued his philosophical reflections and after its end he was ready to publish his first major work, the *Logisch-philosophische Abhandlung,* in Vienna in 1921.[3] It was published in England, with a parallel English translation, in 1922 as the *Tractatus Logico-Philosophicus.*[4] Some of the groundwork leading to the *Tractatus* has been published posthumously as the *Notebooks* 1914-1916.[5]

In 1919, despite the recognition given to his work, Wittgenstein gave up his philosophical career, studied elementary school teaching, and went to teach children in some village schools in Lower Austria, between Vienna and Graz. Having given away a comfortable inheritance he lived in simple quarters and on the barest necessities. In 1926 he thought of entering a monastery and worked for some months as gardener at a monastery at Hutteldorf. At this time in his life, the Socratic, almost Cynical, aspect of Wittgenstein's personality is vividly obvious. Even when he returned to Cambridge, he maintained almost complete indifference to such physical things as wealth, comfort, position, and even social conventions. His years in Austria show the same unconcern one may find in a cryptic passage in the introduction to the *Tractatus*: "How far my efforts agree with those of other philosophers I will not decide. Indeed what I have here written makes no claim to novelty in points of detail; and therefore I give no sources, because it is indifferent to me whether what I have thought has already been thought before me by another."[6]

By 1929, Wittgenstein felt a new interest in, and saw a new approach to certain philosophical questions, and when friends urged him to return to Cambridge, he did so. He taught there until 1936, and his thought at this period has been preserved for us in notes that have been published posthumously as *The Blue and Brown Books*.[7] He left England for Norway in 1936, but returned when war broke out in 1939 and spent the war working in a hospital and medical center. After the war he tried teaching at Cambridge again, but lasted only until 1947. He then went to Galway, Ireland, where he lived a hermit-like existence for several months in a cottage by the sea, and later moved to Dublin. On the invitation of his friend and former student, Norman Malcolm, he made a trip to the United States in 1949. During the last years of his life he was trying to work his thoughts into another book, since he had changed some of the opinions expressed thirty years earlier in the *Tractatus*. He never finished this work in his lifetime, but the material he prepared was published posthumously as the *Philosophical Investigations*.[8] Ludwig Wittgenstein died of cancer at Cambridge on April 29, 1951.[9]

Both in his person and in his thought Wittgenstein was hard to understand. Many people wanted to like him, but he was severe and could be demanding and even, at times, cruel to his friends. Still, those who were close to him were devoted to him, and found that he was capable of a deep, generous, if uncompromising, friendship. He was impetuous and unpredictable. He gave the impression, especially in his classes—which were more discussions than lectures—of awesome intensity and concentration. The same combination of attraction and mystification is to be found in his writings. They seem to be profoundly important, difficult, and subtle. His German style is original and artistic, in its own way. Wittgenstein has been called the greatest philosopher of our century, but it is hard to catch and label precisely the elusive character that makes his thought significant. What has he said that changes philosophy? What effect will it have on subsequent thought? The philosophical trend he stimulated in England seems to have reached a moment of reorientation. The time seems to have come for reflective, critical analysis of his thought. The history of linguistic analysis will be written in the years that lie before us. As the personal impact and impetus of Wittgenstein's life and character recede into the past, historians will be able to give us their critical evaluation of his place in the history of western thinking.[10]

●

Wittgenstein's career is generally divided into two major parts, an early period in which he is said to have professed a "logical atomism" and a "picture theory" of meaning, and a later period in which he abandoned some of his earlier convictions and turned to a more fluid concept of language. In our treatment of his early thought we will bypass the customary metaphors and direct attention on the concept of "logical space" as the focal point of his thought; in discussing his later philosophy we will turn to the metaphor of "language games" as the central presentation of his ideas. Elaboration of these and other metaphors will provide a framework in which to discuss Wittgenstein's thought.

In explanations of the *Tractatus,* the attempt is often made to begin with the atoms that logical atomism is supposed to posit, and then to reconstruct the rest of logic and thought. Such a procedure has at least one serious weakness. Like the atoms of the Greek thinkers, Wittgenstein's primitive linguistic units are not directly experienced. They are posited as necessary philosophical principles, as *archai,* to explain something else that is directly experienced as a problem and can find no adequate solution in the realities of our everyday world. The Greek atomists did not posit atoms because someone saw them, but because the Parmenidean paradox of change and being could not, they felt, be solved unless some such reality as an atom exists. Likewise, Wittgenstein never points to a specific, real atomic proposition; he does not even unequivocally give us an example of a simple name.[11]

He posits them because they are needed as philosophical principles, *archai,* to explain the experience we have of logic, thinking, and language on the macroscopic level. He feels that without simple names, it is impossible to explain the definiteness of sense; meaning cannot be precise unless it is built up of elements that are in themselves wholly precise and simple: "The demand for simple things is the demand for definiteness of sense." [12]

Wittgenstein's argument is similar to that which infers that because we experience material reality as extended, there must be some ultimate piece of matter, an atom, which is itself extended and which acts as the basic component from which macroscopic matter is built. Even if such atoms are never actually experienced, their existence is affirmed on the basis of the implication of what is directly experienced. Thus to begin presentation of Wittgenstein's thought with his logical atomism is to join him at a point where half his philosophical journey has been travelled. Instead of starting with logical atomism as the characteristic of Wittgenstein's early thought, we shall begin with the concept of logical space, and see how logical atomism fits into this context. We can proceed by articulating the ways in which language is like geometrical space.

First, geometrical space sets up certain possibilities in physical reality. It makes certain things and operations possible. When geometrical coordinates are introduced into the world, it becomes possible to speak about physical motion, size, action and reaction (if the latter are considered as pure functions), growth, and other physical operations and processes. It is the presence of geometrical structuration of the world that makes such physical "realities" possible. We do not require specifically cartesian geometry, of course; even a more primitive geometrical space can suffice for rough and vague presence of these things, but some sort of space is necessary. Without some form of geometrical space, the order that is required to be able to speak of physical reality is lacking.

According to Wittgenstein, language introduces into the world a "logical space" which makes certain realities possible. It is language that sets up the order in which it becomes possible for us to speak about things and relationships. Wittgenstein says that language "casts its shadow" on the world, and it is this shadow that brings things into relief.[13] It makes them differentiated, it orders relations among them, and allows us to elaborate our whole network of thought as a representation of reality.

>3.411. The geometrical and the logical place agree in that each is the possibility of an existence.

Let us try to refine further our concept of geometrical space. Instead of talking about the geometrical coordinates themselves—instead of talking about a two dimensional or three dimensional graph, for instance—we can shift our manner of expression into algebraic form. We can use formulas instead of graphs or pictured coordinates. Thus the expression, xy plus 5 equals z, is another way of speaking about a certain physical reality, for instance, a rectilinear path followed by a body under certain conditions. The same reality that can be depicted by a wire model in three dimensions can now be depicted by the more esoteric form of an algebraic formula, and the formula itself can be said to introduce the geometrical space, the geometrical order, that allows the path to exist in our world. The formula is as much a "picture" of the path as the wire model is.The wire framework, with its geometrical dimensions, is found embodied in the formula, even though the formula itself is not a three dimensional thing.

This step brings geometrical space into closer similarity with logical space, for the analogon to the algebraic formula is the proposition in language. The statement, "The beauty of this painting consists in its contrasts of color and shape," is not itself a beautiful statement; there is nothing particularly esthetic about its formulation. And yet, it is able to structure a part of our world in such a way as to bring into this world an esthetic dimension. It makes it possible for esthetic values to be constituted for us. Without the language of esthetics, the beauty of painting or music could only be very rudimentarily experienced, and even such rudimentary experience would require at least a few primitive words of esthetic approval or pleasure. Without the language, claims Wittgenstein, the world of esthetics does not exist. The "logical space" of esthetics is required if we are to experience artistic beauty.

Can we explain how the algebraic formula constitutes geometrical space, and how the language statement constitutes logical space? How this comes about is the central problem in Wittgenstein's early philosophy, and most of his concepts at this period of his thought can best be understood in terms of it.

A first, naive way to solve the difficulty would be to claim that each of the words in a statement names or stands for an element in reality. Likewise, each symbol in an algebraic formula names or stands for a point in the world. Such reference, it might be claimed, is sufficient to provide the link between language and the world. This answer might be adequate if language consisted only of proper names, each of which stands in a one-to-one correspondence with elements in reality. Such a view of language is based on a Lockean concept of the mind as something purely passive, something that receives impressions from outside and then formulates labels which it places on each of them. Mental activity, and more specifically linguistic activity, would be wholly passive and receptive.

A solution like this runs against its greatest difficulty in trying to explain how words that are not names can refer to reality. What happens to logical operations, like "and," "not," "or," "since," etc.? They certainly do not refer to anything in reality, at least not in the same way that proper names refer. The same difficulty arises in regard to algebraic operators; signs for addition, exponents, etc., do not stand for geometrical objects. Thus there is a factor in statements and formulas that is different from simple names: the form or the structure of the statement or equation. Its nature is different from that of names, and its way of expressing reality is different from the way names refer to things. Wittgenstein focuses his attention on this factor of form in expression. The form or structure of a lingustic expression is what constitutes logical space in our world, and it is therefore philosophically the most important element in language. Names make sense only as components within a form. They can carry out their activity of referring to individual things only within the context of the logical space set by the logical form of a statement. The logical structure makes up the "possibility of the existence" of individual things.

2.18. What every picture, of whatever form, must have in common with reality in order to be able to represent it at all—rightly or falsely—is the logical form, that is, the form of reality.

The order within a statement is what orders the world into logical space. The structure in linguistic expressions is what is important and philosophically significant, not the whole expression itself; we must investigate not the formula, but the form.

When Wittgenstein claims that the structure or form of statements is what arranges a logical space in the world, he does not, of course, mean simply the spatial relationships words have to one another in a statement. He refers to the logical relationships existing among words, to that field of possible relationships that each word carries with itself, the relationships that allow the word to be joined in certain ways with some words, forbid it to be connected with other terms, or permit its connection with still other terms in different ways. For instance, esthetic terms are surrounded by a certain penumbra of possibilities; they can be joined with words expressing pleasure or dissatisfaction, they allow a growth or decline in intensity, and they permit comparison. However, they exclude words that imply direct and exact measurement. We cannot measure, in any sort of units, how much esthetic value Vermeer's *View of Delft* possesses. The "logic" of esthetic words does not allow junction with the logic of terms describing mathematical measurements. The gears do not mesh.

Each type of word, therefore, brings along its own logical space. Such logical space is the basis of certain necessary statements we can make about the reality designated by the word.

> 2.0131. . . . A speck in a visual field need not be red, but it must have a color; it has, so to speak, a color space round it. A tone must have *a* pitch, the object of the sense of touch *a* hardness, etc.

The logical space that accrues to words describing sounds is such that some pitch is necessarily implied in them, although the specific pitch a certain sound will have is not necessarily determined. Therefore, to know the meaning of a word, to know the nature of a thing, we must simply know the possible relationships it is capable of entering into. To "explicate" the nature of a certain reality, we need only describe the network of logical possibilities inherent in it, for to know these possibilities is to know the object.

> 2.0123. If I know an object I also know all its possibilities in states of affairs. (Every one of these possibilities must be part of the nature of the object.)[14]

When words are used together in propositions, this field of logical possibilties remains operative, and the juncture of several possibilities sets up a structure peculiar to the type of statement being made. Any statement in language thus carries within itself a network, a structure of logical relationships. The structure depends on the words used in the statement, and on the nature of the statement itself. When proper names or common nouns are imbedded in this structure, it becomes possible for them to refer to things in the world, but it is the structure that first must organize the world into a coherent pattern, into logical space of one sort or another, before the names can carry out their reference. The structure must first "cast its shadow" upon the world before the individual things come into relief and become named.[15]

The way in which linguistic structure casts its shadow and form upon the world is not easy to talk about. The relationship between linguistic form and reality is very subtle in Wittgenstein's thought. Whereas names simply stand for certain objects in an uncomplicated one-to-one correspondence, the relation of the form of propositions is much more creative. Linguistic form does not simply stand for an objective structure that is already there; it constitutes the real structure. It arranges reality into logical space. Linguistic structure is like the order and harmony in a painting, which may help us to see order, harmony, and values in the world that we could not have seen without the aid of artistic creation. But in such a case the structure of the painting does not "name" or "stand for" the structure of the world that we have discovered. Rather, the painting embodies the same form we are to see in the world. It displays that form, and then makes it possible for us to discover the form in the world.

Language works in this way. In a language statement we have

an embodiment of a logical form, and the logical constants express part of this form. But the form is not a "name" of anything in the world, because the structure that it displays is not the sort of thing that can be named. It is not a thing. Hence Wittgenstein says,

> 4.0312.... My fundamental thought is that the "logical constants" do not represent. That the *logic* of the facts cannot be represented.

We cannot simply give a name to the logical space, the structure and order, that is constituted in reality. All that can be done is for language to incorporate, to embody, to mirror, the same form within itself and so display it to us.

> 4.121. Propositions cannot represent the logical form: this mirrors itself in the propositions. That which mirrors itself in language, language cannot represent. That which expresses *itself* in language, *we* cannot express by language. The propositions *show* the logical form of reality. They exhibit it.

The metaphor we have used of a painting is not foreign to Wittgenstein's thought. He speaks frequently in the *Tractatus* of statements as "pictures" (*Bilder*) and uses the word "picturing" (*abbilden*) to talk about the relationship between language and reality. A concrete statement is a picture of reality. It contains individual names which refer to objects, but it also incorporates a logical structure which "pictures" the logical space in reality.

> 3.42.... The logical scaffolding round the picture determines the logical space.

Thus the "picture theory" of meaning attributed to the early Wittgenstein is not a naive epistemological position in which elements of language stand in one-to-one correspondence to elements of reality. The key to the theory is the factor of logical form. The logical form "pictures" or displays a structure that is to be found in reality. Because of this Wittgenstein says, "A picture is a model of reality."[16] They both have the same logical form.[17]

This discussion about logical space now provides a suitable context in which to treat briefly of Wittgenstein's atomism. What does he intend to say when he affirms that there must be simple names, simple objects, and simple propositions? Let us consider the statement, "The book is on the desk." Several inferences can be immediately made from this affirmation: "All the parts of the book are on the desk," "The book exerts a certain pressure on the desk," and so forth. Such statements explicate our first affirmation; they carry out inferences into the logical space surrounding the original affirmation. They are true, meaningful statements implied by and grounded in the statement we started with. However, closer inspection will show that the inferences we have made are not immediately grounded in the words actually used in our original statement. The inferences we have carried out are not derived from "book" and "desk" as such, but from the fact that books and desk are material objects. The inferences could have been made just as well if we had simply said, "Material object X is on material object Y." This is the statement that really allows us to make the derived affirmations.

Thus there is a deeper level within our original statement, and this deeper level of meaning is the one that has logical and philosophical importance, because it is the basis of inferences. Likewise, each of the nouns in the original statement is found to have a deeper level of sense within itself: "book" has the sense "material thing" as a component or nucleus within itself, and the logical space surrounding the work "book" radiates from this nucleus. The words used in our original statement are found to be secondary and derived words. They can and must be analyzed into something more basic and more important philosophically. But can the new, deeper level be traced back to something more fundamental still? If we were Cartesians, for instance, we would say that "material thing" can be analyzed into "extension" as its nucleus, because extension defines what a material thing is. Wittgenstein, of course, does not take sides in this issue. He does not say how far analysis must go and where it must end, but he does insist that it ends somewhere. He does claim that language supposes some final, simple units that cannot be further analyzed and defined. These are the "atomic" elements, the simple names that are the foundation for all language on the complex, macroscopic level.

Wittgenstein does not give an inventory of such simple names, he does not even give one unambiguous example of what they would be like. He affirms their existence in language not because he has found specimens of them, but because the nature of language requires that they exist. Simple names are affirmed because of logical necessity. Wittgenstein feels that the definiteness of meaning that we find in language requires that analysis come to an end at some point, for if a word could be analyzed and defined by another, the second again analyzed and defined by a third, and so to infinity, there would be no explanation for the precision and definiteness of words. Definitions must come to an end somewhere, and the words in which they terminate are called by Wittgenstein simple names.

> 3.26. The name cannot be analyzed further by any definition. It is a primitive sign.

Such primitive, atomic names cannot be defined; any explanation of them is simply the articulation of their logical space. When we try to clarify what such primitive names mean, we do not analyze them into more basic terms; we can only make explicit the inferences and implications the name allows. Thus if "material thing" were to be taken as a simple name, we could not define it in terms of anything more basic. To explain or clarify it, we would simply specify what sort of propositions could be made as inferences from it: a material thing cannot occupy two places at once, it has a surface and internal parts that do not lie on the surface, etc. Such statements could be called clarifications, but they are not definitions of material things.

Another interpretation of Wittgenstein's "simples" can be made. We have interpreted his primitive terms to be names of things like "material objects," "extension," "color," and so forth; names of realities that, in other philosophical traditions, would be called primitive essences. It could be argued that Wittgenstein's simple names refer rather to individual objects, purely as individual. They would be best exemplified by demonstratives like "this" or "that." The simple objects they name would be individual pieces of reality, individual, atomic things. Simple names would be a special class of proper names. Reality would have to be analyzed into such simple pieces, and language into the proper names of such pieces, before we would reach that level of simplicity that assures the definiteness of words in language.[18]

Such an interpretation of Wittgenstein's *Tractatus* is supported by some critical comments he makes about his early work himself in the *Philosophical Investigations*.[19] If it does represent what he thinks, then his atomism runs into serious difficulties when we consider how simple names are supposed to form atomic propositions. Wittgenstein says:

> 4.22. The elementary proposition consists of names. It is connexion, a concatenation of names.
> 4.221. It is obvious that in the analysis of propositions we must come to elementary propositions, which consist of names in immediate combination.

An elementary proposition is said to be formed of two or more names in immediate combination. However, if we simply put two proper names together, we do not form a proposition. "Peter Paul" is not a proposition. What is needed to make it one is the logical space that accrues to words like "color," and "material thing." An immediate combination like, "Material thing colored," can be considered an elementary proposition, if we make allowances for the implied copula. To say that Wittgenstein's simple names are proper names of individual pieces of reality, is to deny them any logical space; but without logical space they cannot form propositions.

A further consideration can be made on Wittgenstein's statement:

> 4.21. The simplest kind of proposition, an elementary proposition, asserts the existence of a state of affairs.[20]

The simple propositions that are formed out of primitive names are supposed to be able to picture a state of affairs. But two proper names placed in immediate combination cannot picture a state of affairs; they lack the logical space that makes such "picturing" possible. They have no form, and it is the form that is essential in a statement's reference to the world.

Most of the *Tractatus* is devoted to showing what language does and to explaining the mechanism by which it functions. However, towards the end of the work, Wittgenstein attempts to draw the limits of language, to point out the realities that cannot be expressed in linguistic form. It makes no sense to try to talk about them, claims Wittgenstein. He discusses this subject in the so-called "mystical" passages at the end of the *Tractatus,* but more material is to be found in the *Notebooks.*[21] Among the subjects that are on the limit of language, and therefore inexpressible within language, are the ego, death, God, and language itself.

Since language is a picture of the world, it functions in such a way as to organize the world we perceive. It arranges objects in the world according to logical patterns. But this implies that language can arrange only objects in the world, that is, objects that stand over and against the knowing subject, the ego who is the user of language. The world exists for him; he is not a thing in the world:

> 5.632. The subject does not belong to the world but it is a limit of the world.

Just as the eye cannot see itself, so the user of language, the ego, cannot turn language on himself.

> 5.633. Where *in* the world is a metaphysical subject to be found? You will say that this is exactly like the case of the eye and the visual field. But really you do *not* see the eye. And nothing *in the visual field* allows you to infer that it is seen by an eye.[22]

Like the transcendental ego of Kant, which accompanies all presentations in consciousness but can never itself be made an object of consciousness, Wittgenstein's subject is the anonymous user of language who can never be directly spoken about. It is much like the transcendental subjectivity of Husserl, which is not a thing in the world but which constitutes the world as an intentional

correlate to itself. Some of Wittgenstein's statements could easily
have been written by Husserl:

> 5.641. Thus there really is a sense in which philosophy
> can talk about the self in a non-psychological way . . . . The
> philosophical self is not the human being, not the human
> body, or the human soul, with which psychology deals, but
> rather the metaphysical subject, the limit of the world—not
> a part of it.[23]

On the issue of solipsism, Wittgenstein states in Husserlian
fashion that the ego is truly to be considered as something cut off
from the world, because it is not an object among other objects in
the world; but the world itself is correlated to and coordinate with
this ego.

> 5.64. Here we see that solipsism strictly carried out co-
> incides with pure realism. The I in solipsism shrinks to an
> extensionless point and there remains the reality co-
> ordinated with it.

The ego uses language to talk about the world, and he cannot
talk about himself because he does not experience himself as part
of the world. Likewise, he cannot talk about his own death, because his death is not simply an event classed among others
in the world. His own death is again a limit to the world, and
therefore cannot be talked about as something in the world.

> 6.431. So too at death the world does not alter, but comes
> to an end.
> 6.4311. Death is not an event in life: we do not live
> to experience death.[24]

Death is like the edge of our field of vision. It is always there,
limiting and surrounding the world that we see, but we can never
look at it directly.

God cannot be conceived as something in the world either, for
that would take away from him that which makes him God, his
difference from any being we experience directly.

6.432. . . . God does not reveal himself *in* the world.

God cannot be classed among things in the world, and furthermore, he does not reveal himself in the world. Wittgenstein implies
that no worldly event can be called a "divine intervention," no
set of facts or circumstances can be called a manifestation of God.
If such were the case, God would be acting as someone in the
world, and would lose his difference with the world. It would
follow that it is impossible for us to speak meaningfully about God
with human language, which is fit only for the organization of
logical space and the naming of objects that do exist in our world.

Most paradoxically of all, Wittgenstein claims that language
cannot talk about itself. The function of language is to mirror
the world; but a mirror does not reflect itself. Hence the supreme
paradox stated at the end of the *Tractatus*: whoever understands
all Wittgenstein's statements in that book will now have come to
see them as nonsensical. The *Tractatus* must lead, by means of
language, to a position where the reader realizes that the language
that has been leading him is meaningless; "he must so to speak
throw away the ladder, after he has climbed up on it." [26] This
explains why the things Wittgenstein tries to say about language
are so difficult to grasp. They are not and cannot be stated in a
forthright way because philosophically language cannot talk about
itself; hence the abundance of metaphors and analogies which serve
more to hint at what language is, rather than bluntly to say so.
The concepts of logical space, of language as a picture or mirror,
of logical scaffolding, even the notion of atomism, are all metaphors that intimate what language is like but do not describe it
directly, as we would describe and express physical or biological
laws. The nature of language simply manifests itself:

6.522. There are, indeed, things that cannot be put into
words. They *make themselves manifest.*[27]

Wittgenstein's metaphors are intimations to help us see how they
manifest themselves.

●

It is difficult to put Wittgenstein's early philosophy into specific, clearly expressed doctrine, and his later thought is even

more unwieldy. The style of the *Philosophical Investigations* is meditative, rambling, and questioning, quite in contrast to the confident pronouncements of the *Tractatus*.[28] In some ways, the *Investigations* resemble the restless, repetitive style of St. Augustine, but differ in not coming to as many answers as Augustine reached.[29] Wittgenstein has few answers in the *Investigations,* but his questions are indeed provocative and rich; much of the value of the work consists in its showing new ways of investigating and questioning our experience of language and the world.

The change in doctrine which is most significant in the *Investigations,* and upon which most of the other discrepancies with the *Tractatus* hinge, is Wittgenstein's rejection of atomism. In the *Tractatus* he feels that, in principle if not in fact, language must be reducible to primary elements which name simple objects. There are certain simple names and simple objects that have an independent existence. They comprise a final, absolute, static realm that is the nucleus upon which our normal language and everyday world is structured. In the *Investigations,* Wittgenstein claims that such reduction to final elements is, in principle, not possible. Such simple and independent elements, whether in language or in reality, cannot exist. Even to look for them has no sense.

> 47. But what are the simple constituent parts of which reality is composed?—What are the simple constituent parts of a chair?—The bits of wood of which it is made? Or the molecules, or the atoms?—"Simple" means: not composite. And here the point is: in what sense "composite"? It makes no sense at all to speak absolutely of the "simple parts of a chair."

The term "simple" can have many meanings, all contingent upon the context in which the term is used. There is no absolute, ideal sense fixed for the term. For instance, if one were to analyze a chessboard into its simple components, one might stop with the squares as one type of ultimate, or with the lines as another, or points of color as a third.[30] Even the atoms from which it is composed could be considered the ultimate "parts" of which it is made. It all would depend on what one means by simple parts.

There is no absolute, final element that exists Platonically apart from any context at all.

To carry through our metaphor, the "logical space" of the *Tractatus* now becomes changed into linguistic "fields of force." [31] Logical space implies a fixed, static structure with a precise pattern that remains the same throughout any operations carred out within it. The logical space of color words is completely determined by the simple words used in its constitution, and all color words have a fixed place within this space. But if we consider words as existing in linguistic fields of force, then this static, clear precision is lost. A word in a certain field of force has a certain use and function, but it can become subject to another field of force which makes the same word operate differently. The verb "to know" has one use in chemistry, and another type of use in the science of history. Its material logic is different within each field, and it would have no sense to ask what the word would mean apart from any field at all. Words have sense in a context. The whole of language, furthermore, is composed of innumerable fields of force interlaced and interacting with each other. [32] There is no ideal, ultimate structure for language.

Nevertheless, words do have logical lines of force in Wittgenstein's new thought. They have a logical structure manifest in the rules that govern their use. Certain inferences and chains of discursive reasoning can be built up upon them, while other inferences may be excluded. Words still have the "logical scaffolding" attributed to them in the *Tractatus,* but the scaffolding is now less fixed than in Wittgenstein's early thought. It is fluid, subject to change and adjustment. Thus Wittgenstein is not an outright behaviorist or psychologist, even though much of what he says tends towards such a position. Words are not simply psychological events or proper names. In his treatment of negation, for instance, Wittgenstein does not accept entirely the behaviorist theory that considers negation simply as a feeling of rejection, a psychological state. Negation has a sense, an objective, logical force, which is shown by the peculiarity that a double negation becomes an affirmation again. As he says, this could not be explained in behaviorist terms; "we do not annul a shake of the head by shaking it again." [33] Behaviorist actions do not suffice to explain logic.

Wittgenstein often treats this logical dimension of words in terms of a person's ability to carry out an indefinite series of applications or uses of a word. I show that I know the meaning of "democracy" not by using the word correctly a definite number of times, but by my ability to continue to use it correctly in new and unfamiliar situations. When we learn the correct use or meaning of the word "red," we must be able to apply it to a series of objects, and then be able to say, "and so forth." It is this "et cetera" that indicates a certain transcendence in words.[34] They go beyond any definite number of instances by virtue of the logical element in them. The understanding of mathematical operations is another example of this:

> 151. Let us imagine the following example: A writes a series of numbers down; B watches him and tries to find a law for the sequence of numbers. If he succeeds he exclaims: "Now I can go on!"

Thus the sense of words is a logcal reality, transcending any finite number of instances.

However, although Wittgenstcin admits the logical dimension of words, he does not want to appeal to a subsistent "meaning," neither as a concept in the mind nor as an aspect of reality, to explain it. He wants to treat it as a function of words. Meaning is not an entity, but something we do with words; the meaning of words is the use to which they are put, and we understand a word when we can use it correctly. Wittgenstein tries to overcome the dichotomy between meaning and language, and his attempt to reconcile the two gives the *Investigations* their piquancy and philosophical interest.

Philosophical concepts of the nature of mind always correspond to a thinker's conception of the cognitive or volitional capacities of man, and Wittgenstein's concept of mind reflects his assimilation of meaning to the use of words. Mind becomes the power man has to use words according to rules. It is not considered as a subsistent entity, a receptacle for concepts. Mental processes, says Wittgenstein, are not to be imagined as shadow actions taking place behind our physical gestures and speech; they are simply the gestures or speech itself, but used according to logical rules.

154. Try not to think of understanding as a "mental process" at all—For *that* is the expression which confuses you. But ask yourself: in what sort of case, in what kind of circumstance, do we say, "Now I know how to go on," when, that is, the formula *has* occurred to me?

Wittgenstein's philosophy in the *Investigations* is much less contemplative than it is in the *Tractatus*. The language he speaks of in his early work is the language of pure science and speculation, the order that is introduced by theoretical thought. In the *Investigations,* language is brought into the current of human action. The rules that belong to words are not only derived from speculation, but arise in human activity and must be placed within that context of activity to be properly understood.

23. Here the term "language-*game*" is meant to bring into prominence the fact that the *speaking* of language is part of an activity, or of a form of life.

Human actions like giving commands, joking, working out puzzles, expressing emotion or thanks, all enter into the context of language, so the use and the meaning of certain words can be recovered only in their proper place in life. This introduction of human praxis makes Wittgenstein's theory of language more socially and historically orientated, for now the type of activity man is made capable of performing by the development of society and culture enters into the construction of language. Thus Wittgenstein's striking metaphor comparing language to a city implies that all the action and history that go into the growth of a city are required to build language.

18. Our language can be seen as an ancient city: a maze of little streets and squares, of old and new houses, and of houses with additions from various periods; and this surrounded by a multitude of new boroughs with straight regular streets and uniform houses.

The root metaphor for Wittgenstein's later thought is, of course, that of language games. Various regions of our language are like distinct games. A game is not simply a physical gesture, it is an activity carried out according to rules. The use of language also involves the physical acts of writing, speaking, or reading according to certain rules, according to the material and formal logical rules that govern the sense of words. But we cannot give any absolute structure for games; there is no such thing as an ideal game with characteristics that all concrete games are supposed to instantiate somehow. Some games are played alone, others with a team, some with a ball or cards or checkers. Rules and even criteria for winning differ from one game to another. What is common to all games? Wittgenstein answers:

> 66. Don't say: "There must be something common, or they would not be called 'games' "—but *look and see* whether there is anything common to all.—For if you look at them you will not see something that is common to *all,* but similarities, relationships, and a whole series of them at that. To repeat, don't think, but look!

There is no ultimate ideal structure for language either, as the *Tractatus* and *Principia Mathematica* maintain. Language is rather a collection of "games" which may have family relationships, general similarities of structure, but no definite, common form. The language game of ethics has peculiarities of usage not found in esthetics, physics has rules different from history, and mathematics is a language game different from telling a story or reprimanding a person. Finally, the element of action is clearly brought out by the metaphor of games; to play a game is to do something, and to use language, claims Wittgenstein, is not to carry out unseen mental acts, it is a concrete human activity using words according to rules.

Having elaborated this concept of language, what does Wittgenstein propose as the function of philosophy? The task he gives it is modest indeed. Philosophy can examine the various language games that ordinary human activity has built up and it can show the type of rules, the logic, that belongs to each game, but it cannot interfere in the formation of language games. It cannot say anything about the nature of what is expressed in specific games, nor can it devise criteria by which to judge the rules established by them.

> 124. Philosophy may in no way interfere with the actual use of language; it can in the end only describe it. For it cannot give it any foundation either. It leaves everything as it is.

Ordinary language builds its own structure with no help or interference from philosophy.

However, Wittgenstein does attribute to philosophy a negative, policeman's role over language. At times the rules of language games go awry; the rules of one game are confused with words and rules of another. This gives rise to a seemingly insoluble problem, whose perplexity is all the greater because we do not know how to go about solving it:

> 123. A philosophical problem has the form: "I don't know my way about."

Ordinary language has definite ways of operating with our activity and experience of the world. When problems in physics, biology, social reality, politics, and the like, occur, we know how to go about solving them. We may not be able to reach the correct answer in a given case, but at least we know how to proceed in looking for it. Such orientation is lacking, Wittgenstein feels, in the case of philosophical problems. We do not know what to invoke as an answer, because the problem itself is not a real one. Talking about philosophical difficulties, Wittgenstein says:

> 109. These are, of course, not empirical problems; they are solved, rather, by looking into the working of our language, and that in such a way as to make us recognize those workings: *in despite* of an urge to misunderstand them. The problems are solved, not by giving new information, but by arranging what we have always known. Philosophy is a battle against the bewitchment of our intelligence by means of language.

Thus all philosophy can do in such cases is clear up the misunderstanding. It examines the language games that have become entangled, and disentangles them. Philosophical problems are not to be solved, but dissolved. Language, claims Wittgenstein, must be brought down from its metaphysical to its ordinary use.[85]

●

Wittgenstein is a contemporary philosopher, but the short history of his thought has already spoken some judgment about him. His early philosophy has been upset in its central doctrine, linguistic atomism, by his own subsequent thought. British philosophy after Wittgenstein has, by the very paths it has taken, also carried out criticism, both positive and negative, of his positions. It has elaborated Wittgenstein's insight into the variety in language by investigating the diversity of argument and methods of proof that exist. The peculiarities of explanation in physics, in history, in esthetics and legal argument have been analyzed in many valuable studies.[36] However, recent British thought has also shown that Wittgenstein stops short in not giving a basis for language, and in not providing an analysis of language-forming consciousness. Ultimately, this will raise the need for a metaphysical analysis of reality as something that can be expressed in words, something that lends itself to language. This development reinforces the conclusion of Plato's own "linguistic" dialogue, the *Cratylus*: names can never be the last word in philosophy.[37] To speak about names or language, and to do so in a philosophically thorough and satisfying way, one must go beyond analysis of words into the study of man and his world. Certainly, language has a unique role in structuring the world and even in forming man, but it is not the only factor.

The need for such further, extra-linguistic elements is brought out by the change that language games undergo. Wittgenstein's later philosophy introduces, implicitly at least, a historical dimension into language, but gives no reason why language should have a history. How can one language game ever be abandoned, or found to be inadequate, unless nonlinguistic factors enter into consideration? We do accept certain innovations in language, and we do reject others; the criteria for such rejection or acceptance cannot be found in language itself. For if language were the only criterion, there would never be any change or development. The language games that are in possession would have no reason to find themselves inadequate, since by their own standards they would naturally be acceptable and correct. Other criteria, other norms, must be introduced to act as a standard against which existing language can be judged. They can be found only in the evidence reality offers to consciousness.[38] And since our concept of mind will be correlative to the type of cognitive power we attribute to man, we cannot say that man is simply the user of language; he must also be capable of insight into reality as a basis of his language. It is true, of course, that the evidence reality offers to us, and our disposition to accept this evidence, are both conditioned by the words we use, even if never overwhelmed by them. It is Wittgenstein's merit to have helped us wonder, philosophically, at the place of language in our thinking and our world.

NOTES

1. 388B. Jowett translation.

2. A certain rhythmic structure in the *Tractatus* is described in E. Stenius, *Wittgenstein's 'Tractatus'* (Oxford: Blackwell, 1960), pp. 3-17.

3. It was published in *Annalen der Naturphilosophie*, 14 (1921), pp. 185-262.

4. (London: Kegan Paul, Trench, Trubner, and Company, 1922). There have been several reprintings of the original text and translation. In 1960 a new translation was made by D. F. Pears and B. F. McGuinness (London: Routledge and Kegan Paul, 1960). In our study, we prefer to use the old translation except for a few instances where the new translation conveys the sense of the original better. We will indicate in a footnote when the new translation is being used.

5. Edited by G. H. von Wright and G. E. M. Anscombe, translated by G. E. M. Anscombe (Oxford: Blackwell, 1961).

6. p. 27.

7. (Oxford: Blackwell, 1958).

8. Translated by G. E. M. Anscombe (Oxford: Blackwell, 1958). Another collection of Wittgenstein's writings are found in his *Remarks on the Foundations of Mathematics*, tr. G. E. M. Anscombe (Oxford: Blackwell, 1956). The material in this volume dates from 1937-1944. His only other publications are, "Some Remarks on Logical Form," *Proceedings of the Aristotelian Society*, Supplement, 9 (1929), pp. 162-171; and a letter to the editor of *Mind*, 62 (1933), pp. 415-416. More publications of Wittgenstein's works are planned.

9. A fine biography and personal description of Wittgenstein is to be found in: N. Malcolm, *Ludwig Wittgenstein, A Memoir,* with a Biographical Sketch by G. H. von Wright (London: Oxford University Press, 1958).

10. Many studies of the *Tractatus* have appeared recently: G. E. M. Anscombe, *An Introduction to Wittgenstein's 'Tractatus'* (London: Hutchinson University Library, 1959); J. Griffin, *Wittgenstein's Logical Atomism* (Oxford: The Clarendon Press, 1964); A. Maslow, *A Study in Wittgenstein's 'Tractatus'* (Berkeley: University of California Press, 1961); D. Favrholdt, *An Interpretation and Critique of Wittenstein's 'Tractatus'* (Copenhagen: Gyldendal, 1964); M. Black, *A Companion to Wittgenstein's 'Tractatus'* (Ithaca: Cornell University Press, 1964); E. Stenius, *op. cit.;* a very useful research tool has been compiled by G. K. Plochmann and J. B. Lawson, *Terms in their Propositional Contexts in Wittgenstein's 'Tractatus'; an Index* (Carbondale: Southern Illinois University Press, 1962). The first work to attempt to present and contrast the early and late philosophy of Wittgenstein is: G. Pitcher, *The Philosophy of Wittgenstein* (Englewood Cliffs: Prentice Hall, 1964). The later philosophy alone has been ably treated by: D. Pole, *The Later Philosophy of Wittgenstein* (London: The Athlone Press, 1958), and E. K. Specht, *Die sprachphilosophischen und ontologischen Grundlagen im Spätwerk Ludwig Wittgensteins* (Cologne: The University Press, 1963).

11. Cf. the treatment accorded this subject in the *Notebooks,* pp. 60-69.

12. *ibid.,* p. 63; cf. *Tractatus* 3.23.

13. Cf. *Notebooks,* p. 27: "The picture (i.e. the proposition in language) must now in its turn cast its shadow on the world."

14. The new translation is used here, chiefly because of the more accurate translation of *Sachverhalt* as "state of affairs" instead of "atomic fact."

15. Things cannot be conceived without a logical space: *Tractatus* 2.013. "Each thing is, as it were, in a space of possible states of affairs. This space I can imagine empty, but I cannot imagine the thing without the space." New translation.

16. *Tractatus* 2.12.

17. Wittgenstein makes some comments on the form of music as similar to the form of words and propositions. Cf. *Notebooks,* pp. 40-41.

18. Cf. Pitcher, *op. cit.,* pp. 31-43. Wittgenstein is dealing with a classical problem in philosophy at this point, the problem of the relationship between universal and individual. It is the same problem that causes difficulty in the ·interpretation of Aristotle's *tode ti,* as in *Metaphysics* 1028 a 10. Plato treats it in his examination of true opinion as a form of knowledge in the *Theaetetus,* 201 C–210 B, and Hegel studies it in the section on consciousness, especially the part dealing with sensory consciousness and certitude, in the *Phenomenology of Spirit.* For Husserl's treatment see no. 14 of the *Ideas.*

19. Cf. n. 46 and n. 47.

20. New translation.

21. Cf. pp. 71-91.

22. New translation.

23. New translation.

24. New translation.

25. Ethics is also relegated to the inexpressible. Cf. 6.421—6.43.

26. 6.54.

27. New translation.

28. However the style of the *Investigations* is not very different from the *Notebooks*. The *Tractatus* is probably so different because it was definitely prepared for publication.

29. Wittgenstein enjoyed reading Augustine and had a high regard for him. Cf. Malcolm, *op. cit.*, p. 71.

30. Wittgenstein uses the example of a chessboard himself. Cf. *Investigations*, n. 47 and n. 48.

31. Wittgenstein uses the analogy of field of force, but only rarely. Cf. *Investigations*, p. 219. Cf. also S. Ullman, *Language and Style* (Oxford: Blackwell, 1964), pp. 23-28.

32. Language is like a single thread made of many fibers. No one fiber is present in the whole thread, and yet the thread is constituted as a unity. Cf. *Investigations*, n. 67: "And we extend our concept of number as in spinning a thread we twist fiber on fiber. And the strength of the thread does not reside in the fact that some one fiber runs through its whole length, but in the overlapping of many fibers."

33. n. 556.

34. Cf. n. 31.

35. Cf. n. 116: "What *we* do is to bring words back from their metaphysical to their everyday use." This way of doing philosophy became known as therapeutic analysis: correction of linguistic confusions by means of analysis.

36. Examples of such studies can be found in the recent work of J. L. Austin, S. Hampshire, G. E. M. Anscombe, N. R. Hanson, W. B. Gallie, S. Toulmin, R. M. Hare, and J. N. Findlay. J. Passmore tries to systematize this type of philosophy in *Philosophical Reasoning* (London: Duckworth, 1961).

37. 439 B: "How real existence is to be studied or discovered is, I suspect, beyond you and me. We must rest content with the admission that the knowledge of things is not to be derived from names. No; they must rather be studied and investigated in their connexion with one another."

38. *ibid.*, 438 D: "But if this is a battle of names, some of them asserting that they are like the truth, other contending that *they* are, how or by what criterion are we to decide between them? For there are no other names to which appeal can be made, but obviously recourse must be had to another standard which, without employing names, will make clear which of the two are right; and this must be a standard which shows the truth of things." D. Pole makes use of the argument from linguistic change in criticizing Wittgenstein's philosophy; *op. cit.*, pp. 79-102. We have also criticized

Wittgenstein's philosophy elsewhere because it fails to account for the unity of language and have suggested that the failure might be corrected by metaphysical analysis of expressions of existence; cf. "La philosophie analytique et la métaphysique," *Revue philosophique de Louvain*, 57 (1959), pp. 596-597.

PHILOSOPHIES OF HISTORY
NICHOLAS BERDYAEV: CAPTIVE OF FREEDOM
ARNOLD J. TOYNBEE AND HIS SYNCRETIC FAITH

nicholas berdyaev

CAPTIVE OF FREEDOM

by Robert Paul Mohan

Reinhold Niebuhr once referred to Nicholas Berdyaev as the outstanding religious personality of our time. Evelyn Underhill and the late Goeffrey Francis Fisher, Archbishop of Canterbury, echoed this sentiment. He has also been called the "supreme Russian philosopher," passionately interested in the moods and ideas of his time. *The London Times* said that in a lifetime he had accepted and denied with equal vehemence more ideas than most men even fleetingly dream of. The *New York Times* called him the most exciting writer on contemporary religious themes. He was a man as pugnacious as Léon Bloy in his search for the Absolute ,but agonizingly aware of freedom and its responsibilities, a "nay-sayer' to life at one moment, and boldly assertive the next; exhibiting an almost neurotic sensitivity at one time, and at another a stoic courage.

This spiritual anarchist, as he described himself, gives us a great insight into his personality in his *Dream and Reality*. He tells his autobiography is not to be a diary in the sense of André Gide's *Journal* or the confessions of Jean Jacques Rousseau and St. Augustine, but rather a philosophical autobiography of what he calls a "history of spirit and self knowledge".

There is an almost Kierkegaardian anxiety in Berdyaev—a persistent feeling of alienation and aloneness despite his constant political and social and ideological involvements. As he once phrased it: "Nothing is my own and all things are mine". He tells that as a child he was never conscious of belonging to his parents, and was repelled by family ties. Even family resemblances he considered an affront to the dignity of the individual human person.

Berdyaev was born in Kiev, the first center of Christianity in Russia, in 1874. He died an expatriate in Paris in March 1948, much to the relief of his fellow emigrés. As a twenty-year old youth Berdyaev turned to Marxism, was arrested twice in the next four years by Tsarist police, and later exiled to Vologda for two years. After the October revolution he was twice arrested by the Soviets, as by this time he had become disenchanted with Marxism, and was not hesitant in saying so. Despite his dislike of Marxism he taught at the University of Moscow, but was eventually exiled to Berlin and later moved on to Paris.

Berdyaev's family though of Muskovite origin, belonged to the aristocracy of the southwest, and were strongly influenced by the West. French was the language of the home. His mother was a beautiful, aloof aristocrat who was never quite convinced that the Berdyaev family into which she had married was normal. His aunt owned a hundred and fifty thousand acres in Kiev, and had palaces in Warsaw, Paris, Nice, and Rome.

As a child of fourteen, the young Berdyaev was devouring Kant, Hegel, and Schopenhauer. Surprisingly enough, he attributes his religious awakening, not to the Bible, nor to the Orthodox Church, but to Schopenhauer, who also brought home to him the tragic sense of the pain of human sensitivity.[1] From his earliest years he was deeply conscious of what was believed to be the destiny of the Russian people; he was conscious of remaining a nobleman even as he sought justice for the oppressed in revolutionary activity.

Through his childhood Berdyaev nursed resentment against the semi-feudal society of his parents, and the Church, which he felt to be a political tool. But although on occasion extremely critical of orthodoxy, Berdyaev seems to have been considerably influenced by the Orthodox Church, and affiliated himself as an expatriate only with those congregations that were linked to the Moscow patriarchate.[2] Basic to his worship was the concept of 'sobornost', a unity born of voluntary togetherness, a common mind of the assembled faithful. His early bias against the church was probably derived from his father's free-thinking tendencies

and Voltairean scepticism. It was probably to Voltaire, discovered in his father's library, that Berdyaev himself owed his
lifelong interest in the philosophy of history.[3] His studies in
history led him to this conclusion that nothing seems to succeed
in history, but that all things acquire their significance in it.[4] ˋ

Berdyaev was not aware of a specific moment of conversion,
although he had no great reluctance for dramatizing his many
great decisions. Philosophically, Kant was a great influence in his
life, and the one whom he regarded as the philosopher of freedom
par excellence. Yet he says in the same breath, "I have never com-
plied with *any* philosophical tradition". Even Karl Marx in his
later days is said to have remarked, "I am not a Marxist." Berdyaev
too, even when he saw in Marxism an articulate protest against
the inequities of his world, never admitted himself to be completely
a Marxist. Not only would his anarchic spirit resist the relentless
restraints on human personality, but idealism was the philosophy
he represented himself as embracing at this period.

This realism was not the idealism opposed to realism in the
traditional philosophic sense; neither does it seem to represent
any abstract metaphysics.

His *Destiny of Man* contains praise of Kant, but he rejects
the Kantian noetic, and actively opposed the neo-Kantianism of
the Russian intelligentsia which he felt reduced authentic Kantianism
thought to a kind of ethical moralism. Kant's greatest contribution
in Berdyaev's opinion was his conviction that true morality was
within and not empirically arrived at.

Berdyaev's disenchantment with Marxism was by no means
based on a regard for capitalism, which he considered the greater
evil, and one doomed to destruction. No party or system could
long interest this restless spirit who was really interested in a
personalistic socialism, free of both collective and individual restraints.

Of enormous influence on Berdyaev was Dostoevsky, whose
character Stavrogin, in *The Possessed,* he longed to be identified
with as a young man. He loved to dramatize himself as the
aristocrat of the Revolution, "the dark haired nobleman gleaming
with life, and wearing the mask of cold aloofness."[5] Dostoevsky he
considered the artist of terror who gave artistic utterance to
the anguish and sense of alienation which Berdyaev never com-

pletely lost. He says: "The heroes in Tolstoy's and Dostoevsky's novels were of greater importance for me than philosophical and theological schools of thought, and it was at their hands that I received Christianity."[6] It is indeed quite questionable, as will be indicated later, how much Christianity Berdyaev actually accepted. His mystical anarchism is well-expressed in the words of Dostoevsky's Ivan Karamazov: "I accept God, but I do not accept His world."

It is perhaps to Dostoevsky that Berdyaev owes his belief in a spiritual freedom in Christianity which is free of restraint from either God or man. In his book on Dostoevsky, Berdyaev states that his turning to Christ was not a turning to the Christ of the Gospels, but to the image of Christ as contained in the story of the Grand Inquisitor.

Tolstoy's influence was perhaps less significant, although his background was more like Berdyaev's own. Tolstoy, a count, was also a member of the repentant, breast-beating aristocracy, deeply disturbed by the social irresponsibility of the landed gentry and the general pointlessness of life as he saw it.

One might concentrate on two particular aspects of Berdyaev's thought which are of more than average importance: his concept of the divine and his concept of freedom.

Reference has already been made to his independent Dostoevskian approach to the majesty of God. Berdyaev never accepted the concept of a transcendent God in the Christian sense. Berdyaev sees God not as Lord, but as Liberator from the slavery of the world.

He says:

> "It is unfortunate that Christians have come to speak or drone in the language of meek obsequiousness called humility, and to conduct themselves accordingly, for this belies the Christian conception of man as a God-like spiritual being."[7]

Berdyaev is a believer in God because he is primarily a believer in man. His is a metaphysics of freedom not of being, for freedom is more ultimate than being itself. His God is a limited God, a God who knows needs and suffering, and who can be enriched by human creativeness. "God has need of man, of his creative response to a divine summons."[8] Or again: "God desires a free creative daring in man.."[9]

He accepted as a motto for his book, *The Meaning of the Creative Act,* the motto from Angelus Silesius: "I know that without me God cannot exist for a single second. If I cease to be, He too, must necessarily cease to be."

God is not reached by reason but by mysticism, and the greatest of the mystics to him was Jakob Boehme from whom the rather bizarre theory of the *Ungrund* is derived. From the primordial Absolute itself God the creator comes. Freedom is not dependent on God, but externally exists in the primordial nothing out of which God creates. It is, in a sense, anterior to God himself. God is powerless over the anterior realm and is thus exonerated from responsibility for evil. As in Whitehead, creativity is strongly emphasized, but there is no theory or analogy by which meaningful parallels of human and divine creativity may be drawn. God to the degree that He is known, is known in the language of symbolism.

Lacking a theory of analogy, Berdyaev's anthropomorphism is one of concept not merely of idiom or methodology. Both the theory of freedom and his theory of the divine result from his agony of being unable to resolve the problem of evil. Berdyaev rejects categorically the idea of Providence, stating that if God is present in evil and suffering, in destruction and misery, in plague and cholera, then faith is impossible and rebellion justified. God reconciles man to the suffering of creation not because he reigns, but because he suffers. All theological attempts to resolve the problem of evil Berdyaev sees as intolerable rationalizations. Evil springs from indeterminacy which Providence itself cannot banish.

Berdyaev also expresses horror at the notion of God's seeing from all eternity the outcome of human history. Man is not merely a creature, but self-creative, and in creating self, creates deity. Hell is rejected as totally incompatible with the notion of divinity. He proclaims with much heat that if hell is a reality than he is an atheist.

Berdyaev describes himself as a seeker of truth, a rebel desirous of freedom to the bondage of life, to things, objects, abstractions, ideologies, and the fatalism of history. His search was for an anti-hierarchical personalism—and he phrases it eloquently:

"As the result of a long spiritual and intellectual journey I have arrived at a particularly keen awareness of the fact that every human personality, the personality of the least significant of men, bearing as it does within itself the image of the highest existence, cannot be a means to any end whatever." [10]

He summarizes his views of the anti-freedom forces in his theory of objectivization. As Spengler's civilization is a sclerosed culture that has lost its creative power, so Berdyaev's objectivized man is a destroyed personality. Objectivization is defined as an operation whereby man is brought to servitude, alienation, law, hostility, impersonality, and death. Personality to him is prior to being itself, for being as conceptualized becomes an abstraction—and consequently an enslaving factor.[11]

Personality, as essentially spiritual, exists in the world of freedom, a subjective force in the world of objects. It is not even caused by God—for this to Berdyaev would be a form of objectivization.[12] Objectivization is impersonality, the "ejection of man into the world of determinism." It creates the sociological realities of community, state, nation, and church and imposes restrictive laws of universal obligation. Man's duty is the duty of "transcension", the by-passing of the world of objectivization to the inner core of existence which is the meeting ground with the reality of God, other people, and interior values.[13]

The vague reality of transcension is defined by Berdyaev as an "active dynamic process", an immanent aloofness from depersonalizing society, a realm of freedom where one achieves alike, strength against catastrophe and a direct confrontation of life's supreme personal values. Transcension thus becomes the realization and fulfillment of personality as objectivization is its negation.

Personality as an "individually unrepeatable form" is forever unique as opposed to the world which emphasizes the restricting common aspect of things.

It is indeed important to note that objectivization extends not only to the material conditions of existence but to any systematized or organized rationalization—hence the existentialistic dislike for any systematic philosophy. Moreover, "the criteria of truth is found in the subject and not in the object."[14] And again: "It is expressly in subjectivity and not in objectivity that primary reality is found."[15]

Objectivization is most obvious in the form of society itself which imposes relationships and restrictions inimical to personality. Especially in organic theories of society is man considered a mere subjected part of a whole.[16]

In culture too human nature is seen by Berdyaev as objectivized, exteriorized, and depersonalized. Creativity and artistic genius is inhibited by the "congested and crystallized conditions of culture."[17]

The state is similarly a great depersonalizing agent, possessing no ontological validity other than the exteriorization of the people themselves, ever ready to encroach upon the rights of the human person.

It would be an oversimplification to see in Berdyaev's thought a simple antithesis between spiritual and natural values, since man's slavery may be to himself as well as to nature, war, nationalization, the bourgeois spirit, collectivism, eroticism, aesthetics, and even history.

Berdyaev remains something of a paradox: a philosopher who despised discursive reason; a cadet who hated the military; a fearful hypochondriac who worked calmly through revolution and bombardment; a lover of God who was never quite at home in God's world. Berdyaev was indeed a man of great religious sensibility, but though he believed that a philosophy of personality could be worked out only on a Christian basis, he was hardly a Christian in any recognizably orthodox sense of the term. A man of great insights and great prejudices, he nevertheless, as has been said, underscored and emphasized the fact of freedom when much of the world was ready to forget it.

NOTES

1. *Dream and Reality.* (New York: MacMillan, 1951), pp. 37, 83.
2. Ibid. p. 177.

3. *Le sens de l'histoire*. (Paris. Aubier, n.d.), p. 13.

4. *Solitude and Society*, trans. by George Reavey. (New York: Chas. Scribner's Sons, 1938), p. 137.

5. *Dream and Reality*, p. 40.

6. Ibid. p. 80. In his St. Petersburg period, Berdyaev was much impressed by a book, *Tolstoy and Dostoevsky*, by Dmitri Marezhkovsky.

7. Cf. *Slavery and Freedom* (New York: Charles Scribner's Sons, 1944). Note the resemblance here to the thought of Marx and Nietzsche for whom Christian humility was a "nay-saying" to life.

8. *Dream and Reality*, p. 181.

9. *The Meaning of History* (London: Geoffrey Bles, 1949) p. 41.

10. *Slavery and Freedom* p. 10. Cf. also pp. 44, 45.

11. Ibid., p. 73.

12. Ibid., p. 26.

13. Ibid., p. 29.

14. Ibid., p. 116.

15. Ibid., p. 116.

16. Ibid., p. 116.

17. Ibid., p. 128.

arnold toynbee

AND HIS SYNCRETIC FAITH

by Robert Paul Mohan

The author of this paper remembers lunching with Mr. Toynbee at Bryn Mawr College in March, 1947, on the morning that the historian had received in the mail the first of D. C. Somervel's now-famous abridgements. Except for the so-called pre-abridgement Toynbeeans, few hardy souls had gone through the set of six volumes that were eventually to total more than 6,000 pages, including some 19,000 footnotes.[1]

The publication of the abridgement had great significance in that it brought Toynbee's work to the masses.[2] In a relatively short period of time the abridgment competed on best-seller lists with volumes more preoccupied with the visceral than cerebral. Toynbee was written up in *Life* magazine, asked to lecture all across the country, and was finally accorded the ultimate accolade—the closest thing our limited American secular society can grant next to immortality itself: a cover story in *Time*.

Toynbee's theme in the first six volumes is now well-known. He considers civilizations the units of historical study rather than nations or periods, and identifies five of these societies—and as well as "fossilized" remnants—as still extant: Western Christian, Orthodox Christian, Islamic, Hindu, and Far Eastern. He studies civilizations from the point of view of their origin, growth, breakdown, and disintegration in a manner somewhat reminiscent of Spengler. He insists, however, that civilizations do not have to die, and that they are not organisms.[3]

Neither these five civilizations, nor any of the twenty-one

which have existed, owe their existence to racial or to environmental factors. A civilization which is essentially a product of wills, arises from successful responses to the various challenges of hard countries, new ground, blows, pressures, and penalizations. If the challenge, however, is overwhelming, the civilization aborts, as it were, and what ordinarily would be an incentive to growth becomes instead an arresting force.

Growth is determined by creative minorities and by creative personalities who withdraw from the society they are destined to re-enter and save. Civilizations do not die as the result of an inevitable biological necessity, but from progressive human inadequacy and loss of command over self and enviornment. The idolization of ephemeral institutions at this stage prevents a dynamic attempt to meet new needs, and disintegration follows.

Spengler once identified his *Untergang* (referred to in the title, *Decline of the West*) as a process that was gradual though inevitable, and compared it to the gradual sinking of a ship. Toynbee's disintegration is similarly not one of catastrophic abruptness—except in a few exceptional cases when a military assault has administered a *coup de grâce* to a civilization already in decay.

Disintegration is the result of schism of the body social into a dominant minority and unabsorbed elements called external and internal proletariats. Schism in the soul, the other great cause of disintegration, is characterized by such factors as abandon, truancy, and sense of drift, the sense of sin, the sense of promiscuity, an escape into the past known as archaism, and an escape into tomorrow known as futurism. It is significant that in this earlier period Toynbee sees hope, not in the savior with the sword, time machine, or philosophy, but in the Savior who is God incarnate in a man. Jesus of Nazareth he sees as the single figure alone capable of effecting a palingenesia or a restorative transfiguration.

This apparent preference for Christianity is by no means found in the second series of volumes, quite different in scope and conception, in which Toynbee claims that he would find it hard personally to choose on any other ground than personal convenience between Christianity and Buddhism.[4] Religion, formerly the chrysalis of civilization is now its fulfillment. God is indeed the Lord

of History and history itself is "God revealing himself." It is also
true that Toynbee speaks the language of Christianity quite
fluently. He recounts a dream in which he saw himself clinging
to the crucifix which hangs over the main altar in the Benedictine
Abbey of Ampleforth while a voice said: "Amplexus expecta."
In his last volume Mr. Toynbee suggests that the advice of the
dream to hang on and wait is the advice to our Western World.
Toynbee indeed calls himself a Christian, and sees Christianity
as the "climax of a continuous upward movement of spiritual
progress." Moreover he sees the possibility of a future transfiguration of society that it might effect. But he insists that Christianity
is but one way to the City of God and has no "monopoly of the
Divine Light."

The stage for Toynbee's bizarre syncretic faith is set in the
historian's contention that "post Christian" civilization is not
going to be saved by a return to Christian orthodoxy as found in
established churches. Such a return he considers an illusory refuge
from contemporary needs. The totality of man's needs can only
be served by the new spirtual species which will be a blend of
higher religions.

Toynbee, an enemy of chauvinistic nationalism, had earlier
claimed that universal states, despite the political unity they
effect, are already marked for death—and, in fact, are brought
about after the decay of civilization itself. The universal state
is but the seed bed of the new significant unit of historical study—
the universal church, which was formerly accorded a secondary
position. The man who formerly deprecated the use of civilization
with a capital C, and who presented a relativist phenomenonology
of equivalent cultures, in his later volumes ends up by advocating
a single syncretic faith, made up of the four "higher" religions
of Christianity, Hinduism, Islam, and Mahayana Buddhism. In
short, civilization is to be superseded by the syncretic faith as history's most meaningful reality. A kingdom of heaven is seen
in Toynbee's chiliastic vision as being realized on earth.

Mr. Toynbee's spiritual odyssey is best seen as charted by
Volume VII of his series, and his Gifford Lectures of 1952 and
1953, published as *An Historian's Approach to Religion.*

In the latter volume he seeks a common spirit in the history
of all religions. Mr. Toynbee sees primitive man as worshipping

nature, while man in process of civilization worships self in the form of idolization of parochial and ecumenical communities, and philosophies. After the disintegration of early civilization, Toynbee sees an epiphany of seven higher religions: Judaism, Christianity, Islam, the three Buddhaic religions of Hinduism, Hinayana and Mahayana Buddhism and Zoroastrianism. He sees the higher religions yielding to the blandishments of Power, Logic, and Self.

When Toynbee speaks of a "higher religion" he means that it must have some vision of the one true God and therefore must be monotheistic in character. A higher religion he sees as arising as a response to strife within the body social.[5]

He would consider Christianity, for instance, as an internal proletariat within an Hellenic civilization whose dominant minority had become preoccupied with political organization.

The existing higher religions of Christianity, Islam, Judaism (sometimes excluded) Buddhism, and Hinduism have greater similarities than existing civilizations, but they do differ significantly among themselves.[6]

The basic insights however, are considered supplementary variations of a single theme. To consider one religion superior to the others is to commit the sin of ego-centricity, for if one religion were universally valid, the others would have been rejected.[7] He sees their exclusion as the chief sin of the Judaic religions.

A passage is sometimes cited from Toynbee to indicate the historian's opposition to religious syncretism.

> "In the light of history, I should not expect to see mankind converted to a "syncretistic" religion, constructed artificially out of elements taken from all the existing religions. Such artificial religions have been, and are being manufactured; but I should not expect to see any of them capture the imagination and the feelings of the imagination of mankind."[8]

A later passage, however, indicates the possibility of a natural syncretism in which the "winning" religion absorbs what is best in the ones that become extinct.[9]

Toynbee sees the supplementary character of the higher

religion dictated by a basic psychological need. Christianity and
Islam are seen as extrovert religions emphasizing transcendence,
whereas Hinduism and Buddhism are introvert religions emphasizing immanence. Adjusting his theory to Jung's typology,
he sees Christianity expressing God as love, Hinduism expressing
the contemplative approach to divine omnipresence, Islam emphasizing sensation, and Buddhism the need for extinction of
desire.

"In the human psyche there are divers faculties and
attitudes that are, all alike, importunate in seeking vent.
These are all to be found in every individual human being,
but this in different combinations and different relative
strengths which display themselves in a variety of psychological types. There is not, and cannot be, any psychological type in which all the psychological elements
can have full play at the conscious level; in every type
there are, and are bound to be, some elements that are
repressed into the Subconscious, and in every type the
repressed elements seize, and are bound to seize, every
opportunity of flooding back, unbidden, into Consciousness.
These psychic phenomena prove to have been reflected
in Religion. Each of the living higher religions, and each
of their principal sects, has been attuned to some particular
psychological type or sub-type; and each religion was ever
seeking, like the psychological type which it served, to
achieve the impossible feat of ministering to the whole
gamut of the Psyche's elemental needs for expression. The
feat was impossible because there was not and could not be,
any spiritual organ capable of playing a psychic diapason;
and therefore any existing higher religion that aspired
to become *the* Universal Religion was doomed to disappointment, while any that claimed already to be the
Universal Religion must be unaware of its own intrinsic
limitations. The heavenly music that would satisfy every
need of the soul was not inaudible on Earth, but it was
never audible in a solo; it could be heard only in a
symphony. The divers higher religions must resign themselves to playing limited parts, and must school themselves

to playing these parts in harmony, in order, between them, to fulfill their common purpose of enabling every human being of every psychological type to enter into communion with God the Ultimate Reality.[10]

It is one of the peculiarities of Mr. Toynbee's thesis that religion yields to the blandishments of Power by serving the interest of universal states, yet he apparently considers the all powerful ecumenical state, despite its forcible imposition of birth control and restriction of liberties, an indispensable prelude to the great turn to religion.

Mr. Toynbee's anti-theological bias is evident in his denigration of logic. He rejects creeds or any immutable deposit of Revelation in favor of modernism's concept of religion as an evolving human experience.[11] His attitude to theology and philosophy betrays anti intellectualism, as philosophies are merely cultural effluvia of their civilization, and theologies represent, at best, verbal attempts to reconcile what he calls scientific and prophetic truths. Toynbee moreover recognizes no theory of the analogy of being, and accuses theologians of anthropomorphism in conceiving of God in terms of feeling, will, and intellect.[12]

The third nemesis of higher religion to Toynbee is self: i.e. the attempt to see a particular religion as unique and ultimate. He cites the wars of religion as the results of such ideological pretension and the cause of the disrepute of religion itself.

Toynbee has left the safe terrain of history for divagations into lesser known areas of philosophy and theology. His syncretic faith is an imaginative but gratuitous formulation of an historian turned prophet—a deeply felt personal belief projected into the history of religion. In short his entire effort converges in the syncretic faith of the future which replaces civilization itself as history's most meaningful reality. Toynbee's theory of religion is non-dogmatic, naturalistic, and evolutionary. Man, religious by nature, moves onward and upward, developing new insights and relations to God, but being free, he tends to idolize temporal institutions and invest them with an ultimacy they do not possess. The development of religion itself is the result of a Hegelian conflict of values; antithesis is at the heart of all religious belief.

Although Toynbee grants to the four extant higher religions

a relative permanence, he considers change as becoming more significant than a closed body of Revelation. But perhaps his most damaging religious concept is his identification of fact with science and reason, and religious truth with faith and the unconscious. Theology thus becomes anti-rational and eventually futile, and creeds are the mischievous ephemeral products of theology.[13]

It is difficult to believe that Toynbee actually considers Christianity one belief, or that each man in the future will respect his neighbor's religion, because it is eventually his own. Father Linus Walker and William F. Albright both see an essential pantheism in Toynbee's "Dweller in the Innermost" approach to divine immanence.[14] Balancing these negative factors is his belief in the love and majesty of a God who is the end of man, Toynbee has reverence for the saints, the dignity and freedom of man, and recognizes the *natura vulnerata* as one in which there is a great disparity between aspiration and performance. Toynbee emerges from his intellectual voyage not as a sober historian of religion, but as a religiously sensitive prophet who has projected his dreams and hopes into his highly personal and highly questionable vision.

NOTES

1. Cf. Martin R. P. McGuire. "Toynbee's *A Study of History*: Fruitful Failure on the Grand Scale." *The Catholic Historical Review*, XLII, 3 (October, 1956), 322-239.

2. Cf. The writer's "Toynbee and the Somervell Abridgments." *The American Ecclesiastical Review*, CXXXVII, 1 (July, 1957), p. 39.

3. Although his work is often compared to that of Spengler, grace and free will in Toynbee replace Spengler's biological determinism. Cf. also *Civilization on Trial*, (New York: Oxford University Press, 1948). p. 9; *A Study of History*, I, 87, 135, 150; III, 221, and especially 383.

4. Cf. *An Historian's Approach to Religion*. (New York: Oxford University Press, 1956) pp. 131-146, 180-182; *A Study of History*, VII, pp. 449, 735; *Christianity among the Religions of the World*, (New York: Charles Scribner's Sons, 1957).

5. Ibid. V, pp. 96-152.

6. *Christianity Among the Religions of Mankind*, pp. 24-28.

7. *An Historian's Approach to Religion*, p. 138.

8. *Christianity Among the Religions of the World,* p. 103.

9. Ibid., p. 110.

10. *A Study of History,* VII, p. 734.

11. *A Study of History,* VII, p. 456.

12. Ibid. pp. 467-468.

13. Ibid. VII, p. 428.

14. Linus Walker, A review of *A Study of History, The Thomist,* XVIII (April, 1955); and William I. Albright *From the Stone Age to Christianity.* (New York: Doubleday. 1951) pp. 5-6.

PSYCHOLOGISTS AS PHILOSOPHERS
JOHN DEWEY: PHILOSOPHER IN THE MARKET PLACE
SIGMUND FREUD AND THE DEVELOPMENT OF
PSYCHOANALYSIS
CARL JUNG: PHILOSOPHER OF THE UNCONSCIOUS

john dewey

PHILOSOPHER IN THE MARKET PLACE
by George C. Reilly, O.P.

Among the twentieth-century thinkers who have had a serious influence on their time, John Dewey occupies a significant place. He has had an impact not merely on philosophy but to a greater extent on education and therefore on our national life. He is, moreover, one of the few American philosophers who have had an effect that extends beyond his own country; this an understandable fact, since it is only in our own time that American philosophy has become of age. This is pointed out at the beginning of this examination of Dewey's thought, not as a mere historical fact but as an important key to the understanding of Dewey's philosophical endeavor. For John Dewey was above all a product of his time and his environment, and he continued in his own fashion the pragmatic tradition deriving from C. S. Peirce and William James. The American dream of success as the true test of the value of any activity, whether it be educational, industrial, financial, social or political, had found in pragmatism a philosophical justification. The real test of the worth of anything must be found in its ability to produce results. Dewey tells us: "The hypothesis which works is the true one."[1] And by the same token, the philosophy of pragmatism seemed to have found objective and experimental proof of its worth in the facts of American life. We had, for example, an industrial system that worked, at least up to a point, and a political system that was stable and worked better than most others. What we seemed to lack was a complete and rounded philosophy that had a direct and obvious relation to this environment, this cradle of activity, this setting of all experience. John Dewey set out to provide one. If he did not have this explicitly in mind at the beginning of his philosophical career, it gradually crystallized in his thoughts until in one of his most important books, published in 1929, he set down what is practically his basic philosophical platform. "Philosophy's central problem", Dewey tells us, "is the relation that exists between the beliefs about the natures of things *due to natural science* to beliefs about values, using that word to designate whatever is taken to have rightful authority in the direction of conduct."[2] In this statement, Dewey clearly indicates the main elements of his philosophical structure and the important currents of thought that were to sway him until the end of his career.

Noticeable at once is the radical empiricism that was to be a dominant feature of his thinking. It would be very hard to find any more devoted partisan of the scientific and experimental method than John Dewey. For him, this is the one method that could lead to advances in knowledge and he applied it not merely to the area of natural bodies, where no one questioned its value, but to all fields of inquiry without exception. There were several influences at hand that made Dewey the most articulate champion of this method and its universal extension. First, it seemed to him that the history of philosophy shows us a long record of controversy and confusion. System succeeds system, philosopher fights with philosopher, and there appears to be no way to settle the endless and fruitless arguments or to bring peace to the vociferous proponents of contradictory opinions and theories. To Dewey's mind, all these views were equally worthless and outmoded; they were sterile and completely divorced from real life; they were in his words "diseased formulations". Secondly, the success, in the practical order, of the American dream was an object lesson in the seeming miracles that could be produced by putting the scientific method to work. The achievements of the modern world in industry, commerce, communications, and transportation, all these were the fruits of the application of the experimental method, which had opened up a new era in all these fields and others with consequent blessings for humanity. Here was a method that really worked; why not use it? Why not apply it to other fields where it was so obviously needed? And so Dewey officiated at the marriage of scientism and pragmatism. It had been said, in times past, that philosophy bakes no bread. If that were true, then so much the worse for an outmoded spectator philosophy which deserved only a decent burial. The new type of thinking would get out into the market place. It would be pragmatic; it would be experimental; and, finally, in Dewey's view it would be socially orientated toward morals and education. In this way the beliefs about the natures of things that we drew from natural science could actually be related to our beliefs about values.[3]

John Dewey is not the clearest writer in the world, and his turgid prose is a constant trial and source of bafflement to the student who is trying to find out what he means. It contains a number of contradictions, many obscurities, and far too many words that Dewey has suddenly and without warning endowed with a new meaning they never previously bore. But if this is noted, and if it is recognized that there is a certain natural development of his thought over the years, there are three basic elements that remain constant in his philosophy. It is always pragmatic, experimental, and socially orientated.

The pragmatism derives from Peirce and James, as Dewey admits,[4] but he greatly disliked all systems and was not at all happy to be classified as a member of any particular school. He even found distasteful the name of pragmatism, and preferred to call his general view instrumentalism, thus stressing the point that knowledge, thoughts, and ideas are instrumental toward action. It is activity that is basic, for in Dewey's thought there is no being but only becoming. There are no inert essences but only events; there is no real stability but only change and evolution. There is no such thing as knowledge for its own sake; knowledge is for action and only for action; without action it is incomplete. The contemplative and the speculative are sterile and useless; it is only the practical and the active that have any importance. Ideas, hypotheses, indeed philosophers themselves, all must be brought before the bar of practice and submitted to the test of practical life. Truth has only an instrumental value; its role is to guide to action; the most certain test of truth is in its practical consequences. This thoroughgoing activism which pervades and controls his whole philosophical outlook is one of the most attractive and easily accepted of Dewey's opinions because it stresses an element of truth. In fact, it is precisely a half truth in the strictest sense because it cuts the human mind in half, eliminating the speculative element in knowledge, and admitting only the practical. This dependence on a half truth guarantees and ensures the characteristic superficiality which pervades all pragmatic philosophy, but it also guarantees an immediate appeal to the superficial mind.

The second dominant trait of Dewey's thinking is experimentalism. At first sight this would seem to refer to a method alone, but for Dewey experience is not only the method of philosophy but also the very content. As method, it is very easy to understand the fascination it had for the mind of Dewey. He had seen and appreciated the practical results of scientific investigation using the experimental approach; he was well aware of the success of modern scientific methods of research, and his very pragmatism forced him to attempt to extend this method to all fields of knowledge and action. Experimental thought is for him the only thought worth while, and in one of his books he tells us: "This book represents the conviction that the needed and steadying factor is found in adopting as the end of the endeavor that attitude of mind, that habit of thought which we call scientific."[5] No other method has any value, and in one of his major works he assures us of the futility of attempting to use any other method: "The problems to which non-empirical method gives rise in philosophy are blocks to inquiry; blind alleys; they are puzzles rather than problems."[6]

The grasp of what Dewey means by experience as the content of philosophy is a bit more difficult. In ordinary discourse we tend to tie up experience with knowledge either directly or indirectly. Thus, when we see or feel something, we would be having an experience, and experience would be something made available to us, at least primarily, by knowledge. For Dewey, however, experience is something much broader than knowledge. In a sense we may say that for him experience embraces all reality. In our terminology it would be co-extensive with being. For Dewey experience means things interacting in certain ways. Both subject and object, mind and matter are all elements of experience, which in the first place has no divisions, but is continuous in an unanalyzed totality. Later on, of course, we do make distinctions as the result of reflection, but knowledge is only a small part of experience, that part which makes it possible for us to control the other elements of experience.

The third dominant feature of Dewey's philosophy is its social orientation, which actually is a necessary consequence of his pragmatic tendencies. For if the purpose of philosophical investigation is not to know reality merely, but rather to control it and thereby to attempt the enrichment and perfection of human life, then there are inevitably tremendous problems awaiting solution in society. Two types of social problems particularly interested Dewey: moral problems and educational problems, and he has left us a respectable amount of writing about each.

To appreciate the singular importance of these three dominant traits of the philosophy of John Dewey, it may help to stress the fact that they are not merely implicit in his writings but are quite explicitly aimed at and glorified. As Dewey read history, there had been in recent times three radical revolutions that had totally changed modern life. These were, first, the intellectual revolution brought about by the discoveries of modern science; second, the industrial revolution growing out of scientific development and consequent upon the invention and production of modern machinery; and third, the social revolution stemming from the growth of modern democracy. The development of science because of the use of the experimental method led directly to the revolution in industry; these two together then prepared the ground for democracy. Hence the three leading ideas in Dewey's view of life: Science, industry, and democracy; and the corresponding dominant trends in his philosophy: experimentalism, pragmatism, and socialism.

Up to this point attention has been concentrated on the main and dominating themes in Dewey's philosophy rather than on specific doctrines, because of our conviction that the main thrust of instrumentalism is more intelligible and more distinctive than many of its individual elements which are apt to be obscure and baffling. There are, however, a number of precise problems to which Dewey offered solutions, and a consideration of several of them will prove advantageous in our attempt to understand what he is saying. His theory of knowledge is, for example, a key element in the entire system.

Dewey wrote at great length on his theory of knowledge and in book after book he makes clear his conviction that the true nature of knowledge is completely missed by the outmoded theories of the past. He is particularly vehement in condemning and deriding what he calls the "spectator theory of knowledge", which to him implied a passive contemplation of a realm of eternal essences and fixed beings somehow distinct from the changing temporal world of experience. His own words are very clear in this connection: "Nowadays if a man, say a physicist or chemist, wants to know something, the last thing he does is merely to contemplate. He does not look in however earnest and prolonged way upon the object expecting thereby that he will detect its fixed and characteristic form. He does not expect any amount of aloof scrutiny to reveal to him any secrets. He proceeds to do something, to bring some energy to bear upon the substance to see how it reacts; he places it under unusual conditions in order to induce some change."[7] Knowledge is the result of activity, of this doing something arising out of a doubtful situation. To know is to do something and the satisfactory outcome of the doing is termed knowledge. Because knowledge is the result of inquiry, it is not something final, settled or static, but like inquiry itself it is progressive. To quote Dewey again: "In scientific inquiry, the criterion of what is taken to be settled, or to be knowledge, is being *so* settled that it is available as a resource in further inquiry; not in being so settled as not to be subject to revision in further inquiry."[8] Knowledge is instrumental and intermediate between the organism and environment, enabling man to gain control over objects. As Dewey remarks: "Men go on thinking only because of practical friction or strain somewhere . . . thinking is essentially the solution of tension."[9] Out of all this, it becomes clear that the ordinary distinctions between sensation and intellection, between concrete and abstract knowledge have no meaning for Dewey. His doctrines of experience and the continuity of all things rule them out. His theory, indeed, as it develops gets into ever more serious difficulties and farther away from reality, to the extent that it has become a target of criticism from all sides. One of his critics has shown that Dewey's theory of knowledge closely parallels the explanation which St. Thomas Aquinas gives of *practical* knowledge directed toward the achievement of a practical end, but that it misses the point as an explanation of knowledge in general.[10]

As for a metaphysical doctrine, the anti-intellectualism which went along with his pragmatism in the early days of his career led Dewey to disparage the validity of any metaphysical speculation. But reality was too much for him and gradually he began to develop a naturalistic metaphysics. In most philosophical constructions, knowledge follows upon reality and reports it, but Dewey's pragmatic bent forces him to make his metaphysics an outcome and a consequence of his theory of knowledge. Since knowledge is instrumental, knowledge must determine reality because it is a tool by which man makes reality amenable to his needs and purposes. There is here no relationship of being and knowing, but rather one of becoming and doing. There are no subsisting beings of which reality is made up. Reality is rather an indeterminate process. "Every existence", Dewey tells us, "is an event."[11] in accord with his principle of continuity he seems to make all things one great flux. All is becoming, all is process. As Dewey expresses it: "Structure and process, substance and accidence, matter and energy, permanence and flux, one and many, continuity and discreteness, order and progress, law and liberty, uniformity and growth, tradition and innovation, rational will and impelling desires, proof and discovery, the actual and the possible ,are names given to various phases of the conjunction."[12] On the other hand he finds himself faced with the common sense opinion that there are actually different things, persons and events in the world of nature. Dewey in this case seems baffled by the contradiction and takes refuge in obscurity to the extent that one of his followers offers this criticism: "These passages indicate that Dewey intends to use 'continuity' so vaguely and to press his assumption of it so far, that he tends to dispose on purely a priori grounds of questions concerning the actual amount of empirical differences there is between things. Whether minds gifted with a faculty of thought exist, or whether awareness occurs and is not described in physical terms—these are questions of fact: you cannot settle them as Dewey seems disposed to do, by merely saying that if they did exist, there would be more discontinuity in nature than you like. Obviously there is some discontinuity in *some* sense." [13]

This sort of criticism of some of Dewey's solutions to specific problems is commonplace among his contemporaries and is documented in a volume entitled *The Philosophy of John Dewey,*[14] which is the first volume of a series called *The Library of Living Philosophers,* in which a number of philosophers comment on the philosophy of one man, who is then permitted a rejoinder. In Dewey's case, although there is a consistent approval of his main themes, there is also steady criticism of his specific answers to certain problems, to which criticism Dewey reacted strongly in his rejoinder. It is not my purpose here to go into detail about these criticisms, but only to note them as part of a pair of paradoxes surrounding Dewey and the acceptance of his work.

He is generally recognized as a representative and important American philosopher, yet very few seem to have any inclination to accept his specific philosophical opinions. This is the first paradox; pragmatism retains some of its general influence, but Dewey's instrumentalism seems a dead issue. But there is a second paradox. Dewey's influence as a philosopher is at the moment very slight, yet his influence as an educator is still extremely strong. Again his specific solutions to philosophical problems are generally rejected, while his general influence in education remains a vital one. There are good reasons for this state of affairs.

As a pragmatic thinker, Dewey was always aware of the practical influence of philosophy on education, indeed for him there was no such thing as a philosophy which merely knew reality or any phase of it. Philosophy had to be practical and to issue in an attempt to change and control the various elements of the human situation. Every philosophical theory naturally develops into an educational theory or else it soon dies, and Dewey saw very clearly that "education is the laboratory in which philosophic distinctions become concrete and are tested." [15] Dewey's educational theories, therefore, are bound to have all the virtues and also all the inconveniences of his general philosophical views. Education thus must be pragmatic, it must be experimental, and ultimately it must be socialized.

While teaching at the University of Chicago, Dewey had been the head of the Department of Philosophy, Psychology and

Education, and it was during this period that he founded a school at the university in which his ideas could be worked out. His foundation came to be known as the Laboratory School, and was the original example of the active and progressive school, in which the child was to learn by doing. When Dewey transferred to Columbia University in 1904, he immediately became associated with the Teachers College of that university. Through his own teaching there, and that of his students there and elsewhere, Dewey's influence on education spread to teachers and administrators throughout the country and, indeed, abroad for his influence has not been negligible either in England or on the continent.

It may be noticed that we have been content up to this point to attempt only an exposition of Dewey's thought, hoping to make it intelligible, with no serious attempt to criticize or evaluate it excepting a few animadversions whose purpose was mainly to aid in the exposition. Now, however, it is time to ask: What is the significance of Dewey, and what is our assessment of his philosophical contributions? Let us admit at once that such assessment is not easy, for the days are long gone when a philosopher's views could be summed up and disposed of in a lengthy syllogism. Dewey's contribution to philosophy, moreover, is a mixed one, containing both good and bad. It may be interesting to preface this evaluation with a passage from one of Dewey's books citing a German critic's description of pragmatism and Dewey's reaction to it:

> Now a recent German critic has described pragmatism as "Epistemologically, nominalism, psychologically, voluntarism, cosmologically, energism; metaphysically, agnosticism; ethically, meliorism on the basis of the Bentham-Mill utilitarianism."[1] It may be that pragmatism will turn out to be all of this formidable array; but even should it, the one who thus defines it has hardly come within earshot of it. For whatever else pragmatism is or is not, the pragmatic spirit is primarily a revolt against the habit of mind which disposes of anything whatever—even so humble as a new method in Philosophy—by tucking it away, after this fashion, in the pigeon holes of a filing cabinet.

Dewey gives a footnote:

> [1] The affair is even more portentous in the German with its capital letters and series of *muses*: "Gewiss ist der Pragmatismus erkenntniss-theoretisch Nominalismus, psychologisch Voluntarismus, naturphilosophisch Energismus, metaphysisch Agnosticismus, ethisch Meliorismus auf Grundlage des Bentham-Millschen Utilitarismus." [16]

From the negative point of view we find it necessary to reject his three dominant themes, at least in the exaggerated emphasis found in his system. His activism and practicalism are overdone, and it is not difficult to see the reason for this in the denial of speculative knowledge and the overemphasis on practical knowledge alone. This splits the human mind and takes one part, and the lesser part at that, as the whole. Knowledge for its own sake, i.e., speculative knowledge, is quite real and in fact is primary; knowledge for use is secondary. In this matter Dewey was badly mistaken; not all knowledge is instrumental, but some knowledge can be instrumental; and even though knowledge must be prior to use, yet some knowledge can be useful. Dewey's restriction of all knowledge to the practical truncates the human mind, and makes all our knowledge unintelligible.

Again experimentalism is badly overrated by Dewey. As a method of investigation it surely has an important role to play, but of its nature it is restricted to matter, and to bodies that can be dealt with by the senses. It properly applies only to things that can be weighed and measured, and it is indispensable in this its proper field. But there is a whole universe of important things to which it can have no application. In the face of this uncomfortable area of reality, Dewey simply ignored or denied its existence. But this will not help, for the fact is that these things do exist; and they can be investigated by the peculiarly human sciences, the sciences of the mind and the spirit, of the moral life, of religion, and of God. These matters are totally outside the scope of the experimental type of research. Just as we do not deny the value of the practical but do reject universalizing it, so we are well aware of the area in which scientific experimentation is useful and necessary, but we also realize that there are many fields of investigation not amenable to this method. Something very similar is true concerning Dewey's concept of society. It is not well balanced but rather leads to an over-socialization. The individual becomes completely subordinated to society and personal destiny is lost sight of. Here again, extreme individualism is a curse to mankind, for man is truly a social animal and naturally so, but it still remains true that the individual is prior to society, and has a destiny that is quite distinct from his social end.

Dewey's dominant themes, therefore, are all partial truths, and the realization of this points up the inadequacy of his philosophical construction. Similar difficulties affect his views of knowledge, of man and of reality in general, and these mistakes in turn are carried over into his moral and educational theories, all of which need careful balancing by truths that Dewey simply ignored. This, however, being said, it is still not the whole story. Whitehead, a better philosopher than Dewey, remarks in his appraisal of Dewey's philosophy that "refutation has its legitimate place in philosophic discussion, but it should never form the final chapter."[17] And so we can recognize and welcome the positive contributions that Dewey has made to the total philosophical endeavor. If he overstresses the practical, perhaps it was because the speculative had been previously overstressed. The lesson for us would be to make certain that the practical receives its due at the hands of philosophers, not to the neglect of the speculative but in complement to it. We are further warned to make much clearer the distinction that Dewey missed; and finally we are made aware of a real lag in the development of those philosophic disciplines that are genuinely practical, the fields of morality and art.

If, again, Dewey overemphasizes the experimental, the lesson for us would be to seek the balanced view by not neglecting that method where it is useful, and by taking advantage of its achievements in all the fields related to the philosophy of nature. If, finally, Dewey overemphasizes the social, the lesson would be never to forget the social nature of man, and the contributions that the philosopher is called upon to make in the solution of social problems. We need not agree with Dewey's thought that philosophy's major task is to help man control his environment, for this is a mistake. But the truth is clear that when the philosopher can bring his knowledge to bear in assisting man to enrich his life, the philosopher's assistance should be at hand.

Apart from these general contributions, which are principally in the line of emphasis rather than specific doctrine, there are many other problems to whose solution Dewey added elements of completion or clarity. His theory of knowledge, for example, is inadequate, but his investigations help to clarify our own views. His metaphysics is superficial and truncated, but his insistence on unity and continuity among all the things that make up reality is an antidote to the exaggerated picture of essences that have no connection one with another. Many other examples might be adduced, but these are sufficient to indicate that no serious investigation, however imperfect, can fail to contribute something to the completion and the perfection of our knowledge.

Writing as one who accepts St. Thomas as his primary guide and master, I find that there is not only a content to be appreciated and maintained, but a vast work of development to be carried on. St. Thomas has made a contribution, a unique contribution, to the philosophic endeavor, but he has not said the last word on anything. His work is never to be a barrier to further knowledge, but rather a beacon pointing the way to the never-ending growth of philosophical knowledge. He himself gives us the guidance to follow in studying and assimilating the opinions of others. He tells us both explicitly and implicitly in his own philosophical procedure:

1. The study of philosophy is directed not to a knowledge of what men think but to how the truth of things stands.[18] The same idea is to be found in many other places in his writings, for example: "In accepting or rejecting opinions, a man must not be influenced by love or hatred of him who proffers the opinions but only by the certainty of the truth."[19]

2. The study of philosophy is advanced not by endless argumentation and denial, but by a careful weighing of opinions, and openness to truth of any kind. "Just as in court," says St. Thomas, "no judgment can be passed before the arguments for both sides are heard, so also it is necessary for the philoso-

pher to heed the opinions and doubts of different authors in
the fomation of a more definitive judgment." [20]

3. The advance of philosophical knowledge does not come about
   only from one system or from a few men, but from the selected fruits of all men's endeavors; not from eclecticism ut
   from development, St. Thomas again puts the matter most
   clearly:

   > We must give ear to the opinions of the ancients, no matter
   > who it is that made the statements. There is a twofold
   > benefit in this. We thereby acquire for our own use what-
   > ever was correctly said by them; and we avoid that in
   > which they erred. [21]

4. In the construction of truth the cooperation of all men is
   needed. On this point St. Thomas is most emphatic:

   > In establishing truth we are aided by others in two ways.
   > We receive direct assistance from those who have already
   > discovered truths. If every one of the earlier thinkers has
   > found an element of truth, then these elements taken
   > together and unified are to the later investigators a power-
   > ful help towards a comprehensive knowledge of truth. We
   > are indirectly helped by earlier investigators in so far as
   > their errors after diligent discussion give us the opportunity
   > of a clearer exposition of the truth in these matters. It is
   > therefore proper that we be grateful to all who have
   > aided us in the pursuit of truth. [22]

With such principles in mind, we can be sure that the small
contribution of any one man can be integrated into the more
general picture. Even philosophers who have often been in error
have made genuine contributions to the development of philosophy.
We are right in glorying in our own tradition and in our own
rich heritage which has drawn nourishment from the main line
of human thought down through the ages, but we shall be the
wealthier if we are eager to accept truth from whatever source,
realizing that each glimpse of partial truth derives from that
truth which is whole and eternal.

NOTES

1. John Dewey, Reconstruction in Philosophy (New York: New American Library, 1952), p. 129.

2. *The Quest for Certainty* (New York: Minton Balch and Co., 1929), p. 256.

3. *Quest for Certainty*, p. 256.

4. John Dewey, "From Absolutism to Experimentalism," in *Contemporary American Philosophy*. Edited by G. P. Adams and W. P. Montague (New York: The Macmillan Co., 1930) Vol. II, 13-27.

5. John Dewey, *How We Think* (New York: D. C. Heath and Co., 1933), p. iii.

6. John Dewey, *Experience and Nature* (New York: W. W. Norton and Co., 1929).

7. *Reconstruction in Philosophy*, p. 100.

8. John Dewey, *Logic, The Theory of Inquiry* (New York: Henry Holt and Co., 1938), p. 245.

9. John Dewey, "Social Psychology," *Psychological Review*, I, (1894), p. 408.

10. E. F. Smith, O.P., *A Thomistic Appraisal of the Philosophy of John Dewey* (Washington, D. C.: Pontifical Faculty of the Immaculate Conception, 1955), p. 141.

11. *Experience and Nature*, p. 69.

12. *Ibid.*, p. 76.

13. W. T. Feldman, *The Philosophy of John Dewey* (Baltimore: Johns Hopkins Press, 1934), p. 84.

14. *The Philosophy of John Dewery*, Vol. I of *The Library of Living Philosophers*, ed Paul Schilpp (Evanston and Chicago: Northwestern University, 1939).

15. John Dewey, *Democracy and Education* (New York: The Macmillan Company, 1922), p. 384.

16. John Dewey, *The Influence of Darwin on Philosophy, and Other Essays in Contemporary Thought* (New York: Henry Holt and Company, 1910. Reprint: New York: Peter Smith, 1951), pp. iii-iv.

17. A. N. Whitehead, in *The Philosophy of John Dewey*, op. cit., p. 478.

18. *In I De coelo*, lect. 22.

19. *In XII Metaph.*, lect. 9. Cf. *In II De coelo*, lect. 17; S. Th. I, 32, a. 1 ad 2.

20. *In III Metaph.*, lect. 1. Cf. S. Th., 97, a. 1.

21. *In I De anima*, lect. 2.

22. *In II Metaph.*, lect. 1.

BIBLIOGRAPHY

I. Works by John Dewey:
Dewey, John. *Leibniz's New Essays Concerning the Human Understanding.*

A *Critical Exposition*. Chicago: S. C. Griggs and Company, 1888. Reprinted in 1902 by Scott, Foresman & Co., Chicago.

————. *The Influence of Darwin on Philosophy and Other Essays in Contemporary Thought*. New York: Henry Holt and Company, 1910.

————. *A Common Faith*. New Haven: Yale University Press, 1934.

————. *Art as Experience*. New York: Minton, Balch and Co., 1934.

————. *Democracy and Education*. New York: The Macmillan Company, 1916.

————. *Experience and Nature*. New York: W. W. Norton and Company, Inc. 1929.

————. *How We Think*. New York: D. C. Heath and Company, 1933.

————. *Logic, The Theory of Inquiry*. New York: Henry Holt and Company, 1938.

————. *The Quest for Certainty*. New York: Minton, Balch and Company, 1929.

————. *Philosophy and Civilization*. New York: G. P. Putnam's Sons, 1931.

————. *Problems of Men*. New York: Philosophical Library, 1946.

————. *Reconstruction in Philosophy*. New York: New American Library, 1952.

II. Works on John Dewey:

Feldman, W. T. *The Philosophy of John Dewey*. Baltimore: The John Hopkins Press, 1934.

Hook, Sidney (ed.). *John Dewey: Philosopher of Science and Freedom, A Symposium*. New York: The Dial Press, 1950.

Ratner, Joseph (ed.). *Intelligence in the Modern World. John Dewey's Philosophy*. New York: The Modern Library, 1939.

Schilpp, Paul Arthur (ed.). *The Library of Living Philosophers*. Vol. I, "The Philosophy of John Dewey." New York: Tudor Publishing Company, 1951.

Smith, Vincent Edward. *Idea Men of Today*. Milwaukee: The Bruce Publishing Company, 1950.

Smith, E. F. *A Thomistic Appraisal of the Philosophy of John Dewey*. Washington, D. C.: Pontifical Faculty of the Immaculate Conception, 1955.

Collins, James. *Three Paths in Philosophy*. Chicago: Henry Regnery Company, 1962.

Sigmund Freud

AND THE DEVELOPMENT OF PSYCHOANALYSIS

by Marius G. Schneider, O.F.M.

Sigmund Freud occupies a unique position among the philosophers whose systems of thought are discussed in this volume.[1] As a psychiatrist, he was not a philosopher by profession. He even denied any philosophical ambition, and attempted to substantiate this denial by a confession of his constitutional incapability of philosophical thought.[2] Yet he alone succeeded in playing that leading role in our society which both the pre-christian and the post-christian philosopher so much desire. Husserl, Heidegger, and Sartre may be known in various academic circles. Freud alone captures the scientific and popular mind alike by his ideas. Whether they bless or curse the influence of psychoanalysis, historians and critics of the American scene are unanimous in admitting the tremendous efficacy Freud's concepts have shown in forming and understanding human behavior in the United States. Freud's "ideas spread," writes a leading American psychologist,[3] "until they pervaded all thinking about human motivation both among the psychologists and among the lay public." "Not one field of the social sciences," states another, "has escaped the impact of the concepts and technics that are included within the term psychoanalysis."[4] Freud's "influence has permeated the mental hygiene movement, social work, child psychology, and even the more formal aspects of education," finds Sears.[5] His ideas have been "employed in the interpretation of normal and abnormal behavior of individuals and groupings of individuals. Persons and epochs of history, crime and delinquency, labor problems and the process of education and re-education have been analyzed in psychoanalytic terms. Many workers in the fields of the social sciences ... would find in psychoanalytic doctrines the key to all social adjustment."[6]

Freud was well aware of the enthusiastic welcome which his far-reaching and revolutionary revelations about human nature received in the United States. However, it was not idle joy that accompanied this observation. The father of psychoanalysis was most grateful for the recognition of his work in American scientific circles. Rejected and ridiculed by the allegedly tradition-minded and authority-fixed European science,[7] he experienced G. Stanley Hall's invitation to speak during the twentieth anniversary celebration of Clark University as an unforgettable personal satisfaction and as a real opportunity for his psychoanalytic movement. This unexpected academic support of his opinions was rewarded with his eulogies of the fair and open-minded American scholar.[8] However, he could not suppress misgivings about the broadminded acceptance and sudden popularity of psychoanalysis in America. Of course, Freud had not the least objection to the propagation and profession of his ideas. His early identification with the "Semitic Hannibal" and his "deeply neurotic" longing for Rome,[9] his hatred of the religious view of man, and his desire to replace it with his psychological completion of the supposed Copernican and Darwinian devaluation of man's position in the universe[10] could find fulfillment only in a popularization of his message. But these psychoanalytic ideas were to represent his doctrine purely and integrally. He believed that there were reasons to doubt that a sincere and serious interest in the genuine meaning of his teaching lay behind the apparent popularity of psychoanalysis in America.

A truly friendly disposition toward psychoanalysis appears questionable, Freud writes,[11] when Americans always seem to have money for every possible and impossible scientific or pseudo-scientific endeavor, but can never be induced to sacrifice a cent for his psychoanalytic institutions. American scientific efforts to solve psychoanalytic problems can also easily be discounted. American contributions to psychoanalytic theory are rare and offer scarcely anything new. Psychoanalysis is used by American psychiatrists and neurologists as a therapeutic method, but as a rule these men show little interest in its scientific problems and cultural importance. What is worse, American physicians and authors reveal a very defective acquaintance with psychoanalysis; all they know is its name and a few of its catchwords, and yet they boast of the authority of their judgment. Hence they confuse psychoanalysis with other doctrinal systems or they create an ugly mishmash of psychoanalysis and other elements, and advance this deplorable procedure as a proof of their broadmindedness, whereas actually it demonstrates only their lack of judgment. Freud believes that the explanation of such unscientific behavior may be found in the general American tendency to neglect theory in favor of hasty practical applications and to study an object like psychoanalysis in sources that are secondary and often inferior instead of in the original texts.

A reader of genuine psychoanalytic sources may sympathize both with the author of these accusations and with the accused. Freud had reason to be dissatisfied with the American popularity of his ideas. Most of the seemingly enthusiastic supporters of his opinions are not seriously interested in psychoanalysis. They in fact use his doctrinal constructions merely as slogans, as clever aperçus, or as oversimplified conceptions divorced from their genuine psychoanalytic meaning.

However, one wonders whether this apparently unscientific manipulation of Freudian doctrines is occasioned only and mainly by American pragmatic preferences. Perhaps American light-heartedness is not completely innocent of a somewhat frivolous use and abuse of Freudian notions, and it could well be that the healthy American commonsense is more responsible for avoiding a serious encounter with the genuine psychoanalytic meaning and sources than is a lack of scientific conscience. If such suspicions are justified, Freud had every reason to fear rather than hope for a scientific study of his teaching. An objective investigation of psychoanalysis would reveal such a completely unfounded, one-sided, hopeless, and loveless picture of human nature and existence, that no American of sound mind would take it as a realistic representation of human reality. Our discussion of the development of psychoanalysis from a psychiatric system to a comprehensive philosophical anthropology may perhaps justify this judgment, in spite of all the limitations imposed by the manifold and complicated aspects of the problem.[12]

Psychoanalysis as a psychotherapeutic method originated about 1880 in the sickroom of the later famous Anna O.[13] This unfortunate but highly gifted young woman had suddenly fallen ill while nursing her dying father. In time she developed almost the entire catalogue of possible hysterical symptoms; for instance, she was unable to swallow water. One evening during hypnosis, which her physician, Dr. Joseph Breuer, usually applied as a means of loosening inhibitions in order to discuss her problems, she started to describe an incident that had happened years before. She had entered the room of her English tutor just as she was offering her little dog water out of her personal drinking glass. With every sign of the revulsion once suppressed out of respect for a disliked authority, Anna seemed to re-experience the forgotten event. At the end of her story she asked for a glass of water, drank healthily, and awoke from the hypnosis to find the glass at her lips. The difficulty in drinking was cured once and for all. Modern psychotherapy was born. The psychogenic origin of hysterical symptoms and a psychological method of treating them were discovered. It was indeed a happy event. Psychoanalysis and the manifold psychotherapeutic systems of our century are the results of the development of the promising discovery made by Joseph Breuer.

Sigmund Freud was at that time not interested in an analysis of human personalities. He was still a student of medicine at the University of Vienna, analyzing nerve tracts of the brain and spinal cords of primitive fishes with the stubborn perseverance and imperturbable concentration characteristic of his approach to any object or idea that fired his imagination.[14] However, he was soon to hear about the discovery of psychological therapy, since Breuer was his friend and financial helper.[15] Later, when forced to give up his academic ambitions and to go into medical practice, he proved himself the driving force behind the new psychotherapeutic movement, and in 1895 succeeded in persuading Breuer to publish together with him the new discovery and an interpretation of it in *Studies on Hysteria*.[16] Psychoanalysis, the Freudian system of psychiatry was on its way.

Psychoanalysis starts as an interpretation of the origin, nature, and cure of hysteria. On the basis of six cases treated by the authors of the *Studies,* the psychogenic character of this type of neurosis is defended against the prevailing neurological understanding of the disease. "Hysterics suffer mainly from reminiscences," reads the thesis.[17] These memories concern "traumas", i.e., distressing experiences of fright, anxiety, shame, or physical pain which were not abreacted, that is, expressed in voluntary or involuntary behavior, and had been forgotten.[18] The pathogenic nature of such unabreacted experiences is explained by way of theoretical assumptions which Breuer and Freud had learned from their teacher Brücke. Faithful to a youthful oath never in his future career as a scientist to admit the existence of other than material forces, Brücke in his physiology courses had reduced manifestations of life to quantitative conditions of physiological processes, identified the psychic personality with the nervous system, and considered the principle of the conservation of energy as the supreme law of a living organism.[19] These doctrines serve his former students for their interpretation of observed hysterical phenomena.[20] Affective experiences represent large quantities of excitation of the nervous system, they declare. The principle of the constancy of energy in the organism demands the discharge of this excitation. Since in traumas the normal abreaction cannot take place, their sum of excitation impinging upon the nervous system enforces an involuntary outlet. The affective energy connected with the distressing experience separates from its forgotten representation and is converted into hysterical symptoms. A cure is achieved when the traumatic energy is reconnected with its original representation and abreacted in a re-experience of the pathogenic event. Since personal or social circumstances of the painful experience rendered the trauma unconscious, the required abreaction can be realized only by way of psychotherapeutic means, which at this stage of the history of psychoanalysis is seen in hypnosis.

Freud soon changed this first theory and therapy of hysteria, but he always remained faithful to its mechanistic conception of psychic life. Qualitative differences of psychic phenomena are more and more disregarded and reduced to quantitative conditions of antagonistic or even of identical instinctual energies. The fate of these instinctual forces, which are lastly identified with somatic or biochemical processes,[21] is determined by their quantity and ultimately by the principle of the conservation of energy, later called the pleasure-principle.

The element most characteristic of psychoanalysis does not play a distinctive role in this first theoretical structure of psychotherapy. Sexuality is listed by Breuer as the most powerful of the organism's physiological needs calling for discharge.[22] But its causal relationship to hysteria is explicitly denied by both authors for some of the six cases dealt with in the *Studies*. However, Freud had already gone far ahead of his friend's discoveries and notions at the time of publication of the book. He suspected sexuality to be an etiological factor not only behind hysteria but behind every form of neurosis.[23] At any rate, sexuality as a possible cause of neurotic disease fired Freud's imagination and he pursued it with the same concentration, perseverance, and forgetfulness of reality which once had characterized his research of fish brains. The unceasing search, which after twenty years of psychoanalytic effort discovered libido behind every manifestation of human life, first demanded a change of theory and therapy of neuroses. The manifold psychic experiences described as pathogenic of hysteria in the *Studies* are reduced to the sexual trauma, and the role of sexuality as the cause of all types of neuroticism was established.[24]

Contrary to a widespread opinion, Freud cherished a rather "old fashioned" view about the meaning of sex. It is true that he often onesidedly identifies psychic health with normal sexuality. However, he considers that the normal sexuality corresponding to the natural purpose of sex is the capability and the healthy exercise of sexual relations between husband and wife. He wrongly denies the ability of such relations to the neurotic, and declares any other form of sexual behavior in adults as either perverse or pathogenic.

Theoretically these views of Freud rest on his principle of the constancy of psychic energy, when this is identified with sexual energy or libido. Sexual stimulation leads to an increase of excitation that necessarily requires a discharge. In normal sex relations this discharge is achieved naturally and results in complete satisfaction; normal sexuality is psychic health. Any interference with the natural performance of the marriage act and every frustrated sexual stimulation either partly or completely prevent the healthy abreaction of the increased excitation. The blocked-in sexual energy is transformed into anxiety, as the simularity of somatic symptoms accompanying anxiety with those of sexual relations reveals to Freud. Anxiety-neurosis, described as "a substitute of the omitted specific sexual action,"[25] is the result. A waste of energy in sexual excesses, on the other hand, leads to exhaustion, and neurasthenia, a state of general nervousness, follows. Obsessional neurosis, with its compulsive ideas and rituals, phobias, paranoia, and hysteria, however, do not allow adult sexual behavior, according to Freud's opinion mentioned before. Such things are explained as abnormal discharges of the energy of sexual tendencies which had to be repressed at the time of puberty. The onset of sexual feelings during adolescence arouses memories of infantile sexual traumas in the later neurotic. These memories associate sexuality with painful emotions and thus occasion a repression, an unconscious, unreflected keeping-out-of awareness of sexuality. Instead of leading to psychic health in normal sex relations, the libidinous energy rages in the unconscious and enforces an outlet in neurotic disease.[26] Its therapy demands the removal of the sexual trauma which is seen in a seduction committed mainly by the father of the patient during the early years of childhood.[27]

The logical consequence of this theory of the sexual etiology of neurosis was the introduction of a new method of therapy. The name psychoanalysis was henceforward to distinguish Freud's psychiatric efforts from other systems of psychiatry.[28] Hypnosis, which had not fulfilled his hopes as a psychotherapeutic means, could not be used for the analysis of the suspected pathogenic experience. For Freud it is an effect of sexuality rather than a means of delivering that pathogenic factor from the bondage of the unconscious. When one of his patients had once embraced him immediately after she awoke from hypnosis, he had no difficulty in recognizing the "mysterious element" responsible for the hypnotic rapport.[29] Moreover, his "persistent search for sexual causes" aroused the resistance of his patients.[30] This resistance had to be mastered by a therapeutic method corresponding to the new conception of the origin of neurosis.

The new mode of treatment is described by Freud as "urging" therapy[31] in order to distinguish it from Breuer's cathartic method. It is primarily "an art of interpretation" of free associations,[32] an analysis of resistance, and an emphatically expressed insistence upon the sexual cause of the disease. The bed in the sickroom of Breuer's patients was to play a role in the new therapy also, and was replaced by the couch in Freud's office.[33] Lying on it, with his face turned away from the therapist, the patient reports on his life, his problems, and his dreams. He is supposed to talk freely about whatever comes to his mind, without any consideration for logical, causal, or emotional connections of his ideas.[34] This free association of ideas, Freud believes on the ground of his "strong confidence in the strict determinism of psychic phenomena,"[35] will necessarily be determined by the dynamically charged repressed, and thus reveal its nature. He admits that the material produced by the patient does not point to the pathogenic source directly. However, he is convinced that free association offers a rich body of ideas which can put the analyst on the track of the forgotten. "With the help of additions and interpretations," Freud writes, the doctor can "conjecture and reconstruct" what has been forgotten.[36] Of course, success on the part of the analyst presupposes a specific analytic attitude, including an abandonment to his own unconscious and an unreflected, merely global attention to the neurotic report.[37] In this way, Freud assumes, the therapist receives the patient's unconscious into his own, and grasps the theme underlying the disease. He then has merely to tell him, and to enforce the admission of, the cause of the neurosis. Insight into the origin of the symptom produces its relief.[38]

Freud's surprise and shock were tremendous when after years of practicing this new, psychoanalytic method of therapy he had to recognize that the "correctly analyzed" infantile sexual trauma, i.e., seduction by the father, represented mere phantasy products of the neurotic mind.[39] He plays with the idea that this "memory" of infantile seduction is probably the result of his own suggestion.[40] Freud's closest friend, Fliess, soon expressed a similar suspicion. "The mind reader reads his own mind in his patients," he told Freud,[41] and like others who disagree with what Freud himself once characterized as his obsessive train of thought,[42] Fliess lost his friendship. The possibility that his own conceptions are the dynamic source of the associations on the couch had to be rejected. It is not even mentioned when soon afterwards his newly constructed theory of the girl's pre-oedipal incestuous love of the mother led to a corresponding change of the seducer in the phantasies of his patients.[43] The temptation to quit his psychotherapeutic work after this disastrous psychoanalytic blunder was soon overcome. The realization that at his age he had "no choice to begin something new,"[44] as Freud writes, helped him to find the reorientation required for a continuation of his research of sexuality. However, he will exercise a more careful control over possible avenues of suggestion in the future. Expression of his conjectures and interpretations, which cost him a hoarse voice after nine to eleven hours of analysis almost every day,[45] would be restricted. The ideal of the analyst functioning as cold mirror reflecting the mental processes of the neurotic psyche would be realized. More attention would be paid to expressions of a genuine insight into the nature of his problems on the side of the patient.

The fact that hysterics reduced their symptoms to invented sexual traumas, as Freud starts his new line of reasoning, manifests the importance of such phantasies in the situation of the neurotic. The problem underlying the disease elicits sexual phantasies about traumatic childhood experiences. Since the father is proved not to be guilty of these invented experiences, Freud concludes that it can only be the baby herself. So infantile sexuality and the Oedipus complex are determined to be the important psychic reality behind the seduction stories.[46] The infantile sexual trauma is replaced by the sexual development of the child, that is, infantile sexuality itself is discovered to be the trauma behind neurotic symptoms.

This renewed but scarcely modified confidence in the objectivity of analytically elicited associations was justified by Freud with the discovery of his own Oedipus complex during self-analysis,[47] which itself is declared to be essentially dependent upon the recognitions gained from the psychoanalytic interpretation of the phantasy products of his patients.[48] Actually, Freud's new interpretation of neurotic phantasies has its foundation in two basic psychoanalytic assumptions. One of them concerns the determination of free association by the infantile past, the other takes sexuality as the only decisive dynamic psychic reality. Only belief that sexuality is the dynamic force of mental life justifies the unquestioned reduction of neurotic sexual phantasies to a sexual problem. For if human problems different from sexual ones are admitted, their hiding behind sexual imaginations is no less possible than the masking of the libido which Freud discovers behind every innocently looking psychic or somatic phenomenon. A scientific conclusion to the existence of infantile sexuality as the determining source of neurotic sexual phantasies is justified only if free associations are also truly determined only by the primitive, unconscious, and unknown past. Experimental findings unknown to Freud disprove this psychoanalytic supposition. Free associations seem to be mainly determined by the present psychic condition of the subject.[49] However, Freud systematically puts his psychoanalytic experience above and beyond common sense and scientific experimentation. His convictions of the complete determination of the future personality by its primitive, remote unconscious and unknown beginnings, and of sexuality as the only dynamic psychic force first enter his psychoanalytic theory as a priori principles. For the time being, the discovery of infantile sexuality offered a comprehensive understanding of perversions and neuroses, as presented in the *Three Essays on the Theory of Sexuality*.[50]

Perversions deviate from normal adult sexual behavior. They are characterized by a dependence of sexual satisfaction upon certain unusual types and modes of activities, as their names like exhibitionism, voyeurism, and fetishism indicate. Some of these activities, Freud observes, play a role also in the marriage act,[51] and what is more interesting, show similarities with common behavior patterns of children before the development of shame, morality, and aesthetic feelings. His suspicion that perversions represent merely a continuation of inherited infantile forms of sexuality finds confirmation in the psychoanalytic research of neurotic symptoms. The infantility of the sex life of hysterics is commonly known, Freud finds.[52] However, their symptoms evidently reveal a relation to activities characteristic of perversions.[53] Hysterical blindness, for instance, is unmasked in psychoanalysis as the conversion of visual sexual curiosity. When sought as object of adult libidinous satisfaction, this curiosity represents the perversion that is voyeurism.

With such psychoanalytic insights into the relationship between infantile behavior and perversions and neurotic symptoms, Freud has to a large extent solved the problem of his libido theory, that is, the psychoanalytic understanding of the psychic manifestations of sexuality.[54] The term libido is introduced in order to eliminate the traditional confusion of sexual and genital, and to indicate that sexuality is not one uniform instinct but a combination of partial drives. These so-called components of libido have a genetic history of their own. Under normal developmental conditions, they are unified into genital sexuality at the time of adolescence.[55] They end in perversion when intensively developed in childhood, or appear in neurotic symptoms when at the experience of the impulsive demands of genital lust sexuality is repressed. Thus the assumed infantile sexuality explains the entire range of sexual manifestations.

Its existence, as conceived in psychoanalysis, is contradicted by anatomical and physiological conditions of the infantile organism, and, as Freud admits, is denied by countless experts in child medicine and neurology. However, such objections rest on a confusion of sexual and genital, he rejoins, presupposing what was denied in the objection.[56] Genital lust represents the greatest pleasure and happiness, but it is only one type of sexuality. There are other feelings of pleasure which are no less sexual than genital lust.[57] The sexual nature of infantile satisfaction is admittedly not accessible to common observation; its discovery is the exclusive result of the analysis of neurotic phantasies of adult patients.[58] However, a psychoanalytically trained observer will easily discover indications of its existence and properties. For instance, Freud finds that an infant's face during sleep after having been nursed by his mother so nearly resembles the look after sexual satisfaction that it evidently reveals the sexual character of oral satisfaction, especially when this blissful look reappears after pleasure-sucking.[59]

The Oedipus complex which had been discovered several years before the publication of the *Three Essays* does not figure as a developmental phase of libido in that work. Its existence is not required for the psychoanalytic reduction of possible sexual phenomena to infantile libido. However, the usefulness of the complex for a radical Freudian disposal of the so-called " 'higher' things in human life" [60] guarantees it a central place in the later elaboration of the psychoanalytic doctrine. It is then described as the core of normal and abnormal development, and "its recognition as the shibboleth distinguishing followers of psychoanalysis from its opponents."[61] Its theoretical significance also determines its therapeutic importance. The analysis of transference, of the patient's identification of the analyst with mother and father, the objects of oedipal experience, becomes the final phase of the ideal psychoanalytic therapy. Feelings of love and hatred which the patient develops during the year-long communication with the analyst are interpreted as repetitions of repressed infantile oedipal relations. Their realistic confrontation is supposed to complete the cure of neurosis.[62]

The psychoanalytic attempt to reduce every type of genuinely human behavior to manifestations of libido was an early aim of Freud's personal ambition. As he told Jung, he had to extol and extend the role of sexuality as a dogma in order to dam the black flood of occultism, that is, of morality and religion.[63] The transformation of psychoanalysis form a psychiatric theory and therapy of neuroses into a system of general psychology was completed around the turn of the century. His interpretation of such common phenomena of everyday life, as dreams, slips of tongue, and forgetting, justifies, Freud claïms, the presentation of psychoanalysis as the psychology of normal as well as of abnormal life. Naturally these common phenomena are considered and explained as neurotic or psychotic symptoms. But such so-called neurotic activities take place in the life of normal people, and thus Freud feels himself entitled to conclude that normal behavior must also be understood psychoanalytically.[64] For instance, the dream, a "transitory psychosis,"[65] is "the (disguised) fulfillment of a repressed wish,"[66] and hence specifically human experiences are effects of the unconscious or compromises between the forces of the unconscious and the energy of the ego-instincts in the conscious system of the psychic apparatus. All manifestations of this psychic machine, called personality, are "automatically" regulated by the pleasure principle.[67] Interpreted psychologically, this economy aspect of the psychoanalytic theory is to express Freud's conviction, that all human behavior is motivated by a desire for lust; understood physiologically, it means that human activity is enforced by the pressure of instinctual energy to find discharge. The reality principle, the other functional law of the Freudian psychic apparatus, is not opposed but subordinated to the pleasure principle. As "only continuing the work of the pleasure principle in a more effectual way,"[68] it secures a more successful or, at least, a disguised fulfillment of the blind instinctual urges of the unconscious. It does this by way of the reality test, that is, by a conscious consideration of the actual possibilities of instinctual satisfaction. Intellectual operations, therefore, do not represent an expression of a specifically human sphere of being, nor do they have a meaning of their own. The only purpose of intellectual life consists in its service for instinctual gratification. Its "fundamental characteristic," described as sythesizing function, clearly reveals to Freud the uniting instinct, libido, as its source.[69] Thought is nothing but masked libido.

With the conception of the psychic apparatus the Freudian reduction of normal psychic life to products of an automatic play of instinctual forces is achieved. However, the psychoanalytic depersonalization of the human individual is not yet complete. Although the responsible human person is replaced by quantitative relations of instinctual energies, the rule of libido has still a partner in the ego instincts, and the so-called "higher things in life" are not yet disposed of explicitly. Such obstacles of a pansexualistic understanding of the human personality await the further progress of psychoanalytic experience. Freud finds the required fact with the help of one of his faithful disciples.

In a discussion with the master, Abraham, a member of the secret inner circle organized by Freud in 1920 with the purpose of protecting the purity of the psychoanalytic doctrine,[70] observes that dementia praecox, a type of schizophrenia, occurring in late adolescence, is characterized by a lack of libidinous cathexes of objects, that is, of erotic relationships. He wonders about the fate of the patient's libido when thus diverted from its objects. To a mind trained in psychoanalytic thought patterns the answer is simple. The object libido of the schizophrenic—who, because of his age, probably had not been in love at all—returns to the ego, Abraham answers, and Freud agrees.[71] Imprisoned in the structure of his abstract, mechanistic conceptions, Freud does not realize that the charge of libido never leaves the subject; he can think of love only as of an investment, transfer, and deprivation of energy, and then wonders about the possible effects of its return. The solution of this psychoanalytic problem marks the beginning of Freud's insistence upon the narcissistic instinct theory. The distinction between libidinous and ego instincts is discarded as superfluous. After all, self-preservation is only the expression of an erotic infatuation with the own ego. Only one type of energy, ego libido or libidinous self love, can be admitted in the organism. From it certain quantities are invested in objects, thus becoming object libido in later life. The greater amount of libido "remains perpetually in the ego." [72]

After the loss of its own energy, the conscious system of the psychic apparatus suffers its extinction as a result of further psychoanalytic insights. Freud observes the unconsciousness of resistance, and then concludes that not only the repressed but also the repressing and resisting forces, and consequently the conscious system from which repression proceeds, must be partly unconscious. The concept unconscious becomes ambiguous, and loses its importance, he writes. [73] The psychic apparatus demands a new structure. Human personality is primarily and essentially Id, the unconscious and unknown, the reservoir of libido, "a cauldron of seething excitement," [74] a libidinous battery by nature impelled to seek discharge of its energy. The surface of the Id is transformed into the mental province of the ego, the subject of consciousness, as a result of material forces impinging upon and modifying the external layers of the Id. As "part of the Id," the ego naturally has no energy of its own. It does not live actively but is lived by unknown untamed forces of the Id. [75] In this "faithful slave" of the Id [76] social influences construct a further province, the Superego. The psychoanalytic experience of the origin of this unique representative of the "higher things in human life" finally offers Freud an opportunity to assign the Oedipus complex a systematic place in his theory of human existence.

Various aspects of genuinely human life had already found sporadic psychoanalytic explanations. Thinking and knowledge, for instance, are declared obvious libidinous derivations of sexual curiosity. [77] Since the object of this first psychoanalytic curiosity is sexual, curiosity itself must necessarily be libidinous. Manifestations of art and appreciations of the beautiful are evidently masked expressions of the waste of libidinous energy in erotic infatuation. [78] No type of love can deny its low ancestry; all such tender feelings are nothing but "inhibited libido." [79] Striving for perfection observed by Freud in rare specimens of the race is obviously the result of a continuous frustration of sublimated libido.[80] Religion is an outgrowth of infantile impotence in the adult personality who in front of a dangerous world projects the ever-ready protecting help of the father as experienced in childhood upon an illusionary father-God beyond the clouds.[81] Character traits are reaction-formations developed as means of protection against libidinous impulses.[82] Naturally all such mental phenomena characterized as sublimation, inhibition, projection, or reaction-formation are merely masked libido, in spite of their hostile opposition to sexuality.

Also the superego itself had already found Freudian explanations which render the psychoanalysis of its oedipal origin superfluous or contradictory. The "latency-period," a time of sex-free innocence, following the polymorphous perversity of the infant around the age of three to five, and the birthdate of shame, incest fear, and morality, is declared to be the product of inherited organic maturation processes[83] due to the interruption of the sexual development of our animal ancestors by the ice age.[84] Or the boy's identification with the father, a mechanism conceived to explain the change of the amoral child into a responsible member of society, is said to be a natural process preceding his incestuous oedipal love.[85]

However, all such features of the Freudian description of human life either completely destroy or do not harmoniously fit into the psychoanalytic picture of human personality. Every trace of the spiritual has to find a place in the very cellar of human personality, Freud tells Binswanger, later to be founder of Existential analysis, who then as a faithful follower of the Viennese master had dared to express doubts about the role of the mind in psychoanalysis.[86] What Freud primarily considers as spiritual, the superego, the incarnate opposition to libido, must find its source in the most perfect creation of the psychoanalytic cellar, namely, in the Oedipus complex.

This superego is a one-sided representative of human moral life. It is not the morality of the mature person who freely attempts to adjust his behavior to the demands of his conscience, reacting in conformity with his personally acquired realistic convictions as to the meaning of his created existence. It is the irrational, compulsive, anxiety-ridden attitude of his neurotic patients towards sex, which Freud identifies with human morality, and tries to explain as "the heir to the Oedipus complex."[87] Thus it is not surprising that he uses a psychotic phenomenon as the starting point of psychoanalytic argumentation about the origin of the superego.

As a result of their disease, melancholic patients frequently torture themselves with most unrealistic self-reproaches on the one hand, and on the other experience and complain about a loss of the emotional contact with their beloved ones. The impression that such psychotic self-accusations, which Freud considers to be manifestations of conscience, are evaluations better corresponding to the behavior of one of the friends of the patient rather than of his own is sufficient for Freud to see a causal relation between the two psychotic symptoms. Overlooking the fact that both phenomena represent effects of the disease, Freud identifies psychotic decay of the affective bond with the environment with loss of a love object, and assigns this loss as the cause of the melancholic self-torture. According to Freud, psychotic self-accusations actually represent reproaches formerly directed against an unsatisfactory love-object. They are redirected against the ego, after the loss of the love-object has enforced an identification with it. Psychoanalysis has revealed that a lover defends himself against the damaging experience of failure in love with an introjection of the beloved person, ascribing to himself the reprehensible characteristics of the beloved.[88]

This psychoanalytic insight into the mechanism of the origin of the pathological "conscience" easily explains the mystery of the beginning of normal moral life.[89] Self-evaluation is first observed in the latency period, or after the failure of the boy's incestuous love affair with the mother. The fear of castration, which the mother threatens that the father will perform, forces the little sexual fiend to repress his libidinous and murderous ambitions. The loss of the infantile love object elicits the defence mechanism of its introjection. Parental authority, which till now had inhibited, forbidden, and punished the sexual impulses of the infant from outside, is established in the ego of the child and continues as superego the moral guidance of his behavior. As a result of the introjection of the first love object the superego represents "the power, the aims and even the methods of the parental function." [90]

As usual, Freud's mechanistic understanding of subjective psychic functions impairs his psychoanalytic reasoning. Psychologically an identification does not mean a transfer of the object of identification and its power into one's own person, but an imitation of this object by one's own power. The person with whom one identifies oneself, becomes the object of imitation, not its subject. However, Freud himself is dissatisfied with this product of his psychoanalytic experience. In his view, the proto-type of moral perfection is the father, since girls maintain their oedipal relations for many years and thus develop an almost negligible sense of moral responsibility. [91] Accordingly, an identification with the mother cannot fulfill the expectations Freud has set on his usual conception of the Oedipus complex. However, psychoanaltyic research finds an exit from the dilemma. Remembering the bisexuality of human constitution, Freud discovers the "complex" Oedipus complex, which involves not only the baby's incestuous love of the mother but also his homosexual love of the father. [92] The assumed repression of this complicated oedipal structure produces also the required identification with the father, and continuation of the moral traditions of society is secured. Civilization can persist at the price of sacrificing satisfaction of the only natural desire of its libido-obsessed subjects.

Actually Freud's forceful attempts to establish the descent of the superego from the Oedipus complex are mere waste of psychoanalytic energy. Years before the publication of *The Ego and the Id,* where he proposes the complex Oedipus complex as source of individual morality, new observations had led to a discovery which made the employment of the complex in this regard superfluous. Libido, which in the narcissistic instinct theory had occupied the entire powerhouse of the personality, again receives a partner, the death instinct. Various reasons induced Freud toward the end of his life to decide upon this destructive or aggressive instinct as the primary dynamic force of human existence. The strange behavior of conscience could now be easily explained. Unless he intends to be cruel and to turn his destructive tendencies toward his environment, man must destroy himself by suicide or by the torture of his conscience. There is no escape from this dilemma. The aggressive impulses are manifestations of that death instinct which by necessity destroys every life. The irresistible power of this instinct is an expression of the disintegrative forces of material particles which produce the phenomena of life by their chance unification but by nature tend to re-establish their original inorganic conditions. Even the pleasure principle, the automatic regulation of life processes by the discharge of libidinous energy, is now recognized as a mere means for the achievement of the destructive purposes of the death instinct.[93] Psychoanalytic depersonalization of human personality and materialistic reduction of every trace of psychic and spiritual life are finally complete.

In the first period of psychoanalytic research man is a freak of nature, a libidinous monster necessarily seeking sexual satisfaction yet almost constantly frustrated and forced by the cruel demands of reality to sublimation, inhibition, or neurotic conversion of libido. During the last two decades of Freud's life man is psychoanalytically revealed as a mere stage in the chance processes of material particles, a trick played by blind cosmic forces of matter. Freud's early identification with the "semitic Hannibal" and his "deeply neurotic" desire to reach Rome, like Hannibal, found fulfillment in a most absurd and pessimistic view of the meaning of human life.

There is no need for an explicit refutation of Freud's philosophical anthropology, since today no one, not even the orthodox Freudian, defends the master's view of human nature. However, as a kind of indirect refutation, a few words about Freud's psychology and psychiatry may be written. On the one hand, the truth of a philosophy of man depends at least to some degree upon general psychology, i.e., empirical study of human behavior, and on the other, it is often maintained that Freud's psychology and psychiatry are independent of his philosophy, and that his greatness as a psychologist is beyond any doubt.

With regard to the relationship between psychoanalytic philosophy and psychology, a certain degree of agreement between empirical facts established by psychoanalysis and Freud's view of human nature cannot be denied. However, this relationship is not identical with a dependence of his philosophy upon his psychoanalytic discoveries but rather with a determination of his empirical studies by his preconceived ideas about human nature. Freud is convinced that human existence is meaningless. "The moment one inquires about the sense and value of life, one is sick," he writes, "for neither of them has any existence."[94] He is consistent enough in drawing the consequences from his conviction. Freud is a radical pessimist. His entire psychoanalytic work is intended as a justification of his pessimistic view of human life. He does not have the physician's passion to help his patients,[95] whom he considers as "often very inferior material,"[96] nor is he in the least interested in a scientific study of human behavior. Psychoanalysis is not primarily concerned with an observation of psychic phenomena—the first condition of a scientific psychology—he declares, but with a discovery of their unknown dynamic causes.[97] His pessimistic, materialistic philosophy does not allow him to take an unbiased look at human reality. It forces him to be selective in the study of the psychic life of his patients and scientific literature, and to manipulate the small section of human behavior accessible to his approach with every possible abuse of the rules of scientific work in order to achieve at least some confirmation of his faith.

With regard to the second problem, one may reasonably list Freud among the great psychologists, since, the greatness of a scientist or philosopher is not necessarily correlated with the truth value of his teaching, and yet deny that his contributions to psychology and psychiatry are independent of his philosophy of man. One can admit, for instance, that it was a great achievement for Freud to enforce recognition of the need and usefulness of psychological therapy by his stubborn perseverance, and at the same time that his use of the psychoanalytic method is dictated by his view of human nature and, because of that fact, questionable. One may recognize that in spite of his careless use of his "psychoanalytic experience" Freud gained new insights into the functioning of the human mind, but one must still insist upon the shortcomings of these insights due to his mechanistic and biologistic conception of human existence. Such insights concern primarily the so-called defence mechanisms, which occasionally are described as permanent psychoanalytic contributions to psychology.

We may elaborate on the effects of Freud's philosophy upon

his psychological and psychiatric achievements. It can easily be shown that the doctrine of repression is determined by his mechanistic and biologistic view of man. His mechanization of psychic life forces him to hypostasize mental phenomena. The repressed wish is conceived as an entity in the unconscious, separating itself from its energy, investing it in mental and somatic symptoms under the influence of another unconscious entity, and waiting for psychoanalysis to find its release from the prison of the unconscious. However, such objectivistic hypostatizations, falsify psychic reality. Memories are not independent entities hiding in a dark system of a psychic apparatus. A man is unable to find a letter that demands an answer, and his forgetting where it is may be due to dislike of its writer. But the psychoanalytic explanation, that the dislike dynamically represses the memory of the letter's localization into the unconscious, which releases it only after the recognition of the dislike, merely insinuates an understanding of the existing situation. The forgotten memory simply does not exist in the mind. It merely means the present inability of the subject to perform a personal act involving the representation of a formerly experienced event. This inability may be due to dislike. But again it is not the dislike paralyzing the normal ability to remember past happenings that explains this inability. It is rather the psychic condition of the subject who, because of his dislike of the writer of the letter, did not fulfill the requirements for a successful use of his normal remembering ability, which represents the psychological explanation. Because of his dislike of the writer, the subject did not pay the normal attention when receiving the letter, nor occasionally think of the demands of the letter as is usually done when one is interested in some project or person, nor make a sufficient effort in the actual attempt of remembering, and is thus unable to perform the required act successfully. As this example shows, the psychic dynamics of human behavior are completely different from the conditions insinuated by the metaphorical descriptions of psychoanalysis. Life processes are performances of a subject; they are not chance results of a struggle or independent, hypostasized instinctual forces. The psychoanalytic dehumanization of the personality and elimination of the subject prevent a grasp of the genuine psychic conditions of normal and abnormal mental phenomena. Psychoanalytic terms like defense mechanism, identification, and sublimation simulate a profound understanding of every manifestation of human life. Actually, they often merely represent psychoanalytic names of the phenomena which they are supposed to explain, or they indicate an explanation which falsifies existing psychic conditions.

Except in rare cases of certain traumatic experiences repression does not involve the existence of an unconscious complex, unaffected by the developing personality and disturbing psychic life, as psychoanalysis maintains. It is more like an immature, unrealistic, and ambivalent attitude toward unavoidable problems in human life, which has to go on and yet cannot proceed in a realistic manner.

Hence the psychoanalytic understanding of the nature of repression and of the functioning of the repressed is not independent of Freud's mechanistic conceptions of life. His determination of the contents of the repressed and the psychoanalytic evaluation of repression clearly reveal his biologistic view of human nature. Only the genuinely dynamic, the decisively important in human beings can be repressed and produce the devastating results in psychic life ascribed to it in psychoanalysis. In conformity with the biologistic philosophy of man, however, this genuinely dynamic entity is seen in the instinctual, the primitive, the infantile, and the "bad," and its repression is consequently considered as bad also. As a result of this onesided view of the nature of the repressed and of the pathogenic role of repression, healthy forms of repression, the repression of other aspects of human existence, for instance, of conscience or religion, and the harmfulness or an inability of repression are disregarded. As is generally known, neurotic patients many times do not suffer from the repressed but from unforgettable memories of past offences or of painful experiences.

Accordingly, it is a psychoanalytic oversimplification, dictated by the Freudian biologistic philosophy of man, to seek the etiology of neurosis exclusively in repression or, worse, in a repression of sexuality. Although repressed libido, in the sense explained before, i.e., as an immature and ambivalent attitude towards sex, may have been the main problem of Freud's hysterical patients, it was not the only cause of their disease, as Freud himself at least indirectly admits by his repeated references to overdetermination. Most certainly the psychoanalytic trauma of infantile sexuality is no more the cause of their disease than the sexual trauma of seduction which Freud had once assumed and was forced to dismiss as an etiological factor. Infantile sexuality, with its Oedipus complex, followed by a supposedly sex-free latency period up to puberty, as conceived by Freud, simply does not exist. Certainly children are sexual beings—after all, they are born as boys and girls. They may enjoy oral and somatic pleasure, give indications of a rivalry with the father for their mother's love, they may turn to "masturbation" in certain unfavorable constitutional or social circumstances. But to explain such phenomena as sexual and as determined by an urge for sexual lust, instead of as expressions of the child's liveliness, egotism, or helplessness and despair, manifests a complete disregard of the physiological and psychological development of a human being, enforced by Freud's a priori conceptions. The retardation of sexual maturation is a natural manifestation of the human form of life, as modern comparative studies of the ontogenetic development of animals and man establish.[98] A comparison of any realistic textbook on child psychology with the crude, reductionistic psychoanalytic theory of infantile development will convincingly show that Freud's philosophy of human existence is the source of his psychology, not vice versa.

Nor is the psychoanalytic method of therapy free from the influence of Freud's philosophical convictions, and because of this it is not the best means of psychological treatment. Let us introduce the best qualified witness for the correctness of this statement, Freud himself. In a letter to Oskar Pfister, a Protestant minister who used psychoanalysis in his pastoral work, he writes: "Lasting success in psychoanalysis certainly depends on the conjunction of two issues: the obtaining of gratification, and the mastery and sublimation of the obdurate instinct.... You are in the fortunate position of leading them (your patients) on to God ... We no longer have this opportunity of settling the matter. People in general ... we also are mostly thoroughly irreligious—and since the other forms of sublimation through which *we* replace religion are commonly too difficult for most patients our cure generally issues in the search for gratification."[99] Pascal seems to be correct, when he writes: "It is dangerous to make man see too clearly his equality with the brutes without showing him his greatness."[100] Of course, Freud is unable, even to imagine that the admittedly regrettable results of his therapy are probably due to an unrealistic understanding of human existence. His convictions of the meaninglessness of human life forces him to identify the genuinely human with its assumed unknown beginnings, its primitive unconscious past. Hence he directs the analysis of his patients to the experience of an illusionary Oedipus complex. Naturally, a patient may profit even from this unrealistic experiment. As Freud writes, his therapy is "in essence a cure through love."[101] In a yearlong intimate communication with an understanding and sympathetic analyst, a patient may learn to recognize his irrational fears and ambitions and his compulsive likes and dislikes, to overcome his childish self-centered and contactless attitudes, and to gain confidence in himself and in his environment, even when such a relationship is interpreted as a re-experience of infantile Oedipal love. However, a therapy based on a realistic notion of human nature and on a correct diagnosis of the patient's personality and actual problems is, as Freud indirectly admits in his letter to Pfister, certainly to be preferred to an analysis dictated by the reductionistic and materialistic psychoanalytic view of man. It will not be determined by preconceived ideas about murderous and incestuous impulses of the patient's infantile past as the only etiological factors of neurotic disease. It will not be blinded by the Freudian prejudice about the utter meaninglessness of human existence, and it will reject the dogma of the absolute determinism of psychic life by instinctual forces. It will thus be in a better position to see a patient's genuinely human problems, and to avoid Freud's therapeutic blunders and their regrettable results which, after all, were mainly the consequences of Freud's philosophy of man.

In a letter to his friend Fliess, Freud once compared psychoanalysis with a mass of iron ore containing unknown amounts of precious metals which still await coining into serviceable dollars and cents.[102] After a review of the development and meaning of psychoanalysis one can scarcely disagree with Freud's evaluation of his creation. Psychoanalysis is a mass of crude theoretical constructions which contain precious insights into both normal and abnormal functionings of the human mind. The psychoanalytic understanding of these insights is determined by those logical constructions; it is not independent of Freud's philosophy. The contributions of psychoanalysis to psychology have to be separated from their mechanistic and biologistic meaning, and reinterpreted psychologically, before they can be incorporated into a realistic and personalistic psychology. The presentation of the crude mass of the Freudian philosophy, psychology, and psychiatry was successful, but still an error. However, it seems that this error is more and more recognized also in the United States where Freudianism had found the first enthusiastic reception. A great disillusionment with psychoanalysis has set in within those same academic circles which had once welcomed Freud into their ranks. Not long ago one of their representatives predicted that twenty-five years from now psychoanalysis "will take its place with phrenology and mesmerism . . . Like them (Gall and Mesmer), Freud had the germ of an idea which flared into a way of life for a time, but then vanished."[103] Such prophecies are probably too optimistic. But we may hope that the innate human desire for truth and the famous restlessness of the human heart will prevail in time, and help to recognize in psychoanalysis what, according to the confession of its author, it truly is: Freud's mythology,[104] and scientific fantasy.[105]

NOTES

1. The writer's primary concern is to offer an appraisal of the philosophical aspects of psychoanalysis rather than an evaluation of Freud's contributions to psychology. However, the problem of the relationship between Freud's psychology and his philosophy of man is discussed in the concluding part of the article.

2. Cf. Sigmund Freud, "Selbstdarstellung" in *Gesammelte Werke* (London: Imago Publishing Co., 1948), XIV, 86. In the following footnotes combinations of Roman and Arabic numbers refer to volume and page of this standard edition of Freud's writings.

3. Edwin G. Boring, *A History of Experimental Psychology.* 2nd. ed. (New York: Appleton-Century-Crofts, 1950), p. 707.

4. A. T. Poffenberger in Foreword to Robert R. Sears, *Survey of Objective Studies of Psychoanalytic Concepts.* Social Science Research Council, New York. Bulletin 51, 1943. Lithoprinted Ann Arbor: Edwards Brothers, 1951. p. VII.

5. Robert R. Sears, *op. cit.*, p. 141.

6. A. T. Poffenberger, *l. c.*

7. Cf. XIII, 223.

8. Cf. X, 70 f; XIV, 77 f.

9. Cf. Sigmund Freud, *Aus den Anfängen der Psychoanalyse* 1887-1902 *Briefe an Wilhelm Fliess* (Frankfurt: Fischer, 1962), p. 203. Hereafter referred to as *Fliess*.

10. Cf. XIV, 109.

11. Cf. XIV, 570 f.

12. For a more extensive philosophical evaluation of Freud's doctrine, confer Marius Schneider, OFM., "An Existential-Analytic Psychiatrist's Appraisal of Psychoanalysis," *The Bulletin of The Guild of Catholic Psychiatrists*, XI (1964) pp. 9 ff, 68 ff.

13. Cf. Josef Breuer and Sigmund Freud, *Studies in Hysteria*. Transl. and ed. by James Strachey (New York: Basic Books, 1957), pp. 21 ff. In the following, this work is referred to as *Studies*.

14. Cf. *Fliess*, pp. 21 f.; XIV, 35 f.

15. Cf. XIV, 42.

16. Cf. Footnote 13.

18. Cf. *Studies*, p. 6.

19. Cf. Ernest Jones, *The Life and Work of Sigmund Freud*. 3. Vol. (New York: Basic Books, 1953, 1955, 1957), *Vol. I.*, pp. 40 ff.

20. Cf. *Studies*, pp. 3 ff., 86, 192 ff.

21. Cf. XIII, 65; XVII, 73, 80.

22. *Studies*, p. 200.

23. Cf. *Studies*, pp. 255 ff.

24. Cf. XIV, 47 ff.

25. I, 338.

26. Cf. Sigmund Freud, *Zur Ätiologie und Theorie der Grossen Neurosen, Fliess*, 79 ff.

27. Cf. XIV, 59.

28. Cf. XIV, 56.

29. Cf. XIV, 51 f.

30. Cf. X, 59.

31. Cf. XIV, 54; 64.

32. XIII, 214 f.

33. Cf. XIV, 59.

34. Cf. V, 5 f.

35. XIII, 214.

36. Cf. XIII, 411.

37. Cf. XIII, 215.

38. Cf. X, 62.

39. Cf. X, 55.

40. Cf. XIV, 59 f.

41. *Fliess*, p. 286.

42. Cf. Ernest Jones, *op. cit.*, III, 446.

43. Cf. Sigmund Freud, *New Introductory Lectures on Pschoanalysis*. Transl. by W. J. H. Sprott. (London, Hogarth Press, 1937), p. 155. Hereafter referred to as *NIL*.

44. X, 55.

45. Cf. *Fliess*, pp. 119, 156, 230.

46. Cf. X, 56; XIV, 60.

47. Cf. *Fliess*, p. 34.

48. Cf. *Flies*, p. 202.

49. Cf. Joseph Nuttin, *Psychoanalysis and Personality* (New York: Sheed and Ward, 1953), p. 23.

50. Cf. V, 27 ff.

51. Cf. V, 49.

52. Cf. V, 64; 76.

53. Cf. V, 65 ff.

54. Cf. V, 118 ff.

55. Cf. V, 108; XIII, 219 ff.

56. Cf. V, 81.

57. Cf. V, 112 ff.

58. Cf. X, 56 f.; V, 77.

59. Cf. Sigmund Freud, *Introductory Lectures on Psychoanalysis*. Transl. by Joan Riviere (London: Allen & Unwin, 1943), p. 263.

60. NIL, p. 90.

61. V, 127 f., Footnote 2.

62. Cf. XIV, 67 ff.

63. Cf. C. G. Jung, *Gegenwart und Zukunft* (Zürich: Rascher, 1957), p. 25.

64. Cf. XIV, 303; XIII, 216; 416.

65. XVII, 98.

66. Cf. XIII, 415.

67. Sigmund Freud, *Introductory Lectures on Psychoanalysis*, pp. 298 f.

68. Cf. Ernest Jones, *op. cit.*, II, 453.

69. *NIL*, p. 101.

70. Cf. Edwin G. Boring, *op. cit.*, p. 712.

71. Cf. Sigmund Freud, *Introductory Lectures on Psychoanalysis*, pp. 346 f.

72. *NIL*, p. 133.

73. Cf. XIII, 244 f.; *NIL*, pp. 92 ff.

74. *NIL*, p. 98.

75. Cf. XIII, 251 ff.; *NIL*, pp. 102 f.

77. Cf. Ernest Jones, *op. cit.*, II, 449.

78. Cf. XIV, 90.

79. Cf. XIII, 232; XIV, 64.

80. Cf. XIII, 44 f.

81. Cf. XIV, 340 f.; 345 f.

82. Cf. *NIL*, pp. 132 f.

83. Cf. V, 78; 127 Footnote 1.

84. Cf. XIII, 263.

85. Cf. XIII, 115; 259.

86. Cf. Ludwig Binswanger, *Der Mensch in der Psychiatrie* (Pfullingen: Neske, 1957), pp. 52 f.

87. XIII, 265.

88. Cf. X, 430 ff.

89. Cf. XIII, 256 ff.; *NIL*, pp. 82 ff.

90. *NIL*, p. 85.

91. Cf. *NIL*, pp. 165 f.

92. XIII, 261 f.

93. Cf. XIII, 35 ff.; *NIL*, pp. 133 ff.

94. Cf. Ernest Jones, *op. cit.*, III, 465.

95. Cf. Ernest Jones, *op. cit.*, II, 446.

96. Cf. Ernest Jones, *op. cit.*, II, 439.

97. Cf. XI, 62.

98. Cf. Adolf Portmann, *Zoologie und das neue Bild des Menschen*
(Hamburg: Rowohlt, 1956), pp. 88 ff.

99. Cf. Ernest Jones, *op. cit.*, II, 439 f.

100. Blaise Pascal, *Pensées* (New York: The Modern Library, 1941),
p. 132, n. 418.

101. Cf. Ernest Jones, *op. cit.*, III, 435.

102. Cf. *Fliess*, p. 141.

103. Cf. the quotation from Lee R. Steiner's paper in O. Hobart
Mowrer, *The Crisis in Psychiatry and Religion* (Princeton: D. van Nostrand,
1961), pp. 69 f.

104. Cf. *NIL.*, p. 124.

105. Cf. Sigmund Freud, *Introductory Lectures on Psychoanalysis*,
p. 349.

carl jung

PHILOSOPHER OF THE UNCONSCIOUS

by Paul F. Nolan

Writers who describe the careers of Sigmund Freud, Alfred Adler, and Carl Jung take pains to show that situations in the lives of these men had important effects on the psychological theories they produced.[1] It has often been remarked, for example, that Freud's theory of the Oedipal complex may well be due to the family circle in which he grew up.[2] His father ruled the family with a good deal of authority.[3] Moreover, there was almost as much disparity in age between Freud's mother and father as there was between Freud himself and his mother.[4] So far as Jung is concerned, we need not conjecture the point because Jung said on more than one occasion that some of his theory is traceable to his biography.

Carl Jung was born in Kesswil, Switzerland, a small town on Lake Constance, on July 26, 1875, the son of Johann Paul Achilles Jung, a liberal Protestant minister with a deep interest in Oriental studies, and Emilie Preiswerk Jung, a member of one of the most respected families of Basel.[5] His paternal grandfather was a professor of anatomy and internal medicine who had come to Basel from Germany as a political refugee in 1822.[6] Jung's father was not the only clergyman and his grandfather not the only physician among his forebears; it is in a family line of ministers that we find the roots of his later interest in philosophy and theology.[7] When Jung first entered the University of Basel in 1895 he intended to be an archaeologist,[8] but after a short time he began studies for a career in internal medicine with special interest in natural science and pathology. In 1896 he became interested in the case of a sonambulistic girl who possessed the gifts of a medium. "The manifestation in her of several distinct personalities aroused his speculation; there must be, he conceived, something in the background, a hidden life of the mind, showing itself in fantasy and dream, a world beyond the conscious world with which she was in contact." [9] Jung received his Doctor of Medicine degree in 1900. As a result of his interest in philosophy and theology and his encounter with the young sonambulist, he chose psychiatry as a field of specialization.

When Jung took up psychiatry as a life work, there was very little information and much less any definite theory to explain what today are called unconscious processes. He needed a theoretical construct, and at first he thought that he had found it in Schopenhauer's theory of the will.[10] Schopenhauer holds that within the universe there is an irrational, eternally pulsating force of life and that this pulsating, irrational force, which he calls will, is the primal root of movement in the world. Jung was convinced that Schopenhauer opens vistas for understanding problems of the unconscious even though he disagreed with the latter's central belief that the primal force in the universe is without any goal.[11] He therefore continued his research in philosophy, and in time concluded that a better foundation for the problem was to be found in the teaching of Eduard von Hartmann,[12] who maintains that the basic force in nature has a very definite goal toward which it is tending, even though this force is not itself aware of its goal. Von Hartmann's theory has both the goal-directiveness and the unconscious process Jung had been looking for. However, he was not yet sure he had enough material to make a workable hypothesis, and so he continued his philosophical and psychiatric researches.

By the time he had read Schopenhauer and von Hartmann, Jung had already begun the association-test experiments for which he later became famous. The test is very simple: Jung would mention a word to the patient and ask him to say the first word coming into his mind. Jung would then record the reaction time for each word the patient gave. By studying the words having the longest reaction-time and by interpreting the words associated with them, he was able to probe more deeply into the recesses of the patient's mind.[13]

In 1900 Freud wrote *The Interpretation of Dreams*,[14] and Jung not only read it at the time but also referred to it in a book he wrote on occultism in 1902.[15] In 1906 he published his well-known work on association tests, and in 1907 he wrote a now-classic work, *The Psychology of Dementia Praecox*.[16] In April, 1906, a regular correspondence was established between Freud and Jung; and in the following year Jung made his first visit to Freud in Vienna.[17] At the outset they had unbounded admiration for each other, and Freud decided soon thereafter that Jung was to be his successor. But in spite of their mutual enthusiasm Jung felt even then that he could not accept Freud's outlook on sexuality, and his difficulty with Freud's position increased even more as time went on. By 1909 a tide of dissension had swept over Switzerland in regard to Freud's sexual theories.[18] In May, 1911, Jung notified Freud that he could no longer accept his narrow definition of *libido,* and that in Jungian language the term would hereafter merely designate general tension.[19] In May, 1902 Jung denied that the incest wishes of a patient should be taken literally and he insisted that they should be interpreted as symbols of other tendencies.[20] In September of the same year he delivered a series of lectures at Fordham University and while he was giving these lectures in New York reports were filtering back to Vienna that during the course of them he was showing strong antagonism to Freud as a person. When Jung returned from the lecture series he sent Freud a note saying that he had been eminently successful in making psychoanalysis more palatable to his New York audience by leaving out Freud's sexual themes. Freud, of course, could not accept Jung's outlook because he was convinced that by it Jung had cut the heart out of psychoanalysis. Nevertheless, before the break occurred Freud and Jung had collaborated on many projects. It may be well to review some of these before presenting Jung's own theory.

In 1909, Freud and Jung were two of several celebrated European psychologists who had been invited by G. Stanley Hall[21] to lecture at Clark University in Worcester, Massachusetts to celebrate the twentieth anniversary of its founding. While they were at Clark University they spent several weeks in daily contact analyzing each others' dreams. Jung found in his own dreams contents which could not be explained by Freud's theory of the unconscious.[22] He had found already contents similar to his own in the dreams and fantasies of his patients, and, as a result of his exchanges with Freud, he began to suspect more than ever that there were major weaknesses in Freud's position. Nevertheless he remained with Freud's psychoanalytic movement, and in 1910, when the International Psychoanalytical Association was established by Freud and his followers, Jung was elected president, and he continued to hold the presidency until 1914. But his own research was carrying him further and further from Freud's and their difference in outlook was apparent to everyone in the psychoanalytic movement when Jung published his "Wandlungen und Symbole der Libido" in 1912.[23] Jung knew then that he was moving off in a different direction; it was a letter from Jung's wife to Freud which alerted Freud himself to the coming break. .

Shortly thereafter the old enthusiasm between Freud and Jung dwindled to nothingness. By June, 1912 Freud was no longer addressing Jung as "Lieber Freund" but as "Lieber Herr Doktor." Early in 1913 they no longer maintained personal correspondence and shortly thereafter they terminated their business correspondence. In April, 1914 Jung resigned his presidency of the International Psychoanalytic Association, and in August of the same year withdrew from membership. Freud and Jung never met again.[24] Both men have written their own accounts of the break.

The major cause seems to have been Freud's pan-sexualism; but Hendrick suggests that the disagreements were probably personal as much as they were scientific.[25] Jung disagreed in theory over more than Freud's pan-sexualism.[26] He could not agree with Freud's view that the individual adult is simply the product of his past experiences. Jung maintained that the human personality must be understood not only in terms of its past, but also in terms of its future. This is why, he says, the eternal aspirations, affections, and fears of man must be taken into account. A man is only partly understood in terms of what has happened to him. Only a dead man can be fully explained in terms of his past.

In spite of the fact that he coined words which nowadays are used by angry young writers, Jung's complete theory is relatively obscure. The obscurity is due partly to Jung himself, because, even shortly before his death in 1961, he refused to summarize his ideas since he felt that a mere summary would be only a distortion.[27] Another source of difficulty is the wide amount of erudition he demands of those who would seek to understand him: His explorations took him into the fields of Yoga, alchemy, astrology, fairy tales, the tribal rites of Pueblo Indians, German philosophy, Zen Buddhism, extra-sensory perception, the cave drawings of prehistoric men, and the analysis of at least 100,000 dreams.[28] Jung was often accused of abandoning psychiatry for mysticism, but he always replied that mysticism is a proper subject for psychiatry because it is part of human experience. After taking up psychiatry he continued research into philosophy and theology, not so much in order to become a philosopher or theologian, but more to discover anything in these fields which might in any way throw light on problems of psychology.[29]

Often Jung's philosophical or theological pronouncements have been taken out of context. We hear, for example, his remark:

> "I have treated many hundreds of patients. Among those in the second half of life—that is to say, over 35—there has not been one whose problem in the last resort was not that of finding a religious outlook on life." [30]

Champions of certain religious groups have concluded from this that Jung on the basis of his psychological theories believed he was confirming the ontological truth of religion; whether he did or not, this was not the point of his remark. He was merely saying that religious thought is so deeply ingrained in the human unconscious that any man refusing to think about religion is headed for trouble because he will be working against one of the most deeply rooted ways of human thinking.[31]

To give another illustration, in 1954, Jung wrote a book called *Answer to Job*[32] in which he commends the proclamation of the dogma of the Assumption[33] not because he believed it to be doctrinally right or wrong, but because he believed such a pronouncement to be psychologically necessary. The majority of Catholic women, he said, at least unconsciously had been demanding the doctrine in order to have a symbol of identification in heaven. Another good illustration of Jung's attitude in this regard can be summarized from a conversation between him and an interviewer at Küsnacht/Zurich, Switzerland, in September, 1960: The interviewer asked Jung his views on God and immortality, Jung replied:

> "If you should find in yourself . . . an ineradicable tendency to believe in God or immortality, do not allow yourself to be disturbed by the blather of so-called 'free thinkers'—but if you find in yourself an equally resistant tendency to deny all religious ideas, do not hesitate to deny them and see how that suits you." [34]

The interviewer then asked Jung, "Then you do not think it necessarily futile for people to place their hope on the possibility of a life after death?" Jung replied, "As there is no possibility of proof, it is just as legitimate to believe in life after death as it is to doubt it. We have experiences which point both ways. The only important thing is to find a philosophy to live by." [35]

The relevance of the points just mentioned may not be wholly clear at this time, so it will be well to review some basic material; first, definitions of the terms "conscious" and "unconscious," as used in everyday speech and in Freud and Jung, and then certain of the chief tenets of Jung's theory can be summarized.

In everyday speech the term "conscious" refers to whatever we are aware of at the present moment, while the term "unconscious" refers to contents that may exist in our minds but but are not here and now in our field of awareness. Suppose, for example, we call into consciousness John Milton's *Paradise Lost*. If we had not been thinking about Milton's poem just before it was suggested, then *Paradise Lost* was at that time an unconscious content of our minds, whereas at the present time it is a conscious content. Among the different contents of the unconscious are those which at the present instant are not in consciousness but which are about to emerge into consciousness. Such contents are called subconscious. The subconscious, then, is part of the unconscious; it is that part which is about to become conscious.

Freud's terminology is somewhat akin to that of popular speech, but it is also different: First of all, he divides the mind into consciousness and unconsciousness, and unconsciousness he divides into two parts: the preconscious and the unconscious.[36] The preconscious (Pcs.) contains not only contents we ordinarily call subconscious; it also contains further elements which ordinary speech would call unconscious; i.e., memories of objects and situations a person may have forgotten for months or even years and perhaps will not recall for many more months. or years. The important point about all the contents of the preconscious is that they can be recalled by the man possessing such contents. It may not always be easy to recall them, but with enough effort he can do this.

For Freud, the unconscious (Ucs.) has contents that no man can recall by himself, and that he can bring up only by the special techniques of psychoanalysis. The contents of the unconscious (Ucs.) are of two kinds: first, repressed traumatic experiences which the man himself has undergone; and, secondly, residual psychological contents of the human race.[37] By the latter Freud means that just as modern man has inherited anatomical characteristics from his earlier forebears, so too, modern man has inherited certain psychological characteristics from his earlier forebears. These psychological characteristics are predispositions for reacting in definite ways to certain situations confronted by prehistoric ancestors, and if modern man is put into circumstances like theirs, he will react in exactly the same way as prehistoric men. Freud's own evidence for this was based on observation of paranoid patients who are acutely aware of any kind of change in their surroundings.[38] A. A. Brill, who introduced Freud to the United States, cites what he says is an example of a mentally healthy modern man reacting like a prehistoric man in a primitive situation. In World War I soldiers had to drive trucks along the front lines in pitch darkness, but even without lights these drivers could detect shell holes ahead on a road by listening for the change in sound echo. According to Brill, when moving along in ordinary traffic, these same men were oblivious to such subtle variations in sound differences.[39]

For Freud's theory, it is the first part of the unconscious (Ucs.), the repressed experiences of a man's own life, that plays the most important role; but for Jung's theory the more important role is played by the racial unconscious. Jung's whole system is vast, and it is impossible to do it complete justice in a short space, but some of its chief features can be given in outline.[40]

For Jung, the human psyche consists of two spheres possessing contrary properties: the sphere of the conscious and the sphere of the unconscious. While their properties are contrary to each other, they do not negate each other; but supplement, complement, and compensate one another.[41] Within these spheres are found several systems, the chief of which are (1) The ego, (2) The personal unconscious with its complexes, (3) The racial conscious with its achetypes, most noted of which are (a) The persona, (b) The *anima* (*animus*), (3) The old man (the earth mother). Finally, there is the self, which is the symbol of the fully integrated personality.

In Jungian psychology the ego is the conscious mind, and is made up of those perceptions, memories, thoughts and feelings which a person may be entertaining at any particular time in his consciousness.[42] It is because a person has a conscious ego that he has a feeling of continuity, that is to say, he has a recognition that the acts performed yesterday and the acts performed today are those of the same person.

The personal unconscious is a region of unconsciousness adjoining the ego. It consists of two different elements, both of which originate from the person's own experiences:[43] first, experiences which were at one time in the field of consciousness but which have been repressed, suppressed, forgotten, or ignored; and secondly, experiences, which were originally too weak to make a conscious impression upon the individual. The contents of Jung's personal unconscious are somewhat akin to those of Freud's preconscious, in so far as the personal unconscious is accessible to the conscious ego. The personal unconscious can also be compared to what Freud calls the unconscious repressed.[44]

Among contents of the personal unconscious special note must be taken of those which gather together into a complex,[45] viz.; a well-organized group of feelings, thoughts, and memories consisting of two main parts, the nucleus and the associated contents.[46] The nucleus group of a complex has contents from two different sources: First, there are inherited racial tendencies to act in a certain way if certain situations arise. Such inherited tendencies come not only from one's immediate ancestors but also from the earliest ancestors of the human race. The second part of the nucleus contains certain emotions, feelings, and memories this person has acquired from his own experiences. For example, with regard to the deeply-rooted tendencies in the nucleus of a mother-complex, human beings have always had mothers, either their own natural mother or someone who acts like a mother toward them. Therefore in the course of thousands of years, Jung says, there has developed in the human mind a residual content which disposes every human child now alive to react toward some human adult in the same way children generally have reacted toward a mother. This Jung calls the mother-archetype. The second part of the nucleus contains emotions, feelings, and memories a human being now has after his own actual relation to the adult who functioned as a mother. The nucleus group attracts further ideas, feelings, and memories which have the same emotional tone as the nucleus.

Everybody has complexes. Some are harmless. Many of them are helpful especially so far as they may supply further energy to reinforce conscious activities. But in some cases a complex will become dangerous if it gathers too great a mass of psychic content which develops into a completely isolated set of character traits and begins acting on its own, apart from and incompatibly with the rest of a person's mental make-up.[47] The complex may even seize control of the whole person and exploit the rest of the personality for its own ends. An example of this is Adolf Hitler, in whose case the complex was a craving for power. The nucleus and many of the associated ideas, feelings, and memories of a complex are unconscious most of the time, but any of the associated ideas, feelings, and memories, and even the nucleus itself, may, and often do, break into the field of consciousness. Whether the complex is healthy or unhealthy, it indicates that the person's psychic life is not yet wholly fulfilled.[48] An unhealthy complex can be removed only by means of psychotherapy, but the presence and depth of any complex can be detected without psychotherapy. One need only apply Jung's word-association test.

The Collective (Racial) Unconscious

Beyond question the theory of the collective unconscious is Jung's best-known contribution to depth psychology. It has been applied not only in that field but to many other areas, especially to history and aesthetics. Jung maintains that the collective unconscious is the most powerful and the most influential part of the total psychic structure. In pathological cases, it overshadows the ego and the personal unconscious.

The collective unconscious, Jung says, seems to be the storehouse of latent memory traces inherited by each man from his ancestors. Not only his human ancestors but also animal ancestors through all the stages of evolution which have contributed to the human body. In brief, the collective unconscious is the psychological residue of man's evolutionary development.[49] It is almost entirely detached from anything personal in the life of an individual,[50] but, as already stated, it may contribute certain contents to the nuclear group of a complex. All human beings have more or less the same contents in their collective unconscious. In each individual the patterns in which the racial contents are arranged may be slightly different, just as in each individual human face there are two eyes, one nose, and one mouth, but they are arranged differently on each face.

Actual memories of events that have conditioned the collective unconscious are not inherited as such. Rather we inherit the possibility of reliving the experiences of past generations.[51] We inherit dispositions toward acting in certain ways to certain situations if, or when, these situations arise in our own lives. These inborn predispositions to react in certain ways may be compared to man's capacity for three-dimensional vision. Just as he develops this capacity by experience and training, so too, says Jung, man is born with many predispositions for thinking, feeling, and perceiving according to definite patterns and contents. The individual develops those predispositions through a series of experiences. While man has all these predispositions, it does not mean that all of them will actually develop. For example, all men are born with fears of the dark and of poisonous snakes, but they do not actually begin to fear the dark or poisonous snakes unless they first undergo a traumatic experience.

Anything a person learns as a result of his own experience is influenced in a major way by his collective unconscious because whatever content he himself acquires will be given a certain bias by the predispositions which are already part of his collective unconscious. Since what he learns constitutes his personal unconscious, it should be evident that the personal unconscious is influenced significantly by the collective unconscious. This is equally true of the ego, since much of the content of the ego arises out of the personal unconscious.

It should be obvious, then, that since it influences a person's reactions to his environment and to individual situations, the collective unconscious can be of immense service to a human being. On the other hand, if the contents of the collective unconscious are ignored by the conscious ego, the collective unconscious may disrupt rational processes. Symptoms, phobias, delusions, and other irrational activities stem from neglected unconscious processes.

The inherited primitive predispositions in the collective unconscious are called archetypes.[52] As has already been noted, these contents are not actual memories of the emotional experiences themselves but they are predispositions to react in the same way to the same kind of experiences our ancestors went through.[53] The archetype usually contains a large segment of emotion.[54] Reference has been made of two archetypes: the mother, and the fear of the dark. The mother archetype is an innate predisposition to act in a certain way toward the mother. In ordinary experience this predisposition toward the mother will be reinforced by the child's actual experience with its mother. The result is that both the archetype and the personal experience reinforce each other and combine to strengthen the person's traits. Usually the archetype and one's personal experience will be compatible with each other because the archetype, after all, has resulted from the usual behavior of the race.

The notion of archetypes may be further illustrated by reference to one that has figured prominently in the past twenty years, namely, the energy archetype. Jung holds that throughout its existence mankind has always been exposed to innumerable experiences of great natural forces such as earthquakes, waterfalls, floods, hurricanes, lighting, and forest fires. Out of these experiences there has developed a predisposition to perceive power, and to be fascinated by it and a desire to create and control it. This archetype is the root of a child's delight in firecrackers, a teenager's preoccupation with high-powered racing cars, and an adult's obsessive interest in atomic energy. For Jung mankind is driven unconsciously to seek out new sources of energy, and the contemporary age might well be described as the age of the energy archetype.

Certain archetypes have already developed so fully in the race that they have become distinct systems within the human psychic structure. These are especially:

(1) The *persona*
(2) The *anima* (*animus*)
(3) The old wise man and the earth mother
(4) The self

Jung's term *persona* is that same Latin *persona* from which our "person" derives. Originally in Latin it signified the mask worn by a Roman actor to indicate the role he was playing. Jung uses the term with much this same root meaning because the Jungian *persona* is the face that each individual presents to his surroundings. It involves a certain amount of necessary and healthy play-acting that eases the tensions between a man's inner world and the world around him. A person has to act the way other people act in his society; if this were not so, the society would become chaotic. Jung once defined the *persona* as a compromise between the individual and society.[55] The *persona* can become injurious only when it dominates the inner personality. In some instances, where it predominates but is not overwhelming, the person's behavior becomes stereotyped and he is impervious to new ideas: In more serious cases of a predominant *persona,* the man who is always play-acting may be repressing some very primitive impulses; if he does not recognize their presence within himself, they may burst out violently at some unexpected time.

The *anima* is the feminine principle in a human male and there is a corresponding *animus,* i.e., masculine principle, in a human female. The *anima* embodies those traits which in our society have usually been considered as female, such as gentleness, appreciation of finer things, pettiness, and rage. The *anima* is the unconscious image in the mind of each male as to what a woman ought to be.[56] The *anima* is the image of a woman that appears and reappears throughout the ages. She is young, yet she has the wisdom of the ages; she is somehow strangely meaningful, clad in an aura of secret knowledge.[57] The *anima* and the *animus* archetypes have been acquired in the course of human history as a result of the interaction and interdependence of the two sexes.

The archetype of the old wise man may appear in dreams or fantasies as a king or a hero, medicine man, magician or savior.[58] In therapeutic situations, the old wise man appears to many patients as the psychiatrist himself. If a man becomes abnormally receptive to the idea of himself as an old wise man, he may become the leader of a wild-eyed revivalist sect with messianic delusions, a Hitler, or a mad-house Napoleon.

Corresponding to the old wise man, there is the feminine archetype called the earth mother. The earth mother is a woman's conception of herself as the very source of life.[59] But if a woman becomes excessively impressed with the notion of herself as the earth mother, and begins to envision herself as endowed with an unmatched capacity for understanding the problems of others, she may become meddlesome, or tighten the circle of her mothering influence until she strangles the objects of her devotion.

At the root of the archetypes by far the most important principle is the self which integrates elements from both the conscious and unconscious and from all the archetypes, and integrates even good and evil. It is a symbol of perfect integration of everything in a person's physical and psychological make-up. The self is arrived at, if ever, as the result of a lifelong process called individuation.[60] In the process of individuation the individual gets to know more and more about his unconscious; and the more he gets to know of his unconscious, the more he is able to give proper values to what had been previously only half-sensed and disturbing urges.

In order to appreciate more fully what Jung means by "the self," account must be taken of his notion of the symbol[61] and return be made to the archetypes to show how the self is the quintessence of symbols. For Jung a symbol differs from a sign: A sign represents some reality other than itself; it is a clear and consciously recognized representation of something other than itself; it represents something that is known. The symbol also represents, but what is represented by the symbol is something mysterious, laden with meaning yet not fully understood.[62] The sign is a product of conscious activity, the symbol is a product of unconscious activity. The symbol is an image that represents an aspect of reality which no concept can encompass, and can be grasped only indirectly and in a nonintellectual form. Jung is not concerned as to whether the mysterious reality behind the symbol really exists in the way the symbol represents; he is merely interested insofar as these symbols exist in the psychological makeup of people.[63] Again, the actual existence of God or of the immortality of the soul is not a proper question in Jung's theory. In Jungian psychology there is an archetype symbol of God and there is another of immortality, but so far as Jung's psychological theory is concerned, there need not be such an actual entity as God or any actual future life.

The reverse of this viewpoint is seen in Jung's notion of evil. For him, as far as some neurotic patients are concerned, evil is something definite and actual. Hence he disagrees violently with philosophers who say that evil is a privation of being, that it is non-being as it were. Jung even proposes the possibility that evil is present in God himself.[64] However, it must be kept in mind that for him a symbol is important only as a psychic reality.

The archetypes are designated by several terms in Jungian psychology. They are sometimes called dominants of the collective unconscious, primordial images, imagos, mythological images and behavior patterns. It was only later that Jung called them archetypes. An archetype is a psychic disposition found in all men and which usually contains a large element of emotion.[65] Archetypes are the permanent deposits resulting from the cumulative and repeated experiences of many generations. But the repeated experiences of these many generations have been conditioned by even deeper roots in what he calls a proto-image which might be compared to what a scholastic philosopher calls the natural appetite of a substance: Among biologists it is a well-known fact that every species of animal possesses certain inborn tendencies to act in certain ways and that these inborn tendencies differ from one species to another. Not only are such tendencies found in lower animals but they are to be found in the human species, which manifests also certain innate patterns of behavior. Jung holds that these patterns must be taken into account by anyone attempting to investigate the deepest roots of human behavior. Such "patterns of behavior" should not be confused with innate ideas. They are rather tendencies to act in a certain way without any prior learning, ". . . just as a chick has an inborn propensity to break out of the egg, or the bird has to build a nest, or an eel to find its way to Bermuda." [66]

Such patterns are not themselves on the psychic level of living functions; but they are the source out of which the psychic originates.[67] They are prior to the individual's own consciousness.[68] They are, of their very nature, unconscious, and will never manifest themselves directly in consciousness. The deep level of processes on which these "primal behavior patterns" are found is called the psychoid. The psychoid may be defined as "an intangible point of transition where biological phenomena are no longer merely biological, but where, on the other hand they are not yet psychological." [69] Out of the psychoid processes develop the instincts and archetypes. Instincts furnish the energy by which the life process of the organism progressively discloses itself whereas the archetype is the pattern according to which the organism's life processes develop. The instinct is the physiological aspect of the innate patterns of behavior while the archetype is the mental aspect of the same innate pattern. In *The Death and Rebirth of Psychology* Progoff says that the psychoid level

> ". . . should be thought of somewhat as a hypothetical substratum of the human organism at which psychological qualities are present but still unformed; they are potential but still undifferentiated in a way that is comparable to the capacity of speech still undisclosed in the human embryo." [70]

Down on this deep level of the psychoid where there is not yet consciousness there is, nevertheless, a purposiveness to the activity. Although not itself conscious, the living being still seems to "know" a goal toward which it is moving. This unconscious innate biological "knowledge" which the living thing possesses is called a proto-image. As Jung describes it:

"It has fixed qualities. The instinct of the leaf-cutting ant fulfills the image of ant, tree, leaf, cutting, transport, and the little ant garden of fungi. If any one of these conditions is lacking, the instinct does not function because it cannot exist without its total pattern, its image. Such an image is an a priori type. It is inborn to the ant prior to any activity at all unless an instinct of corresponding pattern initiates and makes it possible. This schema holds true of all instincts and is found in identical forms in all individuals of the same species."[71]

The proto-image lies deeper than any of the individual's own mental processes, but it is the source out of which arise all his physiological and mental activities. On higher levels the psychoid becomes differentiated into the physiological and psychological aspects, the instincts and the archetypes. Every species of animal contains a proto-image; and in the human species the proto-image is called the self.[72]

The self, then, begins as a darkly purposeful "content of knowledge" by which the human organism "knows" the goal toward which it is moving. In its deepest roots it manifests no consciousness, but on higher levels it manifests itself through psychological activities. It leads the human organism outside of itself because man's very deepest roots lead him to a point where he must transcend himself. He must reach out beyond his own life to an experience of something in which he is encompassed but which he can never define because it is boundless. At these outermost limits man experiences the "boundlessness of the soul" as an evident fact. But only in the rarest cases, says Jung, does a man integrate his total personality so as to arrive at a perfect fulfillment of the self. Nevertheless, the man who does achieve this total integration arrives at perfect harmony with everything about him because there is perfect harmony of everything within him.

The extent in which considerations of the immaterial are significant in Jung's theory is apparent. He is well aware that the past of his patients plays a great role in their present condition, but he is equally aware of how great a role a patient's future goals will play. In this respect he differs from Freud who, in theory at

least, denies freedom of choice and holds that no man can be
other than he is because he is the inevitable product of his past.
Jung's considerations of sex, God, and religious experience are
closer to the facts than Freud's are, but his views on some of
these matters cannot be taken without qualification. The same
may be said of his notion of the collective unconscious; it is not
universally accepted by psychiatrists; and, as propounded by
Jung, it presents certain difficulties. In order to appreciate what
these difficulties are, let us follow Jung as he develops his argument for the archetypes. A major exposition is found in Chapter
I of *Psychology of The Unconscious* which was first published
in 1912.

Jung begins by saying that dream images are to be understood
symbolically; that is to say, they are not to be taken literally
as they appear during sleep but one must surmise the hidden
meaning behind them.[73] When a certain dream content manifests
itself regularly throughout human cultures over thousands of
years, we can be certain that, while this content may not literally
represent some kind of extramental reality, nevertheless this
same content does manifest a psychological reality.[74] In other
words, the content is the product of some kind of psychological
process taking place down on the deeper levels of a human
mind.[75] The dream is "... a *series of images, which are apparently
contradictory and nonsensical but arise in reality from psychologic
material which yields a clear meaning."*[76]

Jung illustrates his point with the case of a girl who, after she
has spent a happy evening at a dance, dreams that a robber
noisily breaks open her door and stabs her with a lance.[77] He
remarks that this theme, whose latent content is obvious, is found
in countless variations. Instead of a lance it may be a sword, a
dagger, or a revolver, and the assault may be represented as made
during a burglary, a pursuit, a robbery, or by someone who had
been hidden under the bed. Frequently the content may appear
in more complicated form. The attacker may be "a horse which
throws the dreamer to the ground and kicks her in the body
with his hind foot;" or the attack may be made by an elephant
with a threatening trunk," or by some kind of a snake.[78] Jung
goes on to say that if the reader is not convinced by the examples
cited, he may seek further evidence in the works of Freud, Stekel,

and Rank. In any case, Jung insists that the existence of dream symbolism is an established fact. He then raises two questions: Why are dreams symbolic? and How is it that dreams are symbolic?

To answer the first Jung resorts to Freud's explanation of the dream as a disguise for wishes that are unacceptable to a person's normal waking state but still seek an outlet in consciousness. Since they cannot arise in their raw state, they emerge under a symbolic disguise. To answer the second question he begins with the observation that symbolism is found in everyday thinking. When we think intensively, for example, we may speak to ourselves or put the problem in writing or outline the problem with diagrams in order to be absolutely clear about what the problem is.[79] Then we think in words, we talk to ourselves as it were, while we mull over the problem, and when the solution is found we express it in words to convince others. Thinking such as this Jung calls "thinking with directed attention."[80] Furthermore, such thinking is manifestly an instrument of modern culture. This raises another question: What happens if we do not think directly? Our thinking then becomes undirected.[81]

Undirected thinking does not tire us, and it leads us quickly away from reality and into phantasies of past and future. "Image crowds upon image, feeling upon feeling; more and more clearly one sees a tendency which creates and makes believe, not as it truly is but as one indeed might wish it to be."[82] The material out of which the mind constructs these thoughts which turn away from reality can be only memory with its manifold contents. Mental activity of this sort is called dreaming. Thus we have two kinds of thinking: directed thinking and dream thinking.

Directed thinking is a phenomenon of modern times, whereas phantasy thinking was the common way of thinking among ancient Greeks.[83] It is difficult for modern man to appreciate how much energy ancient man expended in his phantasy thinking. But this is why the Greeks created not science but mythology.[84] We know, says Jung, that phantasy thinking characterizes childhood.[85] If one accepts the well-established principle of comparative anatomy and embryology that the structure and function of the human body are results of a series of embryonic changes and correspond to similar changes in the history of the human race, then one is jutified in supposing that "... ontogenesis corresponds in *psychology* to phylogenesis."[86] Therefore, it is true to say that the infantile kind of thinking found in a child's psychic life as well as in adult dreams is nothing more than a re-echo of the prehistoric and the ancient. After a long quotation from Nietzsche[87] Jung quotes Freud: "it is probable that the myths correspond to the distorted residues of wish phantasies of whole nations ...". Then, after reference to Rank and Rilkin, he quotes Abraham: "The myth is a fragment of the infantile soul-life of the people."[88] Jung goes on to remark that any unprejudiced reader of the authors cited will conclude that there are definite connections between dream psychology and myth psychology. Myths are so deeply ingrained in the human mind that

> "should it happen that all traditions in the world were cut off with a single blow, then with the succeeding generation, the whole mythology and history of religion would start all over again."[89]

One might destroy a particular manifestation of some myth, but one could never destroy the impulse in the human mind to create myths.[90]

If we ask why the human mind creates myths, Jung again appeals to Freud's theory for the answer. We imagine what we lack, and, he adds, whenever we imagine we find that the contents of our phantasies are mythological themes.

Jung presents his thesis a second time. Just as our bodies retain vestiges of old functions and conditions in various organs, so also our minds, which apparently have outgrown archaic psychologic tendencies, still bear the marks of the evolution passed through, and the very ancient re-echoes at least dreamily in phantasies.[91]

Directed thinking, Jung says, is conscious throughout. But this cannot be said for phantasy thinking. Some of the latter falls in the realm of the conscious but at least just as much goes along "in the half-shadows," and an undetermined amount of it goes on in the unconscious.[92] This latter part discloses itself only indirectly. By means of phantasy thinking

directed thinking is connected with the oldest foundations
of the human mind, which have been for a long time
beneath the threshold of the consciousness.[93]
The known conscious phantasy may be of mythical or other
material; it is not to be taken seriously as such, for it has
an indirect meaning.[94]

Jung wrote another concentrated exposition of the archetype
in 1921 in his *Psychological Types*, where Chapter XI defines
terms that had caused difficulty for his critics. *Image* is one of
such terms; the archetype is sometimes called a *primordial image*.
The image is only an indirect presentation of the object or situation.[95] Ordinarily the image differs from an hallucination in that
the content of the latter is believed to represent an actually-
existent extramental reality, whereas an image content is readily
recognized as suggesting some extramental reality only indirectly.
Although the image may not represent something actually existing at the time in the extramental order, it often signifies indirectly
certain constellated contents deep in the unconscious.[96] However,
the image is not restricted solely to the contents of the unconscious,
but is also

> *a concentrated expression of the total psychic situation*, not
> merely, nor even preeminently, of unconscious contents
> pure and simple.[97]

There is no doubt that the image does express some of the content
of the unconscious, but only that part which at the time is concentrated around the momentary situation in the field of consciousness. Thus it may be said that the image is an expression
of contents from both the unconscious and the momentary conscious situation.

An image is called *primordial* when it possesses an archaic
character; that is to say, when the content of the image is strikingly
similar to that of familiar mythological subjects.[98] In such a case
the image expresses material derived mostly from the collective
unconscious and it shows simultaneously that the momentary
conscious situation is being influenced less from the personal
than from the collective unconscious.

A primordial image, that is, an archetype, is always collective; it is at least common to entire nations or periods. There is evidence suggesting that the most important mythological subjects are found at all times and in all races. Here is Jung's own description of the primordial image:

> The primordial image is a mnemic deposit, an *imprint* ("engramm"—Semon), which has arisen through a condensation of innumerable, similar processes. It is primarily a precipitate or deposit, and therefore a typical basic form of a certain ever-recurring psychic experience. As a mythological motive, therefore, it is a constantly effective and continually recurring expression which is either awakened, or appropriately formulated, by certain psychic experiences.[99]

If we wish to understand Jung's further explanation of the archetype we must keep in mind how much he was influenced by von Hartmann's philosophy of the unconscious. Von Hartmann asserts that the unconscious is the one absolute subject and that it reveals itself in a multiplicity of individuals.[100] Individuals as such are only phenomenal combinations of an organism with the actions of the unconscious directed to the same.[101] Matter and consciousness are phenomenal forms of the unconscious.[102] The world consists only of a sum of activities or will-acts of the unconscious, and the ego consists of another sum of activities or will-acts of the unconscious.[103]

Previous observations on von Hartmann and the excerpts just quoted from his *Psychology of The Unconscious* reveal the roots of Jung's theorizing about archetypes. The archetype is the psychic expression of an anatomically and physiologically determined disposition.[104] Just as the body acquires a definite anatomical structure from surrounding conditions, so in like manner the psyche acquires definite modifications from the surrounding environment.[105] In this way the myth could be related to nature. But we are still left with the problem of why the real content of the myth reveals itself only indirectly.

Jung is convinced that the allegorical contents of the myth point inescapably to an independent collaboration on the part of the psyche because these contents cannot explain themselves as mere imitations of the momentary environment. By this he means that the given brain-structure of a human being owes its particular nature to not only surrounding conditions but also to the peculiar and autonomous quality of living matter of constantly reorganizing, renewing, and adapting itself.[106]

> The organism confronts light with a new formation, the eye, and the psyche meets the process of nature with a symbolical image, which apprehends the nature-process just as the eye catches the light. And in the same way as the eye bears witness to the peculiar and independent creative activity of living matter, the primordial image expresses the unique and unconditioned creative power of the mind.[107]

The primordial image is "a recapitulatory expression of the living process."[108] It coordinates both the immediate content of the senses and the unconscious contents of the psyche; it constructs a meaningful pattern which serves to guide actions; it liberates and channels life energy.[109]

Jung then distinguishes between the idea and the primordial image. The idea is the product of directive thinking, it is the product of the formulating reason. It is marked by some degree of clarity, whereas the primordial image is known only vaguely. The primordial image is superior to the idea in that the former has vitality since it is, after all, "an inherited organization of psychic energy."[110]

Jung asserts that if the term primordial image is substituted each time for the term idea, then Schopenhauer may be quoted to describe the Jungian primordial image:

> The idea is never known by the individual as such, but only by the man who is exalted above all willing and above all individuality to the pure Subject of knowledge: thus it is attainable only by the genius, or by the man who has achieved mainly through the works of genius an elevation of his pure gift of cognition into a temper akin to genius: it is, therefore, not absolutely, but only conditionally, comunicable, since the idea conceived and reproduced

in an artistic creation, for instance, only appeals to every man according to his intellectual powers, etc.

The idea is unity split up into multiplicity by virtue of the temporal and spatial form of our intuitive apprehension. The concept is like an inanimate vehicle, in which the things one deposits lie side by side, but from which no more can be taken out than was put in: the idea, on the contrary develops within the man who has embraced its conceptions which in relation to its homonymous concept are new: it is like a living, self-developing organism endowed with creative force, bringing forth something that was never put into it.[111]

Jung establishes his theory of archetypes on data acquired from his own experience as a psychiatrist and from the findings of anthropology. Thus he is able to conclude in *Psychological Types* with the words:

I am myself so profoundly convinced of this homogeneity of the human psyche that I have actually embraced it in the concept of the collective unconscious, as a universal and homogeneous substratum whose homogeneity extends even into a world-wide identity or similarity of myths and fairy-tales; so that a negro of the Southern States of America dreams in the motives of Grecian mythology, and a Swiss grocer's apprentice repeats in his psychosis, the vision of an Egyptian Gnostic.[112]

Here is one of the most frequently quoted examples proposed by Jung to show that a mythological theme recurs among different peoples throughout the ages. If we look at Nietzsche's poem, *The Beacon,* we find that libido is represented in that poem as a flame.[113] A rearing snake is a phallic image of libido, and is also a symbol of impatience. The combination of flame and snake is found in an ancient image of the sun possessing a phallus. Among the Egyptians the sun god is a creator. In Mithraic liturgy there is found a passage that reads:

In like manner the so-called tube, the origin of the

ministering wind, will become visible. For it will appear to you as a tube hanging down from the sun.[114]

Jung remarks that this passage would be strange and meaningless if it did not have the phallic meaning. The tube is the place of origin of the wind, which, like the sun, is a fructifier and a creator. Jung also finds this symbol of the tube coming down from the sun in a medieval German painting of the Immaculate Conception, where a tube is shown as coming down from heaven and passing beneath Mary's dress, and the Holy Spirit in the form of a dove is shown flying down in the tube.

Jung then reports the case of one of Honneger's paranoid patients who saw the sun an "upright tail," or something like an ithyphallus. Whenever the patient moved his head back and forth, the object in the sun moved back and forth, and that, said the patient, is how the wind arises. Only after he learned about the Mithraic liturgy could Jung make any sense out of this patient's hallucination. In fact the patient's hallucination seemed to clarify an obscure text in the Mithraic liturgy.[115]

Jung comments that the word *orama* signifies the thing seen, and that the term *apophora* signifies carrying away. Then he conjectures that the meaning of the text, according to this "might be" that

> the thing seen may be carried sometimes here, sometimes there, according to the direction of the wind. The *orama* which is "the tube, the place of origin of the wind," which turns sometimes to the east, sometimes to the west ...

This vision of the insane man, Jung claims, corresponds astonishingly with the Mithraic description.

Jung refers in a footnote for the same passage to the case reported by Rilkin, one of his colleagues, of

> a paranoic who passed over into a manifest megalomaniac in the following way: She suddenly saw a strong light, a *wind blew* upon her, she felt as if "her heart turned over," and from that moment she knew that God had visited her and was in her.[116]

This corroborative evidence has been quoted in detail because it is considered one of the best cases that Jung has presented in favor of his theory, but the evidence is not absolutely convincing. First of all, Jung inaccurately identifies a picture of Pentecost or the Annunciation as one of the Immaculate Conception, and secondly, he merely conjectures the meaning of the Mithraic text. Thirdly, he explains the experience of Rilkin's patient in terms of the Mithraic liturgy when it could just as easily be explained in terms of the New Testament account of Pentecost if the patient was a Christian or at least had heard of Pentecost.

In recent times much more anthropological evidence has been provided to show that certain themes recur in the cultural experience of many civilizations. Some of the best evidence has been produced by Mircea Eliade,[117] who has shown that certain natural objects and events serve regularly as symbols throughout human history. The egg is a symbol of regeneration; fire and water are symbols of death and rebirth for the obvious reason that any human culture is surrounded with the presence of water and fire whose natural powers of disintegrating and reintegrating matter soon become evident. Eliade's data have been suggested as corroborating Jung's theory. But do they? Would it not be just as acceptable an argument to say that objects of everyday experience are often used metaphorically in human thinking? One immediately thinks of Christ's use of parables.

If Jung could show that mythological contents and dream contents are markedly identical in more ways than he has submitted for evidence, the weight of the argument would be more in his favor. At the present time it cannot be said that the theory is right or wrong. It is a brilliant conjecture, a possible interpretation which at some time may have greater value on the basis of more evidence. It can still be accepted for what it was intended to be—a fruitful hypothesis. Jung's attitude toward his theory is best summarized in a quotation he placed at the front of *Psychology of the Unconscious*:

> Therefore theory, which gives to facts their value and significance, is often very useful, even if it is partially false, for it throws light on phenomena which no one observed, it forces an examination, from many angles, of facts which

no one had hitherto studied, and it gives the impulse for more extended and more productive researches.

It is, therefore, a moral duty for the man of science to expose himself to the risk of committing error and to submit to criticism, in order that science may continue to progress. A writer has attacked the author of this very severely, saying, here is a scientific ideal very limited and very paltry. But those who are endowed with a mind sufficiently serious and impersonal as not to believe that all that they write is the expression of truth absolute and eternal, approve of this theory which places the aims of science well above the miserable vanity and paltry "amour propre" of the scientist.[118]

Jung was always open to new ideas. While he still lived, the works of Binswanger,[119] Boss,[120] Caruso [121] and Frankl,[122] to name only four writers, were adding refinements to his work, and since his death even newer contributions to psychiatric theory have been offered.[123]

NOTES

(For the benefit of readers who may be unfamiliar with German, citations are given in reference to authorized English translations. Where there is no authorized translation, citations are left in German.)

1. The literature on this point is abundant. The following are a few citations. Otto Rank shows how this is true for Freud in *Beyond Psychology* (New York: Dover Publications, 1941), p. 288. With special regard for Jung, cf. W. Daim, "Der Grundfehler C. G. Jungs, *"Wissenschaft und Weltbild,* VI (1953), pp. 58-66. With regard to Adler, cf. Ira Progoff, *The Death and Rebirth of Psychology* (New York: The Julian Press, 1956), pp. 115-119. Progoff recognizes his indebtedness for this view to Phyllis Bottome whose biography of Adler is the most definitive as yet, cf. Phyllis Bottome, *Alfred Adler: A Biography* (New York: Putnam, 1939). Writing on this point to Aniela Jaffé, Jung remarks: "My life has been in a sense the quintessence of what I have written, not the other way around. The way I am and the way I write are a unity. All my ideas and all endeavors are myself. Thus the 'autobiography' is merely the dot on the i." C. G. Jung, *Memories, Dreams, Reflections,* tr. by Richard and Clara Winston (New York: Pantheon Books, 1961), p. xii. This is a posthumous book and may be considered, literally in some cases, as "the last words" Jung had to say on certain subjects.

2. Cf., for example, Ernest Jones, *The Life of Sigmund Freud,* Vol. I

(New York: Basic Books, 1955), p. 11, and Progoff, *op. cit.*, pp. 27-28, 39.

3.Jones, *op. cit.*, p. 7.

4. Freud's father was born on December 18, 1815, his mother on August 18, 1835. Freud himself at 6:30 p.m., May 6, 1856. Freud's mother was his father's second wife, and he had a half-brother, Paul, whose first child was older than Freud.

5. Elizabeth S. Sergeant, "Doctor Jung: A Portrait," *Harper's Magazine,* Vol. 162, (May, 1931), p. 741.

6. "Jung," *Current Biography,* 1943.

7. Sergeant, *op. cit.*, p. 742.

8. "As a youth Jung first entered his name on the Philosophy faculty of the University of Basel with the intention of becoming an archaeologist." *Current Biography* (1943). Jones, *op. cit.*, (Vol. II, p. 141), speaks of Jung's early interest in archaeology. It is significant to note that Freud also had much enthusiasm for antiquities. In fact, his chief reason for accepting G. Stanley Hall's invitation to lecture at Clark University in 1909 was his desire to see the New York Metropolitan Museum's collection of Greek antiquities and to visit Niagara Falls. Cf. Jones, *op. cit.*, Vol. II, p. 56.

9. Sergeant, *op. cit.*, p. 745. He later used the case of this girl as the subject for his doctoral dissertation. "Jung," *Current Biography,* 1953.

10. Arthur Schopenhauer, *Die Welt als Wille und Vorstellung.* Schopenhauer's sämmtlike Werke, Hrsg. von Julius Frauenstädt, 2. aufl., Neue ausg ... (Leipzig: F. A. Brockhaus, 1891), Vols. 2 & 3.

11. Sergeant, *op. cit.*, p. 745.

12. Karl Robert Eduard von Hartmann, *Philosophie des Unbewussten* (Berlin: C. Dunker, 1882). A survey and appraisal of von Hartmann's work was completed at the Catholic University of America this year by a doctoral candidate, Denis Kennedy Darnoi. *Eduard von Hartmann's Metaphysics of The Unconscious.* Washington; C. U. A. Press, 1964.

13. Two points should be kept in mind about the word association test: (1) the unconscious material which emerges is relatively close to consciousness before its appearance; (2) while this test is most frequently linked to Jung, similar tests can be found earlier in the works of Galton and of Wundt. Jung's test emphasizes· affective connections between the contents whereas Galton's and Wundt's emphasize conceptual relations.

14. This work of Freud's seems to have received almost as cool an initial reception as David Hume's *A Treatise of Human Nature,* and it is said that only 228 copies of the work were sold during the first two years cf., I. Hendrick, *Facts and Theories of Psychoanalysis* (3rd edition) (New York: Knopf, 1958), p. 324. Freud's *Studien über hysterien* also remained almost unknown for some time after it was published. Only 626 copies were sold in the first 13 years. Freud's royalties amounted to 85 dollars.

15. G. Jung, *Zur Psychologie and Pathologie Sogennanter Occulter Phänomene.* (Leipzig: O. Muntze, 1902). This was his doctoral dissertation prepared for public dissemination and its publication qualified him to be a lecturer at the University of Zürich.

16. G. Jung, *Über die Psychologie der Dementia Praecox* (Halle, Marhold, 1907). The most recent English translation is to be found in Volume 3 of Jung's *Collected Works*. C. G. Jung's *The Psychogenesis of Mental Disease - tr.* by R. F. C. Hull (New York: (Bollingen Series III) Pantheon Book, 1960). Prior to Hull's translation of this work the best known was that of A. A. Brill.

17. At ten o'clock in the morning on Sunday, February 27. Their warm friendship continued for some time after this meeting. The meeting which occurred when Freud visited Jung at Burghölzi (September, 1908) is said to have been the second most cordial session they ever had.

18. Jones, *op. cit.*, Vol. II, p. 141. Jones also mentions two letters dated February 15 and May 15 written to him by Jung expressing dissatisfaction with Freud's theories.

19. *Ibid.*, p. 143. By 1930, after Jung's *Contributions to Analytic Psychology* had come out in English, Lydiard H. Horton, writing in *The Journal of Abnormal and Social Psychology*, was able to say that "what Jung is really announcing by this new display of old material in a refreshing rearrangement is that Libido now more than ever means psychic energy in the broad sense of Aristotle's energeia (the exercise of faculty)." "A Critique of 'Contributions to Analytic Psychology'," *Journal of Abnormal and Social Psychology*, XXIV, 4 (Jan.-March, 1930), p. 443.

Watson says that Jung's definition of Libido includes"... the whole range of drives, being all embracing in nature, close in spirit to Plato's *Eros* or to Schopenhauer's will to live than to Freud's more restricted meaning." Robert I. Watson *The Great Psychologists, Aristotle to Freud*, New York: Lippincott, 1963. pp. 466-467.

20. Jones, *op. cit.*, p. 144. These lectures comprise Freud's *The Theory of Psychoanalysis*.

21. Granville Stanley Hall (1844-1924), first president of the American Psychological Association (1892) and founder of *The American Journal of Psychology* (1887), was head of the Department of Psychology at Clark University at the time. Among others attending this celebration were Sandor Ferenczi, E. B. Titchener, J. McK. Cattell, William James and William Stern.

22. Sergeant, *op. cit.*, p. 746.

23. "Wandlungen und Symbole der Libido, *"Jahrbuch für Psychoanalytische und Psychopathologische Forschungen*, III and IV. It was printed in volume form in Leipzig in 1912 by Deuticke, and translated into English as *Psychology of the Unconscious* by Beatrice M. Hinkle (New York: Moffett Yard, 1916; London: Kegan Paul, 1916). At the time of its publication Freud recognized that Jung's opinions were radically different from his own, but he dismissed the book as merely a case of a son revolting against his father.

24. The break with Jung was extremely painful to Freud, who had already broken with Adler and Stekel. The break with Adler and Stekel gave Freud nothing but relief. Jung, on the other hand, had a much better

grasp of psychoanalysis than they, and Freud had expected Jung to make major contributions.

25. Hendrick, *op. cit.*, pp. 333, 346.

26. Cf. Jung's *Contributions to Analytical Psychology* (New York: Harcourt Brace, 1928), p. 313.

27. Cf. Jaffé's "Introduction" to Jung's *Memories, Dreams, Reflections,* p. xiii. It should be kept in mind that while Jung's own writings comprise almost 20 large volumes, he did give his approval to at least two brief summaries written by associates. Cf. footnote 40.

28. To illustrate Jung's wide background with a few more examples: He spent six months among native tribes in North Africa in 1921 and returned in 1926 to spend another nine months. He visited the United States six times. During these visits, he was so delighted with American words and the American way of speaking English that he lectured almost entirely in American English when he returned to his seminars in Switzerland. He was always in close contact with Richard Wilhelm, director of the China Institute in Frankfurt and their mutual scholarly interests culminated in the joint publication of a translation of *The Secret of the Golden Flower* from Chinese into German in 1929. *Das Geheimnis der goldenen Blüte.* (München: Dorn, 1929). Jung was also a close friend of the great authority on Indian philosophy, Heinrich Zimmer. He wrote a foreword to the latter's posthumous work, *Der Weg zum Selbst* (Zurich: Rascher, 1944). Moreover intellectual indebtedness to Jung has been acknowledged by Paul Tillich, Arnold Toynbee, Philip Wylie, Lewis Mumford and Paul Radin.

29. In the opening of his Terry lectures at Yale University in 1937, Jung disavows any claim to being a philosopher, at least in the sense in which he understood the term. "Notwithstanding the fact that I have often been called a philosopher, I am an empiricist and adhere to the phenomenological point of view." These lectures are published in volume form: C. G. Jung, *Psychology and Religion* (New Haven: Yale University Press, 1938). The quotation above is on page 1.

30. *Modern Man In Search of a Soul*, tr. by W. S. Dell and C. F. Baynes (New York: Harcourt Brace; London: Kegan Paul, 1933), p. 264. It may clarify a point to mention that for Jung a religious person is anyone who has either actually undergone a transcendent experience or at least admits the possibility of it; he need not be a member of any organized religious group.

31. C. G. Jung and Carl Kerenyí, *Essays on the Science of Mythology,* tr. by R. F. C. Hull, Bollingen Series XXII (New York: Pentheon Books, 1949), pp. 105-106.

32. *Answer to Job*, tr. by R. F. C. Hull (London: Routledge, Kegan Paul, 1954).

33. He calls it ". . . the most significant religious event since the Reformation." p. 169.

34. Gordon Young, "Advice for Living," *The American Weekly*, Feb. 19, 1961, p. 11.

35. The following quotation from Jung may clarify further his ap-

proach: "The quality of personal immortality so fondly attributed to the soul by religion is, for science, no more than a psychological *indicium* which is already included in the idea of autonomy . . . the immediate meaning of 'immortality' is simply a psychic activity that transcends the limits of consciousness. "Beyond the grave'. . . means, psychologically, 'beyond consciousness.' There is positively nothing else it could mean, since statements about immortality can only be made by the living, who, as such, are not exactly in a position to pontificate about conditions 'beyond the grave'." "Anima and Animus," in *Two Essays on Analptical Psychology,* tr. by H. G. Baynes and C. F. Baynes (New York: Dodd, Mead & Co., 1928), p. 189. Two Catholic writers Raymond Hostie and Victor White have written appraisals of Jung's views on religion: Raymond Hostie, *Religion and the Psychology of C. G. Jung,* tr. by G. R. Lamb (New York: Sheed & Ward, 1957). Victor White, *God and the Unconscious* (Chicago: Henry Regnery & Co., 1960). Jung subsequently presented more fully his opinions on religion and religious matters in *Memories, Dreams, Reflections.* Although this work was published after the Hostie and White books, Jung does not say anything in it which would force them to change essentially what they had written.

36. S. Freud, *The Basic Writings of Sigmund Freud,* tr. by A. A. Brill (New York: The Modern Library, 1938).

37. S. Freud, *The Ego and the Id,* tr. by Joan Rivière (London: The Hogarth Press, 1950), p. 52.

38. Cf. A. A. Brill, *Lectures on Psychoanalytic Psychiatry* (New York: Alfred A. Knopf, 1949), p. 73. How these psychological dispositions can be passed down from one generation to another is not clear in Jung's writings. T. V. Moore, here at The Catholic University of America, expressed his doubts in *The Nature and Treatment of Mental Disorders* (New York: Grune and Stratton, 1951), pp. 58-59. Cf. also E. Glover, *Freud or Jung* (New York: Norton, 1950), *passim.*

39. Brill, *op. cit.,* p. 73.

40. Brevity requires omitting a detailed treatment of functions and attitudes but no discussion of Jung's pschology would be complete without some mention of them. Functions are thought processes; they are four irreducible kinds of mental activity discoverable in the human psyche, called thinking, feeling, sensing, and intuiting. In thinking a man seeks to understand his own nature and the nature of his environment by establishing conceptual relations and logical deductions. By feeling he reacts emotionally to things around him. By sensing he looks for concrete facts and concrete representations, he becomes aware of the particular individuated data of objects. By intuiting he goes beyond feelings and concepts and treats his environment as something involved in a far deeper mystery. To illustrate the differences between the four functions let us suppose that four men, each one representing one or another of these types, as standing on the rim of the Grand Canyon. The thinking man studies the canyon in terms of its geological structure. The man of feeling undergoes a sense of awe, grandeur, and breath-taking beauty. The sensation-type man examines the canyon

closely and notes all the details like a camera. The man of intuition grasps the canyon as a mystery of nature, possessing deep significance and one whose whole meaning could be understood only during a mystical experience.

Jung says that every man is born with all four functions but early in life one of these becomes dominant in consciousness, and is called the superior function. There are definite relations among the four functions. The thinking function is diametrically opposed to feeling, sensation is diametrically opposed to intuition. These relations are important because the function opposite a man's superior function is located in his unconscious. This is called his inferior function, is poorly developed, and is not directly under his control because it is outside of consciousness.

Besides his superior function each man makes use of another called his auxiliary function. Both superior and auxiliary functions are conscious and are subject to control by the will. The opposite to the auxiliary function can be raised into consciousness and every time it comes up it brings with it influences from the inferior function. Whenever the poorly developed function breaks through into consciousness, it brings with it infantile primitive and archaic material.

While the functions are basically only four in number it is not necessary that every man's functions be pure types. That is to say, one man's superior function may be the sensation type, another's may be the thinking type, and a third man's may be a sensation-thinking type rather than a pure sensation or a pure thinking type. The third man's inferior function in this case would be an intuition-feeling type.

The attitudes are patterns of. adjustment according to which a man bases his behavior on norms prevalent in his own time, place and society, or according to norms he has established from principles within himself. The first of these is called an extravert, the second is called an intravert. A man whose conscious behavior is extraverted will behave like an intravert on the unconscious level and the intravert will behave like an extravert on the unconscious level. Attitudes are more firmly established at birth than the functions are.

General summaries of Jung's position may be found in most works discussing theories of personality. There are three books which concern themselves exclusively with Jung's theory, and the first two of these have Jung's *imprimatur* on them. Frieda Fordham, *An Introduction to Jung's Psychology* Baltimore: Penguin Books, 1961). Jolande Jacobi, *The Psychology of C. G. Jung* (new revised edition) (New Haven: Yale University Press, 1961). Cf. also Ira Progoff *Jung's Psychology and Its Social Meaning* (New York: Grove Press, 1955). Fordham's book has a very good summary of the attitudes and functions in Chapter 2.

41. Jacobi, *op. cit.*, p. 10.

42. "The Ego is a complex of representations which constitutes the centrum of my field of consciousness and appears to possess a very high degree of continuity and identity." C. G. Jung, *Psychological Types* (London: Kegan Paul, 1933), p. 540.

43. Jung and Kerenyí, *op. cit.*, p. 102. Cf. also, C. G. Jung, *Two Essays on Analytical Psychology*, pp. 67-68.

44. Jung says that it contains "forgotten repressed, subliminally perceived thought and felt matter of every kind." *Psychological Types*, p. 616.

45. From the time of Bleuler the term "complex" had been used frequently and with several meanings in psychology. In his original work on association tests (*Diagnostische Associations studien*, Leipzig: Barth, 1906), Jung uses the term "feeling-toned complex" which he later shortened to "complex."

46. A detailed treatment of the Jungian complex is to be found in J. Jacobi's *Complex, Archetype, Symbol in the Psychology of C. G. Jung* (New York: Pantheon, 1959).

47. C. G. Jung, "Factors Determining Human Behavior, "*Harvard Tercentenary Conference on Arts and Sciences* (Cambridge: Harverd University Press, 1937),

48. Jung, "A Psychological Theory of Types," *Modern Man In Search of a Soul*, p. 91.

49. Cf. Nietzsche's statement in *Human All Too Human*". . . we pass through the whole thought of earlier humanity," which Jung quotes in "Symbols of Transformation," *Collected Works*, (Vol. 5), (New York: Bollingen Foundation, 1953), p. 23.

50. "The contents of the Collective Unconscious are not acquired during the lifetime of the individual; they are inherited instinctual forms, primordial forms of apprehension, the so-called archetypes of basic images." Jung: *Contributions to Analytical Psychology*, p. 260.

51. "Again and again I encounter the mistaken notion that an archetype is determined in regard to its content, in other words that it is a kind of unconscious idea (if such an expression be admissible). It is necessary to point out once more that archetypes are not determined as regards their content, but only as regards their form and then only to a very limited degree. A primordial image is determined as to its content only when it has become conscious and is therefore filled out with the material of conscious experience. Its form, however, . . . might perhaps be compared to the axial system of a crystal, which, as it were, preforms the crystalline structure in the mother liquid, although it has no material existence of its own. . . . The archetype in itself is empty and purely formal, nothing but a *facultas praeformandi*. . . ." Jung, *The Archetypes and the Collective Unconscious*, p. 79 f.

52. According to Jacobi, Jung adopted the term *archetype* from the Greek term he found in Dionysius the Pseudo Areopagite's *De divinis nominibus*, iv, 6. She also says that Jung found the notion of them in St. Augustine's *De diversis quaestionibus*, q. 46, and suggests a parallel between the Jungian archetypes and the Platonic *Ideas*. Cf. Jacobi, *The Psychology of C. G. Jung*, p. 42.

53. Jung, *Psychological Types*, p. 379. Some of the better-known archetypes are the following: birth, rebirth, the child, God, the old wise man,

the earth mother, the demon, the hero, the animal, death, and magic. Cf.
Jung, *Symbols of Transformation, passim.*

54. Jung, *Civilization in Transition.* This volume is in preparation, it
was projected for publication in 1962 but is still in manuscript.

55. Jung, "The Relation between the Ego and the Unconscious," in
Two Essays on Analytical Psychology, pp. 156, 190-191.

56. Jung holds that, apart from psychological considerations, there is a
physiological basis for the *anima/animus* in that the male body, while containing a majority of male genes, does possess also a certain amount of
female genes. The opposite is true for the female body. Cf. "Archetypes
of the Collective Unconscious," *The Archetypes and the Collective Unconscious,* pp. 27-28. Jung holds further that the *anima* of the male shows up
in inexplicable moods of pettiness, craftiness, and cattiness, and that the
animus of the female shows up in moods of belligerence and infallibilism.
"The Syzygy: anima and animus," *Aion,* tr. by R. F. C. Hull, Bollingen
Series, XX (New York: Pantheon Books 1959), pp. 15-16. Cf. also, "Anima
and Animus," *Two Essays in Analytical Psychology,* pp. 206-208.

57. Cf. Jung, "Archetypes of the Collective Unconscious," *The Archetypes and the Collective Unconscious,* pp. 25-27.

58. Jung, "The Phenomenology of the Spirit in Fairy Tales," *The Archetypes and the Collective Unconscious,* p. 216. Jung maintained that the
Greek notion of the king-philosopher resulted from a fusion of two archetypes: the hero and the old wise man.

59. Jung, "Psychological Aspects of the Mother Archetypes," *The
Archetypes and the Collective Unconscious,* p. 106.

60. "I use the term 'individuation' to denote the process by which a
person becomes a psychological 'in-dividual,' that is, a separate, indivisible
unity or whole." Jung, "Conscious, Unconscious, and Individuation," *The
Archetypes and the Collective Unconscious,* p. 275. "Individuation means
becoming a single, homogeneous being, and, insofar as 'individuality' embraces our innermost, last, and incomparable uniqueness, it also implies becoming one's own self. We therefore could translate individuation as 'coming
to selfhood' or 'self-realization'." Jung, "The Function of the Unconscious,"
Two Essays on Analytical Psychology, p. 171.

61. The major source for Jung's ideas concerning symbols is the nineteenth-century cultural historian, J. J. Bachofen (1815-1887).

62. "Now a symbol is not an arbitrary or intentional sign standing for
a known and conceivable fact, but an admittedly anthropomorphic—hence
limited and only partly valid—expression for something suprahuman and
only partly conceivable. It may be the best expression possible, yet it ranks
below the level of the mystery it seeks to describe." Jung, *Psyche and
Symbol,* ed. by Violet S. de Laslo (New York: Doubleday and Company,
1958), pp. 152-53.

63. "Jung has remarked elsewhere that there must be a continual misunderstanding between the theologian and the empirical psychologist over
their use of the word 'God,' for 'the theologian will naturally assume that

the metaphysical *Ens Absolutum* is meant,' while the empiricist 'just as naturally means a mere statement, at most an archetypal motif which performs such statements.' It appears, then, that Jung employs names like *Yahweh* and nouns like *God* to function not as signs but as things (to adopt modern terminology): as second, not first intentions (to adopt scholastic terminology)." Victor White, "Jung on Job," *Blackfriars,* XXXVI (March, 1956), p. 56. Jaffé, in her introduction to Jung's, *Memories, Dreams, Reflections,* writes in much the same vein as Fr. White. She cautions her reader to distinguish between Jung writing as a man who has had what he calls "an immediate experience" of God and as "the scientist who consciously restricts himself to what may be demonstrated and supported by evidence," p. xi.

64. Victor White, "Frontiers of Theology and Psychology," *God and the Unconscious,* p. 75. Jaffé may be quoted again as offering a perfect parallel to White's statement: "Jung's concept of religion differed in many respects from traditional Christianity—above all in his answer to the problem of evil and his conception of a God who is not entirely good or kind." Jung, *Memories, Dreams, Reflections,* p. x.

65. Jung, *Civilization in Transition.*

66. Introduction to M. Esther Harding's *Woman's Mysteries: Ancient and Modern* (New York: Longmans, Green & Co., 1935), pp. ix-x.

67. Jung, "Instinct and the Unconscious," *The Structure and Dynamics of the Psyche* (New York:, [The Bollingen Foundation, Vol. 8] Pantheon Books, 1960), p. 133. The term "psychic" as used here is coextensive with ordinary usage of the term "mental."

68. "The material contained in this area is *not* derived from the life-experience of the person, but from the life experience of the person's progenitors, *all of them,* and therefore, of the entire human race. The whole history of human psychic functioning, the collective experience of humanity, is the inheritance of each individual psyche. "Archetype," *Psychiatric Dictionary,* 3d edition. Ed. by Leland E. Hinsie and Robert J. Campbell (New York: Oxford University Press, 1960).

69. ". . . the collective unconscious . . . represents a psyche that . . . cannot be directly perceived or 'represented' in contrast to the perceptible psychic phenomena, and on account of its 'irrepresentable' nature I have called it 'psychoid'." C. G. Jung, *The Structure and Dynamics of the Psyche,* p. 436.

70. Progoff, *The Death and Rebirth of Psychology,* p. 168.

71. "The Spirit of Psychology," in *Spirit and Nature.* Papers from the Eranos Yearbooks, I (New York: [Bollingen Series XXX, 1] Pantheon Books, 1954, London: Routledge, 1955), p. 411.

72. C. G. Jung, *Psychology and Alchemy,* tr. by R. F. C. Hull (New York: [Bollingen Series XII] Pantheon Books, 1953), p. 175.

73. *Psychology of the Unconscious.* p. 8.

74. *Ibid.* pp. 8-9.

75. As Jung remarks, the dream content "*is* not literally true, but is

true psychologically." p. 9. Again he remarks that ". . . the dream arises from
a part of the mind unknown to us, but nonetheless important. . . ." *Idem.*

76. Italics Jung's.

77. *Ibid.* p. 10.

78. *Idem.*

79. *Ibid,* p. 13.

80. *Ibid.,* p. 14.

81. This doctrine is directly out of Eduard von Hartmann's *Philosophy of the Unconscious,* tr. by William Chatterton Coupland. London:
Routledge & Kegan Paul, Ltd. 1931. Volume II, p. 47.

C. K. Ogden points out in the Preface to this edition how broadly
von Hartmann's book influenced subsequent theories, especially in Psychology. Von Hartmann's original German work was published in 1869.

82. *Psychology of the Unconscious.* p. 21.

83. *Ibid.,* p. 24.

84. Jung fortifies his argument here by reminding the reader that "in
ancient times the sun was the Great Father of heaven and earth and the
moon was the faithful Good Mother. Even the sun was given wings in order
to illustrate movement." *Ibid.,* p. 24.

85. *Ibid.,* p. 25.

86. *Ibid.,* p. 26. Italics ours.

87. *Ibid.,* p. 28. This is the same passage from *Human All Too Human*
referred to previously in footnote 49.

88. *Ibid.,* p. 29.

89. *Ibid.,* p. 30.

90. *Ibid.,* p. 30.

91. *Ibid.,* p. 35.

92. *Ibid.,* p. 36.

93. *Idem.*

94. *Ibid.,* p. 39.

95. *Psychological Types.,* p. 554.

96. *Ibid.,* p. 555.

97. *Idem.*

98. *Idem.*

99. *Ibid.,* p. 556.

100. *Philosophy of the Unconscious.* Vol. I. p. 5.

101. *Ibid.,* Vol. II. p. 250. Cf. also ". . . all plurality . . . only belong(s)
to the phenomenon, not to the essence which posits the former, but this is
the Absolute Individual, the single existence *which is All* whereas the world
with its glory (is) reduced to the bare phenomenon. Vol. II. p. 223.

102. *Ibid.,* Vol. II. p. 223. Cf. also, "Matter, Consciousness, and Organic
Formation, Instinct (are) comprehended as three modes of action or modes
of appearance of the Unconscious, and the latter (is) the essence of the
world." Vol. II. p. 240.

103. *Ibid.,* Vol. II. p. 242.

104. *Psychological Types.,* p. 556.

105. *Idem.*

106. *Ibid.*, p. 557.

107. *Idem.*

108. *Idem.*

109. *Idem.*

110. *Ibid.*, p. 558.

111. Arthur Schopenhauer, *The World As Will and Idea.* Vol. I. s49.

112. *Psychological Types.* p. 624. Note that this homogeneity refers only to the unconscious and not to consciousness.

113. *Psychology of The Unconscious.* p. 107. Note that the expression "burning desire" is common in English.

114. *Papyrus Anastasi,* leaf 7. Paris: Bibliothèque Nationale. Greek Supplement of the *Raccolta Magica,* n. 574.

115. "And towards the regions westward, as though it were an infinite Eastwind. But if the other wind, towards the regions of the East, should be in service, in the like fashion shalt thou see towards the regions of that side the converse of the sight." The Greek text follows shortly after the quote referred to in note 114. The translation given here is that found in G. R. S. Mead, "A Mithraic Ritual," *Echoes From the Gnosis.* London: Theosophical Publishing Society, 1906. p. 22.

117. Mircea Eliade, *Images and Symbols,* tr. by Philip Mairet. London: Harvill Press, 1961, *The Sacred And The Profane,* tr. by Willard R. Trask. New York: Harper Torchbooks, 1961; *Shamanism.* tr. by Willard R. Trask. New York: Pantheon Books. 1964. These works are representative of Eliade's.

118. *Les Lois psychologiques du symbolisme.* 1895. Preface,

119. Ludwig Binswanger, *Ausgewahlte Vortrage und Aufsatze,* 2 vols. Bern, Franke, 1947-55.

120. Medard Boss, *Psychoanalysis and Daseinanalysis,* tr. Ludwig B. Lefebre. (New York: Basic Books, 1963).

121. Igor A. Caruso, *Bios, Psyche, Person; eine Einführung in die allgemeine Tiefenpsychologie.* (Freiburg: Karl Alber, 1957).

122. Viktor Frankl, *Man's Search for Meaning: An Introduction to Logotherapy,* tr. by Ilse Lach (Boston: Beacon Press, 1963).

123. Cf., for example, Karl Menninger's recent work in which he attempts to reduce the presently enormous and cumbersome classifications of mental illness down to five basic types and offers a theory to justify his simpler categories. Karl Menninger and Paul Pruyser, *The Vital Balance* (New York: The Viking Press, 1963).

In addition to books and articles cited in the notes, the following works are recommended:

Agostino Gemelli, *Psychoanalysis Today,* tr. by John Chapin and Salvator Attanasi. New York: P. J. Kenedy & Sons, 1955.

Josef Goldbrunner, *Individuation.* New York: Pantheon, 1956.

Jung Institute, *Studien zur analytischen Psychologie C. G. Jungs.* Zurich: Raschner, 1955.

Calvin S. Hall and Gardner Lindzey, *Theories of Personality*. New York: Wiley, 1957.

John Macquarrie, *Twentieth Century Religious Thought*. New York: Harper & Row, 1963.

Patrick Mullahy, *Oedipus Myth and Complex*. New York: Grove Press, 1955.

Howard L. Philip, *Jung and the Problem of Evil*. London: Rockliff, 1958.

Anthony Storr, *The Integrity of the Personality*. New York: Atheneum, 1961.

Johannes Van der Hoop, *Character and the Unconscious*, tr. by Elizabeth Trevelyan. New York: Harcourt Brace & Co., 1923.

James Vandervelt and Robert P. Odenwald, *Psychiatry and Catholicism*. New York: McGraw Hill Book Co., 1952.

THE EXISTENTIALIST MOVEMENT
MIGUEL DE UNAMUNO: THE TRAGIC SENSE OF LIFE
JEAN PAUL SARTRE: PHILOSOPHER OF NAUGHT AND
NAUSEA
MAURICE MERLEAU-PONTY AND PHILOSOPHY
PAUL TILLICH: PHILOSOPHER OF CONTEMPORARY
PROTESTANTISM

miguel unamuno

THE TRAGIC SENSE OF LIFE

by Felix Alluntis, O.F.M.

According to Miguel de Unamuno it is impossible to know the thought of a philosopher without previously knowing his concrete, existential life. The reason he gives is that a man philosophizes "not only with reason but also with will, with intellect, with flesh and bones, with soul and body. The whole man philosophizes."[1] Undoubtedly this affirmation contains a great deal of truth but it is equally true, as a general rule, that one who philosophizes has been influenced by previous philosophies. This is obvious from what Unamuno adds. Our philosophy of the world and life, he says, stems from our feelings concerning life, and life, like everything affective, has subconscious or perhaps unconscious roots. Although it is said that man is a rational animal, what possibly distinguishes him from other animals is sentiment rather than reason. "I have seen a cat reasoning more often than smiling or crying. Perhaps it cries and smiles within itself, but perhaps too the crab within itself solves equations of the second degree."[2] This conception of man as an affective animal and of philosophy as an affective task presupposes a definite conception of the nature of both man and philosophy.

From his premise that the whole man philosophizes Unamuno draws the conclusion that our ignorance of the history of philosophy stems from our ignorance of the philosophers' lives; if instead of immediately and directly studying systems, we investigated the intimate biographies of their authors, this procedure "would explain more things for us." As an illustration he mentions the case of Kant, who as a philosopher rejects rational proofs of the existence of God but as a man worries about his destiny and the immortality of his soul, "rebuilds with his heart what his reason had destroyed," and in the *Crtitique of Practical Reason* "from the immortality of the soul deduces the existence of God." [3] After having first embraced positivism, Unamuno later rejected it as well as absolute idealism, because both are vitiated by the original sin of assuming that reason alone operates in the philosophical endeavor and as a consequence offer us only dead ideas instead of living reality. [4]

That the intimate biography of a philosopher reveals his thought or feeling better than his works is undoubtedly true of Unamuno himself. His whole philosophy is the expression of a vital experience, his inner tragic life. For this reason we shall outline, first, the main events of his life and, second, some of his final and cardinal thoughts or sentiments. This latter task will not be easy, for we will meet with cryptic expressions, abrupt interruptions of thought, and conscious contradictions. "Someone will see a basic contradiction in everything I am saying... Contradiction? Of course! The contradiction of my heart, which says 'yes' and my head, which says 'no'! Contradiction, naturally... After all, we live on and by contradiction; life is a tragedy,... a contradiction." [5] Nor are all the real or apparent contradictions we find in Unamuno's writings the result of the conflict between his head and his heart, or between reason and faith, but rather of his paradoxical and contradictory mind and the religious, social, political, and literary factors that constituted the concrete situation in which he wrote.

I

THE MAN

1) FROM OVER-CONFIDENCE IN REASON TO AGNOSTICISM AND ATHEISM

Miguel Unamuno was born in Bilbao, capital city of the Basque province of Biscay, Spain, on September 6, 1864. [6] He received a thorough and rigorous religious and moral education. His family also succeeded in infusing into him at an early age an extraordinary thirst for knowledge, for during his fifteenth and sixteenth years while living an intensely religious life as a member of the Congregation of St. Luis Gonzaga and following the regular courses at the *Instituto Vizcaíno,* he read the books in the library of an uncle who was a priest. Unamuno himself tells us of his intellectual voracity and his desire both to know everything and to rationalize his religion. Philosophy above all interested and attracted him, and he read the works of Jaime Balmes and Donoso Cortés; through Balmes he was introduced to French materialism and sensism, British empiricism, Kantianism, and the idealism of Fichte, Schelling, and Hegel.

During this period Unamuno went to Mass daily and received Communion monthly. One day it occurred to him to open the Gospels and put his finger at random on a passage. The passage read: "Go and preach the Gospel to all nations." He repeated the experience on another day and the text then read: "I told you; why do you want to know it again?" Unamuno tells us that he cannot explain the deep impression he received from these experiences; he interpreted them as a call to the priesthood and they remained with him and worried him for the rest of his life. The fact that he did not follow the divine call, or what he thought to be a divine call, has been interpreted as a resistance to and refusal of divine grace, and as the cause of his subsequent loss of faith.[7] But as Hernan Benítez and Charles Moeller have noted, a vocation to the priesthood is never a command and God never abandons a soul for having refused to follow the evangelical counsels.[8]

After graduating from the *Instituto Vizcaíno* at the age of sixteen, a sad and nostalgic young Unamuno left Bilbao and enrolled in the school of philosophy and letters at the Central University of Madrid. The philosophy taught at the university was Krausism; and the European thinkers who then and later influenced intellectual circles were, in order of popularity, the positivists Spencer, Renan, Taine, and Wundt; the materialists Vogt, Moleschott, Büchner, and Haeckel; the historical materialists Marx, Engels, and Lasalle; the post-Kantians Lange, Liebmann, and Cohen; the empirio-criticists Mach and Avenarius; the philosopher of the unconscious, Eduard von Hartmann; the pragmatist William James; and especially the philosopher of vital values, Nietzsche.[9] Kierkegaard, Dilthey, and Brentano were not yet known. Apparently the courses at the university did not particularly appeal to Unamuno, for he makes hardly any reference to them. During his first year in Madrid Unamuno continued to go to Mass every day and to receive Holy Communion once a month. At the same time he continued in his efforts to rationalize his faith: he sought mathematical certitude in matters of faith— an error of method or, as St. Thomas Aquinas calls it, "a sin against the intellect," to which the too intellectualistic and almost rationalistic apologetics of the nineteenth century greatly contributed.

After failing in his efforts, Unamuno went to the opposite extreme. Since the truth of faith cannot be proved, he concluded, faith can in no way be based on reason. Thus by trying to rationalize his faith, Unamuno saw it evanesce and disappear, probably in 1882, and gave up all religious practice. He embarked with new fervor on the study of philosophy, first of Hegel, then of Spencer, and ended by embracing positivism and a radical "scientism:" "Seek first the kingdom of science and its justice and everything else will be given to you besides." In his opinion, assertions of God's existence and the immortality of the soul cannot resist rationalistic attacks. Kant's philosophy—in the writer's opinion the most decisive and permanent influence on Unamuno's final thought and sentiment—convinced him that proofs of God's existence and all rational speculations are sophistical in character.

In 1884, after obtaining his doctorate in philosophy and letters, he returned to Bilbao. He also returned to the practice of religion, apparently to spare his mother's sufferings but without a real faith and only for a short period; he then definitively abandoned the liturgical and sacramental exercise of any religion. He occupied himself in private tutoring and writing, but above all in study with the immediate aim of obtaining a university position. He studied physics, chemistry, biology, mathematics, the Italian and British poets,[10] and particularly philosophy and psychology.[11] His previous positivism and scientism weakened and around the year 1886 his thought took an existential turn.[12] He failed in successive competitive examinations for the chairs of psychology, logic and ethics, and metaphysics. As his friend Arzadun describes, in all these examinations Unamuno brilliantly gave the different answers to each problem, but instead of stopping

there he always added, "But in my opinion . . ." and proceeded
to deny all existing theories. The members of the tribunal recognized and attested to his knowledge but refused to entrust
the youth of Spain to such a "wild beast."[13] Later Unamuno
tried unsuccessfully to obtain a chair of Latin, but finally won
one in Greek at the university of Salamanca. The economic
security this event brought to him allowed him to marry Con-
cepción Luzarraga, a simple and devout girl from Guernica whom
he had loved for many years. As Unamuno himself writes, his
wife was a real blessing for the rest of his life, especially as an
antidote to his hypochondriac tendencies and as a support and
comforter in moments of crisis. She was for him not only his wife
but also his mother, his "virgin mother."

2) CRISIS IN SALAMANCA, AND CREATION OF A NEW FAITH

Unamuno took possession of his chair at Salamanca in 1891
without any intention of dedicating himself to Greek scholarship.
Remarking that Greek scholars were the least of the needs of
Spain and that he knew more than enough Greek to introduce
his students into the language of Plato, he wrote on everything
except classical linguistics. In 1896 he became father to a hydro-
cephalic son and saw in him a divine sign of the failure of a man
who lost his faith. This fact, together with the vital dissatisfaction
he was already experiencing, caused in Unamuno a severe crisis
which exploded in full intensity in March, 1897. It was primarily
of a religious character,[14] and the idea of death became an obsession with him. One night he awoke with violent palpitations,
thinking he had the angina pectoris and feeling himself "in the paws
of the angel of nothingness," and was overcome by abysmal
anguish. Unamuno interpreted this crisis as a divine call and
retired for three days to the Dominican monastery of San Esteban
at Salamanca, where he sought the advice and counsel of the
great mystical theologian, Father Arintero. He also wrote to his
former spiritual director, Father Juan José Lecanda, who invited
him to spend Holy Week with him in Alcalá de Henares. During
these days Unamuno wrote in his *Diary* numerous spiritual
thoughts on death, repentance, humility, grace, faith, divine
paternity, the role of Christ in our return to the Father, and the

Mystical Body. During the Holy Week ceremonies he devoutly followed the liturgical texts and assiduously prayed for the recovery of his faith but without success. He wrote: "To receive communion in this condition, without faith in the sacrament . . . would it not be a sacrilege and the fruit of the most refined pride?"

After Unamuno returned to Salamanca the crisis lost its intensity but did not disappear altogether. While, as he says, "God remained silent," he was tortured by perpetual doubts; he was terrified at the thought of nothingness, and at the same time thoughts of suicide occurred to him. He despaired of ever recovering his lost theological faith, but was resolved to follow the divine call in some way, and broke with the previous, superficial, and inauthentic life he had led as an unbelieving intellectual. He was acutely aware of the ridicule to which he would be subjected by other intellectuals and by his own reason, but, like another Don Quixote, he was ready to face it. He developed a sentimental faith which fed upon doubts and consisted not in believing but in willing to believe and in creating its objects. He devoured the works of Protestant liberal theologians, particularly Ritschl and Harnack, who attached a paramount role to the act of faith.[15] He recalled the evangelical text, "Go and preach the Gospel to all nations," and became a lay preacher of his religion of sentimental faith, of hope in despair, and of the tragic sense of life.

Different authors have tried to analyze or explain the reasons for Unamuno's failure in his search for faith. Vicente Marrero attributes the failure to Unamuno's spirit of contradiction and rebellion.[16] Charles Moeller attributes it, in a great extent, to the state of Catholic theology in Spain and, with a few exceptions, in Europe in general.[17] He suggests that if Unamuno had known Cardinal Mercier or Maurice Blondel, the final outcome of the crisis could have been very different.[18] It also has been asked whether Unamuno was sincere in adopting the new life of tragic sentiment that he had constructed. Antonio Sánchez Barbudo denies it. According to him, Unamuno's later public life was farcical.[19] Armando Zubizarreta and Charles Moeller reject such an interpretation and believe in the religious honesty and tragic sincerity of Unamuno.[20] We have no doubt that in spite of his agnostic reason he sincerely willed to believe, sincerely hoped in

despair, sincerely sought in the tragic sense of life the meaning of
his earthly and future life, although most probably without success.
In the year 1901 Unamuno was named rector of the university
and held this post until 1914 when he was removed for political
reasons but continued as a vice rector.

3) EXILE, NEW CRISIS, AND DEATH

Because of his attacks on the monarchy and the dictatorship of
General Primo de Rivera, Unamuno was deported in 1924 to
Fuerteventura in the Canary Islands. A few months later he escaped to France, where he lived until 1930, first in Paris, then in
the Basque town of Hendaye. During his first two years in France
(1924-1925) he suffered another crisis.[21] The obsession of angina
pectoris and death returned, he could not sleep, he could hardly
write, he felt more strongly than ever the anguish of nothingness,
and the thought of suicide came back. Exile and what he considered to be his political failure contributed to the crisis, but
the religious factor and the feeling of the failure in his personal
life also played an important role. "God remains silent," he wrote,
"because he is an atheist."

Antonio Sánchez Barbudo interprets this crisis as the result
of the farce Unamuno's life had been up to that point. According
to him, in the work Unamuno wrote shortly after his crisis, *How
a Novel is Made,* as well as in his subsequent works, *The Other,
Brother Juan, St. Manuel,* all of which are highly autobiographical,
Unamuno contraposes the authentic Unamuno, a solitary and
convinced atheist, and the inauthentic and theatrical Unamuno,
an insincere and hypocritical man. Armando Zubizarreta, on the
contrary, interprets Unamuno's crisis as the failure of his political
and historical mission and of his intimate life, and in the four
works named he does not see the contraposition of the authentic
and false Unamuno but "the tragedy of a divided personality that
cannot find the unity of meaning of his life," "in which [per-
sonality], brutally contraposed, a feeling of freedom and culpability
and a feeling of painful ignorance of the limits of imputability play
their parts .. [and] a feeling of an obscure plan and a feeling
of fatality fight against each other."[23]

In 1930, after the fall of the dictatorship, Unamuno returned to Salamanca as a hero, and in 1931 he was reelected rector of the university. From 1931 to 1933 he was deputy in the Constituent parliament (*Cortes*) of the new republic as a member of the Republican bloc but was not allied to any specific party. At the outbreak of the nationalist revolution in 1936 he at first declared himself in its favor, but later, at the inauguration of the academic year, took a public stand against it, and as a consequence was confined to his home. On December 31, 1936, moments after telling Bartolomé Aragón Gómez, who was visiting him, that "God could not turn his back on Spain," he died suddenly. Death came to him as he had anticipated many years before in his poem "Two Home Incidents" (1907):

> It is night, in my study
> And I say to myself: Perchance soon when
> they will come to tell me
> my evening meal is waiting
> They will find here a body
> pallid and cold . . .[24]

II

THINKER OR FEELER

1) OBJECT OF PHILOSOPHY

For Unamuno the object of philosophy is man; not an abstract concept of man, such as rational animal, political animal, or featherless biped, but the concrete, existing man, "the man of flesh and blood, the man who is born, suffers, and dies—above all dies—the man who eats and drinks and plays and sleeps and thinks and loves, the man who is seen and heard, the brother, the true brother." [25] Unamuno likes to repeat Terence's dictum, *Homo sum; nihil humani a me alienum puto,* I am a man, nothing human is foreign to me, although he would prefer to change it into, *Homo sum; nullum hominem a me alienum puto,* I am a man; and I do not consider any man a stranger to me.[26] He dislikes abstract adjectives and nouns, like 'human' and 'humanity'; he is interested in the concrete, individual man with all his weaknesses and sufferings. The fact that Unamuno makes man, the existential man, the object of philosophy does not mean that he excludes

from the realm of philosophy every other reality, for he sees in
every man the need of attaining a comprehensive vision of the
whole world. But he regards every other reality as secondary, as
a sub-object, so to say, with regard to the man of flesh and
blood.[27]

In the individual existing man, Unamuno distinguishes between
individuality, which signifies the container, limits, and finitude,
and personality, which signifies content, inner richness, infinity.
One may enjoy a strong individuality with hardly any personality,
and vice versa.[28] He says he knew many human pachiderms. The
truly real and substantial reality in the concrete man is his personality, which Unamuno also calls consciousness, the ego, the
spirit, the soul. He conceives it as a product of vital activity and
as constantly growing.[29] Unamuno likes to identify consciousness
with dreaming. Among the several quotations from classical
literature concerning the dreamlike texture of life, he prefers
that of Shakespeare, which states not only that we dream our
lives, but that we ourselves are made of "such stuff as dreams
are made on."[30]

According to Julian Marías, by identifying life with a dream,
Unamuno wishes to point out the peculiar reality of consciousness, which approaches the texture of the dream rather than the
massive constitution of material things. Unamuno must have
the same purpose, the purpose of clarifying the peculiar reality
of consciousness as opposed to other types of reality, when he
places on the same level fictional beings and real persons, Cervantes and Don Quixote, Shakespeare and Hamlet, Unamuno and
Augusto Pérez. For life or consciousness is something that is
constantly *in fieri*. It is a history, and under this aspect the concrete
man coincides with literary characters, with fictional beings, rather
than with stones or trees. Fictional beings are lives, histories; they
have biographies; their mode of being and ours are similar in
the sense that both are historical, temporal, and personal; both
are in the making and can be narrated. To be Don Quixote is
not to have such and such physical characteristics, but to act,
to think, and to feel in a particular way. The being of a fictional
character, like my own being, is a product and result of history.[31]

Charles Moeller interprets Unamuno's identification of consciousness with dream as an effect of the emotion of nothingness

which accompanied him as an obsession and caused him an abysmal anguish.[32] Perhaps we should add that Unamuno's paradox that conceives life as a dream is connected with his relegation of substantial life to the realm of faith and "biotic," for the means faith uses to express its creations are plays, novels, and poetry whose objects are shadows and dreams.

Does consciousness disappear with death or does it survive beyond the tomb? If consciousness ceases at death, Unamuno says, nothing is more absurd than human existence and nothing has any value. Hence the problem of consciousness and personality is ultimately reduced to the problem of immortality. The thought of personal annihilation always terrified Unamuno. When he was still a young boy, he tells us, the possibility of ceasing to exist disturbed him much more than the fear of hell. However, the problem of immortality became the great problem for Unamuno after the severe crisis he suffered in 1897, during which, in spite of extraordinary efforts, he did not succeed in recovering the supernatural faith of his youth. Hunger for immortality, Unamuno writes in *The Tragic Sense of Life,* is the very essence of man. "We wish to be, and to be forever."[33] He likes to repeat the words of Spinoza: *Unaquaeque res, quatenus in se est, in suo esse perseverare conatur; conatus, quo unaquaeque res in suo esse perseverare conatur, nihil est praeter ipsius rei actualem essentiam.* All things, according to Unamuno's interpretation, strive to persevere in their being, and the effort by which they try to persevere in their being is their actual essence.[34]

Man's longing for immortality, Unamuno says, manifests itself in different ways, in his desires for name and fame, to perpetuate himself by generation, and for personal immortality. The first two types of perpetuation are only apparent, deceitful substitutes for real perpetuation. Immortality of name and fame is sought by those who do not believe in the substantial world of spirit and bow to the dictates of reason, namely, to absolute death. They are the so-called "cultural" men whom Unamuno despises and often derides: "Instead of looking straight in the face of the sphinx, they spend their time counting the hairs of its tail." Sexual perpetuation is only partial; moreover, sexual love always implies a certain amount of greed which is opposed to real perpetuation. The only perpetuation worthy of the name, Unamuno concludes, is personal immortality, and it must include both body and soul.[35] This hunger for immortality has originated and maintained the different religions, for every religion arises from a cult of the dead, that is, from a cult of immortality. When men were building straw or clay huts for themselves, they were erecting monuments to the dead. What distinguishes man from other animals is that he preserves his dead; he is a "dead-keeping" animal, and he keeps the dead because he believes in their survival.[36] Not only religion, but the whole universe is interpreted by Unamuno on the basis of his longing for immortality; even in rocks and plants he detects consciousness and a desire to exist forever.[37] In his hunger for immortality he also includes hunger for totality, that is, every individual man desires not only to be forever but also to be ever more, to be all things but without losing his identity and distinction.[38]

Unamuno's constant wrestling with the problem of immortality explains his obsession with death to the point that his philosophy has been described as *meditatio mortis,* a meditation on death. After all, the problem of whether or not we will survive is posed by the fact that all men die. The idea and feeling of death is always present in Unamuno's essays and poetry, and in his novels he multiplies the deaths of the characters. Undoubtedly he tries to detect what happens at that supreme moment and to solve the mystery by imaginatively anticipating the fatal hour. The role death plays in his philosophy is therefore very different from its role in, for example, the philosophies of Heidegger and Sartre.

2) REASON, FAITH, AND THE TRAGIC SENSE OF LIFE

When, as a boy of 14, 15, 16 years, Unamuno endeavored to comprehend and rationalize his faith, he had an exaggerated trust in reason. When he became convinced of the impossibility of the task, he went to the opposite extreme, to the positivistic and Kantian irrationalism which he never abandoned. He removed from the scope of reason not only the mysteries of faith but also truly philosophical or rational problems. Reason, he says, cannot apprehend life; it tends rather to death, since it seeks to reduce everything to identities and genera and attaches to each concept one and the same content in every place, time or relationship.[39]

Reason, which feeds upon dead ideas, can neither apprehend the living man of flesh and blood nor satisfy his burning desire to know whether or not he will die completely. There is no rational way of proving the immortality of our consciousness or the existence of God. Unamuno attempts to refute the traditional proofs for the immortality of the soul and also certain empirical proofs drawn from psychic facts and spiritistic phenomena that favor the substantiality, spirituality, and immortality of the soul.[40] Such criticism, which he borrows chiefly from Kant, contains no novelty. He concludes that within its own limits, reason not only cannot prove the immortality of the soul but in fact proves its mortality.[41] However, he immediately adds that this conclusion should not discourage us because life has exigencies that are above reason. Beyond the boundaries of the rational stands the contrarational, and beyond and against logic stands "biotic" and sentimental faith.[42]

There is some confusion among Unamuno's interpreters as regards the meaning and nature of Unamunian faith. A few identify it with his previous Catholic faith, others with the faith-trust (*fides-fiducia*) of Lutheran theologians. There is evidence to the effect that his loss of faith always worried Uuamuno, but apparently it did not too acutely affect his psychological life until the severe crisis he suffered in 1897. This crisis was primarily religious and Unamuno made extraordinary efforts to recover the faith of his happy youth. Having failed in this endeavor, he sought consolation in a new type of faith, namely, one of sentiment. This faith, he tells us, does not consist in believing but in willing to to believe—*Credo, Domine, adiuva incredulitatem meam*—and it is "the flower of the will." [43] Obviously such faith is not Christian faith and Unamuno explicitly distinguishes it from his previous supernatural faith. Those who identify Unamuno's with Catholic faith misunderstand either his sentimental faith or Catholic supernatural faith or both. Those who link Unamuno's new faith with Lutheran faith-trust base their interpretation on his own texts.[44] José Luis L. Aranguren and Charles Moeller, among others, see a definite connection between Unamuno's doctrine and Lutheran theology as presented chiefly by Harnack.[45] Undoubtedly Unamuno was influenced by Protestant theology, but he never incorporated it into his own thought or sentiment without having substantially changed it. Unamuno's faith implies trust or confidence, but it is not identical with Lutheran faith-trust. According to Lutheranism, a man believes in the real existence of the person, God or Christ, in whom he trusts. This is also true of Kierkegaard and his leap into the absurd or abyss. Unamuno's faith, on the contrary, does not consist in believing but in willing to believe; it does not trust in someone whose existence it does not question; it trusts that God exists. Nor does Unamuno's faith hope to reach something it certainly admits but rather hopes in its existence. We are of the opinion that Unamuno's faith is essentially Kantian. For Kant too faith is an act of the practical reason, of the will, and the immortality of the soul and God's existence are postulates, hypotheses, objectifications—creations, so to say—of our will. Hence Kant, like Unamuno after him, wrote that each one should imagine God according to his own desires.

Unamuno's relegation of the vital problem to the realm of faith seems to contradict his affirmation that the whole concrete man philosophizes. True, he identifies faith with "biotic" or the total activity, but he opposes faith and "biotic" to rational activity, whose function is limited to formulating the creations of faith and injecting doubt and despair into them; yet reason is also a part of the whole concrete man. Does faith and "biotic" include an intuitive activity of the intellect? At first the reader may be inclined to answer affirmatively. Unamuno also uses the term "cardíaca" (cardiac) as synonymous with "biotic," in a sense similar to Pascal's coeur, which implies intelligence. But a careful reading of Unamuno's explanations of faith excludes, it seems to us, not only logical reason but also the intuitive activity of the intellect and its pre-logical, connatural, magic, or "nocturnal" exercise.

The fact that Unamuno relegates substantial reality to the realm of faith explains his use of novels and poetry as means of philosophical inquiry and expression. At the end of The Tragic Sense of Life he tells us that he presents as mythology what he believes to be true substantial reality for fear of the inquisition of science and his own reason, just as Galileo presented his work on the movement of earth to the Grand Duke of Tuscany "as poetry or dream."[46] But the reason why Unamuno uses poems, plays, and existential novels as tools of philosophy is his conviction that living reality can only be grasped by irrational acts or "faculties," whose means of expression are not syllogisms, and his persuasion that the reality of life and consciousness is much more similar to the temporal, historical, *in fieri,* reality of a fictional being than the massive reality of, for example, a stone.[47]

Although Unamuno relegates the capture of substantial reality and immortality to sentiment, will, and faith, he is not a fideist, who, having rejected reason, rests peacefully on faith. This is obvious from the very meaning of his faith, which does not consist in believing but in willing to believe and furnishes us not with any proofs or relief but rather with despair. Moreover, although immortality belongs to the antirational domain and is outside the rational sphere, reason, which is also a part of our life, constantly injects doubt, uncertainty, or denial into the creations of faith. Thus we have "rational skepticism and sentimental despair facing each other like brothers in war."[48] Reason denies immortality, but vital desire reacts to it and affirms it—*Credo quia absurdum*—and hopes in despair. From this tragic embrace springs a fountain of life, of tragic life in which reason says "no" and the heart says "yes," of the only possible true and substantial life.[49] Furthermore, reason or logic denies the possibility of our becoming everything else, of our becoming God, without losing our identity and distinction, while vital desire unceasingly strives for totality, and this conflict adds to the tragic sense of our life.[50] Even eternal life and the "beatific vision" are conceived by Unamuno as tragic.[51] In *The Agony of Christianity* the term "agony" is used in its etymological sense of fight or conflict, and Unamuno deals with the tragic sentiment of life or the struggle between faith and reason in individual Christians and exemplifies it with the inner religious tragedies of St. Paul, Pascal, and the ex-Carmelite Hyacinth Loyson, as he interprets them.[52]

3) GOD, RELIGION, AND THE MORAL ORDER

Personal immortalty, claims Unamuno writing under Kant's influence, is unthinkable without the existence of an eternal being who will save us from annihilation.[53] Thus the problem of God is for him subordinated to the problem of our immortality. He warns us against confusing the true God, who is felt as a

person, as a consciousness outside us, although surrounding and
sustaining us, with the idea of God.[54]

Unamuno contends that rational God, the supreme being of
"theological philosophy," is only an idea of God, not the real
God, that the traditional rational proofs of God's existence refer
to this God-idea or logical God, to God *via remotionis*; and that
they prove at most the existence of the idea of God. He stops
to criticize some of the traditional proofs for God's existence, but
his criticism, inspired by Kant, offers little novelty. Reason, he
concludes, far from proving God's existence, denies it; our reason
is atheistic.[55] Apparently not even God's reason can grasp his
own true being, for Unamuno repeatedly says that "God is an
atheist." However, he adds, the fact that our reason cannot reach
God, and rather denies his existence, should not dishearten us, for
God does not belong to the domain of reason but to the realm
of sentimental faith and despairing hope and is reached by a vital
way, through suffering and love, through our feeling of his
absence.

Unamuno feels God as the conscience of the universe and as
a limited, finite, tragic being who also constantly strives for freeing
himself from matter, for becoming everything else without losing
his identity and distinction.[56] Therefore, although in Unamuno's
writings there are pantheistic expressions, he is a panentheist
rather than a pantheist. Since he conceives or rather feels God
as an objectivation or creation of our will and sentimental faith,
which cannot offer proofs, Unamuno cannot affirm the extramental or "extracardiac" existence of God. "This question [whether
or not God exists] is unanswerable. Reason should be satisfied
with not being able to prove the impossibility of his existence. To
believe in God is to desire his existence and to behave as if he
exists.[57] This again is Kantianism.

Religion implies a relationship between God and man. For
Unamuno the main term in this relationship is man, who postulates
God.[58] Religion depends upon the sentiment of religious man and
is compatible with the most diverse doctrinal tenets and even with
superstition.[59] Among the different definitions of religion he
prefers that of Schleiermacher who defines it as a feeling.[60] Ultimately religion consists in a sentimental union with God.[61]

For Unamuno religion is and must be eschatological. Hunger

for personal immortality is as essential to religion as is hunger for the existence of God, our immortalizer. Unamuno cavils about the different ways in which eternal life and the "beatific vision" can be felt; he pays special attention to the possible ways of imagining or feeling "apocatastasis," the restoration of all things in God, and "anakefalaiosis," the recapitulation of everything in Christ-man, of which St. Paul speaks. He concludes that although such theological fantasies—he presents them as such—may appear absurd to reason, we must believe in another life in which each one will feel his consciousness united with all others in God and ever growing. We must believe in the other life in order to bear and give meaning and finality to this life and perhaps to deserve it, and we must so behave that if nothingness is reserved to us, it must be an injustice, as Senancour wrote in his *Obermann*.[62]

In regard to the moral life Unamuno rejects rational ethics. For him the only foundation for moral activity is a doubtful faith. We must behave morally, not because we think that a principle of action is valid or that the spiritual world is true, but in order to make the one valid and the other true. Virtue is not based on dogma, but rather dogma is based on virtue. Faith does not make martyrs, rather martyrs create faith.[63] The practical norm of morality might be formulated as follows: Act so that in your own judgment and in the judgment of others you may merit eternity; act so as not to merit death. It could also be formulated with the words of Senancour in his *Obermann*: "Man is perishable. That may be; but let us perish resisting, and if it is nothingness that awaits us, let us not act in such a way that it would be a just fate.[64]

Unamuno rejects as absurd Kant's proposition that we have come into the world not to be happy but to fulfill our duty. If we are in the world for something, Unamuno replies, this *for* or finality can be derived only from the essence of our will which looks for happiness—happiness in agony—and not duty as the ultimate end. "Cultural men, those pedants who are resigned to absolute death, will laugh at this; but there remain a few poor savages like ourselves who do not resign themselves to the idea of one day having to disappear.[65]

From the given norm of morality it follows that according to Unamuno an act is morally good if it favors either directly or

indirectly our hunger for immortality; it is evil if it goes counter
to this vital desire. In other words, moral life is the same as
authentic or substantial life, which is that of those who live
from within, anguished by the problem of immortality and conscious of the tragic sense of life. An immoral life is identical
with an inauthentic or merely apparent life, viz., the life of those
who live superficially and in time, unconcerned about their
true being and destiny, and absorbed by the material world, which
aims at the suffocation or annihilation of our consciousness.[66]
Unamuno compares the material world, as well as the so-called
cultural man, to Helen in Marlowe's *Faust;* just as Helen drew
forth the soul of Dr. Faustus with her kisses, matter and rationistic
culture attempt to suck out our very soul, and we must fight
without truce against their allurements.

For Unamuno, the only real and efficacious sanction would be
annihilation of consciousness in one who destroys or neglects to
nourish his natural aspiration to eternal life. He stresses the
importance of intention in our moral activity, and considers the
matter of our acts as indifferent or unimportant. In other words,
his ethical doctrine is formalistic, although in practice he accepted
a material ethics; personally, like so many representatives of formal ethics—Kant, Kierkegaard, Heidegger, Jaspers, and others—
he lived according to the dictates or tenets of strict Christian
morality.[67]

III

CONCLUSION

Non-idealistic and non-positivistic philosophers reject the irrationalism that pervades Unamuno's whole philosophy, his relegation of the problems of life, God, and immortality to the irrational realm of sentimental faith, his idealism concerning the
validity of scientific knowledge properly so-called, his conception
of substantial personality as a project, or rather as the product
of vital activity, and his denial or neglect of material ethics. Most
Christians—and I say "most Christians," for there are nowadays
those who call themselves Christians and do not even accept
the spirituality of the soul—will condemn as unorthodox Unamuno's interpretation of the Scriptures and his phantasies on eternal

life and the beatific vision. Christians and many non-Christians will criticize this image of God as a limited, suffering, ever-growing, somehow material being. Philosophers of all tendencies will belittle him for his naive efforts to bare human life on a sentimental faith which obviously cannot create its objects and for having spent his life in preaching the gospel of the tragic sense of life. Atheists will accuse him of hypocrisy for pretending to believe. All such criticism, except the last, are valid and should not be overlooked in evaluating Unamuno's work.

However, there are also positive points in his thought and life. As we have seen, Unamuno anticipates many themes of existentialist philosophy. He proclaims as the object of philosophy concrete individual man, concrete individual life and existence. He conceives human existence as a project; he distinguishes between authentic and inauthentic existence; he attaches a unique epistemological role to suffering and anguish. He spoke of hunger for totality many years before Sartre started to write. Kierkegaard, it is true, expressed similar ideas many years earlier. Unamuno knew Kierkegaard's work, and as a matter of fact he learned the Danish language in order to read Kierkegaard. However, most of those who have studied the problem of the relationship between the two thinkers have concluded that Unamuno had already developed his fundamental ideas and feelings before he read Kierkegaard's works in 1900, although they subsequently helped him in the further development of his thought.[68] Unamuno, therefore, had an uncommon vision of the problems of our times, for the success of existentialism is due, in a great extent, to the fact that when we read the writings of its exponents we get the impression that they are talking about us and our problems. Unamuno uses poetry, plays, and novels to express his ideas or feelings, a method or technique which has become general among existentalists. According to Julian Marías, Unamuno created the existential or personal novel, as opposed to the traditional psychological novel.[69]

As Ernst Robert Curtius, Charles Moeller, and Julian Marías point out, it is Unamuno's outstanding achievement to have proclaimed the problem of immortality as a real, in fact as the only, philosophical problem at a time when a great portion of the prevailing philosophy and science rejected it as an illusion.[70] Unamuno has been rightly criticized for having relegated this problem to the antirational realm of a sentimental faith. However, even this deficiency contains a positive dimension. His listeners were victims of the same antirationalism as he was, and they would never have listened to, for example, the Thomistic rational proofs of the immortality of the soul. In other words, Unamuno spoke to them in a language they could understand and accept, and many did listen to him. The same can be said of his constant preaching on God and religion in a purely naturalistic environment, since this preaching stirred many consciences and led them to the true God.[71]

Finally we should touch on a debate which has been going on as to whether Unamuno is a philosopher in the strict sense of the term and deserves to be included in the history of philosophy. All agree that he deals with philosophical problems, not only in his essays but also in his poems, plays, and novels, and that he really lived those problems. However, there are those who either deny or doubt that Unamuno is a strict philosopher, because, they say, he never follows a rigorous philosophical method. We think with José Ferrater Mora and others that if Kierkegaard or Nietzsche, for example, are accepted as philosophers, Unamuno likewise must be regarded as a true philosopher. The historians of philosophy seem to be of the same opinion, for recent histories, dictionaries, and encyclopedias of philosophy prominently include Don Miguel de Unamuno.

What cannot be doubted is that Unamuno's works are today as actual as when they were first published and by their intense, concrete, and agonized human vitality continue to stir the souls and hearts of their readers. He was right when he wrote:

> When you think me quite dead
> I shall tremble in your hands
> I leave you herein my soul-book, . . .
> When all of you vibrates,
> It is I, reader, who vibrates in you.[72]

NOTES

1. *Del sentimiento trágico de la vida en los hombres y en los pueblos* (Buenos Aires: Colección Austral, 1937), p. 28.

Unamuno's important works are the following: *En torno at casticismo* (1895), *Paz en la guerra* (1897), *De la ensenanza superior en Espana* (1899), *Tres ensayos* (1900), *Amor y pedagogía* (1902), *De mi país* (1903), *Vida de Don Quijote y Sancho* (1905), *Poesías* (1907), *Recuerdos de ninez y mocedad* (1908), *Mi religión y otros ensayos* (1910), *Rosario de sonetos líricos* (1911), *Por tierras de Portugal y Espana* (1911), *Solliloquios y conversaciones* (1911), *Contra esto y aquello* (1912), *Del sentimiento trágico* (1913), *Niebla* (1914), *Ensayos* (7 vols., 1916-1918), *Abel Sánchez* (1917), *El Cristo de Velázquez* (1920), *Tres novelas ejemplares y un prólogo* (1920), *De Fuerteventura a Paris* (1925), *La Agonía del Cristianismo* (1931), *Cómo se hace una novela* (1927), *Romancero del destierro* (1928), *Dos artículos y dos discursos* (1930), *Nada menos que un hombre* (1925), *El otro* (1932), *San Manuel bueno, martir y tres historias más* (1933), *El Hermano Juan o el mundo es teatro* (1934). There is an edition of the complete works of Unamuno; sixteen volumes have been published so far. Miguel de Unamuno, *Obras completas* (Madrid: Afrodisio Aguado, 1951-   ). Among the unpublished works of Unamuno his *Diario* (Diary) is of capital importance for the understanding of his life and works.

2. *Del sentimiento trágico*, p. 8.

3. *Ibidem*, p. 11.

4. *Ibidem*, pp. 2, 7, 232; "Sobre la filosofía espanola," *Obras Completas*, II, p. 487.

5. *Del sentimiento trágico*, p. 7.

6. For Unamuno's life see Nemesio González Caminero, *Unamuno*, I (Comillas: Universidad Pontificia, 1948), pp. 33-117; Charles Moeller, *Littérature du XXe siècle et christianisme*, IV (Casterman, 1961), pp. 47-146. Moeller uses the unpublished Diary of Unamuno discovered by Armando Zubizarreta, and also some unpublished letters and articles of Unamuno; Armando Zubizarreta, *Unamuno en su nivola* (Madrid: Taurus, 1960).

7. Cf. José María Pemán, "Unamuno o la gracia resistida," *ABC* (Madrid, May, 1949).

8. Hernán Benítez, *El drama religioso de Unamuno* (Buenos Aires: Universidad de Buenos Aires, 1949), pp. 163 ff.

9. Cf. Julián Marías, *La escuela de Madrid* (Buenos Aires: Revista de Occidente, 1959), pp. 45 ff.

10. Cf. Charles Moeller, *l. c.*, p. 67, n. 19. The literary figures preferred by Unamuno were Ibsen, Carducci, Senancour, Leopardi, Antero de Quental, and Carlyle. Cf. N. González Camminero, *l. c.*, pp. 99-114.

11. Cf. Charles Moeller, *l. c.* Among philosophers and thinkers, Unamuno preferred Spinoza, Hume, Berkeley, Joseph Butler, Kant, Fichte, Schelling, Hegel, John Stuart Mill, Le Dantec, Darwin, Schopenhauer, Rousseau, Voltaire, Papini, Kierkegaard, Bergson, W. James, and Croce. Cf. Nemesio González Camminero, *l. c.*, pp. 82-99.

12. Cf. Charles Moeller, *l. c.*, p. 79, n. 3.

13. *Ibidem*, pp. 67-68.

14. Cf. Armando Zubizarreta, *l. c.*, pp. 262 ff; Charles Moeller, *l. c.*,

pp. 79 ff.

15. Cf. Charles Moeller, *l. c.*, p. 95. The theologians preferred by Unamuno were Manuel Swedenborg, Frederick William Robertson, Boehme, Sabatier, Tyrrell, Loisy, Schleiermacher, Herrmann, Harnack, and Ritschl. Cf. Nemesio González Caminero, *l. c.*, pp. 114-117.

16. Cf. Vicente Marrero, *El Cristo de Unamuno* (Madrid: Ediciones Rialp, 1960) pp. 245 ff.

17. Charles Moeller, *l. c.*, p. 100.

18. *Ibidem*, pp. 100-101.

19. Cf. Antonio Sánchez Barbudo, *Estudios sobre Unamuno y Machado* (Madrid: Ediciones Guadarrama, 1959), pp. 93, 111, 127, 129, 131, 133.

20. Armando Zubizarreta, *l. c.*, pp. 262-276, and 391, n. 49; Charles Moeller, *l. c.*, p. 93.

21. Cf. Armando Zubizarreta, *l. c.*, pp. 262-276; Antonio Sánchez Barbudo, *l. c.*, pp. 83 ff.

22. Antonio Sánchez Barbudo, *l. c.*, p. 121.

23. Armando Zubizarreta, *l. c.*, p. 278.

24. Cf. *Poems by Miguel de Unamuno*, trans. Eleanor L. Turnbull (Baltimore: The John Hopkins Press, 1952), p. 143.

25. *Del sentimiento trágico*, p. 7.

26. *Ibidem*.

27. *Ibidem*, p. 31.

28. *Ibidem*, p. 133; "El individualismo español," *Obras Completas*, III, pp. 390-391.

29. *Del sentimiento trágico*, p. 128; "Adentrol," *Obras Completas*, III, p. 210; *La agonía del cristianismo, Obras Completas*, IV, p. 829.

30. *Del sentimiento trágico*, ch. V.

31. Cf. Julián Marías, *l. c.*, pp. 68 ff.; 334 ff.

32. Charles Moeller, *l. c.*, p. 111.

33. *Del sentimiento trágico*, p. 179.

34. *Ibidem*, p. 13.

35. *Ibidem*, p. 179.

36. *Ibidem*, pp. 37 ff.

37. *Ibidem*, p. 111.

38. *Ibidem*, ch. VII.

39. *Ibidem*, pp. 73 ff.

40. *Ibidem*, pp. 65 ff.

41. According to Unamuno, the scientific knowledge, which is the field of reason, is limited to the phenomenal order. As regards its objective value or the existence of its objects, Unamuno states that there is something outside our mind and consciousness, for the matter of our knowledge comes from the exterior world. But it is impossible, he says, to know how this matter is, since to know is to inform matter, and the formless as such cannot be known. It is likewise impossible to know whether rational and systematic knowledge actually reflects an external systematic reality, for to solve the

problem it would be necessary to place ourselves outside the system itself, which is impossible.

42. *Del sentimiento trágico,* p. 100.

43. *Ibidem,* pp. 91 ff; 145 ff.

44. Cf. Miguel de Unamuno, "La fe," *Obras completas,* III, pp. 227 ff; etc.

45. Cf. José Luis L. Aranguren, *Catolicismo y protestantismo* (Madrid: Revista de Occidente, 1957), 196; Charles Moeller, *l. c.,* pp. 87 and 91.

46. *Del sentimiento trágico,* p. 228.

47. Cf. Julián Marías, *l. c.*

48. *Del sentimiento trágico,* p. 94.

49. *Ibidem.*

50. *Ibidem,* ch. VII.

51. *Ibidem,* pp. 157 ff.

52. *La agonía del cristianismo, Obras completas,* III, pp. 819 ff.

53. *Del sentimiento trágico,* p. 10.

54. *Ibidem.*

55. *Ibidem,* pp. 123 ff; "Intelectualidad y espiritualidad," *Obras completas,* III, p. 465; "Qué es verdad?", *Obras completas,* III, p. 697; "Mi religión," *Obras completas,* III, p. 821.

56. *Del sentimiento trágico,* p. 160.

57. *Ibidem,* p. 143; "Qué es verdad?", *Obras completas,* III, p. 697.

58. *Del sentimiento trágico,* p. 121; cf. "Epistolario Unamuno-Ilundain," in Hernán Benítez, *El Drama religioso de Unamuno,* pp. 241 ff.

59. *Del sentimiento trágico,* p. 168; "Plenitud de plenitudes," *Obras completas,* III, p. 509.

60. *Del sentimiento trágico,* p. 168; "Mi religión," *Obras completas,* III, p. 819.

61. *Ibidem.*

62. *Del sentimiento trágico,* pp. 170 ff.

63. *Ibidem,* pp. 200 ff; *Vida de Don Quijote,* pp. 132, 237.

64. *Del sentimiento trágico,* p. 201.

65. *Ibidem,* p. 204.

66. *Tres novelas ejemplares, Obras completas,* II, pp. 986-987; "Sobre la consecuencia la sinceridad," *Obras completas,* III, p. 747.

67. Unamuno contends paradoxically and with obvious exaggeration that his philosophy is the philosophy of quixotism. In quixotism he sees "a complete method, a complete epistemology, a complete esthetics, a complete logic, a complete ethics, and above all a complete religion, that is to say, an absolute hope in that which is rationally absurd." The hunger for immortality, Unamuno says, was the incentive of all the heroic deeds of Don Quixote. His madness was the madness of those who rule their lives independently of the norms of reason. His actions derive from sentiment, will, faith. He reached the substantial world of consciousness, unique and irreplaceable, whose destiny troubles us by means of suffering and anguish. He considered it to be his duty to awaken so many merely apparent men,

unconcerned with the substantial world, and to instill in them the tragic sentiment of life. He did not act according to any rational ethics, his behavior created morality, not vice versa, his activity derived from passion and the end of his justice was forgiveness. Thus he sees the main theses of his philosophy actualized in the life of Don Quixote as interpreted by Unamuno, which is often contrary to the mind and even to the explicit words of Cervantes. Cf. *Vida de Don Quijote,* (Buenos Aires: Colección Austral, 1939), pp. 266 ff; *Del sentimiento trágico,* pp. 236 ff.

68. Cf. Charles Moeller, *l. c.,* p. 79, n. 3.

69. Julián Marías, *l. c.,* p. 79, n. 3.

70. Cf. E. R. Curtius, *Kritische Essays zur europäischen Literatur* (Zurich, 1954), pp. 239-240; Charles Moeller, *l. c.,* p. 126.

71. Cf. Julián Marías, *l. c.,* p. 93.

72. *Poems by Miguel de Unamuno,* p. 225. The writer wishes to thank the editors of New Scholasticism for allowing him to use his article "The Philosophical Mythology of Miguel de Unamuno," *The New Scholasticism,* XXIX, 3 (1955), 278-317.

jean paul sartre

PHILOSOPHER OF NAUGHT AND NAUSEA
by *Allan B. Wolter, O.F.M.*

Perhaps the most common reaction at first reading Sartre's philosophical works is one of bewilderment, shock, or even disgust: bewilderment at his baffling formulations, his inordinate penchant for paradox, his considered courting of obscurantism—Simone de Beauvoir says of the boy Sartre, "He was particularly happy when he could not understand what he was writing"[1]—shock at his obvious exaggerations, his deliberate use of half-truths—"There is an element of cheating in all writers," he admits and "The law of rhetoric is that one must lie in order to speak the truth."[2] — disgust at his morbid fascination with sexual perversity and his ghoulish delight in probing the deviate's miasmatic mind. It may well be one of those self-reflections that he sees mirrored in Genet when he writes of the latter that he "knows that he shocks us" and "secretly enjoys doing so."[3] And again: "By infecting us with his evil, Genet delivers himself from it. Each of his books is a cathartic attack of possession . . . but with each work he masters increasingly the demon that possesses him. His ten years of literature are equivalent to a psychoanalytic cure."[4]

Why does Sartre write one of his longest prose works, some 550 pages, to introduce the collected works of Jean Genet, confessed thief and pervert, whose writings were so obscene that even in France they were sold under the counters? Is it simply be-

cause "I have a passion to understand men," as he tells us, or is
it perhaps in analyzing writers like Baudelaire and Jean Genet, he
is analyzing himself? Why should one read a man like Genet? he
asks. It is because

> we have been kings of shadows and shams ... Since we
> cannot escape from the objectivity that crushes us nor
> divest ourselves of the subjectivity that exiles us, since
> we are not allowed even to rise to the plane of being or
> sink into nothingness, since we are, in any case, *impossible
> nullities,* we must listen to the voice of Genet, our fellow
> man, our brother. He carries to an extreme the latent,
> masked solitude which is ours; he inflates our sophisms
> until they burst ... He exaggerates our dishonesty to the
> point of making it intolerable to us; he makes our guilt
> appear in broad daylight.[5]

Though Sartre addresses these words to the philosophical world
in general, one can scarcely doubt that he is speaking of himself
as well. This seems certain of the closing paragraph of the work,
where he writes:

> We spent our time fleeing from the objective into the
> subjective and from the subjective into objectivity. This
> game of hide and seek will end only when we have the
> courage to go the limits of ourselves in both directions
> at once. At the present time, we must bring to light the
> subject, the guilty one, that monstrous and wretched bug
> which we are likely to become at any moment. Genet
> holds the mirror up to us: we must look at it and at our-
> selves.[6]

1. FROM OBJECTIVITY TO SUBJECTIVITY

"Fleeing from the objective into the subjective" well describes
the early life of Sartre. Born in Paris, June 21, 1905, Jean Paul
was half-orphaned when his Catholic father, a naval officer, died
from intestinal fever contracted in Cochin-China. His mother

went back to live with her parents, first at Meudon, later in 1911
in Paris where her father, Charles Schweitzer, uncle to Albert
Schweitzer, founded the *Institut des Langues Vivantes* to provide
for his wife, daughter, and Jean Paul. So attached was he to the
boy that he found various pretexts to provide for his schooling
privately until he was ten and a quarter years old. Plagued with
ill health and having no other children to play with, the boy
seems to have lived in a world of fantasy. At six he was writing
his own adventure stories, and by nine he was sketching historical
novels, in which make-believe world he starred as hero, martyr,
and saint. His conduct with real people was limited largely to his
mother and his maternal grandparents.

It is not surprising then that the undue affection they lavished
on this only child caused him to develop a spoiled and effeminate
character. What must have been the effect of his mother's remarriage on this sensitive, demanding eleven-year old? Is what
he writes of Baudelaire an echo of his own youth? Left fatherless
at the age of six, Baudelaire's life became centered on his mother.
"I lived in you," he writes. "You were everything to me; an idol,
a companion."[7] Surrounded with every care, Sartre explains,
Baudelaire did not yet realize that he existed as a distinct person.
Far from feeling himself a vague, superfluous existence, he regarded himself as a son by divine right. A year later the boy's
mother remarried and young Charles was sent away to board.
Here, Sartre points out, was the turning point in Baudelaire's life.
He is thrust rudely into personal existence. He discovers he is
one, alone, that life has been given him "pour rien." Solitude is
his destiny. Abandoned and rejected, Baudelaire, instead of
suffering solitude passively, embraces this state, choosing it as his
own. Having experienced himself as other by this harsh revelation
of his individual existence, the boy by an original and free choice
takes to himself this otherness. He feels and wishes to feel unique,
even though this brings with it a feeling of dread and terror.[8]
"Each of us," Sartre goes on to say, "has been able to observe
in his childhood the unannounced and shattering appearance of
the consciousness of his own self."[9] Though all children discover
their subjectivity as a shock, the majority hasten to forget it.
But the child who has discovered himself in despair, fury, and
jealousy, as did Baudelaire, will tend to base his whole life on

this unwholesome, Narcissus-like concern with his formal singularity.

It has been suggested that Sartre suffered such a trauma when his own mother remarried and they moved to La Rochelle where he was sent to school. He seems to have suspected, contrary to all evidence, that he might be an illegitimate child. This theme of "bastardy" appears in many of Sartre's later works where it is used to explain the behavior of his "heroes." In his psychoanalytic biography of Jean Genet, Sartre gives a graphic description of the impact of such a suspicion upon a physically weak and sensitive youngster.

> Genet's origin is *a blunder* (there would not have been a Genet if someone had used a contraceptive), then *a rejection* (someone rejected that hated consequence of a blunder), then *a failure* (the child was unable to integrate himself into the milieu that received him). Blunder, rejection, failure: these add up to a *No*. Since the child's objective essence was the No, Genet gave himself a personality by giving himself the subjectivity of the No; he is the absolute opponent, for he opposes Being and all integration. Although he is a taboo object for everyone, he becomes a sacred subject for himself, and the subjectivity which he claims is the proud internalization of the object's pure being-gazed-upon.[10]

Thrown in with stronger and older schoolmates at La Rochelle, Sartre was not inclined to come out of his shell of subjectivity. Dempsey and others have suggested some unfortunate incident at this time may account for Sartre's later morbid preoccupation with inversion.[11]

Be that as it may, his first published work as a graduate philosophy student at Paris is a short story called *L'ange du morbide* (1923). It tells of a university professor's fascination with morbidity which causes him to pursue an affair with a victim of tuberculosis. Only the horror of the disease frightens him back to some measure of respectibility. As Spiegelberg comments: "It sounds like the defeat of the intellectual libertine in his attempt to conquer Being in one of its more nauseating aspects."[12]

More important for understanding Sartre's philosophical outlook at this time are the open letter sent to *Les Nouvelles Littérai-
res* dated February 2, 1929 and the semi-philosophical essay
Légende de la verité.[13] The latter proposes the view that in
the history of mankind truth is but a transition stage like the age
of commerce. It will eventually be replaced by the standard of
the "probable." The open letter, addressed to an inquiry then
current among his fellow students, is even more indicative of
Sartre's state of mind at this period.

> It is the paradox of the human spirit [he writes] that man,
> whose task it is to create the necessary, cannot elevate him-
> self to the level of being ... That is why I see the root of
> both man and nature melancholy and boredom. This does
> not imply that man does not think of himself as *un être*.
> Quite the contrary, he makes every effort to do so. Hence
> the Good and Evil, ideas of man working upon man. Vain
> ideas! Also a vain idea is that determinism which tempts
> us strangely to synthesize *existence* and *être*. We are free
> as you please, yet powerless ... Everything is too weak:
> all things tend to die.[14]

In an editorial of the same issue, Sartre characterizes his generation
in comparison to the preceding with the words: "We are more
unhappy, but inspire greater sympathy."

During Sartre's first years of teaching philosophy at Le Havre,
this sentiment seems to have continued. It finds its graphic expression in the thinly disguised autobiographical novel *Nausea*.
Roquentin (Sartre), seemingly without cause as he picks a moist
pebble from the beach, is suddenly overcome by a feeling of
metaphysical nausea. This disgust with his own existence runs
the gamut from ennui to a positive loathing and reaches its
climax at the sight of the sprawling roots of the chestnut tree in
a public park. They suddenly lose their character as recognizable
familiar objects and become "a black, knotty mass, entirely
beastly," something frightening and absurd. In that moment,
Roquentin discovers the "key to existence" and to his nausea.
"The world of explanations and reasons is not the world of
existence."[15] For everything, including himself, is "born without

reason, prolongs itself out of weakness and dies by chance."[16] This disgust seizes him even as he looks at the "obscenity" of his upturned hand.

> I see my hand out on the table. It lives—it is me ... Lying on its back, it shows me its fat belly ... like an animal turned upside down ... I feel its weight on the table which is not me. It's long, long, this impression of weight, it doesn't pass ... It becomes intolerable. I draw back my hand and put it in my pocket; but immediately I feel the warmth of my thigh through the stuff. I pull my hand out of my pocket and let it hang against the back of the chair. Now I feel a weight at the end of my arm. It pulls a little, softly, insinuatingly it exists ... No matter where I put it it will go on existing. I can't suppress it, nor can I suppress the rest of my body, the sweaty warmth which soils my shirt, nor all this warm obesity which turns lazily, as if someone were stirring it with a spoon ... It's frightful—if I exist, it is because I am horrified at existing. *I am the one* who pulls myself from the nothingness to which I aspire: the hatred, the disgust of existing.[17]

The source of this nausea is the "Thing" (*La Chose* spelt with a capital C). Its massive, opaque, sprawling existence is essentially senseless and absurd. Not merely a harmless nuisance, it becomes something aggressive, swooping down on man, oppressing him, seeking to reduce him to passivity. It threatens his freedom; it tries to turn him into a thing. In this disgust not only with existence, but with every human being (who in *Nausea* appears not only as a bore but at times as loathsome) we find the reasons Sartre "flees from objectivity to subjectivity." With somewhat less exaggeration, Sartre describes this period in his life as dominated by a "theological attitude." Not that he was still searching for God, since by his own admission he was an atheist at eleven (significantly the year of his mother's remarriage). His search is rather for some transcendent absolute, a search that will lead him first to evil and then to "nothingness."

Like his creation Goetz in *Le Diable et le bon Dieu,* Sartre seems to have made some kind of Faustian pact, deliberately choosing, as did Jean Genet, "to be all evil." "As a being who thinks about being," he explains, "I am a creature of God, as nothingness thinking nothingness, I am my own cause."[18] Coupled with this deliberate choice of evil is an intentional rejection of truth and an attempt to live in the fanciful world of appearance.

> If I discovered a truth, it would belong to everyone and no longer to me. And if, to suppose the impossible, I created being, this being would continue in its being without me, through inertia or with the help of God. But appearance is not I; it steals from being its transcendency, and yet it sticks to the skin of my consciousness as does a cataract to an eye; it depends on me alone. Appearance is satanic, because it caricatures being and because it is all that man can produce by his own means ... The hounded child lets himself sink into the absolute solitude of a long evil dream where no one can follow him.[19]

Perhaps it was at this point where the young philosophy professor discovered in phenomenology the promise of what he was looking for. Does it not enable him to see in the "seizure of each phenomenon a certain contact with being itself, the presence of *an absolute* in the relative?" And it is only by escaping from "the relative condition of humanity" he tells Jeanson, that one "becomes a man."[20]

With a two year grant to the *Institut Français* in Berlin, Sartre began the serious study of Heidegger, Scheler, Jaspers, the psychoanalysts, and above all Husserl.[21] Indeed, when he returned to France, it was with the conviction that Husserl's *Ideen zu einer reinen Phänomenologie und phänomenologischen Philosophie* was the most important philosophical book he had come across. In his first major philosophic work *L'Imagination,* Sartre refers almost exclusively to Husserl, crediting him with pioneering the way for his own studies on the imagination. No treatise on the subject can afford to "neglect his rich observations on the subject; today we must start from zero and disregard the whole prephenomenological literature."[22] It is Husserl too who taught him the Cartesian approach to truth. As he later wrote of this period,

Our point of departure is indeed the subjectivity, and that for strictly philosophical reasons. It is not because we are bourgeois, but we seek to base our teaching upon the truth, and not upon a collection of fine theories, full of hope but lacking real foundations. And at this point of departure there cannot be any other truth than this, *I think, therefore I am,* which is the absolute truth of consciousness as it attains to itself. Every theory which begins with man, outside of this moment of self-attainment, is a theory which thereby suppresses the truth, for outside the Cartesian *cogito,* all objects are no more than probable, and any doctrine of probablities which is not attached to a truth will crumble into nothing. In order to define the probable one must possess the true. Before there can be any truth whatever, then, there must be an absolute truth, and there is such a truth which is simple, easily attained and within the reach of everyone; it consists in one's immediate sense of one's self.[23]

With the discovery of phenomenology, Sartre's thought enters a new phase. His writings become more scholarly and concrete. Truth no longer appears as just a legend. It reveals itself as a core of certainty working its phenomenological way into the penumbra of empirical theories and scientific probabilities. Even the victim of *Nausea* is on the way to some kind of cure as the novel closes. Listening to a jazz recording, Roquentin confesses:

I no longer think of myself. I think of the man out there who wrote this tune, one day in July, in the black heat of his room ... He had troubles ... I find his suffering and sweat ... moving ... This is the first time in years that a man has seemed moving to me ... I think of [him and the negress who sings his song] with such gentleness ... They are a little like the heroes of a novel; they have washed themselves of the sin of existing. Not completely, of course, but as much as any man can ... I feel [joy] brush against me lightly and I dare not move because I am afraid it will go away ... [Could I not justify my] existence then? Just a little? ... In another medium? It would have to be a book: I don't know how to do anything else. Not a history book: history talks about what has existed—an existant can never justify another existant. Another type of book . . . which would be above existence. A story, for example, something that could never happen, an adventure. It would have to be beautiful and hard as steel and make people ashamed of their existence.[24]

This theme of art, of beauty (works of the imagination), as an escape from a nauseating and unjustifiable existence appears again in the closing lines of *L'Imaginaire.*

Though he will later ridicule this concept of literature as a means of metaphysical salvation for the gifted and isolated individual,[25] a concept which undoubtedly inspired his own efforts as a playwright and novelist, Sartre's strictly philosophical works of this period are perhaps his best. They include in addition to *L'Imagination* (1936), *La Transcendence de l'égo* (1936), *Esquisse d'une théories des emotions* (1939) and *L'Imaginaire* (1940). Comparatively free of neologisms and the paradoxical style of *L'Etre et le néant,* they show Sartre adept at using Husserl's eidetic and transcendental reduction techniques to reveal a hard core of certain truths of psychology and philosophy. In his discussion of the "transcendental ego" (which Descartes discovered through reflection), Sartre stresses that this is not the real *cogito* or starting point of philosophy, since it is itself an object. It is created by, and hence presupposes, a more fundamental form of consciousness which can be called direct or prereflective. In analyzing consciousness itself, he argues that since it can imagine (i.e., can make an "image" of) things, it must be something other than existence (which is the characteristic of *La Chose*). To present something to us as an image, then, consciousness must somehow "negate existence." For we recognize the image for what it is, something other than the real or existing object of which it is the image. If consciousness can do this, then it must be irreducible to the category of "thingness" or being (*être*) and hence it is also free of the determinism that rules the world of things. Thus Sartre introduces one of his characteristic tenets, the basic freedom of the self. It is here that he first identifies this free creative source with "nothingness"—a theme that will reach its full development in *L'Etre et le néant*. In the essay on the emotions, he rejects the Freudian thesis that they are irresistible forces determining our behavior. They are rather a form of escape mechanism, a device which we deliberately use to invest the harsh and disagreeable features of the world with a kind of "magic" that makes reality bearable. They do not destroy our basic freedom, however, and to pretend that they do is simply a form of self-deception or "bad faith." This is a thesis that, like that on the origin of negation and nothingness, will be fully developed in *L'Etre et le néant*.

The latter book is the most extensive and ambitious expression of Sartre's early philosophy. Though subtitled "An essay on phenomenological ontology", it could better be described as "much ado about nothing"—over 700 pages to be precise. For despite an introduction captioned "the pursuit of being", it reveals that its author is still largely concerned with "naught" rather than "nausea", i.e., with subjectivity or inner consciousness as opposed to existence or the realm of objects. This is not surprising, since the book was some thirteen years in the making. Though most of its ideas antedate 1943, the year of its publication, it still reflects something of Sartre's postwar change of attitude, his concern with a real world and real people.

To analyze the contents of this immense work even in summary fashion would take us far beyond the scope of this study. The interested reader is referred to some of the numerous commentaries to be found on this subject.[26] I should only like to note that if it has been ridiculed along with Heidegger's works as a horrible example of what logical empiricists refer to as meaningless metaphysics,[27] it has the undoubted merit of having introduced Heidegger, Husserl, and Jaspers to the French-speaking world. Despite its neologisms, which grate upon the sensitive French ear, or its needless and seemingly deliberately obscurity[28] and obvious exaggerations, it is clearer than Heidegger, and it contains a number of important phenomenological insights, among which is Sartre's analysis of "nothingness".

For Aristotle and the scholastics negative knowledge is never primary. Negations are known by way of affirmations. Syncategorematic terms like "not" have no independent meaning. But for all that not even the semanticists want to eliminate all negative terms and expressions. Is there something about reality itself that makes convenient to use negative expressions. Does our immediate experience confront us with phenomena that call for such negative expressions? Husserl suggests that such judgments have their basis in certain prepredicative experiences such as the disappointment of some hope or prior anticipation. Heidegger goes further, and attempts to prove that nothingness has a peculiar mode of existence called "naughting" (nichten) which is on a a par with being. It is particularly through the experience of anxiety that it is manifested.

Though Sartre uses Heidegger's terminology of "naughting" (*néantisation*), his account of the positive experience of an absence of a void, comes closer to that of Husserl. Not every instance of non-existence is experienced in this way, but only such instances as those where we are looking forward, for instance, to meeting a friend. Sartre cites the example of his having an appointment with Peter at four o'clock. He himself arrives fifteen minutes late, only to find that his friend has not showed up. The café with its patrons, its tables and booths, its glittering lights and mirrors, the murmur of voices mingled with the rattling of saucers and clink of glasses, the various odors and smoky air—this appears as a "fulness of being." At first this *plein d'être* seems to be all that is here. Yet in every perception, as the Gestaltists have shown, there are figure and ground, the former emerging from the latter. Now when I enter this café to search for Peter, says Sartre, all the objects therein merge with one another to form a common background from which Peter, or more precisely his nothingness or not-being-there, will emerge as a figure does from the ground. Sartre accepts the traditional view that negativity, even such as has an immediate phenomenological basis in experience, is not really primary. It appears only against some prior positive experience. So too with the absence of Peter. What is peculiar to Sartre's account is that it explains awareness of the absentee as an intuition of a double act of nihilation. The first *néantisation* occurs when the café and all its patrons and furnishings are fused into a common ground. Each element of the setting, says Sartre, each person, table, chair, and so on, attempts to isolate itself, to emerge as a distinct form only to fall back and be swallowed up once more by the general background. The latter is merely the object of peripheral or marginal attention. Yet this primary nihilation whereby each distinct object is melted down into a neutral ground is a necessary condition for Peter's appearance as the principal form. I am immediately aware of and intuit this nihilating process, Sartre insists. I witness the successive disappearance of all the objects at which I look, especially the faces which detain me for a moment ("Could this be Peter?", I ask), but quickly decompose because they "are not" the face of Peter. And yet if I found Peter, my intuition would suddenly be arrested by his face and the whole café would organize itself about him as a discreet presence.

But Peter is not here and his absence is not associated with this or that precise spot but with the café as a whole. His absence, in short, emerges as the central figure against the background of the entire place. This emergence is a second or further act of nihilation. "It is Peter," Sartre explains, "raising himself as a void upon the ground of the [primary] nihilation of the café. So what is offered to intuition is a flickering of nothingness, the nothingness of the ground, which when nihilated demands and calls for the appearance of the figure. And it is the figure, the nothingness, which slips as a *nothing* to the surface of the ground." It is this that serves as the empirical basis for the judgment "Peter is not here!" We intuit a double nihilation, due to the fact, says Sartre, that I expected to see Peter and "my expectation has caused the absence of Peter to *occur* as a real event about the café. It is an objectve fact that I now *discover* this absence and the absence presents itself as a synthetic relation between Peter and the setting in which I look for him. Peter's absence haunts this café and is the condition for its self-nihilating organization as ground."[30]

From this rather straightforward phenomenological analysis of a felt absence, Sartre pushes on to more precarious and questionable interpretations. Since it is only *for us* that Peter is absent, we are the nihilators, and we can nihilate because we have nothingness at our core. Our acts have nothingness between them, precisely because they do not form part of a continuous, deterministic whole, in which each act is necessitated by what precedes. As Mathieu, the hero of Sartre's novel *Le Sursis,* expresses it, "freedom is not a being, it is the being of a man, that is his own *non-being."* Naught, or more precisely, the power of "naughting", is nothing else than free consciousness, the great challenger of "being" as the source of nausea. We are thus presented with the great struggle between the free self as the "For Itself" (*pour soi*) and the objective world of being as a whole, designated as the "In Itself" (*en soi*).

In the second part of *L'Etre et le néant,* Sartre attempts an analysis of the structure of consciousness in terms of its "facticity", "temporality" and "transcendence" or passing beyond itself, toward being. It is here that we have the beginnings of that second phase or counter movement, the return to objectivity.

2. FROM SUBJECTIVITY TO OBJECTIVITY

It is essentially in the third part of the work, that Sartre lays the groundwork for the "return" in a detailed discussion of how one's own consciousness is related to that of others. If Sartre comes closest to Heidegger in the preceding section, in this portion of his work he goes beyond him. Here we find a new type of being, *pour autrui,* in which the self becomes an object *for another.* In this connection, we have another one of Sartre's more original and remarkable phenomenological descriptions, viz., of the human gaze. For one who adopts the Cartesian or subjectivist approach to reality, and is continually in danger of falling into solipsism, the felt experience of another's gaze is an enigma. Other persons should appear to us as any other object. Their gazing upon us should be reducible to the experience of seeing their eyes turned in our direction. But this is not the case. Consider only the shame that goes with being surprised by another in an embarrassing situation, the shock of being looked at. Here I become the object, and another the subject. It is this experience that indubitably proves the existence of other selves and is an empirical refutation of solipsism.

But from this sound phenomenological starting point, Sartre again proceeds to more questionable conclusions. Instead of including some of the more healthy and ordinary features of "being-seen-by-the-Other", such as a friendly recognition, or a warm smile, or the light of joy in another's eye, Sartre concentrates, almost with relish, upon the more sinister aspects of the human gaze. He speaks of it as "petrifying" or "curdling" its object, of "enslaving" it, and so on. In his play *Huis clos,* with its infamous theme that "hell is other people", we have some striking illustrations of this phenomenon.

It is perhaps Sartre's descriptions of the interpersonal relationship in *L'Etre et le néant* that have proved most nauseating and unreal to his readers. The drama of human kind is represented as a fundamental conflict between irreconcilable freedoms. Any true "I-thou" relationship of love becomes impossible, since to retain my character as a "self" rather than an object I must treat the other as object; for if the other is treated as another "self", then I am reduced to the status of object and am no longer free. Union with another through any Christian form of love becomes a dream or an illuson. To *love* another (as opposed to *desiring* another sexually) means I regard them as a free agent and not an object. And to fascinate, attract, or please my beloved, I become an object. But the other wants me not as object only but as free; yet, unwilling to give up an iota of his or her freedom, the other must resent my freedom regarding him or her as object. Failing in love, the lover turns either to sadism or masochism accordingly as one or the other of these irreconcilable drives predominates.

This concern with freedom is perhaps the most characteristic feature of Sartre's philosophy. Not only does the idea of man's absolute freedom and his consequent responsibility dominate *L'Etre et le néant,* but it recurs again and again in the novels that make up the trilogy *Les Chemins de la liberté* [31] and the two plays, *Les Mouches* and *Huis clos,* which appeared in 1943. As Simone de Beauvoir puts it:

> Many persons envy the sleep of trees or stones and try to resemble them; they put their consciousness to sleep; they make no use of their liberty. Sartre can be defined, on the contrary, as a person who passionately refuses to exist in the mode of things and tries to affirm himself as consciousness and pure liberty. [32]

In the fourth and last part of *L'Etre et le néant,* under the heading "Having, Doing, and Being", Sartre stresses the activistic features of human existence that stem from his being "pure liberty". Man's being is derived from his doing and what he does is always based upon some free, original choice. To analyze the root cause of all human behavior in terms of such a "free decision" a new, non-Freudian technique is needed, which Sartre calls "existential psychoanalysis" and which he will illustrate in such subsequent works as those on Baudelaire, Jean Genet, and his own autobiography.

The work concludes with that concern which has plagued thinkers from the time of Descartes. Having so sharply differentiated the free and active, inner consciousness or *pour soi* from the passive, inert, deterministic outer world, the *en soi,* Sartre finds that it was "difficult to establish a bond between them and we feared that we might fall into an insurmountable dualism."[33] But the very fact that we are aware of both realms, of being and nothingness, of naught and nausea, is indicative of a connection between the two. It is the conscious *pour soi* that bonds the two together.

> The For-itself and the In-itself are reunited by a synthetic connection which is nothing other than the For-itself itself. The For-itself, in fact, is nothing but the pure nihilation of the In-itself; it is like a hole of being at the heart of Being.[34]

This conception of naughting is nothing new, being found already in *L'Imaginaire*. What is new, and indicative of the return to objectivity, is the universal and cosmic consequence of this naughting. Using an analogy suggested by certain popularizers of science who say the annihilation of a single atom would result in a catastrophe extending to the entire universe, Sartre points out that if the *pour soi* is "like a tiny nihilation" at the very "heart of Being", this "nihilation is sufficient to cause a total upheaval to *happen* to the In-itself. This upheaval is the world."[35]

As Simone de Beauvoir explains, though this new interest in the world and active concern with his fellowmen had its beginnings shortly before the second world war,[36] it was his stay in a German camp that brought about its rapid growth.

> Determined to be a free man [she explains], he never married, never acquired any possessions . . . In the early days, the freedom thus achieved had a negative character.

Because he believed that nothing mattered except his work, Sartre was trying not to become involved in life; he took no interest in politics and even refrained from voting.[37]

By contrast, his new concept of human freedom and involvement, she continues,

> led him to play an active part in the resistance movement, but this was only the outward sign of a changed attitude. He has come to feel that instead of seeking a refuge from the horror and inadequacy of things in an imaginary world, one should seek it in the heart of man.

In lieu of Sartre's own account of this period of his life, I believe we can turn with profit to that illuminating chapter in *Saint Genet* entitled "I went to theft as to a liberation, as to a light", a quotation from Jean Genet.[38] In this psychoanalytic account of Genet, Sartre shows how his decision to become a thief reversed the inward movement that began in Genet's childhood and "set him on the path of evil", making him "a strange dreamer, turned in on himself, impermeable to experience, dragged along in his inner whirlwinds."[39] But in freely and deliberately turning to theft, "he opens himself to the world, to life."[40] Sartre stresses that Genet's choice entails considerable risk, yet he accepts this danger deliberately. Genet is no longer passive, an *object* for others, as when prior to this choice, he begged for a living. As a burglar, he is active, working, one who "deals primarily with things." He even becomes a specialist, says Sartre, entering "a corporation which has its rules and its professional honor. For the first time he is entitled to say *we*."[41] His passive obedience is replaced by a spirit of initiative, mystical thinking by rationalism and "he carries out by and for himself the Revolution of 1789."[42]

Compare this account with what happened to Sartre. He was drafted in 1939, not an active gesture, perhaps, but it got him into the war, and his weak eyes prevented him from being anything but an army nurse. Captured in Lorraine on his thirty-fifth birthday, he spent nine months in prison before being sent back as a noncombatant to Paris where he resumed his teaching. But—and this is important—he freely joined the resistance movement.

Like Genet, he was taking risks and doing so freely. Like him, too, he could refer to his comrades in the underground as "we". One of the first works in which this new attitude towards the human race manifests itself is the essay "Existentialism is a Humanism."[43] Here he reveals an anxiety for someone other than himself. He speaks of each man's freedom to choose, but stresses that in whatever he chooses to be or become, he is choosing not only for himself, but "for all mankind."

In the closing paragraphs of *L'Etre et le néant,* Sartre hints at a "new ethics" which, if not determined by his ontology—since "ontology itself cannot formulate ethical precepts"[44]—will take into consideration what it reveals about the origin and nature of value. It is freedom of the *pour soi* which acknowledges its radical contingency and in accepting and exulting in it, turns this contingency into a personal adventure that is the only true and absolute value.[45] This new ethics of authenticity is stated more explicitly, and dogmatically, in the essay on existentialism and appears again in the play *Le Diable et le bon Dieu* (1951). But with his growing involvement in political issues in the postwar period, a subtle change in Sartre's social philosophy becomes apparent. He no longer stresses the deadly conflict of freedoms in human relationships, nor is he primarily concerned with his own freedom, but with the freedom of the least free members of society, the proletariat. As he told Wilfrid Desan in an interview in 1956,[46] "Every philosopher is a man who is 'involved' [with his fellowmen] and who must attempt to offer a solution" viz., to the problems of his country, of Europe, and the world. The brash moralist of the earlier period has become less sure of himself. As Desan remarks, though constantly obsessed with ethical problems, Sartre is hesitant about offering any "global dogmatical slogans as a cure-all of evils." He recognizes "the position of the moralist is a serious one and cannot be held without anxiety."

Is the *enfant terrible* of French existentialism finally growing up? It would seem so! Already in *Saint Genet* which was published in 1952, we find hints of his own metamorphosis. Of Jean Genet, he writes:

> He has reread his books and finds them bad. This disgust is the last stage of the ascesis, the last renouncement . . .

Anything can come out of his present state of indecision:
a Trappist monk or a completely new writer.[47]

Has the philosopher of "naught" looked long enough on "the
frightening face of negativity," on the "strange hell of beauty",
to which Genet refers? Has his long look at Genet shown him
only too clearly "the monstrous and wretched bug we are likely
to become at any moment"? Only a decade ago, he wrote this
revealing passage:

> We all hide within us a scandalous breach ... beaten in
> argument we have all constructed whirligigs and sophisms
> to postpone the moment of objective defeat, when we
> already knew in our hearts we were beaten, yet to mantain
> our error, our nothingness against the blinding evidence ...
> we became kings of shadows and shams.[48]

The theory of love presented in *L'Etre et le néant* Sartre now
recognizes as "hellish" and acknowledges that there are other
joys that spring from a saner and sounder "I-thou" relationship
that he once seemed to believe possible. Some of these, like those
associated with the virtue of "generosity", Genet has finally discovered.

> In giving [he explains], Genet puts himself above those
> who maintained him below themselves, and to be sure
> generosity has its joys, as does creation, but there are
> other joys that this taut and lonely spirit which is brilliant
> out of necessity, will never know; that of receiving, that
> of sharing.[49]

Not insignificant, perhaps, is Sartre's admission that he agrees
in principle with Genet that "the only vile or ugly acts are those
that are not completed."[50] His morality, at this stage, Jean Paul
explains is that:

> One must will an act to the very end. But act is alive, it
> changes. The goal one sets at the beginning is abstract and
> consequently false. Little by little it is enriched by the

means employed to attain it, and ultimately the concrete goal, the true goal, is what one wants at the finish. The interrupted act spoils and depreciates, just as the truth that stops midway changes into error. In willing himself, unreservedly, to be a thief. Genet sinks into the dream; in willing his dream to the point of madness, he becomes a poet; in willing poetry unto the final triumph of the word, he becomes a man; and the man has become the truth of the poet as the poet was the truth of the thief.[51]

Is Sartre's original choice to become a writer working its way out to a measure of sanity in a similar fashion? Has he ceased to be the "false bastard" he once called himself, and is he seeking readmittance to the legitimate society of men? Has he set his foot on the final path towards the goal that will give the ultimate interpretation, the *truth,* as he calls it, to his earlier works? For that we must wait to read his promised *L'Homme,* his ethical theory,[52] or until he completes the existential psychoanalysis of himself he has just begun.[53] Though *Les Mots* gives us the story of only the first decade of his childhood, we see already in its caustic self-criticism signs of a wiser and more healthy minded man. Like Genet, Sartre appears to have "reread his books and finds them bad." While it may be too much to expect a Trappist monk to emerge from his present state of indecision, there is hope that we may have "a completely new writer."

NOTES

1. Simone de Beauvoir, "Jean Paul Sartre: Strictly Personal," *Harper's Bazaar,* LXXX (January, 1946), 158.

2. J. P. Sartre, *Saint Genet, Actor and Martyr,* trans. B. Frechtman (New York: George Braziller, 1963), p. 518.

3. *Ibid.,* H 558.

4. *Ibid.,* 544.

5. *Ibid.,* 597-598.

6. *Ibid.,* 599.

7. J. P. Sartre, *Baudelaire* (Paris: Gallimard, 1947), p. 18.

8. *Ibid.,* 19-21.

9. *Ibid.,* 217.

10. *Saint Genet,* 596.

11. P. J. R. Dempsey, *The Psychology of Sartre* (Westminster, Md.:

The Newman Press, 1950), p. 23.

12. H. Spiegelberg, *The Phenomenological Movement* (The Hague: Martinus Nijhoff, 1960), p. 460.

13. The only survivor of a collection of lost *Essais,* this work was published eight years later in *Bifur* (8 juin 1931).

14. This letter was republished in Simone de Beavoir's *Mémoirs d'une fille rangée* (Paris: Gallimard, 1958), pp. 341-342.

15. J. P. Sartre, *Nausea,* trans. L. Alexander (Norfolk, Conn.: New Directions, 1959), p. 174.

16: *Ibid.,* 180.

17. *Ibid.,* 134-135.

18. *Saint Genet,* 160.

19. *Ibid.,*

20. F. Jeanson, *Sartre par lui-même* (Paris: Ed. du Seuil, 1955), p. 175.

21. According to Spiegelberg, *op. cit.* p. 463, there is no evidence that Sartre studied under Husserl or even made his personal acquaintance since he had been in retirement for four years.

22. J. P. Sartre, *L'Imagination* (Paris, Presses Universitaires de France, 1936), pp. 139, 158.

23. From Sartre's lecture "L'Existentialisme est un humanisme," translated by W. Kaufmann in *Existentialism from Dostoevsky to Sartre* (New York: Meridian Books, 1957), p. 302.

24. *Nausea,* 236-237.

25. See Sartre's essay "Qu'est ce que la littérature?" (1947), but especially his *Les Mots* (Paris: Gallimard, 1964), the first part of his long promised autobiography.

26. One of the best detailed accounts of the work in English is to be found in Wilfrid Desan's *The Tragic Finale.* This doctoral dissertation, originally published by Harvard University Press in 1954, has been revised for the paperback edition as a "Harper Torchbook" (New York: Harper and Brothers, 1960). For a briefer analysis see Hazel Barnes's introduction to her translation of the work, entitled *Being and Nothingness* (New York: Philosophical Library, 1956); Spiegelberg, *op. cit.,* pp. 467-473; K. F. Reinhardt, *The Existentialist Revolt* (Milwakee: Bruce Publishing Co., 1952) pp. 156-165.

27. To illustrate what he meant by the nonsensical character of metaphysics, Rudolf Carnap cites such texts as "The Nothing is prior to the Not and the Negation" and "The Nothing itself nothings" from Heidegger's *Was Ist Metaphysik?* See his "The Elimination of Metaphysics through Logical Analysis of Language" in *Logical Positivism,* ed. A. J. Ayer (Glencoe, Illinois: The Free Press, 1959), pp. 69-70. Commenting on *L'Etre et le néant,* J. Passmore remarks that many of its sentences "read like a parody of positivist parodies of metaphysics." See his *A Hundred Years of Philosophy* (London: Gerald Duckworth and Co., 1957), p. 477.

28. Even as sympathetic a commentator as Spiegelberg cannot help remarking on the changed style Sartre adopts in this work. He attributes

Sartre's fondness for verbal paradox and baffling formulations to the impact of Hegel, whose work seems to have enjoyed a certain measure of popularity among the French philosophers at the time. "There are also times," he writes (*op. cit.*, p. 447) "when I cannot suppress the feeling that Sartre enjoys the shock and bewilderment that he can evoke in his more conventional readers. In fact he may even enjoy surprising himself." Others have suggested that he was trying to prove to his French contemporaries that he could "beat the Germans at their own game" of ontologizing, appealing to such descriptions as that of consciousness as "that which is what it is not, and is not what it is" (Cf. *L'Etre et le néant*, Paris: Gallimard, 1943, p. 515).

29. *L'Etre et le néant*, p. 45. For the Barnes translation, see *Being and Nothingness*, p. 10.

30. *Ibid.*,

31. They are *L'Age de raison* (1945), *Le Sursis* (1945), and *La Mort dans l'âme* (1949). *Les Chemins* was planned as a tetrology but the fourth volume remains to be published.

32. *Harper's Bazaar*, LXXX (January, 1946), p. 113.

33. *Being and Nothingness*, p. 617: (*L'Etre et le néant*, p. 711). *Ibid.*

35. *Ibid.*, 618 (*L'tre*, 711).

36. In a brief article in the January, 1939 issue of *Nouvelle Revue Française*, entitled "Une Idée fondamentale de la phénomenologie de Husserl: L'intentionalitè," we have an indication of this change of attitude. He credits Husserl with having "reinstated horror and charm in the objects. He has restored to us the world of the artists and of the prophets: terrifying, hostile, dangerous, with its harbors of grace and love. Here we are liberated from the inward life." The article has since been republished in *Situations*, I (Paris: Gallimard, 1947), pp. 31-35.

37. Simone de Beauvoir, *loc. cit.*, p. 158.

38. *Saint Genet*, 402 ff.

39. *Ibid.*, 402.

40. *Ibid.*, 403.

41. *Ibid.*

42. *Ibid.*, 404.

43. Originally a lecture given at Paris in 1945 it was published together with the subsequent discussion as *L'Existentialisme est un Humanisme* (Paris: Editions Nagel, 1946).

44. *Being and Nothingness*, 625 (*L'Etre*, 720).

45. Man must renounce the "spirit of seriousness" which seeks values in the world of being as opposed to the self. To subjugate itself freely to such means that the self or *pour soi* must become an *en soi* without ceasing to be a *pour soi*. This implies a contradiction. Consequently, man in renouncing this *l'esprit de sérieux*, affirms his own freedom and thus becomes sufficient unto himself. *Ibid.*, 626 (*L'Etre*, 721).

46. See the foreword to the Torchbook edition of Desan's *The Tragic Finale*, p. xviii.

47. *Saint Genet,* 575.

48. *Ibid.,* 597.

49. *Ibid.,* 583.

50. *Ibid.,* 581.

51. *Ibid.,* 582.

52. As Sartre told Desan in their interview in 1956, "It will take me ten more years to finish it." See W. Desan, *op. cit.,* p. xviii.

53. See J. P. Sartre, *Les Mots* (Paris: Gallimard, 1964) or *The Words,* trans. B. Frechtman (New York: George Braziller, 1964). Originally published in the 1963 October and November numbers of *Les Temps Modernes,* this account of his early childhood is perhaps the most readable and charmingly written piece Sartre has done so far.

maurice merleau-ponty

AND PHILOSOPHY

by John F. Smolko

Introduction. In the past few years Maurice Merleau-Ponty has become the object of heightened interest on the American philosophical scene. Two of his principal works, *The Phenomenology of Perception* and *The Structure of Behavior,* appeared in English translations in 1962 and 1963 respectively.[1] His *In Praise of Philosophy* was recently chosen by John Wild and James Edie to begin their series, *Northwestern University Studies in Phenomenology and Existential Philosophy,* the work being characterized by these editors as a "fitting introduction" to this collection which "will be concerned with a *new* way of thinking relevant to the situation and problems of our time."[2] The same series is to include translations of three other volumes by Merleau-Ponty, *Signs, Sense and Non-Sense* and *The Primacy of Perception,* as well as works by Georges Gusdorf, Henri Duméry, Aron Gurwitsch and Paul Ricoeur. The sheer quantity of material by Merleau-Ponty that will thus become available in English as well as the central role assigned him in relation to his compatriots as an exponent of a "new way of thinking" renders him an apt subject for any consideration of twentieth-century thinkers of stature.

The Man. Because of both the translation barrier and his untimely death at an age when his thought was just reaching its maturity, Merleau-Ponty is perhaps not as well known outside his own country as some of the other thinkers discussed in the present volume. Born into a family with medicine and the military in its background at Rochefort-sur-Mer on the western coast of

France on March 14, 1908, he grew up in a tightly-knit household in one of Paris' *quartiers* not far from the lovely Bois de Boulogne. He had lost his father on the eve of the First World War and was strongly attached to his brother and sister and particularly to his mother. If we are to accept Sartre's report, her death later in 1953 had a profound effect on Merleau-Ponty.[3] After an outstanding record at the Janson and the lycée Louis-le-Grand, he entered the École Normale Supérieure in 1926 and became an *agrégé* in philosophy, completing his studies there in 1930.

A "tala" or practising Catholic at the École Normale, he was even a member of the early *Esprit* groups during his student years. As a "militant" of the *Jeunesse Étudiante Catholique* he protested vigorously against the obscene songs traditional at the "Freshman Day" rites of the École's students. His actions led to his being bullied until one of the upperclassmen, admiring his courage, stepped in to rescue him. This proved to be the beginning of a close friendship which was to have a profound effect on Merleau-Ponty's life and thinking. The name of the upperclassman was Jean-Paul Sartre. Merleau-Ponty's religious difficulties slowly grew into doubts, and he gradually separated himself from the Catholic faith, becoming a non-believer about 1935. Despite the Church ceremonies at his funeral and implications superficially drawn by some from his final works, he remained an "agnostic humanist" to his death.[4]

After military training in 1930-31, he taught at the lycée de Beauvais from 1931 to 1933, during which time he became particularly interested in Husserlian studies and perfected his knowledge of German.[5] He spent one school year, 1933-34, in work at the Caisse Nationale de la Recherche Scientifique, then returned to teaching as a professor of philosophy at the lycée de Chartres in 1934-35 and as an *agrégé-répétiteur* at the École Normale Supérieure from 1935 to 1939 where he made a vivid impression on both his students and elders.

During these formative years of the thirties German Gestalt psychology, especially via the work of Paul Guillaume and Aron Gurwitsch, along with the ideas of Max Scheler, Max Weber, Kurt Goldstein and others held Merleau-Ponty's attention. He was attracted to Hegel through Kojève's lectures, strongly influenced by Martin Heidegger and Gabriel Marcel, particularly by the latter's *Être et avoir,* and was continuously involved with Sartre's budding existentialism though not as a wholly uncritical admirer. It would be some years before Merleau-Ponty would be recognized as more than an academic disciple of his more widely known friend. The principal influence of the period, however, remained Husserl, particularly the last phase of Husserl's thought. Especially important was the partial publication in *Philosophia* (Belgrade) in 1936 of the incomplete *Die Krisis der europäischen Wissenschaften und die transzendentale Phänomenologie (The Crisis of the European Sciences and Transcendental Phenomenology),* a work of Husserl's centering on the very problems preoccupying Merleau-Ponty. Though he never studied in Germany nor did he ever meet Husserl, he did considerable research, beginning in March, 1939, in the Husserl Archives at Louvain.[6] Profound as was Husserl's influence, both directly and indirectly via Sartre, it did not result in Merleau-Ponty's becoming simply a follower of phenomenology's sire. What came forth was a highly critical, selective and radically reworked version of some of Husserl's central themes.

La Structure du Comportment (The Structure of Behavior), the first of Merleau-Ponty's two theses for the doctorate, was completed by 1938 though not published until 1942. War service as an officer with the Fifth Infantry Regiment took up the winter of 1939 and the spring of 1940. From 1940 to 1945 he taught philosophy at the lycée Carnot while working at the same time with various Resistance groups. For his degree of *docteur ès Lettres* he presented at the Sorbonne in July, 1945, his principal thesis, *La Phénoménologie de la Perception (The Phenomenology of Perception),* joining it to the secondary thesis mentioned above. In October, 1945, he became a *maître de conférences* at the University of Lyons and in January, 1948, was promoted to professor. He moved to the Sorbonne in Paris for the school year of 1949-50 to teach child psychology and pedagogy and remained there until his election to the Collège de France at the end of 1952 where he was to succeed Louis Lavelle in the chair of philosophy previously held by Bergson, Le Roy, and Gilson. The youngest man ever to hold that chair, he taught there until his death.

On the heels of World War II he joined with Sartre, Simone

de Beauvoir, and Francis Jeanson in founding *Les Temps Modernes,* a political and cultural review for the extreme left. His political sympathies were by and large Communist with nuances from 1935 until 1953 when he broke with Sartre and *Les Temps Modernes,* refusing to accept the dictatorship of the proletariat as an explanation for the numerous Stalinist excesses that culminated with the Korean War. This "friendly secession" occasioned the explicit statement of Merleau-Ponty's basic philosophical and ideological differences with Sartre in *Les Aventures de la dialectique* (1955) where Sartre is taken to task for stressing the Cartesian subject-object dichotomy and introducing a subjective absolute via his notion of freedom, while the usual Marxist description of the historical process is judged illusory in its conjuring up a crude, objective, materialistic absolute. Simone de Beauvoir's bitter rejoinder in *Les Temps Modernes* (vol. 10, 1955, pp. 2072-2122) under the title, "Merleau-Ponty et le pseudo-sartrisme", contended that Merleau-Ponty confused the earlier and later Sartre, a charge that gives some idea of the nature and extent of the rupture.

Merleau-Ponty's later political tendencies can be gathered from his association with the partisans of Mendès-France and his articles for the Socialist weekly newspaper, *L'Express.* Even here he broke with the U.F.D. (*Union des forces démocratiques*) in September, 1960, refusing to sign the "Manifesto of the 121" against the Algerian War though he called for negotiations with the rebels. On the afternoon of May 3, 1961, at the age of 53, he died suddenly of a heart attack while working at his desk on a text of Descartes and a few days later joined many of France's "immortals" in Paris' Cimetière du Père-Lachaise. There was no eulogy at the graveside.[7]

Thought.[8] Though subordinate to his principal thesis, *The Phenomenology of Perception, The Structure of Behavior*[9] was completed and published first and, as De Waelhens argues so well in his preface, represents a pedagogically prior introduction to the later and better-known work.[10] It likewise serves as a useful starting point for any summary exposition of Merleau-Ponty's thought, and its content goes far to explain its attraction for Wild, Edie and others as a new and relevant way of thinking.

In this work Merleau-Ponty begins with a thorough, knowledgeable, and highly perceptive review of the deliverances of the various natural sciences on the topic of behavior. Gradually, methodically, through the inadequacies of these various scientific explanations which this close scrutiny exposes the problem of behavior is posed anew. This reworked problematic springs not only from the partial or erroneous explanations of the various natural sciences. It flows from their very nature and methodology— the reductionist ontological framework which they adopt more or less spontaneously and more or less explicitly.[11] This reductionist tendency is not only bad philosophy; it produces bad science, or better, destroys the very possibility of natural science. Merleau-Ponty writes, "If one refuses to take into consideration, as the object of science, every property of phenomena which is not manifested in the intuition of a particular case and which appears only to reflective consciousness—by an analysis of the varied concordances or by a reading of the statistics—it is not anthro-pomorphism which is excluded, it is science; it is not objectivity which is defended, it is realism and nominalism. Scientific laws which are not *given in* the facts but which one finds *expressed* in them, would be subject to the same grievance. When one speaks of the structure of the situation and its meaning, these words evidently designate certain givens of human experience and are consequently suspect of anthropomorphism. But 'colors,' 'lights,' and 'pressures' or their expression in physical language are no less so. It is clear that all the terms of which we can make use refer to phenomena of human experience, naive or scientific. The whole question is to know whether they are truly constitutive of the objects intended (*visés*) in an inter-subjective experience and necessary for their definition."[12]

It is precisely this approach that commends Merleau-Ponty to Wild and Edie, an approach that in their eyes establishes, "justifies", a distinctive domain for the humanistic disciplines, philosophy included—"the exploration of the original life-world, or *Lebenswelt*"[13]—and proposes and exemplifies the proper method or mode of understanding for such "human sciences"—phenomeno-logy.[14] In the words of Wild, all this points to "a new style of philosophizing, and a revival of philosophy itself in all its various levels and branches."[15]

The argument of *The Structure of Behavior* has two parts:

first, a lengthly description and criticism of experimental psychology's physical explanation of behavior, and, secondly, a briefer positive highlighting of and building upon those aspects of behavior, of the form or structure of behavior, overlooked by so many natural scientists. These overlooked aspects of behavior are shown to be the ground or basis of the data studied in the various sciences.[16] That is, scientific data or experience turns out to be based upon our natural perceptions, our natural experience, and for Merleau-Ponty the key to understanding this natural perception is form, Gestalt, functional structure. Hence, if ultimately "our goal is to understand the relations of consciousness and nature: organic, psychological or even social,"[17] we should study the behavior which, as it were, bridges consciousness and nature—perception. Only by a careful phenomenological description of our primitive, ante-predicative, natural, ingenuous experience, in short, only by a phenomenology of perception can we lay bare (and in a sense ground) the presupposed data or constituted "world" of the natural sciences. In this way *The Structure of Behavior* prepares for and ultimately rests on *The Phenomenology of Perception,* the latter work extending the brief positive treatment of the former both by its lengthly detailed analyses and its somewhat different emphases.

In the critical portion of *The Structure of Behavior* Merleau-Ponty begins by pointing out the inadequacy of the purely mechanical, physiological, behavioristic, reflex-arc explanation of behavior, of lived, existential behavior. This Watsonian (though Merleau-Ponty would tend to absolve John Watson himself at least partially) causal, purely objective, materialistic and "realistic" appreciation of behavior in terms of only objective stimuli fails to take into account what the Gestaltists were quick to point out, namely, that the organism determines via the overall Gesalt or form the stimuli that can affect it and vice versa. Only this factor would permit transcending the numerical particularity of the stimuli which otherwise would never act as stimuli given the non-recurrence of what are actually in fact unique situations. Response and stimulus are *involved* one with another. The behavior is dynamically structured, has a form. Consciousness and nature, subject and object, the "mental" and the physiological, the idea and the thing, all are involved one with the other and in the other; and the "neutral" unity which transcends the duality of *pour-soi* and *en-soi*, of meaning and matter, is structured behavior, the being-in-the-world which is perception.[18]

Pavlov's conditioned reflexes and more sophisticated behavioristic attempts to explain "higher" types of behavior yield in like manner before the onslaughts of totality, form or Gestalt. Witness the evidence of Gelb and Goldstein on the structural or systematic character of disorders following cortical lesions such as that suffered by the celebrated Schneider.[19] Yet even Gestalt psychology, especially as formulated by Wolfgang Koehler, ultimately falls back upon a naturalistic, causal explanation set in the universe of mechanics, of physical objects, of things. "To this very extent one is no longer thinking according to 'form'," and one can no longer "ask of form itself the solution to the antinomy of which it is the occasion, the synthesis of matter and idea."[20] Thus, we must go beyond the causal explanations of all the experimentalists, both behaviorists and Gestaltists, and by carefully examining the phenomena given in direct experience arrive at a philosophy of the form or Gestalt.

Avoiding the objectivist extreme of the natural scientists does not mean that Merleau-Ponty opts for the subjectivist solution to reduce behavior to consciousness and to regard form as some mental, psychical or spiritual substance, an absolute meaning or signification. Contrary to Sartre's limpid *cogito,* our psychic activities are incarnate. Neither psychic nor physical structures independently or in parallel are the ultimate ground, explanation, of behavior.[21] "Empiricism and intellectualism carry over into primitive modes of behavior structures which belong to a very high level: structure of pure juxtaposition—the atom—or structure of pure interiority—the relation . . . . The preceding chapters teach us not only not to explain the higher by the lower, as they say, but also not to explain the lower by the higher."[22] The dualistic dichotomy of the *pour-soi* and the *en-soi,* presupposed in fact if not in theory by Sartre, is overcome by an adequate study of behavior. "*Behavior,* inasmuch as it has a structure, is not situated in either of these orders. It does not unfold in objective time and space like a series of physical events; each moment does not occupy one and only one point of time; rather, at the decisive moment of learning, a 'now' stands out from the series of 'nows,' acquires a particular value and summarizes the groupings which have preceded it as it engages and anticipates the future of the behavior; this 'now' transforms the singular situation of the experience into a typical situation and the effective reaction into an aptitude. From this moment on behavior is detached from the order of the in-itself (*en-soi*) and becomes the projection outside the organism of a *possibility* which is internal to it. The world, inasmuch as it harbors living beings, ceases to be a material plenum consisting of juxtaposed parts; it opens up at the place where behavior appears."[23]

But lest this attack on the mechanical and atomic *en-soi* conception be misunderstood, Merleau-Ponty hastens to add the balancing qualification in the same text: "Nothing would be served by saying that it is we, the spectators, who mentally unite the elements of the situation to which behavior is addressed in order to make them meaningful, that it is we who project into the exterior the intentions of our thinking, since we would still have to discover what it is, what kind of phenomenon is involved upon which this *Einfühlung* rests, what is the sign which invites us to anthropomorphism. Nor would anything be served by saying that behavior 'is conscious' and that it reveals to us, as its other side, a being-for-itself (*pour soi*) hidden behind the visible body." The argument for this approach is expressed by the following words of this same key text as an alternative interpretation, a valid phenomenological description of what in fact occurs—and here Merleau-Ponty's critique transforms its negative tone and takes up the positive strain that will be fully developed only in the later *The Phenomenology of Perception*—"The gestures of behavior, the intentions which it traces in the space around the animal, are not directed to the true world or pure being, but to being-for-the-animal, that is, to a certain milieu characteristic of the species;[24] they do not allow the showing through of a consciousness, that is, a being whose whole essence is to know, but rather a certain manner of treating the world, of 'being-in-the-world' or of 'existing'. A consciousness, according to Hegel's expression, is a 'penetration in being,' and here we have nothing yet but an opening up .... It is only at the level of symbolic conduct, and more exactly at the level of exchanged speech, that foreign existences (at the same time as our own, moreover) appear to us as ordered to the true world; it is only at this level that, instead of seeking to insinuate his stubborn norms, the subject of behavior 'de-realizes himself' and becomes a genuine *alter ego*. And yet the constitution of the other person as another I is never completed since his utterance, even having become a pure phenomenon of expression, always and indivisibly remains expressive as much of himself as of the truth. There is, then, no behavior which certifies a pure consciousness behind it, and the other person is never given to me as the exact equivalent of myself thinking. In this sense it is not only to animals that consciousness must be denied .... In fact I am aware of perceiving the world as well as behavior which, caught in it, intends numerically one and the same world, which is to say that, in the experience of behavior, I effectively surpass the alternative of the for-itself (*pour soi*) and the in-itself (*en soi*)." Thus, not only mechanism is vanquished; every hint of mentalism or spiritual monism is banished.

This overcoming of the classical matter-spirit dualism, of the objective-subjective dichotomy, radically separates Merleau-Ponty's enterprise from that of Sartre. The in-itself and for-itself of Sartre, the *être* and *néant* division, is for Merleau-Ponty fundamentally untrue. There are not two basically different structures or ontological principles. For Merleau-Ponty the only reality is the being-in-the-world, which is to say, man-in-the-world. A careful description, a phenomenology of man-in-the-world, of the structure or form of behavior, will in fact turn out to be, again for Merleau-Ponty, a phenomenology of perception—which is already to give some hint of the extended meaning that Merleau-Ponty attaches to "perception."

The critical portion of *The Structure of Behavior* has both negatively prepared for and already given some positive indication of this phenomenology of perception, a description which constitutes the latter portion of this book and which will become the central theme of the author's principal work, *The Phenomenology of Perception*. In many ways the fundamental ideas of the earlier work erect a framework which both sets forth and limits the discussion of the later book. The ontological status of the object of the later phenomenological inquiry is presented in firm strokes in *The Structure of Behavior* once the restrictive metaphysical monisms presupposed by the mechanistic natural scientists or by the mentalistic philosophers have been dismissed. *The Phenomenology of Perception* never does, in fact, get beyond the ontology of the earlier work, and this is of particular importance for anyone attempting to come to grips critically with Merleau-Ponty's thought. His other works, for example, *In Praise of Philosophy,* either presuppose or reproduce in schematic terms and a more popular dress the fundamental lines set down in *The Structure of Behavior.* It is to this positive argument, this philosophy of form, this phenomenology of the structure of behavior, that we now turn.

The philosophy of form is given in four steps. There is, first of all, a group of general statements regarding "form". There follows a typology of form or classification of the levels of behavior. Next, there is a careful description of the "orders" of the forms of behavior, that is, of the regions or orders of experience. Finally, there is a critical study of past views on the mind-body problem with Merleau-Ponty's own contrasting views included.

In general, by interpreting "form" as structure, as functional-structure, he believes he avoids the consciousness-nature antinomy. "Structure" has a *sens,* a word which in French carries the double denotation of "direction" and "meaning". Yet form or structure is not meaning. It implies at the same time subject and object, finality and substance, yet is none of these. The form is not *a* being, not a reified dynamism, not a frozen intentionality. It is neither an absolute idea nor an absolute atom. Rather it is the dynamic, dialectical interpenetration of subject and object, of meaning and nature, of soul and body. It is dynamic because it is living, a "lived" behavior, *vécu,* not conjured up in the artificial isolation of some laboratory though all the scientist's experiments presuppose it. The form is the functional synthesis of the idea and nature. Its truth as phenomenon, as appearance to consciousness, is precisely this, a totality where the change of one part is the change of all and where the change of all parts can leave the totality unchanged. What is needed is study of "these original properties of wholes in behavior." [25] "Since the decomposition into real parts can never be completed," [26] each of these whole-properties 'is never . . . an individual physical reality; . . . it is always . . . a structure." [27]

Yet there is more to these general considerations, and once again we see the care with which Merleau-Ponty avoids subjectivist, mentalistic conclusions cast its share of light on the situation, a light of unknowing and obscurity. "The structure of behavior as it presents itself to perceptual experience is neither thing nor consciousness; and it is this which renders it opaque to the mind."[28] Ferdinand Alquié was the first to characterize Merleau-Ponty's philosophy as a "philosophie de l'ambiguïté", and the phrase became the title of De Waelhens' study of the philosopher.[29] In these early thoughts on form the ontological roots for this characterization were already laid down. Merleau-Ponty continues his text: "The object of the preceding chapters was not only to establsh that behavior is irreducible to its alleged parts. If we had nothing other in view, instead of this long inductive research—which can never be finished, since behaviorism can always invent other mechanical models with regard to which discussion wiïl have to be recommenced—a moment of reflection would have provided us with a certitude in principle. Does not the *cogito* teach us once and for all that we would have no knowledge of any *thing* if we did not first have a knowledge of our thinking and that even the escape into the world and the resolution to ignore interiority or never to leave things, which is the essential feature of behaviorism, cannot be formulated without being transformed into consciousness and without presupposing existence for-itself (*pour soi*)? Thus behavior is constituted of relations; that is, it is conceptualized and not in-itself (*en soi*), as is every other object moreover; that is what reflection would have shown us. But by following this short route we would have missed the essential feature of the phenomenon, the paradox which is constitutive of it: behavior is not a thing, but neither is it an idea. It is not the envelope of a pure consciousness and, as the witness of behavior, I am not a pure consciousness. It is precisely this which we wanted to say in stating that behavior is a form. Thus, with the notion of 'form' we have found the means of avoiding the classical antithesis in the analysis of the central sector of behavior as well as in that of its visible manifestations. More generally, this notion saves us from the alternative of a philosophy which juxtaposes externally associated terms and of another philosophy which discovers relations which are intrinsic to thought in all phenomena. But precisely for this reason the notion of form is ambiguous."[30] "Ambiguity" here refers not to the property of some linguistic expression but in a radically Heideggerian sense to the characteristic aspect of the human being inserted in a situation yet in some way going beyond it. "Situation and reaction are linked internally by their common participation in a structure in which the mode of activity proper to the organism is expressed. Hence they cannot be placed one after the other as cause and effect: they are two moments of a circular process . . . . If behavior is a 'form,' one cannot even designate in it that which depends on each one of the internal and external conditions taken separately, since their variations will be expressed in the form by a global and indivisible effect."[81] The fundamental opacity of form, contrasted with the clarity of Sartre's *pour-soi,* flows from "what sort of being can belong to form."[32]

Thus, the general consideration of form brings out its "totality" aspect and its radical ambiguity. These "properties" will be controlling the remainder of Merleau-Ponty's development. Like the Heraclitean *Logos,* the forms "are lived as realities . . . rather than known as objects."[33] In fact, Merleau-Ponty never gets very far from, though he deepens, the notions he borrowed from Ehrenfels: "Forms . . . are defined as total processes whose properties are not the sum of those which the isolated parts would possess. More precisely they are defined as total processes which may be indiscernible from each other while their 'parts,' compared to each other, differ in absolute size; in other words the systems are defined as transposable wholes."[34] Following these general remarks on "form", Merleau-Ponty undertakes an examination of what might be loosely termed the subjective pole of the subject-object dichotomy overcome by the "philosophy of form". That is, we are given a typology of form or classification of the levels of behavior. The third stage of the philosophy of form has to do with the "objective" portion of this division, with the regions or orders of objects, types of structure, experienced. This manner of treating the second and third steps of the philosophy of form finds its basis, once again, in form. "The analysis of perception will lead to re-establishing a demarcation—no longer between sensation and perception, or between sensibility and intelligence, or, more generally, between a chaos of elements and a higher system which would organize them—but between different types or levels of organization."[35] Translating this into the language of the philosophy of form as given above, Merleau-Ponty writes: "It is necessary ... to classify behavior, no longer into elementary and complex behavior as has often been done, but according to whether the structure of behavior is submerged in the content or, on the contrary, emerges from it to become, at the limit, the proper theme of activity. From this point of view, one could distinguish 'syncretic forms,' 'amovable forms' and 'symbolic forms.' "[36]

This leads to Merleau-Ponty's detailed treatment of the second stage of the philosophy of form, namely, the typology of form or classification of the levels of behavior under the rubrics just cited. On each level the general characteristics of form as outlined above are verified. Briefly, syncretic forms are found when stimulus and response are so closely wed that any change in the stimulus inhibits the response, a behavior associated with lower organisms. Amovable or removable forms, the basis of signals, characterize behavior where the response is elicited not by the identical stimulus but by its Gestalt in relation to the whole situation, the "totality". In these removable or movable forms animals react more to the structure of the sign-Gestalt than to the physical content or matter of the stimulus, e.g., when monkeys relate means to ends in concrete instances within their field of vision. "In animal behavior signs always remain signals and never become symbols."[37] With symbolic forms we pass to the level usually associated with human behavior. "The true sign represents the signified, not according to an empirical association, but inasmuch as its relation to other signs is the same as the relation of the object signified by it to other objects."[38] Here the behavior not only has meaning; "it is itself signification."[39] The structure of behavior, because of its systematic character, its relations internal to the systems of signs and objects signified, is patient of translation within the sign system. In other words, the symbol signifies an object not via some empirical link but by its relations to other signs when the object it signifies or symbolizes is related to the objects they signify by the same structure, i.e., in the same way. Yet this three-step typology of behavior-structure should not be pressed too far. "These three categories do not correspond to three groups of animals: there is no species of animal whose behavior *never* goes beyond the syncretic nor any whose behavior *never* descends below the symbolic forms. Nevertheless, animals can be distributed along this scale according to the type of behavior which is most typical of them . . . . The fundamental dimensions of space and time are found, if you like, at the three levels which we have just distinguished. But they do not have the same meaning at each level." [40]

If we turn now to the third stage of the philosophy of form, to the "objective" pole of form, the orders of nature, the regions of experience, we find once again the general characteristics of form, the ambiguous totality, verified. Any stimulus, any response, any stimulus-response totality, may be considered as belonging to any one of three orders or regions of experience: the physical, the vital, the mental. None of the three orders or fields requires new substantial principles; an order is not a state or kingdom but merely a restructuring, another configuration, another level of meaning, of the stimulus-response totality. The orders are incarnate dialectics, newly re-ordered, restructured, re-related, excluding any reification or "thing-ness", whether it be mechanistic materialism, naturalism, mentalism or angelism. With this renunciation of substance, the distinction of the three orders has to be accounted for solely by means of structural differences. "Matter, life and mind must participate unequally in the nature of form; they must represent different degrees of integration and, finally, must constitute a hierarchy in which individuality is progressively achieved." [41] To lose sight of their structural difference or to explain it in terms of substances, of things, is ultimately, according to Merleau-Ponty, to eliminate the original distinction. Form is the dialectical ordering principle that alone accounts for the differences.

The physical form—not a thing, not an *en-soi,* not a structure found *in* a nature nor the structure of isolable individuals—is defined in the same way as "physical system", "an equilibrium obtained with respect to certain given external conditions, whether it is a question of topographical conditions . . . or of conditions which are themselves dynamic." [42] It is a system of forces without itself being a force, the internal circulation of an ensemble of forces "such that no law is formulable for each part taken separately and such that each vector is determined in size and direction by all the others."[43] It is composed of partial totalities joined in a unity of correlation, of laws, each partial totality tending toward a relative equilibrium. Since no law is formulable for any part taken singly or for the whole system, "science must be linked to a history of the universe in which the development is discontinuous."[44] As with form nature, the physical order, is not a thing, an *en-soi*. Reverting to his earlier criticism of the "natural scientist's" approach to reality, Merleau-Ponty adds: "The form itself, the internal and dynamic unity which gives to the whole the character of an indecomposable individual, is presupposed by the law only as a condition of existence; the objects which science constructs, those which figure in developed physical knowledge, are always clusters of relations. And it is not because structure, by its essence, resists expression that physics only barely succeeds in formulating the laws of certain structures in mathematical language; it is because the existential solidarity of its moments renders the experimental approach difficult, prevents acting separately on one of them, and demands that a function which is appropriate to all of them be found initially. One cannot even say that structure is the *ratio essendi* of the law which would be its *ratio cognoscendi,* since the existence of such a structure in the world is only the intersection of a multitude of relations—which, it is true, refer to other structural conditions."[45] It is because of this that structure and law are but two moments of the dialectical historical process which is the physical system or order, not two powers of being found in this order of physical nature. "What is demanded by physics is in no case the affirmation of a 'physis'—either as the assemblage of isolable causal actions or as the place of structures—or the power of creating individuals in-themselves (*en-soi*). Form is not an element of the world but a limit toward which physical knowledge tends and which it itself defines."[46] Thus, form, and in its wake the universe of history and perception, is indispensable for physical knowledge since the latter intends and determines it. "Form is not a physical reality, but an object of perception; without it physical science would have no meaning, moreover, since it is constructed with respect to it and in order to coordinate it."[47]

The vital order, order in the proper sense of the word, obtains in organisms where equilibrium is had not with regard to real and present conditions but with regard to conditions that are only virtual, conditions which the structure itself brings into existence. "The physico-chemical actions of which the organism is in a certain manner composed, instead of unfolding in parallel and independent sequences . . ., instead of intermingling in a totality in which everything would depend on everything and in which no cleavage would be possible, are constituted, following Hegel's expression, in 'clusters' or in relatively stable 'vortices'—the functions, the structure of behavior—in such a way that the mechanism is accompanied by a dialectic." [48] Here the dialectic is one of the individual and his environment, and the unity of vital structures is one of meaning in terms of this dialectic. The organism gives its environment meaning and is made "organism" by its environment. The laws of the physical order become norms for the vital level of experience, norms governing the circular action-reaction, the interaction of organism and environment, irreducible to a model drawn up in terms of the laws of the physical order.[49]

With the human order we come to the level of symbolic experience in the full sense of the words. Just as the vital order escapes the purely physical system, so here the mental or symbolic cannot be adequately reduced to the physical and physiological. The partial totalities of the physical system—occasion and effect— and the partial totalities of the vital order—lived situation and instinctive response—arrived at an equilibrium, a total structure, definable in terms of the interaction of these partial totalities. This same dialectical equilibrium of interaction obtains on the human or mental level between the partial totalities, partial forms, consciousness and object of consciousness, the milieu of consciousness. In the case of the vital or animal order, "the mutual exteriority of the organism and the milieu is surmounted along with the mutual exteriority of the stimuli. Thus, two correlatives must be substituted for these two terms defined in isolation: the 'milieu' and the 'aptitude,' which are like two poles of behavior and participate in the same structure." [50] "While a physical system equilibrates itself in respect to the given forces of the milieu and the animal organism constructs a stable milieu

for itself corresponding to the monotonous *a prioris* of need and
instinct, human work inaugurates a third dialectic." [51] This dialectic
is between the partial totalities of perceived-situation and work,
taking the latter word in its Hegelian sense. The third dialectic
projects, between man and the physico-chemical stimuli, "use-
objects" (*Gebrauchobjekts* of Husserl) such as clothing, chairs
and gardens, and "cultural objects" such as books, musical
instruments and language. These objects constitute man's proper
milieu and lead to new cycles of behavior incapable of being
reduced to physical or physiological activity. "Work", then,
is the link of consciousness and action, human action in its radical
meaning and concrete content, "the ensemble of activities by
which man transforms physical and living nature." [52] The equilibrium on the human level is a function of man's intentions as
expressed in the cultural world. Consciousness, here "perception",
is "a moment of the living dialectic of a concrete subject; it
participates in its total structure and, correlatively, it has as its
original object, not the 'unorganized mass,' but the actions of
other human subjects .... Nascent perception has the double
character of being directed toward human intentions rather than
toward objects of nature or the pure qualities (hot, cold, white,
black) of which they are the supports, and of grasping them as
experienced realities rather than as true objects. The representation
of the objects of nature and of their qualities, the consciousness
of truth, belong to a higher dialectic." [53] Therefore, the possession
of some representation or the exercise of an act of judgment is
not the same as consciousness, the life of consciousness. A wider
notion of consciousness is called for, and this in turn is responsible for enlarging our conception of action beyond vital
action to embrace "work." Yet, it is not simply "work" but the
possibilities opened up by "work," the behavior which it grounds,
renders possible, that sets off the human order of experience.
"What defines man is not the capacity to create a second nature—
economic, social or cultural—beyond biological nature; it is
rather the capacity of going beyond created structures in order
to create others. And this movement is already visible in each
of the particular products of human work." [54] Man is not limited
by his physical and physiological makeup to a determined, given
situation but through his symbolic capability, his "power of

choosing and varying points of view ... to create instruments, not under the pressure of a *de facto* situation, but for a virtual use and especially in order to fabricate others," [55] can take possession through his human work of a world of things visible for each and every "I" from a variety of viewpoints, the world of an indefinite time and indefinite space. The essential character of the acts constituting the dialectic of the human order is, therefore, man's capacity to orient himself to the possible, going beyond his limited environment.

But even here the characteristics of form are verified. This human dialectic is essentially "ambiguous." [56] Though it manifests itself through the social and cultural structures it creates and in which in a sense it imprisons itself, yet "its use-objects and its cultural objects would not be what they are if the activity which brings about their appearance did not also have as its meaning to reject them and to surpass them." [57] It is this ambiguity which will provide the transition to the fourth step of Merleau-Ponty's exposition of the philosophy of form, for this same ambiguity hovers over and is in fact the problem of perceptual consciousness. This is a key text for understanding not only the basic thought of *The Structure of Behavior* but also that of *The Phenomenology of Perception* which develops this fourth step of the philosophy of form. "Correlatively, perception, which until now has appeared to us to be the assimilation of consciousness into a cradle of institutions and a narrow circle of human "milieus,' can become, especially by means of art, perception of a 'universe.' The knowledge of a truth is substituted for the experience of an immediate reality. 'Man is a being who has the power of elevating to the status of objects the centers of resistance and reaction of his milieu ... among which animals live entranced.' (Scheler) But the knowledge of a universe will already be prefigured in lived perception, just as the negation of all the milieus is prefigured in the work which creates them. More generally, the life of consciousness outside of self which we have described above, on the one hand, and, on the other, the consciousness of self and of a universe, which we are reaching now—in Hegelian terms, consciousness in-itself (*en soi*) and consciousness in-and-for-itself (*en et pour soi*)—cannot be purely and simply juxtaposed. The problem of percepton lies completely in this duality." [58] It is a

problem which might be termed one of "bootstraps": **how can**
one pick oneself up by one's own bootstraps? How **can a develop-**
ment, dependent on a discontinuous yet progressive **structuration**
of behavior,[59] endow man with higher patterns of behavior which
effectively enable him to surpass and transcend lower, more
elemental patterns at the same time that these higher structura-
tions, reorganizations of conduct, develop, grow out of, the lower
structures? How can the higher grow out of the restructuring of
the lower without thereby being decomposable into juxtaposed
elements of the lower?

But lest this structural opposition be pushed too far, lest some
hint of reified, substantial principles be introduced by these remarks, Merleau-Ponty is quick to add: "Neither the psychological
with respect to the vital nor the rational (*spirituel*) with respect
to the psychological can be treated as substances or as new
worlds. The relation of each order to the higher order is that of
the partial to the total . . . . The advent of higher orders, to the
extent that they are accomplished, eliminates the autonomy of
the lower orders and gives a new signification to the steps which
constitute them." [60] The higher and the lower, the three orders,
are not external to each other so as to explain one another, but
are "inseparable terms bound together in the living unity of an
experience which a pure *description* reveals." [61] We have here not
three orders of being but three dialectics. Their functional opposition may be obscure but nonetheless it is the only genuine
diversity. Hence, applying these general principles of the philosophy
of form to his findings with regard to the human or mental order,
Merleau-Ponty consistently concludes: "Mind is not a specific
difference which would be added to vital or psychological being
in order to constitute a man. Man is not a rational animal . . . . Man
can never be an animal: his life is always more or less integrated
than that of an animal. But if the alleged instincts of man do not
exist *apart* from the mental dialectic, correlatively, this dialectic
is not conceivable outside of the concrete situations in which
it is embodied." [62] Here we have the charter, the theme, not
only for the final portion of *The Structure of Behavior* but also for
the whole of *The Phenomenology of Perception*. Once again, we
are reminded that underlying this whole conception is Merleau-
Ponty's notion of form: "One does not act with mind alone.

Either mind is nothing, or it constitutes a real and not an ideal transformation of man. Because it is not a new sort of being but a new form of unity, it cannot stand by itself." [63]

These remarks already point out the first steps of Merleau-Ponty's reply to the "bootstraps" problem outlined above. In true Hegelian fashion, we find not only a functional opposition of orders. Careful thought shows that this hierarchy is established via and through this opposition, this negation. It is by negating that preceding orders are surpassed in the advent of higher ones. This negation in restructuration, re-interpretation, will ground the ambiguity of the whole of Merleau-Ponty's thought. The obscurity remains, yet negation is the key to the double relation "which both liberated the higher from the lower and founded the former on the latter." [64] Mind is not nothing; it is a real transformation of man, of embodied experience, and this transformation is achieved through negation. But this negating is and has a history.

Having established the general basis for his treatment of the mind-body problem, Merleau-Ponty comes to the fourth step of his philosophy of form: a critical and contrasting review of past thought on this question. He attempts to steer a middle course between the classical solutions of a causal naive realism and that of a constituting critical idealism. In terms of our analysis above, these extremes are in effect but the reformulation of the subject-object dichotomy, the idealist-realist extremes, already dismissed. *The Phenomenology of Perception* is to continue this criticism of empiricist and intellectualistic "prejudices." In the earlier work Descartes, both correctly understood and as misunderstood by the pseudo-Cartesians, along with Kant are the foils for Merleau-Ponty. For Merleau-Ponty the dichotomy vanishes in terms of the higher unity of form. "Since the physical, the vital and the mental individual are distinguished only as different degrees of integration, to the extent that man is completely identified with the third dialectic, that is, to the extent that he no longer allows systems of isolated conduct to function in him, his soul and his body are no longer distinguished." [65] They are no longer distinct substances but are "relativized," [66] their duality a function of the form which unites or integrates them, overcoming their division by its negation. In the functional, dynamic structure which is form, consciousness and nature are united. To appreciate this, to see it "clearly", this form must be described, that is, examined phenomenologically. And this examination of nature and consciousness, of the unity of exterior and interior turns out to be none other than a phenomenology of "perceptual consciousness." "The status of the object, the relations of form and matter, those of soul and body, and the individuality and plurality of consciousness are founded in it." [67] What leads us to reduce all this to perceptual consciousness? The answer— to be worked out in greater detail in *The Phenomenology of Perception*—is simply this: "If one understands by perception the act which makes us know existences, all the problems which we have just touched on are reducible to the problem of perception." [68] But to know existences for Merleau-Ponty is necessarily to encounter ambiguity, an irreducible radical ambiguity. For, though form "has" meaning it is enmeshed in the contingency of reality, the lived perspectives which of necessity "limit our access to eternal significations." [69]

We shall not follow out in detail Merleau-Ponty's development through phenomenological description of the primacy of perception. This presence-to-the-world (*au monde*), our insertion into our world, is studied with great care and becomes a "preconscious," "pre-personal" body-subject, the body-as-lived and expressive or meaning-giving. All conscious life is shown to be rooted in this fundamental pre-conscious phenomenon. "Bodily existence which runs through me, yet does so independently of me, is only the barest raw material of a genuine presence in the world (*au monde*). Yet at least it provides the possibility of such presence, and establishes our first consonance with the world. I may very well take myself away from the human world and set aside personal existence, but only to rediscover in my body the same power, this time unnamed, by which I am condemned to being. It may be said that the body is 'the hidden form of being ourself', or on the other hand, that personal existence is the taking up and manifestation of a being in a given situation. If we therefore say that the body expresses existence at every moment, this is in the sense in which a word expresses thought. Anterior to conventional means of expression, which reveal my thoughts to others only because already, for both myself and them, meanings are provided for each sign, and which in this sense do not give rise to genuine communication at all, we must, as we shall see, recognize a primary process of signification in which the thing expressed does not exist apart from the expression, and in which the signs themselves induce their significance externally. In this way the body expresses total existence, not because it is an external accompaniment to that existence, but because existence comes into its own in the body. This incarnate significance is the central phenomenon of which body and mind, sign and significance are abstract moments." [70] A close examination of this text—and of the whole of *The Phenomenology of Perception*—will show that here we have a developed, a richly developed, notion of form, one, however, which remains totally within the ontological or metaphysical perspective set out by Merleau-Ponty in his earlier work. The ambiguity of form is now the ambiguity of the body-subject, worked out in the later work with greater detail, but ambiguity nevertheless. The same type of "Hegelian existentialism" is found in the lines of *In Praise of Philosophy* and the other works of Merleau-Ponty. Neither man, nor society, nor philosophy is ready-made, a clear idea or a clear consciousness of ideas, but a dialectic, a life-given-over-to-finding-an-understanding-of-itself-as-given, a meaning-giving-to-*facticité,* an ambiguity, a side-long glimpse or perspective. In the face of this radical ambiguity of form, there is no absolute, there can be no absolute, no system. The philosopher is the man who rests in the movement, the reciprocal movement, between knowledge and ignorance; this is the "good ambiguity." [71] Like Socrates, "he knows only that there is no absolute knowledge, and that it is by this absence that we are open to the truth." [72] This becoming-of-truth-in-us is the absolute, or rather this contingency is related to us absolutely. [73] The philosopher rests in this becoming because he is the man who understands-and-chooses this ambiguity. [74] To the end, then, Merleau-Ponty retained as the foundation of his thought his philosophy of form.

Appreciation. The power and the richness of Merleau-Ponty's thought can best be felt only by following him through his wealth of concrete examples, his highly articulated functional structures. Within a few pages we could but sketch the basic metaphysical perspective which was his—his philosophy of form—, and it is to an appreciation of this that we now turn. The real value of his individual analyses must be overlooked for the moment in order to come to grips with his philosophy of form in its most general and significant properties. Again, our criticism itself will remain on the most general level without attempting to enter into detailed arguments for its own counterpositions. The contrast established by the horizon invoked in our discussion should be suggestive enough of the paths more detailed evaluations would have to follow.

What, then, is the basic position of Merleau-Ponty? What is the fundamental metaphysical meaning of his philosophy of form? What is the value of his metaphysics? Though the problematic conceived in these terms may be alien to idiom of Merleau-Ponty, a sketch of the metaphysical horizon may help orient the discussion and locate his position thereon. In the face of our experience, sensory-intellectual, of the reality-given-to-us, five fundamental positions are in principle possible. First, we can attempt to describe this experience in its most general terms and refuse to proceed further. For the moment, it is irrelevant whether the intentional relation, the given-as-other, is recognized or not. Our experience directly yields to us a-material-substance-which-exists-and-changes. If one demands that for consistency even the note of materiality be dropped from this description so that no division, no dichotomy, whether of subject and object, of matter and spirit, be admitted (since the idealist might argue that what we experience are in fact spiritual ideas), and by the same token if one were to require an ontological position prior to the distinction of substance and accident, this formula would become "a-changing-being-which-is-and-changes". Again, if in the name of consistency we are asked to go beyond the separation of change and being and to replace our formula in a simple, non-prejudicial way which would not tend to import this very separation into our mode of conception as soon as the formula was pronounced, we find ourselves at a loss for such a simple formula as our language offers none. Falling back upon our own resources, let us fashion our own term, "abgos", to name our direct experience, anterior to any distinction and separation. "Abgos", then, is equivalent to "a-changing-being-which-is-and-changes" in meaning and reference. It names the given, the *datum,* the *déjà-là,* in the most general way. By the first of the five fundamental metaphysical positions, abgos is all, and there is nothing more. Nothing more can be said; nothing more is or changes. Abgos. The position is perfectly consistent and perfectly sterile. It is incapable of either direct or indirect refutation. It is the position, if such could be formulated, of Aristotle's famous plant with regard to first principles, the plant which maintains that all judgments are alike false and true, mean nothing, and in fact cannot be made, the plant which thinks and does not think, or in our terms the plant which experiences and does not experience. The position is perfectly consistent in its radical inconsistency and, hence, as Aristotle adds, is held by no thinker with any degree of sincerity. (*Metaphysics* 1008 b 6-12) It is a position which can never be said as a position. Abgos.

A second position can mean in saying "abgos" that all is change. A third position in characterizing our present, direct experience as "abgos" can mean that all is being. In each of these positions, an apparent element of the original experience is regarded as illusory or as simply not given. The Aristotelian work cited above handles these pure positions in terms of Heraclitus and Parmenides. The historical validity of these ascriptions does not interest us here. What is of importance is the attempt by Aristotle of an indirect refutation, indirect as no direct proof is possible of truly "first" principles or notions.

A fourth position—and this is of greater interest to us here since we regard Merleau-Ponty as one who closely approaches this theoretical possibility—is that which by "abgos" means "a-changing-being-which-is-and-changes is grounded ultimately in, is for, change, becoming." Relative being, relative density, relative structures, are admitted in this option, but they dissolve in the radical contingency of existence, their meaning vanishing in the flux which underlies all substantiality. The philosophy of form makes a form such an "abgos", a relatively, dynamically, functionally structured being which is grounded, rests on, becoming, on the body-subject-living-in-the-world (*au monde*). If absolute being in its transcendentality is the ultimate ground for the intrinsic knowability (ontological truth) of reality, then, in this fourth option, no such intrinsic knowability is available since becoming and not being is ultimate. Being and knowability are

admitted but only as relative structures which are surpassed by
and dissolve into an abyss of becoming or change. It is not
strange, therefore, that a variety of philosophers of absolutist
persuasion, materialists as well as idealists, realists of several
stripes and subjectivists, while treating of particular questions
analyzed by Merleau-Ponty, such as language or the aesthetic
experience or the nature of psychological knowledge, or occasionally while surveying his thought as a whole, have taxed it as a
"philosophy of irrationalism."[75] In this fourth option, whether
it be a question of being, truth (knowability), goodness (value)
or beauty, the "bootstraps" problem, the emergence of higher
from lower, finds its effective solution in change, becoming, history,
with the concomitant negation of being as such, of goodness as
such, etc., in other words, with the negation of any absolute
distinction between "higher" and "lower". The problem is solved
by being dissolved much as truth in the hands of pragmatists and
linguistic meaning in the thought of the later Wittgenstein vanish
into the whirlpool of historical flux. The "goodness" of ambiguity
is only relative. Ultimately there is only the dank and total opacity
of the absurd.

There is a fifth possibility. In the face of abgos, it distinguishes and separates the "ab"-element of reality-as-experienced
from the "gos"-element. This separation, so natural to us that
it pervades all our judgments in the form of the subject-predicate
couple, is that of change and being. Change is not being. Ab is
not gos if we may lapse into unfamiliar terminology so as to
force us "to bump our heads" into that which is most difficult to
see—that which is most obvious. "The aspects of things that are
most important for us are hidden because of their simplicity and
familiarity. (One is unable to notice something—because it is
always before one's eyes.) The real foundations of his enquiry
do not strike a man at all. Unless *that* fact has at some time struck
him. And this means: we fail to be struck by what, once seen,
is most striking and powerful."[76] In its positive formulation this
fifth option maintains that being is, that change is for, is ultimately
grounded in, is ultimately knowable through, being. In other
words, changing-being is for being. If being is and if change in
a sense both is and is-not, then change is for being. More fully,
change is for changing-being-which-is-and-changes, and the chang-

ing-being-which-is-and-changes is for, is ultimately grounded in, being. If being is insofar as it is, being is being insofar as it is and being is not not-being or non-being insofar as being is. Further, being is true (intrinsically knowable), good, etc., insofar as it is, running down the table of the transcendental "attributes" of being. But if change is and is-not, and if changing-being-which-is-and-changes is and is-not, then neither change nor changing-being (abgos) it totally true, that is, totally knowable intrinsically. In other words in more familiar terminology, no finite being, no changing-being, is its own sufficient reason. But, if contrary to the option of Merleau-Ponty, being is, then being is true, that is, the *omnitudo realitatis,* the totality of reality, is *ultimately* ontologically true or intrinsically knowable. Consequently, changing-being finds its sufficient reason in the Being which is completely, totally intrinsically true of itself, the not-changing-Being or God. This unchanging and unchangeable Being is the ultimate ontological (in the order of being) ground of all reality and gives to changing-being its knowability, ontological truth, hence, its being—which is the usual definition of the causal relation.

With this as our horizon we can better appreciate the place of Merleau-Ponty. He is an enemy of all dualisms because ultimately for him abgos is not for being but for change, which is to say there is never any real distinction within abgos, only dynamic, functional moments or poles. This also points out the great value of such a philosophy. It serves to remind us of the all-pervading becoming which haunts our entire direct experience. If changing-being is not totally knowable in itself, then of necessity *our* knowledge of it (as long as it alone is the direct object of our experience) is obscure and confused, and indeed our knowledge of the unchanging-Being remains obscure and confused as long as we are what we are, changing-beings, *and* as long as we know the unchangeable-Being via the medium of or through analogy with changing-being.[77] Since the interaction which joins us to the other substances of our world is for Merleau-Ponty ultimately identical with the one abgos which is reality, he cannot grant a real numerical distinction of substances let alone recognize their specific variety or hierarchy. If change cannot be separated from being, then there is no radical duality or plurality, only an "interworld", an abgos. If there are no substances, there is no interiority and all vanishes into the dynamic relations which pour out interiority completely into exteriority.

The fifth position goes further, and this also in contrast with Merleau-Ponty's philosophy of form. Each of the substances in its concrete existence is regarded as a changing-being-which-is-and changes. If change is for being, to explain such a being is ultimately to explain change in terms of being, which, simply speaking, it is not. This leads to the whole paradoxical theory of act-potency with its incomplete, intrinsic principles of being, the traditional "transcendental relations." Merleau-Ponty, like Descartes before him, would have nothing to do with such entelechies. And yet— obscure and confused as it may seem, paradoxical as it may appear on first presentation, the theory corresponds to precisely what one would expect of any explanation of changing-being with its "built-in" obscurity, its relative non-knowableness. If Merleau-Ponty denies any substantial distinction in his levels of behavior and his orders of perception, he homogenizes reality by denying the real distinctions which often are available in these areas, the real distinctions of intrinsic principles of being, unusual and mysterious though they may be, yet totally consonant with the ultimate metaphysical character of the realities of our experience. Many of his finest insights take on a breath of life when reinterpreted in terms of the interpenetration of transcendental relations, of intrinsic principles of being whose inter-activity is already signified by the primary (in the order of our knowledge) analogate in our analogous knowledge of such principles: changing-being. Fleeing the clarity and distinction of the substantial body and substantial mind which Descartes proposed, Merleau-Ponty has ended in the extreme of total non-substantiality, total flux. His philosophy of form can offer no other solution. The explanation via intrinsic principles of being, for all its limitations, remains true to the facts of our experience. He is not the first to succumb before the unusual features of form when the latter is regarded as an intrinsic principle of being. Kant, struggling with the very same Cartesian problematic, fumbled with the changing-being" character of form.[78] Form as functional-structure has dazzled and puzzled many a philosopher with its *clair-obscur* face, especially as it is vividly known connaturally by man, himself a changing-being.

Finally, it is the separation of change and being, of history and meaning, all the while recognizing the role of change for being, of history for meaning, which establishes the possibility of objective knowledge, thereby solving the "bootstraps" problem. Through the separation a changing-being, man, has access to ultimate and absolute truth, unchanging and eternal, though such access always occurs in time, history, change. History has a *sens;* change is for being. This applies *a fortiori* to the history of philosophy and, in particular, to the encounter of the fourth and fifth possibilities on our metaphysical horizon, to the dialogue between the thought of Merleau-Ponty and our own. In this we have the issue of our appreciation of Merleau-Ponty's views, a "new way of thinking" which in fact contributes to that which is perennial. "The process of Becoming or development attends upon Being and is for the sake of Being, not *vice versa.*"[79]

NOTES

1. *The Phenomenology of Perception,* trans. Colin Smith (New York: Humanities Press, 1962), and *The Structure of Behavior,* trans. Alden L. Fisher (Boston: Beacon Press, 1963).

2. John Wild and James Edie, "Preface" to Maurice Merleau-Ponty, *In Praise of Philosophy,* trans. John Wild and James Edie (Evanston: Northwestern University Press, 1963), pp. xxiii and xi (italics added).

3. Jean-Paul Sartre, "Merleau-Ponty vivant," *Les Temps modernes,* XVII (1961), 357.

4. Cf. *La Croix* (Paris), May 6, 1961, p. 2: "Sa pensée était celle d'un incroyant pour qui l'Eglise et la religion étaient exclues de la recherche intellectuelle." Also, X. Tilliette, "Maurice Merleau-Ponty ou la mesure de l'homme," *Archives de Philosophie,* XXIV (1961), 412-13, and the interview given to Madeleine Chapsal, *Ecrivains en personne* (Paris: Julliard, 1960).

5. Maurice de Gandillac, "In Memoriam: Maurice Merleau-Ponty (1908-1961)," *Revue philosophique de la France et de l'Étranger,* CLII (1962), 104. Cf. Herbert Spiegelberg, *The Phenomenological Movement: A Historical Introduction* (Hague: Nijhoff, 1960), II, 529, where Sartre's return from Germany in 1935 is given as the occasion for Merleau-Ponty's introduction to Husserl. Spiegelberg's observations on the role of Aron Gurwitsch and Alfred Schuetz tend to bear out de Gandillac's account.

6. Cf. H. L. Van Breda, "Maurice Merleau-Ponty et les Archives-Husserl à Louvain," *Revue de Métaphysique et de Morale,* LXVII (1962), 410-30.

7. It should be noted that the date of Merleau-Ponty's death is incorrectly given in several published accounts.

8. Relatively complete lists of the works of Merleau-Ponty can be found in André Robinet, *Merleau-Ponty, sa vie, son oeuvre avec un exposé de sa philosophie* (Paris: Presses universitaires de France, 1963) 67-74, and in Remy C. Kwant, *The Phenomenological Philosophy of Merleau-Ponty* ("Duquesne Studies: Philosophical Series," No. 15; Duquesne: Duquesne University Press, 1963) 245-47. Though the former characterizes its list as complete (p. 121), a few of Merleau-Ponty's works are in fact missing from both bibliographies. Cf. Spiegelberg, *op. cit.*, p. 517, n. 2; p. 519; pp. 528-30.

9. Cf. *supra*, note 1.

10. But see the distinction drawn between the two works by Paul Ricoeur, "Hommage à Merleau-Ponty," *Esprit*, June, 1961, p. 1119.

11. Cf. the "Introduction" to Merleau-Ponty, *The Structure of Behavior*, pp. xxv-xxvi, where De Waelhens writes, "*The Structure of Behavior* accepts another debate. It takes hold of the image which is traced of us—in colors which are not always harmonious—by the principal schools of experimental psychology (above all Gestalt psychology and behaviorism) and devotes itself to proving that the facts and the materials gathered together by this science are sufficient to contradict each of the interpretative doctrines to which behaviorism and Gestalt psychology have implicitly or explicitly resorted. *The Structure of Behavior* is situated, therefore, not at the level of natural experience, but at that of scientific experience, and undertakes to prove that this experience itself—that is, the ensemble of facts which, brought to light by scientific investigation, constitutes behavior—is not comprehensible within the ontological perspectives which science spontaneously adopts. (15) One succeeds in obtaining a coherent view of behavior only if it is interpreted with the help of a conception which places no more credit in the hypothesis of a behavior-as-thing than that of a behavior-as-manifestation of a pure mind. From this it must be concluded that the notion of an involved-consciousness, such as will be revealed later by the description of natural or ingenuous experience, is found to be already implied, indeed imposed, by the interpretative critique of scientific experience." Note 15, cited in this quotation, runs as follows: "The scientist cannot make the rejoinder here that he thinks without ontological background. To believe that one is not doing metaphysics or to want to abstain from doing it is always to imply an ontology, but an unexamined one—just as governments run by 'technicians' do not make political policy, but never fail to have one—and often the worst of all." (p. xxviii)

Later in the same "Introduction," p. xxvi, De Waelhens continues: "Access to the conception defended by the author is hardly easy and, although it does not jar a certain spontaneous feeling of our being, it goes directly counter to what modern philosophy has taught us to *think* concerning this being. In order to understand him correctly, therefore, it is well not to neglect certain detours and to be persuaded ahead of time that, concerning the problem of perception and its prolongations, the solutions of the modern tradition are decrepit."

Concluding his "Introduction," p. xxvii, De Waelhens writes: "If Merleau-Ponty unstintingly collates and examines the facts given us by scientific experimentation or psychiatry, it is with the single aim of making the onto-logical frames of reference—generally implicit—in which they are presented literally fly to pieces. This does not mean that the author wants to impose the tasks or responsibilities of the metaphysician upon the scientist. It simply signifies that for this philosophy, the scientist—as any man—spontaneously thinks in terms of an ontology—and that, in the present circumstances, this ontology—which seems self-evident because of a long habituation—is in radical opposition to the views which natural and ingenuous experience—in which all scientific experience is rooted—seems to impose when we undertake to understand it without prejudice. (18)" This final citation, Note 18, is of a text from *The Structure of Behavior* itself, p. 219,: "All the sciences situate themselves in a 'complete' and real world without realizing that perceptual experience is constituting with respect to this world."

12. *The Structure of Behavior*, 102.

13. *op. cit.*, xii.

14. Cf. *ibid.*, pp. xii-xiii and pp. xxii-xxiii. Cf. also the "Foreword" of John Wild to *The Structure of Behavior*, pp. xvi-xvii.

15. "Foreword," *The Structure of Behavior*, p. xvii.

16. Maurice Merleau-Ponty, *ibid.*, 144-45 and 219.

17. *ibid.*, 3.

18. *ibid.*, 24-28 and 224.

19. *ibid.*, 65-71.

20. *ibid.*, 137; cf. 150-51.

21. *ibid.*, 133.

22. *ibid.*, 124.

23. *ibid.*, 125. Cf. p. 137: "With form, a principle of discontinuity is introduced and the conditions for a development by leaps or crises, for an event or for a history, are given." As Spiegelberg, *op. cit.*, 542, writes: "What this metaphor means is apparently that behavior is less of a break in the texture of the universe than full consciousness, which, according to Hegel and more recently to Sartre, is not only a hollow (*creux*) but a hole (*trou*) in the framework of being. Behavior indicates a decompression in the compact fabric of being which allows it to become centered in focal points. Thus existence, as Merleau-Ponty understands it, expresses a pre-conscious type of behavior, a transition between the massive In-itself and the perfectly transparent For-itself (consciousness). Existence is thus by no means restricted to human beings. All living beings have some kind of existence, although different from its human form."

24. Cf. Merleau-Ponty, *The Structure of Behavior*, p. 30: "Thus, animals and men react to space in an adapted manner even in the absence of adequate actual or recent stimuli. 'This space is bound up with the animal's body as a part of its flesh. When the animal moves itself in this space to

which it is adapted, a melody of spatial characteristics is unfolded in a continuous manner and is played in the different sensory domains.'" Compare this with Merleau-Ponty's later remarks on the constitution of the body-subject.

25. *ibid.*, 103.

26. *ibid.*

27. *ibid.* Though this text of Merleau-Ponty deals explicitly with a specific situation, it aptly expresses his general doctrine.

28. *ibid.*, 127.

29. A. De Waelhens, *Une Philosophie de l'ambiguïté, l'Existentialisme de Maurice Merleau-Ponty* (Louvain: Publications Universitaires, 1951), p. v.

30. *The Structure of Behavior*, 127.

31. *ibid.*, 131.

32. *ibid.*, 136.

33. *ibid.*, 168.

34. *ibid.*, 47.

35. *ibid.*, 93.

36. *ibid.*, 103-104.

37. *ibid.*, 120.

38. *ibid.*, 121-22.

39. *ibid.*, 122.

40. *ibid.*, 104.

41. *ibid.*, 133. Cf. p. 137: "Matter, life and mind must be understood as three orders of signification."

42. *ibid.*, 145.

43. *ibid.*, 137.

44. *ibid.*, 139.

45. *ibid.*, 142.

46. *ibid.*

47. *ibid.*, 147.

48. *ibid.*, 153.

49. *ibid.*, 161.

50. *ibid.*

51. *ibid.*, 162.

52. *ibid.*

53. *ibid.*, 166. Cf. p. 168: "Primitive objects of perception ... are lived as realities ... rather than known as true objects."

54. *ibid.*, 175.

55. *ibid.*

56. *ibid.*, 176

57. *ibid.*

58. *ibid.*

59. *ibid.*, 177.

60. *ibid.*, 180.

61. *ibid.*, 190.

62. *ibid.*, 181.

63. *ibid.*

64. *ibid.*, 184.

65. *ibid.*, 203.

66. *ibid.*, 210.

67. *ibid.*, 210-11.

68. *ibid,* 224.

69. *ibid.*

70. *The Phenomenology of Perception,* 165-66.

71. *In Praise of Philosophy,* 5.

72. *ibid.*, 39.

73. Cf. *ibid.*, 5 and 44.

74. Cf. *ibid.*, 60-64.

75. Cf. Eugene F. Kaelin, *An Existentialist Aesthetic: The Theories of Sartre and Merleau-Ponty* (Madison: University of Wisconsin Press, 1962), p. 213 and notes 5, 30 and 35 (pp. 428-30).

76. Ludwig Wittgenstein, *Philosophical Investigations,* trans. G. E. Anscombe (Oxford: Blackwell, 1953), n. 129.

77. Cf. Reginald Garrigou-Lagrange, *Le sens du mystère et le clair-obscur intellectuel* (Paris: Desclée de Brouwer, 1934) *passim.*

78. Cf. Charles W. Hendel, "Introduction" to Ernst Cassirer, *The Philosophy of Symbolic Forms* (New Haven: Yale University Press, 1953) I, 9-11.

79. Aristotle, *De Generatione Animalium,* trans. Arthur Platt ("The Works of Aristotle translated into English," ed. J. A. Smith and W. D. Ross, Vol. 5; Oxford: Clarendon Press, 1912) V, 1, 778 b 5-7. Cf. Aristotle, *De Partibus Animalium* I, 1, 640 a 10 ff; *Nicomachean Ethics* I, 12, 1152 b 25-1153 a 18; Plato, *Philebus* 54 a 9 ff.

paul tillich

PHILOSOPHER OF CONTEMPORARY PROTESTANTISM

by George F. McLean, O.M.I.

In his growing self-awareness, contemporary man has come to realize that, in a pluralistic society, one understands himself only to the degree that he gains an insight into the thought, spirit, and striving of others. Because the religious field embraces the most profound significance of all areas, insight in its regard is both particularly needed and particularly difficult to attain. Hence, there is a unique and universal significance in the life and thought of an individual who, by personally living the crisis of his own day, has come to grips with the most profound contemporary problems and made explicit their religious significance. Paul Tillich is such a person.

On the American scene, the crisis has been described by a Protestant historian, Walter M. Horton, as the disintegration of modern culture. This is reflected in the intellectual realm where the various fields no longer are viewed in their relation to the whole and the various sciences are left without principles or common cultural core. "Educators and sociologists who address themselves constructively to this agonizing problem of cultural disruption are almost forcibly driven into the camp of the Catholic neo-Thomists." There would seem to be almost no other alternative to the dilemna: "go Catholic or stay in chaos! . . . If there is one Protestant theologian capable of stepping into this breach, it is Paul Tillich."[1]

If Tillich was able to construct such an alternative for the American scene, it is because in Germany he himself had lived through a similar crisis to which the only alternatives seemed to be "the Roman Church or national heathenism in Protestant garb." [2] It was in the face of these alternatives that Tillich developed his own statement of Protestant thought.

By reviewing these crises in Europe and in America, it should be possible to understand better the universal dimensions of the problem he faced. This in turn should shed light on the way in which he proceeded to develop a philosophy which would be religious, Protestant, and contemporary. Finally the understanding of this thought in relation to the contemporary crisis should clarify the precise relevance of this philosophy to other present forms of religious thought.

The Genesis of Tillich's Philosophy:

Just as one would miss the implications of the thought of Paul Tillich if one were to consider it in isolation from the general contemporary crisis and other forms of contemporary religious thought, so one would fail to grasp the particular significance of his thought if one failed to relate it to the rich strains of past philosophical and theological thought. This understanding of present problems in the light of past achievements of the human mind has been a characteristic attitude of mind from his early student days.[3]

While preparing for his doctorate in philosophy (1911) and licentiate in theology (1912) and for ordination in the Evangelical Lutheran Church (1913), he drank deeply in the thought of the past. What he absorbed was not so much the continuing body of traditional Protestant thought in the Calvinistic and Lutheran tradition. His interest turned more to a combination of an ethical humanism and a dialectical idealism.

The ethical humanism had been developed extensively by Ritschl and Troeltsch. They accepted Kant's situating the religious ·question in the realm of the will and practical reason, rather than in that of the intellect and pure reason. On this basis religious issues were to be understood according to the religious and ethical personality which would be considered ideal according to the culture of the time. Naturalism and historicism were special notes of this thought.

The dialectical idealism was especially that of F. W. Schelling, whose collected works Tillich read in their entirety and wrote upon for his philosophy and theology degrees. In the light of this thought he deepened his appreciation of the divine presence in all things, which according to the structures of the dialectic were, in turn, a dynamic expression of the divine.

This appreciation of the progressive and developing manifestation of the religious in and through culture stood at the center of his teaching in theology, philosophy, philosophy of religion, and philosophy of culture in the great German universities of Berlin, Marburg, and Frankfort during the 1920's.

It was this same appreciation which was at the root of his adherence to religious socialism. According to this thought, the defeat of Germany at the conclusion of the First World War had cleared away all that was opposed to, or substituted for, God. In this way the Kairos or moment of time had been prepared when the divine would be manifested once again. This time, however, it would not be in the church, but in the people or proletariat. Such hopes were shattered in the early 1930's as the socialist ideal became concretized in the National Socialism of the Nazi party. As the nation and the race were put in the place of God, what had been looked forward to as a new manifestation of the divine became its ultimate denial.

As this situation became clear Paul Tillich could not but express strong disagreement in his many public speeches throughout Germany, with the result that he was dismissed from the University of Frankfort when Hitler came to power in the early 1930's. Looking back to that time, Dr. Tillich sees those developments which bound together the two World Wars as more than merely personal or even national events. "Neo-Protestantism is dead in Europe. All groups, whether Lutheran, Reformed, or Barthian, consider the last 200 years of Protestant Theology essentially erroneous. The year 1933 finished the period of theological liberalism stemming from Schleiermacher, Ritschl, and Troeltsch."[4]

In personal terms this disillusionment led him to consider becoming a Catholic as the only alternative to "national heathenism." Instead, he came under the influence of Karl Barth's neo-orthodoxy and its affirmation of God as transcendent. Tillich never allowed this affirmation to remove all religious significance from the dialectic of culture. But he did recognize the way it transformed that dialectic by opening it to strongly negative existential elements and to the acid criticism, developed by Kierkegaard, Nietszche, and Marx, of dimensions of meaning. Barth's emphasis on the transcendence of God made it possible to recognize these negative elements in culture without negating the divine itself. But for Tillich this was not enough. In all his previous thought he had seen God as positively manifested through nature. If now nature must be considered meaningless, then the problem becomes more difficult, but not essentially different. To put it quite simply, the contemporary religious problem has become the way in which God is manifested through and in this very meaninglessness itself.

This thought pattern was not at all unrelated to the American scene upon Tillich's arrival in the United States in 1933, for America itself was in a similar crisis. During the deceptive prosperity of the 1920's, there had been a certain religious parallel to the German situation as the search for God tended to be gradually substituted by the impression that the natural progress of the era was itself God. Ths tendency was especially marked in the Social Gospel Movement which, under the influence of the pragmatism of the Chicago school, had become a relativistic humanism. The task of theology was reduced to that of generating convictions which need not be Christian or even concerned with God, as long as they were pragmatically efficient and apologetically defensible.[5] It was the depression which spelled the end of this direction of religious thought. After that it was no longer possible to identify God as the next stage of progress. Rather, it became necessary to find God in the negation of values in ever widening circles stemming from their initial collapse in the economic realm.

This was a situation in which Paul Tillich had already had personal experience and deep reflection. The religious perspective which he had begun to elaborate proved, in fact, to be particularly relevant. It joined the incipient trend, begun in America by the Neo-Naturalist, to recall men from mere humanism to a theocentric philosophy of religion. But where the Neo-Naturalists were satisfied with a God who was a process wholly immanent in the universe, the Neo-Supranaturalist evolution which Tillich's thought had recently undergone in Europe allowed him to carry further this appreciation of the divine by identifying its transcendent character. In turn, while joining the Neo-Orthodox in their recogntion of the divine transcendence of God and in their critique of culture, Tillich retained the positive interest in and appreciation of nature, intellect, and philosophy which had characterized his earlier period and which was now characteristic of the Neo-Liberals.

This combination, together with the resultant concern for the meaning of the transcendent divine in relation to all dimensions of contemporary culture, has made Dr. Tillich one of the most broadly relevant and avidly read religious thinkers on the American scene. In another context, it has even excited the wish expressed by a noted historian of American Protestantism: "May he be the new Aquinas who will find place within his system for the truth in all our contending theological schools."[6]

Specifications for a Contemporary Protestant Philosophy:

Out of the crisis through which he had lived in Germany and into which he entered on the American scene, Paul Tillich was able to draw the characteristics which must pertain to any body of religious thought which would be at the same time both Protestant and contemporary. As religious it would have to understand the presence of God in all things and their relation to Him. For this, the thought must be both philosophical and theological.

He would disagree with the naturalists and humanists because his strong appreciation of the transcendent character of the divine, and consequently of Christian revelation, excludes any possiblity of philosophy being an adequate statement of religious thought. If, however, the transcendent be considered an answer, it is the answer to a question constituted by that crisis which is the present existential situation. In the analysis of this crisis and the identification of this question of the ultimate lies the proper task of philosophy. Theology cannot become totalitarian, for it exists in a situation of co-relation with philosophy as the answer to philosophy's most profound questions of being and meaning.[7]

This need for philosophy extends to the realm of metaphysics and epistemology, both for philosophers and for theologians. Every philosopher, according to Tillich, actually has an implicit understanding of what "is" means, of the nature of being which logically precedes all statements about what participates in being, and of the universe as universe. The question is not whether or not one works with such positions; it is simply whether one is willing to reflect upon them sufficiently to make his knowledge of them as precise and well-founded as possible. This is also true of biblical theologians, for not only do they treat some problems which are so fundamental that they appear in the mythical phase of human thought before either philosophy or the bible, but they need precise philosophical reflection in order to understand the content of their terms and the relation of these terms to reality.[8] Religious thought must then always be philosophical as well as theological.

Furthermore, Tillich sees reasons why the notion of participation, which is at the center of all religious thought, should be Protestant in character. Positively this would center on Luther's notion of divine forgiveness as received in the center of man's personality and basing there the total personal return to God by which man receives his meaning.[9] Negatively this Protestant character would join the traditional notion of the total depravity of human nature and constitute the Protestant principle by which the identification with God of anything created is definitively rejected.[10] Religious thought which is authentically Protestant must conciliate these two poles: personal reception and divine transcendence.

Finally, the synthesis must be contemporary, that is, it must find the divine in a way which is relevant to the present situation. For Tillich, this situation is that of the crises described above. In fact, these merely concretized the earlier philosophical critiques by which the Neo-Protestant synthesis of naturalism and historicism was bereft of its social foundation by Marx, its moral foundation by Nietszche, and its religious foundation by Kierkegaard. These critiques left man a mere empty object or space without meaning. When this finally was brought home by the concrete circumstances of the 1930's the question could no longer be which values were true, nor could the solution be found in the simple realignment of old forms. God had been pronounced dead, "and with him the whole system of meanings and values on which man lived."[11] Human existence had fallen into utter meaninglessness.

A contemporary Protestant philosophy as a religious philosophy must place the question of meaning. As a Protestant religious philosophy, it must do this in the person, but without making the person divine. As contemporary Protestant religious philosophy, it must place this question in the personal situation of meaninglessness, delving into meaninglessness itself. There can be now no privileged sanctuary, no place outside or beyond meaninglessness where meaning would be found; it must be found within meaninglessness itself. These are the specifications provided by the present crisis for a contemporary Protestant philosophy.

It was the work of Paul Tillich to provide just such a body of thought. Having identified the contemporary religious problem as that of the manifestation or participation of God in the contemporary situation of meaninglessness, it now becomes possible to outline in detail the structure of the philosophical question and the response. The philosophical understanding centers on the clarification of the meaning of God, of man in his essential presence to God and in his present existential alienation from the divine, and of the revelation of God to man in this state.

God:

Tillich approaches the understanding of God in three ways: one is phenomenological, another epistemological, the third ontological. Phenomenologically God is man's ultimate concern. This is an element common to all of man's approaches to God. Whether he be called "being itself" by the scholastics, the "universal substance" by Spinoza, "absolute spirit" by Hegel, or "progressive integration" by Wieman, all express God as man's ultimate concern.

As "concern" the divine is a matter of passion and interest, the question of which one can avoid only by being completely indifferent. "Whatever concerns a man ultimately becomes god for him, and, conversely . . . a man can be concerned ultimately only about that which is god for him."[12] Of itself this might still be open to a naturalist interpretation, according to which any natural reality, whether it be tennis or politics or religion, can become a god simply because it occupies one's subjective interest.

As "ultimate," however, the meaning does not cease with the immediate concern. In terms of this concern it opens beyond to that which integrates all meaning and gives sense to otherwise meaningless lives and activities. As "ultimate" God is unconditioned and free of the particularities of time or place. This means that he cannot be exhausted by any time or place, but in a more positive sense it also means that he can be present to any time and place. The divine is depth, ground, and root of all meaning. For a more precise insight it will be necessary to proceed beyond this phenomenological approach to epistemological and ontological considerations.

The epistemological clarification of the significance of the ultimate concern is attained in the search for the basis of truth. This can be begun by observing the general correspondence as regards *logos* or structure which all philosophies recognize between the knowledge in the subject and the reality of the object. The explanation of this correspondence between subject and object is had only in the recognition of a *logos* which is prior and transcendent to both in power and meaning.[18] This is the divine *logos,* participated in by both self and world as they acquire their being. In this way God, the ultimate concern, is identified as the ground of truth.

The ontological approach constitutes the proper clarification of what was indicated in the phenomenological and epistemological approaches. Both point to something in the order of being. The ultimate concern is that which has the power of threatening, determining, and saving one's being and meaning. The *logos* is the key to the union of subject and object in knowledge because it is the ground of being. Hence, the mind is carried inexorably to the ontological consideration of God as being itself. This is the only nonsymbolic statement of God.

All other expressions are predicated upon a relation to something else. As "ultimate concern" God is related to the attention of man; as "power of being" he overcomes nonbeing; as "substance" he appears in every rational structure as the meaning of all; as "infinite potentiality of being and meaning" he pours himself into the rational structures of mind and reality in order to actualize them; as "ground" he is creative in every rational creation; and as "abyss" he is inexhaustible in any creation or number of creations.[14] All are particular ways of expressing God who is being itself, the ultimate concern, and ground of all truth and meaning.

Since an element in the constitution of the present crisis has been the identification of God with human and finite nature, Tillich has been concerned to state the transcendence of God. "This power of being is the prius which precedes all special contents, both logically and ontologically."[15] The divine is ontologically transcendent as the ground and power of all being, the answer to any and all concerns. Consequently, it cannot be one being among others, for then it would be subject to the structures of being and would itself call for an ultimate power. Neither can it be alongside others, without itself being one among them; nor can it be above them, for this is only another way of being alongside and among them. Finally, it cannot be the totality of beings, without itself being subject to the structures of being as a particular being. Rather, for Tillich, the divine is the depth of being, the analytic depth dimension and ground from which all beings spring.[16] As such, the divine is transcendent as the inexhaustible abyss, and on this is based his justification of the Protestant principle that no thing, even the bible as bearer of the holy, can claim divine status.

From the logical or epistemological point of view also, God is transcendent. The limited categories of reason, which base the objective and common element in knowledge, would limit God and reduce Him to the status of simply one more field of reason. The divine must be the prius of both subject and object, the depth of both being and reason.[17] For this reason, God can be attained, not by knowledge, but only by a personal (Protestant), subjective, individual, and intuitive awareness. Man cannot set out to seize God by reason; he can only place the question, thus opening himself to be seized by the divine. This is the situation of revelation. But in order to understand its contemporary mode, it is necessary to clarify the essential and existential situations of man which stand in relation to revelation as thesis and antithesis.

Essence and Existence:

In the approaches to the divine mentioned above, there has been a continuing contrast between the inexhaustible character of being itself and the finite, structured, and *logos* character of particular beings and concerns. There has been a further recognition of the foundation of the *logos* structure of mind and being in being itself. All of this expresses the reality of essence and the relation of these essences to the divine. As a first element of creation, the essences are placed in the divine where they are considered in a potential state, called one of "dreaming innocence." [18]

In the subsequent state of existence, these essences will have to leave the divine ground and "stand upon" it. Nevertheless, the positive aspect of essence can never be lost without the simultaneous destruction of both mind and body. Consequently, essence always constitutes a radical foundation for participation in the divine and the finite always retains the power to point to the infinite power of being and of reason. This participation is an absolute prerequisite for anything religious.

The necessity of a distinction of the state of existence from that of essence appears whenever one recognizes a distinction of the real from the ideal. In the past, this state of existence has been understood as a simple expression and manifestation of essence. The modern experience, however, has been one of life as shattered and fragmentary, of the individual as lonely and continually driven more into himself, of the person as isolated rather than as participating in being. This has manifested the state of existence to be a contradiction rather than expression of essence. It has stamped existence with the note of estrangement, applied to the individual by Kierkegaard, to society by Marx, and to life as such by Nietzsche and Schopenhauer,

The ontological reality of this estrangement is based on nonbeing. This, along with being, was present in God producing the dynamic qualities of life, but there it was dialectically overcome. In man, however, it is not overcome. He has a heritage of nonbeing; as a creature he comes from and goes toward nonbeing.

Estrangement is mediated to the level of consciousness by anxiety which is ontic, spiritual, and moral.[19] Ontic anxiety is the awareness of the contingency according to which one lives under the threat of death. Spiritual anxiety consists in the awareness of the loss of the concrete content or meaning of particular beliefs; today it reflects the loss of that very center of meaning which makes possible a serious question of meaning. Moral anxiety is the result of that freedom by which man must decide whether, on the one hand, not to choose and hence not to actuate his essence and potentialities, or whether, on the other hand, to choose with the realization that he will not choose according to values which express his essence. From this moral anxiety comes guilt[20] and moral meaninglessness, and from the combination of all three anxieties there derives the situation of despair.

Can such a state be called religious? There are two senses in which it can and must. Even in this situation of estrangement the positive element of essence still remains as an initial expression of the ground of being. More important at this point, however, is the negative sense in which this stage may be called religious in as much as it constitutes a question of God. Since this is a contradiction of essence and constitutes a tragically guilty state of estrangement from God, truth in this situation must be "just that subjectivity which does not disregard its despair and exclusion from the objective world of essence, but holds to it passionately."[21] It is this truth which constitutes the contemporary philosophical question of God to which theology and revelation are the answer.

Revelation:

To a considerable degree the above has delimited the nature of the participation in the divine which man can receive in his situation of despair. Such a participation can in no way be produced by man, nor could it result from an analysis of human experience. Not only would this imply a humanistic, naturalistic, or dualistic approach to God, but in the contemporary crisis the very meaning of being and reason have been questioned. Consequently, God must come to man.[22] He must enter this situation of human existence from "beyond it."

Objectively this entrance of the divine is called "revelation." It takes place in the very midst, and almost by means, of the situation of the shock of nonbeing and the anxiety of death, meaninglessness, and guilt. At that very point at which the normal balance of the mind is disrupted and one is forced to the boundary line where he openly faces nonbeing, if one is serious about anything at all, he must accept and affirm himself as facing nonbeing and meaninglessness. This acceptation itself is a meaningful act, and can be made only by the power of being[23] overcoming nonbeing and manifesting the divine therein.

In this act there is realized the meaning of Luther's phrase that "he who is unjust is just." In the midst of nonbeing it constitutes a personal "sign-event" which, without contradicting the rational structures of reality, produces numinous astonishment and ecstacy. In this is realized the manifestation of the presence of transcendent power, which, being of that which is beyond both subject and object, is absolutely personal and, hence, absolutely incommunicable. This reception of the divine is personal in the strictest sense.

What is received is the divine; it is the ultimate power and depth dimension of reality which has broken through the contradictions of existence. Furthermore, it is the divine which has determined the circumstances of this breakthrough and the extent and degree to which it will be participated. Non-symbolically it is "being itself" which is the point of immediate awareness. Symbolically and in relation to one's anxiety, this is the ultimate and unconditional concern; in relation to one as threatened by nonbeing, it is the power and ground of being.

As concrete content, this concern may be the nation, god, or the God of the bible. As a matter of concrete content, however, it could not be the ultimate as such, but would, instead, fall within the subject-object dichotomy. Hence, it would not be certain and as time goes on could be found to be finite. This itself produces an existential doubt, which introduces a lasting element of insecurity. This existential doubt, together with the certainty concerning the unconditioned, is subsumed in faith as the one state of ultimate concern.[24]

Within this over-all framework, Paul Tillich interprets the various elements of Christianity. God becomes manifest not only to individuals but to mankind. He has done so through the early history of mankind in a series of revelations which can be called "preparatory" because they are related to the definitive or final revelations in Christ. It was in and through the very act of negation which was the cross that the divine was definitively made manifest. In the cross the existential estrangement of being was transcended. There nonbeing, anxiety, and despair were definitively overcome in the "New Being."[25]

Since that time individuals have participated in this New Being only fragmentarily[26] and under the conditions of their existential predicament. Nevertheless, the central event has taken place; the victory over nonbeing has been won in principle. From it there flows a series of receiving revelations in which the victory is rendered specially present at particular points in the subsequent history of mankind. On a continuing basis the church becomes the bearer of the new being so that all of its sacraments and practices are symbols which bear this new being and make it present to men.[27]

In this view morality is provided with an ultimate directive goal: the expression of the transcendent ground of being. The particular contents of morality are related to the particular culture and no ethical directive, beyond that of manifesting the divine depth dimension, attains more than preliminary and relative value.

This summary of the historical challenge which occasioned the religious philosophy of Paul Tillich and of the pattern of thought with which he responded manifests its character as radically religious, penetratingly philosophical, positively Protestant, and creatively contemporary. No more need be said to summon forth for Paul Tillich the honor which is his due as a great twentieth-century thinker.[28]

NOTES

1. "Tillich's Role in Contemporary Theology" in *The Theology of Paul Tillich*, eds. Charles W. Kegley and Robert W. Bretall (The Library of Living Theology, vol. I; New York: Macmillan, 1956), 44-45.

2. *The Interpretation of History*, trans. N. A. Rasetzki and Elsa L. Talmey (New York: Scribner's, 1936), pp. 24-25.

3. Autobiographical Reflections," in *The Theology of Paul Tillich*, pp. 10-11.

4. "The Present Theological Situation in the Light of the Continental European Development," *Theology Today*, VI (1949), 299.

5. H. S. Smith, "Christian Education" in *Protestant Thought in the Twentieth Century, Whence and Whither?*" (New York: Macmillan, 1951), pp. 110-11.

6. Walter Horton, "Systematic Theology: Liberalism Chastened by Tragedy," *ibid.*, p. 121.

7. Paul Tillich, *Systematic Theology*, I (Chicago: Univ. of Chicago Press, 1951), 18-28 and 59-66.

8. *Ibid.*, p. 21.

9. Paul Tillich, *The Courage To Be* (New Haven: Yale Univ. Press, 1952), pp. 63-64.

10. *Systematic Theology*, I, p. 227.

11. *The Courage To Be*, pp. 142 and 152-53. See also "The Present Theological Situation," *loc. cit.*, pp. 299-302.

12. *Systematic Theology*, I, 211.

13. *Ibid.*, p. 79. See "Participation and Knowledge, Problems of an Ontology of Cognition," *Sociologica*, eds. Theodor W. Adorno and Walter Dirks (Frankfurter Beiträge zur Soziologie, vol. I; Stuttgart: Europaische Verlagsanstalt, 1955), 201-209.

14. *Systematic Theology*, I, 79.

15. Paul Tillich, *Theology of Culture*, ed. Robert C. Kimball (New York: Oxford Univ. Press, 1959), p. 25.

16. *Systematic Theology*, I, 207.

17. Paul Tillich, "Religious Symbols and Our Knowledge of God," *The Christian Scholar*, XXXVIII (1955), 192.

18. *Systematic Theology*, I, 238 and 255.

19. Paul Tillich, "The Conception of Man in Existential Philosophy," *Journal of Religion*, XIX (1939), 211-14; *Systematic Theology*, I, 189 and II, 74.

20. Paul Tillich, "Freedom in the Period of Transformation" in *Freedom: Its Meaning*, ed. Ruth Nanda Anshen (New York: Harcourt, Brace, 1940), pp. 123-24 and 131-32.

21. *The Interpretation of History*, pp. 63-64.

22. *Systematic Theology*, I, 64-65.

23. *The Courage To Be*, pp. 63-64.

24. Paul Tillich, "The Problem of Theological Method," *Journal of Religion*," XXVII (1947), 22-23; *Dynamics of Faith* (New York: Harper, 1957), p. 18.

25. Paul Tillich, *The New Being* (New York: Scribner's, 1955).

26. *Systematic Theology*, II, 118.

27. *Ibid.*, I, 138-44.

28. For some critical comments on dangers of subjectivism in the episte-

mology and of pantheism in the ontology see "Paul Tillich's Existential Philosophy of Protestantism" by the present author in *Paul Tillich in Catholic Thought,* eds. Thomas A. O'Meara and Celestin D. Weisser (Dubuque: Priory, 1964), pp. 69-84, and a response by Dr. Tillich in his "Appreciation and Reply," *ibid.,* pp. 301-11.

index

A NOTE ON THE PRODUCTION
OF THIS BOOK

The text is set in Times Roman, a Linotype face that has been adopted by every kind of medium for the printed word since its introduction to the linotype family. Times Roman is a very good text type for it has a forward motion which speeds the eye from letter to letter, word to word.

This book was designed, composed, printed and bound by the Pauline Fathers and Brothers at their own publishing plant in Staten Island. The Society of St. Paul was founded to teach and influence mankind by means of the press, radio, motion pictures. Alba House is staffed by them as a part of this Communications Apostolate. Further information can be obtained by writing: The Pauline Fathers and Brothers, 2187 Victory Blvd., Staten Island, N. Y. 10314.